BLACK VIENNA

BLACK VIENNA

THE RADICAL RIGHT IN THE RED CITY, 1918–1938

JANEK WASSERMAN

CORNELL UNIVERSITY PRESS
Ithaca and London

First published 2014 by Cornell University Press
First printing, Cornell Paperbacks, 2017

Library of Congress Cataloging-in-Publication Data
Wasserman, Janek, 1980–
    Black Vienna : the radical right in the red city,
1918–1938 / Janek Wasserman.
        pages cm
    Includes bibliographical references and index.
    ISBN 978-0-8014-5287-1 (cloth : alk. paper)
    ISBN 978-1-5017-1360-6 (pbk. : alk. paper)
    1. Right-wing extremists—Austria—Vienna—History—
20th century. 2. Political culture—Austria—Vienna—
History—20th century. 3. Vienna (Austria)—Intellectual
life—20th century. 4. Vienna (Austria)—Politics and
government—20th century. 5. Austria—Politics and
government—1918–1938. I. Title.
    DB855.W37   2014
    320.53'3094361309041—dc23   2014000747

Cornell University Press strives to use environmentally
responsible suppliers and materials to the fullest extent
possible in the publishing of its books. Such materials
include vegetable-based, low-VOC inks and acid-free
papers that are recycled, totally chlorine-free, or partly
composed of nonwood fibers. For further information,
visit our website at www.cornellpress.cornell.edu.

Contents

Acknowledgments   vii

List of Abbreviations   ix

Introduction: Reconsidering
"Red Vienna"   1

1. The Emergence of Black Vienna   15

2. The Austro-Marxist Struggle for
   "Intellectual Workers"   47

3. The Spannkreis and the Battle for
   Hegemony in Central Europe   74

4. The Verein Ernst Mach and the
   Politicization of Viennese
   Progressive Thought   106

5. Österreichische Aktion and the
   New Conservatism   132

6. The Rise and Fall of Politically
   Engaged Scholarship in Red
   Vienna, 1927–1934   158

7. The Triumph of Radical
   Conservatism in the Austrofascist
   State, 1933–1938   188

   Conclusion   218

Bibliography   227

Index   247

ACKNOWLEDGMENTS

Many people contributed to the completion of this book. Gerald Izenberg served as my primary reader and commentator. Hillel Kieval was involved the entire way, helping to keep my arguments and prose sharp. Malachi Hacohen read all sections of the book and offered constructive feedback and encouragement. I am also grateful to Howard Brick, Paul Michael Luetzeler, Vincent Sherry, and Corinna Treitel for reading the manuscript and providing the initial suggestions for its improvement.

The book benefited greatly from the feedback and assistance of numerous scholars around the world. Mitchell Ash served as my *Betreuer* in Vienna in 2008–9 when I was a Richard Plaschka fellow; he recommended I look at Viennese conservatives. Gary Cohen took an early interest in the project and invited me to a provocative workshop at the Center for Austrian Studies. Samuel Moyn aided me during the article submission process at *Modern Intellectual History,* which resulted in a tighter second chapter. Jerrold Seigel acted as an outstanding host at the New York Group in European Intellectual and Cultural History, where I first presented work on the monarchists. While I was there, James Chappel, Thomas Ort, and Richard Wolin offered insightful criticisms. Katie Arens has been an ideal interlocutor on the Vienna Circle at Austrian Studies Association conferences. Fritz Stadler generously opened the Institut Wiener Kreis archives to me.

Dozens of friends and colleagues have read and engaged with this project. I thank the anonymous readers of my first two articles—for *Modern Intellectual History* and *Central European History,* respectively—and the readers who reviewed the manuscript for Cornell University Press for their extensive and constructive comments. At Washington University, Sara Jay, Bryan Knapp, Jacob Labendz, and Emma Moran were all intensively involved with early drafts of this work, and I am indebted to them for all the questions and suggestions. Heather Morrison and Erin Hochman have been my most frequent intellectual foils, particularly after long days in the Viennese archives. At the University of Alabama, Holly Grout, Daniel Riches, and Jenny Shaw closely read my work in our European History Workshop. John Beeler, Steve

Bunker, Teresa Cribelli, Jimmy Mixson, and Josh Rothman have made Tuscaloosa a delightful environment for research and recreation. A special thanks goes to Margaret Peacock. Our daily exchanges about all things European history and our simultaneous negotiation of the publication process have made the experience more bearable.

I thank the staffs at the libraries and archives I used for tracking down countless sources and directing me to other potential documents. George Thompson has been an amazing adviser on publication questions for the past year, guiding me sagely through the entire process. I also thank John Ackerman at Cornell University Press for his help from day one. His intensive and conscientious attention has greatly improved the finished product.

I have received outstanding institutional support along the way. The Department of History at Washington University funded several research and conference trips. The Bundesministerium für Wissenschaft und Forschung in Austria granted me a Richard-Plaschka-Stipendium to spend a year in Austria. The Austrian Cultural Forum in New York has twice funded conference trips to the German Studies Association to present research. A Research Grants Council fellowship from the University of Alabama permitted me a trip to Central Europe in 2012.

Finally, I thank my family for their emotional support during this entire process. This book would not have been possible without their love and forbearance.

ABBREVIATIONS

AZ	*Die Arbeiter-Zeitung*
CS	*Der christliche Ständestaat*
FD	*Der Freidenker*
JÖA	*Jahrbuch der österreichischen Arbeiterbewegung*
JÖLG	*Jahrbuch der österreichischen Leo-Gesellschaft*
K	*Der Kampf*
MAK	*Museum für angewandte Kunst Plakat-Sammlung*
Kultur	*Die Kultur*
NR	*Das neue Reich*
ÖV	*Der österreichische Volkswirt*
RP	*Die Reichspost*
SL	*Das ständische Leben*
SZ	*Die schönere Zukunft*
VL	*Das Vaterland*
WPB	*Wiener politische Blätter*

Introduction
Reconsidering "Red Vienna"

On Election Day in April 1927, the conservative Viennese newspaper *Die Reichspost* featured Chancellor Ignaz Seipel's final political announcement to Austrian voters on its front page. Seipel called on the Austrian people to vote for the Einheitsliste, the antisocialist coalition of bourgeois parties, in order to counteract the nefarious intentions of the Austrian Social Democrats: "The victory of the Einheitsliste will guard the Austrian people against the greatest evils. It will hinder the superfluous and harmful tension that still exists between Red Vienna and the other provinces. It will mean that Austria will not appear to a disapproving world as a domain of 90 percent Bolsheviks and an outpost of 100 percent Bolshevism."[1] Seipel attacked the "Soviet-style" socialization measures of the Social Democrats and castigated the educational and cultural programs of the Austro-Marxists as unfruitful and damaging to the nation. On the next page, *Reichspost* editor Friedrich Funder continued Seipel's assault, likening the socialist leaders in Vienna to an elephant in a china shop, destroying all the city's good qualities.

The virulence of these attacks was nothing new; the choice of terminology was. For the first time in a major publication, the term "Red Vienna"

---

1. Ignaz Seipel, "Der Sieg der Einheitsliste," *RP,* April 24, 1927, 1. Translations mine unless otherwise noted.

was employed, pejoratively describing the municipal government and its socialist leadership. Previous epithets had focused on city hall and its radical, partisan policies—for example, "city hall dictatorship," "city hall Bolshevism," "proletarian dictatorship," "red city hall," "class dictatorship," and "tax and finance terrorism." In 1927 conservatives cast Vienna itself as a bastion of revolutionary socialism, a threat to the good people of Austria, and an enemy to the rest of the world. The Red Vienna strategy produced mixed results at best. The Social Democrats recorded their best showing of the First Republic, garnering 42.3 percent of the vote and seventy-one mandates in parliament, yet the Einheitsliste—which consisted primarily of the Christian Social and Greater German People's Party but also included monarchist organizations and factions of the Austrian National Socialist Party—won the election and maintained control of the federal government.

Austrian politics took a radical turn in 1927; conservatives intensified their attacks on Red Vienna thereafter. On July 15, angry protesters set the Viennese Justizpalast ablaze after the acquittal of three right-wing paramilitary men on trial for the murder of two people in Schattendorf. In the ensuing chaos, the police opened fire on the crowd, killing eighty-nine people and injuring more than five hundred. The socialists condemned the action and called for a general strike and the resignation of the police chief. The country seemed on the verge of civil war, yet the Social Democratic leadership hesitated to engage in violence.[2] With the help of the fascist paramilitary organizations, known collectively as the Heimwehr, the government broke the general strike and restored order. Neither the police commissioner nor the police force faced recriminations for their violent actions. Seipel and the conservatives had recognized the reluctance of the socialists and stepped up their own violent assaults. This included increased pressure on Red Vienna. Seipel called for the introduction of "true democracy"—an authoritarian, one-party state—and advanced constitutional amendments that would strengthen the executive at the expense of parliament and the federal states. Austrian politics had begun its authoritarian turn, which culminated in successive fascist regimes—the Austrofascist Ständestaat between 1934 and 1938 and the Nazi state thereafter.

During this period of heightened tensions and emergent fascism, conservatives regularly deployed the term "Red Vienna" while socialists refrained from using it, fearing it would reinforce conservative claims that the core of the socialist project in Austria was Marxist, Bolshevik, Masonic, and Jewish.

---

2. Hanisch, *Der große Illusionist,* 240–54. On July 15, see Botz, *Gewalt,* 107–11; Gulick, *Austria,* 725–31, and Leser and Wlasits, *1927.*

In 1929, Eduard Jehly, a Viennese Christian Social party member, wrote a pamphlet lamenting the ten-year anniversary of socialist rule in Vienna titled *Zehn Jahre rotes Wien.* The broadside enumerated a list of grievances against the municipal government, employing antisocialist and anti-Semitic tropes to account for the decline of the city.[3] When the socialist city council member Robert Danneberg wrote a rebuttal, he avoided the term "Red Vienna," referring instead to "New Vienna." Austro-Marxists writers rarely used the "red" descriptor outside of party rallies, lest they conjure images of Bolshevism.[4] The battle over the Red Vienna brand attested to the existence of powerful countervailing forces against the socialists in the city and across the nation.[5] This book looks at the struggle for the intellectual soul of Vienna waged by the socialist and progressive "reds" against the hegemonic, conservative "blacks."

Ironically, in the six decades since it was coined, the rubric "Red Vienna" has carried mostly positive connotations. This reflects a series of changed circumstances. Politically, socialists have controlled Vienna since World War II and the Red Vienna of the First Republic is seen as a glorious antecedent.[6] The period's cultural and intellectual achievements, inextricably linked to the interwar Austro-Marxist milieu, are today acknowledged as a golden age in the history of Austrian thought. Some of the twentieth century's most influential thinkers (for example, Ludwig Wittgenstein, Sigmund Freud, Karl Popper, and Hans Kelsen) were engaged with socialist projects, while others (Ludwig Mises, Friedrich Hayek, Joseph Schumpeter, and Eric Voegelin) challenged these initiatives. The brain drain that resulted from the persecution, emigration, and murder of the 1930s and 1940s transformed interwar Vienna into a second Austrian "world of yesterday." This recoding began shortly after the destruction of the First Republic in 1933–34, when conservative forces defeated the socialists in the February civil war. The exiled socialist leadership defended their achievements in articles, books, and memoirs.[7] Moreover, thousands of intellectuals, many of Jewish origins, emigrated between 1934 and the start of the Second World War. They reinforced this view, recollecting Vienna as a "fortress" or "ghetto" of cosmopolitan, progressive and even

3. Jehly, *Zehn Jahre rotes Wien.*

4. Danneberg, *Zehn Jahre neues Wien.*

5. Siegfried Mattl, "Die Marke 'Rotes Wien,'" in Kos and Békési, *Kampf um die Stadt,* 54–63.

6. Today, the encyclopedia for the Viennese Social Democrats is located at http://www.dasrotewien.at; The Social Democratic history portal (http://www.rotes-wien.at) chronicles the achievements of interwar Vienna. The mayor of Vienna, Michael Häupl, proclaims his government to be the heirs of Red Vienna: "90 Jahre Rotes Wien ist nicht genug!" (25 April 2009).

7. Mattl, "'Rotes Wien,'" 54–63.

radical ideas.[8] As the sociologist Marie Jahoda recalled, almost everyone with whom she interacted was a socialist or socialist sympathizer.[9] Finally, since the 1960s scholars have been drawn to the currents of Red Vienna and Austro-Marxism; their extensive research has given us a robust understanding of the socialist sphere of influence.[10]

These developments have had two major consequences. First, interwar Vienna began to move out of the long shadow cast by its illustrious fin-de-siècle predecessor.[11] Studies of interwar Austrian movements in philosophy, psychology, economics, literature, and theater multiplied.[12] Scholars concluded that a thriving "late Enlightenment," sociocultural milieu existed, consisting primarily of Jews, socialists, and liberals, which produced the hothouse culture of Red Vienna.[13] According to this interpretation, this group dominated the Austrian cultural and intellectual landscape. The second consequence has been that ideas originating outside this milieu have received less attention. Although there are significant works on interwar Austrian conservatism and Catholicism,[14] the role of conservative thinkers and their influence on intellectual debates in the capital have not been fully appreciated.[15] This relative discounting of the conservative milieu has led scholars

---

8. See the contributions in Leser, *Das geistige Leben Wiens,* especially the "Symposion." See also Malachi Hacohen, "Kosmopoliten," in Konrad and Maderthaner, *Werden der Republik,* 281–316. On Austrian emigration, see Stadler, *Vertriebene Vernunft,* and Ash and Söllner, *Forced Migration.*

9. Jahoda, *"Ich habe die Welt nicht verändert,"* 36. See also "Symposion," in Leser, *Das geistige Leben Wiens,* 148–59.

10. On Austro-Marxism, see Leser, *Zwischen Reformismus und Bolschewismus;* Albers, *Otto Bauer und der "dritte" Weg;* Loew, "Austro-Marxism"; Glaser, *Austromarxismus;* Bottomore and Goode, *Austro-Marxism.* On the achievements of Red Vienna, see Weihsmann, *Das rote Wien;* Frei, *Rotes Wien;* Rabinbach, *Crisis;* Gruber, *Red Vienna;* Gardner and Stevens, *Red Vienna.*

11. Carl Schorske's *Fin-de-Siècle Vienna* inspired a generation of scholars to investigate Vienna 1900. See particularly Boyer, *Culture and Political Crisis,* and Beller, *Rethinking Vienna 1900.* Interwar Vienna is frequently presented as part of a "long," liberal fin-de-siècle moment, stretching from 1848 or 1867 to 1938. Examples of this include Johnston, *Austrian Mind;* Beller, *Vienna and the Jews;* Janik and Toulmin, *Wittgenstein's Vienna,* 239–62; Luft, *Robert Musil;* Steinberg, *Austria as Theater;* and Coen, *Vienna.*

12. See Gruber, *Red Vienna;* Stadler, *Studien zum Wiener Kreis;* Hacohen, *Karl Popper;* Timms, *Karl Kraus,* vol. 2; Danto, *Freud's Free Clinics;* Silverman, *Becoming Austrians;* Pyrah, *Burgtheater;* Beniston and Vilain, *Culture and Politics in Red Vienna;* Holmes and Silverman, *Interwar Vienna.* Holmes and Silverman rightly argue that Vienna suffered from unfavorable comparisons to Weimar Berlin and became an example of cultural backwardness. See *Interwar Vienna,* 1–18, especially 5–6.

13. Friedrich Stadler, "Spätaufklärung," in Kadrnoska, *Aufbruch und Untergang,* 441–73. See also Hacohen, *Karl Popper,* 23–61.

14. See Wandruszka, "Österreichs politische Struktur," in H. Benedikt, *Republik Österreich,* 289–485; Diamant, *Austrian Catholics;* Klemperer, *Ignaz Seipel;* Hanisch, *Ideologie des politischen Katholizismus;* Siegfried, *Universalismus und Faschismus;* Steinberg, *Austria as Theater;* Beniston, *Welttheater.*

15. Recent scholarship has begun to examine the tensions of interwar Austrian and Viennese life. See Thorpe, *Pan-Germanism;* McEwen, *Sexual Knowledge;* Schmidt-Dengler, *Ohne Nostalgie;* Pyrah, "Consensus vs. Control," in Beniston and Vilain, *Red Vienna,* 293–315; Seefried, *Reich und Stände.*

to underemphasize the extent of ideological conflict in interwar Viennese intellectual life.

This book addresses this shortcoming, arguing that one cannot begin to understand the richness of Red Vienna without its opposite number, "Black Vienna." It reconstructs the origins and development of a "Black Viennese" oppositional field by elaborating its institutional and cultural evolution and by examining points of contact and conflict with Red Vienna. It shows that the overwhelming focus on a liberal Viennese political and intellectual heritage has downplayed the radicalism of authoritarian intellectual currents in the academy, press, civic associations, and government.[16] By no means challenging the significance of the "red" cultural field—in fact, this book argues for new ways of appreciating the convictions of progressive intellectuals—this project argues for a revision of our understanding of Red Vienna that takes oppositional movements seriously. It adjusts the late Enlightenment image of Vienna by investigating the political and intellectual commitments of Viennese thinkers from across the cultural landscape. In light of the stiff resistance that Red Viennese intellectuals faced in their professional and political endeavors, their counterhegemonic achievements in philosophy, science, and social reform appear all the more impressive.

The inclusion of a Black Viennese cultural field also recasts the engagement of interwar Austrian intellectuals in a more radical, politicized light. It shows that the most significant ideas from the period did not develop independently of the political, social, and economic turmoil of the interwar years. Understanding Black Vienna and the struggle of intellectuals for hegemony helps us to better understand the impetus behind the rise of Austria's "two fascisms" and the destruction of the First Republic.[17] By engaging in intellectual and political projects in Austria and abroad, Viennese intellectuals participated in the debates over democracy, capitalism, anti-Semitism, and fascism that dominated European affairs. At stake for these intellectuals was not only scholarly impact but also political and social influence. Using relational and transnational models that stress similarities between different cultural organizations and across national boundaries,[18] this book shows Vienna to be a crucible of European ideological debates and a microcosm of interwar historical developments.

---

16. Hacohen, "Viennese Science," 369–74, 391–96. Pauley, *Prejudice to Persecution,* 89–100, stresses the role of anti-Semitism in academic violence.

17. Mann, *Fascists,* 208.

18. Thorpe, *Pan-Germanism,* 1–6, demonstrates the benefits of this approach for fascist studies.

What Was Black Vienna?

While the concept of Red Vienna has been well-defined, Black Vienna, has not been so clearly circumscribed. The term "black" itself possessed multiple valences in late nineteenth and early twentieth century Austria and Europe. Historically, black was the traditional color of the Austrian Christian Social party and European Political Catholicism, leading Ivo Andics to call the Vienna of Karl Lueger "*schwarzes Wien.*"[19] While Black Vienna centered on the right wing of the Christian Socials and radical Catholic priests and theologians, it represented more than a political orientation.[20] As Robert Pyrah rightly observes, interwar Viennese politics and culture did not map onto one another perfectly.[21] This was particularly true of Viennese conservatism. Many writers and thinkers kept their distance from political parties and church-sponsored social movements even as they advocated for radical programs. The Social Democrats recognized the disjuncture between party politics and ideology, exploiting the complexity of "blackness." In a 1932 campaign poster, "Ho-ruck nach links," a red worker pushed a lever toward "Rotes Österreich/Rotes Wien" and away from "Schwarzes Österreich." Lurking behind "Black Austria" was Hitler (in traditional Austrian *Trachten*).[22] "Black" therefore implied fascism—both the Italian variety and Hitlerism. It could also allude to the German nationalism, or "Pan-Germanism," of the Greater German People's Party, the university fraternity the Deutsche Studentenschaft, or the social association the Antisemitenbund. Last, it could refer to the black and yellow colors of the Habsburgs and the monarchists, with their distinctive (Austrian) German nationalism. In short, Black and Black Vienna were rich symbolic complexes and represented a range of positions and phenomena.

While hardly monolithic, the Black Viennese cultural milieu was far more expansive and inclusive than traditional understandings of Austrian culture and politics have allowed. The ideas represented within its institutions ran a broad spectrum, yet its discourse centered on radical anti-Semitism, German nationalism, *völkisch* authoritarianism, anti-Enlightenment (and antimodernist) thinking, and corporatism. The potential for collaboration between Catholic conservatives and German nationalists has only in recent years begun to attract scholarly attention. As Julie Thorpe shows, both groups' demonization of Jews and ethnic minorities, grounded in German

---

19. Andics, *Luegerzeit.*
20. See Boyer, *Karl Lueger*, chap. 8, and Hanisch, *Ideologie des politischen Katholizismus.*
21. Pyrah, "Consensus vs. Control," 308.
22. Victor Theodor Slama, "Ho-ruck nach links," MAK, PI 1820.

nationalism, is particularly noteworthy.[23] Elke Seefried has revealed that ideas about a Central European German Reich united ethnic Germans of various political and social convictions.[24] While some Black Viennese thinkers supported the interwar republics of post-Versailles Europe, most rejected liberal democracy as a negative byproduct of the French Revolution and an import alien to German *Mitteleuropa*. They preferred authoritarian leadership under a strong führer and militated against the new order. Attached to this political vision were corporatist social and economic theories.[25] Taking their cue from nineteenth-century Catholic social theory and the Romantic political theories of Adam Müller, Friedrich Schlegel, and Joseph de Maistre, Black Viennese intellectuals advanced a radical program for overcoming capitalism and achieving organic social unity. These concepts defined the limits of Black Viennese discourse. While not everyone possessed the same understandings of these terms, all Black Viennese intellectuals expressed themselves using some definition of them.[26]

The ideas that made up the Black Viennese platform had their origins in the late imperial period, gaining a broad following with the rise of the Christian Social and Pan-German movements. These subjects have been studied in discrete political and religious histories and biographies, yet they have not been approached as part of a thriving interwar ideological landscape. This situation results not solely from the enduring preference of contemporary historians and intellectuals for progressive ideas but also from the belief that the interwar period signified the eclipse of Black Vienna. In the 1880s and 1890s, German nationalists and Christian Socials had ridden a wave of mass politics, "politics in a new key," to electoral success.[27] The growing appeal of the Christian Social party to the Viennese bourgeoisie and intelligentsia culminated in Karl Lueger's mayoral victory in 1895, while Georg von Schönerer reanimated calls for a greater German Reich.[28] After fifteen years of growth, however, the Christian Socials lost ground with the broadening of the electorate in 1907 and Lueger's death in 1910. After the Great War and

---

23. Thorpe, *Pan-Germanism,* chaps. 5–6.

24. Seefried, *Reich und Stände.*

25. Ibid. On corporatism, see Maier, *Recasting Bourgeois Europe.*

26. On Catholic social theory, see Diamant, *Austrian Catholics,* and Boyer, *Political Radicalism,* 166–80. Anton Staudinger, "Austrofaschistische 'Österreich'-Ideologie," in Talos and Neugebauer, *"Austrofaschismus,"* 28–52, offers a helpful outline: "ideological traditions of the völkisch, anti-democratic, anti-Semitic Catholic Right and its projections of the establishment of a new German Reich" (47).

27. Schorske, *Fin-de-Siècle Vienna,* 116–80.

28. Boyer, *Political Radicalism,* ix–xiv, 1–39, 411–21. Andics, *Luegerzeit,* also views the late Empire as the Golden Age of Black Vienna.

the fall of the Habsburg Empire, they lost their mandate in Vienna. Meanwhile, German nationalists lost much of their support when Austria lost millions of Bohemian, Moravian, and Silesian Germans to Czechoslovakia and Poland.[29]

Nevertheless Black Vienna hardly lost its broader influence, especially in cultural and social organizations.[30] In popular academic societies (the Leo-Gesellschaft and Deutsche Studentenschaft), social organizations (Antisemitenbund, Österreichische Aktion), and intellectual weeklies (*Neues Reich, Schönere Zukunft*), Black Viennese intellectuals mobilized a growing constituency for their radical ideas. Writers, philosophers, priests, historians, scientists, and civil servants—representatives from all segments of the educated bourgeoisie (*Bildungsbürgertum*)—made their voices heard. While conflicts often arose between individuals within the conservative cultural field, they were united in their antipathy to Red Vienna and the First Republic. Black Viennese intellectuals committed to a common program: defeating social democracy, replacing democratic, capitalist Austria, excluding Jews and foreigners, and restoring German and Austrian greatness. Only once these basic goals were achieved in the mid-1930s did major fissures emerge, for by that point there was no longer any place for moderate conservative positions. As the intellectual debates of the Austrofascist years reveal, the *Ständestaat* always stood on precarious ideological grounds in the battle between Austria's two fascisms. Black Viennese thinkers generally wanted more radical solutions than the Austrofascists offered and militated for more expansive changes. In this way, the ideas of Black Vienna paved the way for the Austrofascist coup *and* the *Anschluss*.

The identification of a significant, relatively unified, and radical conservative Black Viennese field challenges the standard historiography of First Republic Austria. Dating to Adam Wandruszka's seminal essay, historians have represented interwar Austrian politics, society, and culture using a three-"camp" (*Lager*) model: Christian Social-conservative, socialist, and (German) nationalist. Wandruszka characterized this division as stable throughout the First Republic; it was "Austria's natural or God-given division" (*natur- oder gottgewollten Dreiteilung Österreichs*).[31] This emphasis on difference over similarity, particularly between the Christian Social and German nationalist camps, stems primarily from a post-1945 tendency to exculpate non-Nazi

---

29. Boyer, "Boundaries and Transitions in Austrian History," introduction to Bischof, Plasser, and Berger, *From Empire to Republic,* 18–20, and "Silent War."

30. On the explosion of civic associations in the late imperial period and early Republic, see Cohen, "Nationalist Politics."

31. Wandruszka, "Österreichs politische Struktur," 291–300.

conservatives and German nationalists of their pre-1938 misdeeds. As the "Austrian victim myth" goes, the shared suffering of Catholic conservatives and socialists at the hands of the Nazis in the concentration camps had created a common Austrian identity.[32] A new emphasis on the two-part division of interwar Austrian life challenges the victim myth and situates this book within a growing body of literature that has investigated the discursive and cultural similarities across camps, particularly across the Catholic conservative and German nationalist divide.[33]

Given the unity of the Black Viennese field, not only does the *Lager* model require correction, but interpretations of interwar Austrian identity that emphasize a culturally distinct (non-German) "Austria" also need revision.[34] The Catholic and national *Lager* split only *after* Austrians had developed their own radical—and fascist—conservatism. Austrian scholarship has stressed the antinationalist (and anti-German) sense of Austrian identity that evolved in the interwar years, yet this development took place only late in the First Republic, if at all.[35] The relative unity of Black Vienna highlights the ambiguities of Catholic views on race, nation, and state in interwar Europe.[36] Whereas Nazism represented a bridge too far for many Catholic intellectuals, their fascist predilections shone through in most of their discursive and political practices. Black Viennese intellectuals distanced themselves from the First Republic and its political parties, engaging in a radical politics of culture. They turned the city's universities, schools, scholarly societies, and journals into ideological battlegrounds. Inviting radical participants from across Europe, they advanced debates on conservatism and fascism. Their ideas contributed mightily to the fascist turn of Austrian politics and culture. An investigation of the struggle for intellectual and political hegemony in Vienna provides a comparative, transnational example that complements recent work on the relationship between religion, politics, and ideology.

---

32. One of the more evenhanded of these articles is Pelinka, "The Great Austrian Taboo." On Austrian victimhood, see Utgaard, *Remembering and Forgetting Nazism.*

33. Boyer, "Boundaries and Transitions," 18–23. On German nationalist and Catholic conservative parallels, see Thorpe, *Pan-Germanism,* and Seefried, *Reich und Stände.* See also McEwen, *Sexual Knowledge;* Schmidt-Wendelin, *Ohne Nostalgie;* and Pyrah, *Burgtheater.*

34. Staudinger, "Austrofaschistische 'Österreich'-Ideologie," makes a similar point. On recent interpretations of Austrian identity, see Gellott, "Recent Writings."

35. See Bruckmüller, *Österreichbewusstsein;* Heer, *Kampf um Österreichs Identität;* Stourzh, *Vom Reich zur Republik;* Pelinka, *Zur österreichischen Identität;* Bischof and Pelinka, *Austrian Historical Memory;* Steinberg, *Austria as Theater.*

36. This subject has been addressed by John Connelly and others. See Connelly, *From Enemy to Brother,* particularly chaps. 1–3. See also Spicer, *Hitler's Priests;* Phayer, *Catholic Church;* Hastings, *Roots of Nazism;* Feldman, Turda, and Georgescu, *Clerical Fascism.*

Austria's interwar "new Right" figured prominently in this Europe-wide turn and deserves a prominent place in the scholarship of these phenomena.[37]

The Struggle for Hegemony and the Importance of "Intellectuals" in Interwar Europe

As an intellectual history of a city that was deeply divided culturally, socially, and politically, this book relies on Antonio Gramsci's model of hegemony to help us better understand the dynamics of ideological conflict. Gramsci argues that effective control over the state and economy derives not only from the use of violence and coercive power but also from consent achieved in civil society. Representing the public sphere between the state and economy, civil society is where people engage with one another as private individuals. Controlling this space requires an ongoing struggle in educational, academic, cultural, and social affairs. For Gramsci, the key actors in the ideological conflict are intellectuals, broadly construed as any individuals who perform mental work as part of their social function. This includes "traditional" intellectuals (clerics, artists, bureaucrats, etc.) and "organic" ones, who represent the interests of their socioeconomic class. The latter group includes politicians and social activists. While politicians confront one another in contests for state control and intellectuals contend for academic and cultural preeminence, there is also constant overlap and interaction between these two fields: politicians strive to win intellectuals for their educational and social programs; intellectuals seek state support for their ideas. Therefore, for Gramsci, political and intellectual life are inextricably intertwined, with civil society serving as the central battleground for hegemonic control.[38]

In interwar Vienna, this type of struggle for hegemony unfolded between black and red camps on the political and intellectual levels. As conservative and socialist politicians vied for parliamentary majorities nationally and within Vienna, educational, social, and cultural matters took center stage. Intellectuals became increasingly involved in these discussions, and politicians actively sought intellectual support for their ideologies. Heated debates raged across the political spectrum over the role and definition of "intellectuals" and "intellectual workers." The "question of intellectuals"[39] addressed a broader segment of the Austrian populace than typically assumed. Meanwhile,

---

37. See (among others) Payne, *Fascism in Spain;* Hanebrink, *Christian Hungary;* Soucy, *French Fascism,* vols. 1 and 2; Blinkhorn, *Fascists and Conservatives,* especially 1–49; Cornwall and Evans, *Czechoslovakia;* Hastings, *Roots of Nazism.*

38. Gramsci, *Prison Notebooks,* 142–47, 154–55, 206–16.

39. Collini, *Absent Minds,* 1–3.

intellectuals also faced off in academic societies, newspapers, and books as they pursued a limited number of academic and cultural appointments. In this way, political and intellectual struggles reinforced and enriched one another. Attracting intellectual supporters preoccupied politicians; intellectuals themselves recognized the need for political patronage. A dialectical relationship of intellectual engagement evolved. Political leaders recruited intellectuals through patronage structures. Intellectuals used these to combat ideological opponents and to build their respective visions of a better order. As Malachi Hacohen argues, "there was no escaping politics in interwar Vienna."[40] In fact, most Viennese intellectuals did not seek an escape. They created engagé cultural fields to explore radical alternatives to the status quo. Karl Popper, Otto Neurath, Helene Deutsch, and others embraced not only socialism but also a transformative idea of "revolutionism."[41] They pressed their friends and colleagues to take up the radical cause against the "metaphysical and theologizing tendencies" of the country.[42] In Black Vienna, Othmar Spann, Richard Kralik, and Joseph Eberle employed "fighting science" in support of their worldview. A closer examination of the dynamics of intellectual debate reveals the intimate interaction between politics, science, philosophy, and religion. Tracing the interactions and conflicts between intellectual groups sheds light on more general trends in Central European history. It tells the story of radicalizing and politicizing intellectual groups engaged in a European-wide struggle for ideological supremacy.

The use of the concept of hegemony forces us to recast our understanding of Viennese intellectual life in a more political fashion. The complex interplay between intellectual and political associations in interwar Vienna reveals that self-professed "apolitical" Viennese intellectuals, especially the conservatives, were hardly neutral bystanders during the Republic. Battles for intellectual hegemony dated to the late imperial period, when the Christian Socials and Social Democrats first began cultivating ties to Habsburg intellectuals over school reform, social policy, and electoral change.[43] Vienna quickly became a hotbed of intellectual activity, with intellectual circles springing up all over the city. Conceiving of postwar Vienna as a "system of microcircuits," this work looks at the evolving cross-disciplinary and political engagements of

---

40. Hacohen, *Karl Popper,* 290.

41. Deutsch, *Confrontations with Myself,* 82, quoted in Danto, *Freud's Free Clinics,* 3, 31.

42. Rudolf Carnap, Hans Hahn, and Otto Neurath, "The Scientific Conception of the World: The Vienna Circle," in Neurath, Neurath, and Cohen, *Empiricism and Sociology,* 317.

43. Boyer, *Culture and Political Crisis.* On the continuities between the imperial and republican eras, see "Forum: Habsburg History," 232–35.

intellectuals.[44] As Edward Timms notes, postwar Viennese circles created a vibrant counterculture, challenging the hegemony of conservative Austria.[45] This makes it all the more urgent to understand those forces that Red Viennese cultural movements *countered*. Doing so obliges us to take a fresh look at how cultural and political forms of capital were produced and accumulated.[46] This interdisciplinary history explores Vienna's polarized intellectual life and the radicalization and politicization of its culture. In doing so, it argues for the importance of Vienna for our understanding of interwar European intellectual trends.

To achieve a relational understanding of cultural fields, red and black Viennese milieus are interpreted as dynamic, historically contingent constellations of thought, not as discrete, monolithic entities. Not only were intellectuals affected by historical events, but their ideas also shaped the world around them. In Red Vienna, intellectuals initially engaged passionately but eventually grew disillusioned with the Austro-Marxists as democracy and socialism failed to take root and radical conservatism gained in strength.[47] Red intellectuals fought a rearguard action against conservatives in the corridors of knowledge and power, producing remarkable scholarship yet failing to turn the intellectual tide. Nevertheless, black intellectuals felt threatened by the red counterculture and lamented the decline of Austrian values. While they reasserted their hegemony in Vienna and Austria, they dreamed of European influence, which eluded them. While most conservatives advocated for fascist solutions and celebrated the destruction of the First Republic, the Austrofascist state satisfied few. Black Viennese intellectuals continued to advocate for even more radical solutions. Ironically, the "successful" struggle for hegemony waged by the Blacks led to the collapse of the vibrant, hothouse culture of interwar Vienna and indirectly to the rise of Hitler.

Outline of the Book

The book advances chronologically through the years 1918–38, alternating between black and red chapters. Chapter 1 explores the evolution of Black Vienna in the early interwar years. Focusing on the Austrian Catholic scientific society, the Leo-Gesellschaft, and the most influential Central

---

44. Edward Timms, "Cultural Parameters between the Wars," in Holmes and Silverman, *Interwar Vienna,* 23–29, and "School for Socialism," in Beniston and Vilain, *Red Vienna,* 36–59.
45. Timms, "Cultural Parameters," 26.
46. This relational approach draws on Bourdieu, *Field of Cultural Production.*
47. Rabinbach, *Crisis,* and Hanisch, *Der große Illusionist,* highlight this fatalism.

European conservative journal *Das neue Reich,* it examines how conservatives defined the concept of "the intellectual" and appealed to that class. It reveals that although interwar Vienna voted red, blacks maintained hegemony in intellectual and cultural life. Intellectuals, divided before the war over questions of German nationalism and the place of Catholicism in Austrian and German conservatism, came together to combat the socialism, "Judaism," and capitalism of the First Republic. The Black Viennese field radicalized over time in response to worsening economic and political conditions. The successes of radicals like *Das neue Reich* editor Joseph Eberle showed the weakness of democratic and moderate ideologies in Austrian conservative thought and foreshadowed Austria's fascist turn.

Chapter 2 looks at the recruitment efforts undertaken by the Austro-Marxists to win "intellectual workers" to the socialist cause in the early Republic. In the wake of the 1918 Austrian Revolution and their 1919 electoral victory, the Social Democrats believed they had an opportunity to win traditional, nonsocialist intellectuals with their social and economic policies. Over the next few years, socialists filled the pages of their theoretical journal *Der Kampf* with articles about intellectual work and recruited non-Marxist, progressive intellectuals to contribute to their movement. Despite the successful recruitment of progressive, Jewish, and "free-floating" intellectuals from outside the corridors of knowledge and power, the Austro-Marxists struggled to attract the broader intellectual class discussed above.

Chapter 3 explores the popularity of authoritarian and fascist ideas in Central Europe through an investigation of the one of the most influential Black Viennese circles, the Spannkreis, centered on the sociologist and philosopher Othmar Spann. Spann's holistic ideology enjoyed widespread academic support in Austria, the Sudetenland, and parts of Germany. Never content with mere academic influence, Spann curried favor with radical political movements, including the Austrian Heimwehr, the Italian Fascists, and the Nazi Party. The robustness of Spann's connections—both intellectual and political—demonstrates the close interaction between science and politics in interwar Central Europe. It also shows the relative unity of Viennese conservatives in a common front against Red Vienna.

One of the groups that challenged the Spannkreis was the Vienna Circle of logical empiricists. Chapter 4 examines the social activities of members of the Verein Ernst Mach (Ernst Mach Society), the public arm of the circle. It contests the claim of Moritz Schlick, one of the group's founders, that the society was "absolutely unpolitical" by showing how its members engaged in social and political struggles in adult education and welfare centers and intellectual societies. The group brought together people from radical, antiestablishment organizations committed to the defeat of the hegemonic "metaphysical and theologizing leanings" of Black Vienna. The involvements of its members demonstrate that progressive science and philosophy had politicized and radicalized by the late 1920s in reaction to the continued conservative predominance in the academy and state.

Chapter 5 investigates the emergence of the monarchist movement the Österreichische Aktion, situating Viennese radical conservatism in the larger context of European authoritarianism and fascism. Traditionally portrayed as a moderate force in Austrian life, the Aktion in fact drew on the work of the proto-fascist Action Française and the Italian Fascists in crafting a "new conservative" movement. Despite its anti-Prussian and pro-Habsburg rhetoric, the group's ideology reinforced notions of German supremacy in Central Europe that overlapped with other contemporary German nationalist and Catholic conservative views. Therefore the chapter calls into question traditional three-*Lager* interpretations of interwar Austrian culture by demonstrating the relative coherence of conservative thought through the 1930s.

Chapter 6 investigates the rise and fall of social and political engagement by progressive intellectuals in the face of Austria's fascist turn in the late 1920s. The chapter argues that the intellectual work of Red Viennese men and women cannot be separated from their practical activities and must be understood against the backdrop of worsening political and economic conditions in Europe. Intellectuals initially believed the time was ripe for transformation and the social democratic movement provided the best means for realizing their intellectual and social goals. As the Austro-Marxists faced repeated setbacks in the late 1920s and 1930s, Red Viennese intellectuals became more critical and distant from the movement. The chapter challenges the idea that "apolitical" science existed in interwar Vienna, contending that disengaged thought became possible only after the decline of Austro-Marxism and the triumph of fascism.

The last chapter looks at the split within the Black Viennese camp and the triumph of its most radical members during the Austrofascist years. Focusing on the struggles between the radicals around Eberle and the more moderate thinkers around Dietrich Hildebrand, the chapter shows that most figures in the Black Viennese field had embarked on the road toward fascism and *Anschluss* by the early 1930s. Intellectuals thus paved the way for a Nazi takeover. This chapter and the conclusion examine the implications of the Black Viennese triumph on the First and Second Republics and on Austrian collective memory. These sections argue that the relative lack of attention to problematic aspects of interwar Viennese culture has contributed to a slow "coming to terms with the past" (*Vergangenheitsbewältigung*).

CHAPTER 1

The Emergence of Black Vienna

On 1 October 1922, the historian and author Richard Kralik celebrated his seventieth birthday, and the Viennese Catholic community took the opportunity to honor their hero and extol the strengths of their intellectual movement. The author Hermann Bahr and the Swiss anthropologist Wilhelm Oehl each wrote laudatory pieces in the Christian Social newspaper, the *Reichspost*. The following day, a full-page spread recounted the festivities from the "Kralik-Feier," hosted at Kralik's manor in Grinzing, a wealthy district of Vienna.[1] According to the article, the celebration attested to the "cultural sense and will" of Austrian Catholics while displaying their commitment to Kralik's German and Christian ideals.[2] Similar professions appeared in the intellectual journal he had helped found, *Das neue Reich*. It proclaimed Kralik's significance for Austria, Catholicism, and *Deutschtum*, lauding his pioneering work in literature, philosophy, and history.[3] Kralik was portrayed as the most important intellectual figure in contemporary Austria and a man of world-historical stature, the equal of Goethe or Leibniz. Finally, the Leo-Gesellschaft, an Austrian academic society for

---

1. Hermann Bahr and Wilhelm Oehl, "Richard Kralik," *RP,* October 1, 1922, 3; "Die Kralik-Feier in Wien," *RP,* October 1, 1922, 3–4.

2. "Kralik-Feier," 3.

3. See *NR* 5, nos. 1–4 (1922–23).

Catholic scholars that Kralik had popularized, ran a series of lectures devoted to his life and work.[4]

Not everyone agreed with this hagiographic outpouring. Karl Kraus, author and editor of the journal *Die Fackel,* leveled an acidulous broadside against Kralik and his acolytes. Kraus lampooned the festivities, eviscerated the Catholic intellectual community, and cast their hero as an exemplar of the worst Austrian traits, an intellectual lightweight and a failure. With few exceptions, Kraus asserted, one could honestly say "that Christian Social and German National literature conducts itself with dilettantism as a spiritual direction and illiteracy as an artistic principle; it is a blinkered worldview and thoroughly blockheaded."[5] Kraus noted a significant overlap between the work of conservative Catholics and German nationalists, which manifested itself in their chauvinistic enthusiasm for German culture and the Habsburg Reich. He assailed their banality and suggested that under normal circumstances, "talents" like Kralik would be hidden from the public by embarrassed family members.[6] He mocked the *Reichspost* and its attempt to portray Kralik as a neglected universal genius. Kraus satirized Kralik, the so-called guarantor of Austrian rebirth, and the man "whose name is synonymous with Austria": "One may see that good ideas in history always come too late, because, rather than this country being condemned to carry along with the name 'Austria' the odium of the monarchy and the bloodbath it perpetrated, one could have advanced the proposal at Saint Germain to name the country 'Kraliksreich' and all would have been ameliorated."[7] Kraus was referring to the outrage conservatives felt about the Paris Peace Accords and their dislike for republican Austria. Kraus rejected conservative claims that Kralik and his movement could "restore" Austria, instead holding them responsible for the First World War and its aftermath.

By honoring Kralik above all other Austrians, Kraus continued, the *Reichspost* also demonstrated how little respect it had for its countrymen, for Kralik was actually talentless. He dismissed Kralik's universality, instead suggesting that his apparent breadth of knowledge stemmed from an utter lack of depth. Kralik's search for the connections between all things always revealed "black-gold" threads—restorationist sympathies. In Kraus's eyes, Kralik was a nothing but a reactionary hack.[8]

---

4. See *JÖLG,* 1924.
5. Karl Kraus, "Kralikstag," *Die Fackel* 601 (1922): 110–11.
6. Ibid., 114.
7. Ibid., 115.
8. Ibid., 116–17.

Despite this anti-Kralik vitriol, Kraus's real target was the *Reichspost*. Kraus had long viewed it as his primary enemy in his one-man war on bad journalism.[9] He did not typically concern himself with Christian Social and German nationalist literary publications since he considered the writers morons "incapable of meaningful communication."[10] In fact, this screed was the sole extended discussion of Kralik and the institutions associated with him—the Leo-Gesellschaft, the Gralbund, and the weeklies *Das neue Reich* and *Die schönere Zukunft*—in Kraus's voluminous writings.

The underestimation and dismissal of conservative Vienna, represented here in Kraus's work, typified progressive Viennese views during the interwar era. Red Viennese thinkers did not fully appreciate the intensity or tenacity of Austrian conservatism's antidemocratic, antimodern, and anti-Semitic ideology. They also missed the developing consensus drawing together the two main camps of Austrian conservative thought: the German nationals and the Catholic Christian Socials.[11] As political and economic conditions worsened in the immediate postwar years, authoritarian intellectuals only gained in influence, with disastrous results.

Kraus's verdict on the conservative Viennese intelligentsia nevertheless still enjoys pride of place today in Austrian scholarship. Journals like Joseph Eberle's *Das neue Reich* and its spin-off *Die schönere Zukunft* remain "beyond the pale"[12] of inquiry on Viennese intellectual life, whereas Kraus' *Die Fackel* remains a standard point of reference.[13] Undoubtedly, *Die Fackel* was one of the most significant interwar Viennese cultural institutions: for example, its circulation during the First Republic has been estimated at around ten thousand copies.[14] As memoirs from the era attest, Kraus's writings were a touchstone for First Republic intellectuals.[15] Ironically, the journals that Kraus so readily dismissed had an even wider readership among the educated classes. They were among the largest intellectual publications in interwar Europe. Beyond their popular support, the journals also attracted leading conservative writers, academics, and politicians.[16] Twenty percent of all contributors were university professors, mostly from Vienna, and 40 percent had some form

---

9. Timms, *Karl Kraus,* 2:268–286, especially 268–73.

10. Timms, *Karl Kraus,* 2:95.

11. Wandruszka, "Österreichs politische Struktur," 291–300.

12. Timms, *Karl Kraus,* 2:95.

13. In addition to the Timms biography, see Janik and Toulmin's *Wittgenstein's Vienna.*

14. Alda, *Karl Kraus' Verhältnis,* 14–15. Other estimates put the journal's circulation at between 8,500 and 10,000.

15. Elias Canetti's memoir explicitly pays homage to Kraus.

16. Hofer, "Joseph Eberle," 106–9.

of advanced degree.[17] Although this participation by no means guaranteed sophisticated discussions, it challenges Kraus's assertion that these conservatives were rank dilettantes and "morons."

To better understand Red Vienna and the landscape of interwar Viennese intellectual life in its complexity, we need a fuller investigation of Kralik's Black Vienna. The intellectuals of this field occupied important academic, cultural, political, and religious positions during the First Republic. Overwhelmingly Catholic and German nationalist,[18] stridently antidemocratic, antirepublican, anticapitalist, and anti-Semitic, they helped push the politics of the First Republic toward authoritarianism, culminating in civil war and the Austrofascist *Ständestaat*. Their social and political views, expressed in scholarly efforts they characterized as unpartisan and apolitical (*überparteilich, unpolitisch*) actually revealed the politicization of intellectual life in Central Europe.

This chapter examines the development of several important conservative Viennese intellectual milieus from the late Habsburg Empire to the early years of the Republic. In the late imperial period, the Christian Social party under Karl Lueger and Albert Gessmann dominated politics and culture in Vienna. A younger generation of activists emerged, pushing Christian Socialism toward a greater commitment to Catholic social values and political Catholicism. They saw Vienna as the central battleground in an ongoing Habsburg *Kulturkampf* between religious (German Catholic) forces and secular (Jewish, liberal, socialist) ones.[19] As part of this struggle, Catholic intellectuals formed the Leo-Gesellschaft, a scholarly society that disseminated Christian, scientific ideas and counteracted modern science and socialism. After the First World War, the dissolution of the Habsburg Empire, the Austrian Revolution, and the "tragedy" of the Paris Peace Accords, the society, like Austrian conservatism more generally, underwent politicization and radicalization. Members saw themselves as defenders of the "Austrian idea" against the materialism and atheism of Red Vienna. Despite their continued popularity in the universities and among the educated public, these intellectuals felt embattled by the masses and "Bolshevik" ideologues. The sustained growth of Black Viennese intellectual outlets suggests that conservative ideas may have suffered a setback in the early years of the Republic when the socialists established Red Vienna, but they nevertheless remained entrenched in Viennese cultural affairs.

---

17. Werner, *"Das Neue Reich,"* 9–10.
18. On German nationalism, see Thorpe, *Pan-Germanism,* 5–8, 30–8.
19. Boyer, *Culture and Political Crisis,* 298–330, 448–58.

The weekly *Das neue Reich,* run by Joseph Eberle, was another outlet for the emergent radicalism of Black Viennese conservatism. What began as a cultural appendage of the Christian Social party quickly established itself as an independent voice for a more strident worldview. A closer analysis of ideas presented in the work of *Neues Reich* intellectuals—particularly Eberle, Kralik, and the philosophers Hans Eibl and Johannes Messner—elucidates the ideological orientation of this milieu. Though these men did not share the same views on all subjects, their individual views delimited the conservative ideological spectrum on issues of democracy, dictatorship, capitalism, anti-Semitism, and more. The significant confluence of German nationalist and Catholic conservative ideological strains within the capital, evidenced especially by discussions of the German Reich, suggests the need for a revision of the traditional historiographical categories of the First Republic.[20] The analysis of the origins of Black Vienna suggests that Austrian conservative intellectuals—whether "German national" or "Catholic conservative"—formed a relatively coherent and influential ideological space, designed to subvert the political and cultural order of the First Republic. While hardly monolithic, this cultural field was more integrated than has been assumed, especially before 1933.

The chapter concludes with a look at the origins of the schism that dominated Austrian conservatism in the 1930s. While a minority of Black Viennese intellectuals supported "moderate" Christian socialism and democratic values, the ultimate victory of Eberle's new publication, *Die schönere Zukunft,* suggests that a new Right actually predominated in Vienna. In sum, this chapter challenges the long-held view that interwar Vienna was a fortress of progressive, red thinking. The city was an intellectual and ideological battleground where the reds gained only a partial victory over the blacks, primarily in municipal politics.

Prewar Beginnings: The Leo-Gesellschaft and Gralbund

In 1930, the editors of the *Arbeiter-Zeitung* lamented, "One has experienced that membership in the Leo-Gesellschaft is decisive for appointment to professorships in the medical faculty and that the habilitation of lecturers [*Privatdozenten*] in physics is denied by Germanists and historians who reject the candidate's political views."[21] Although this may have been an exaggeration by the socialist press, the Leo-Gesellschaft did enjoy overwhelming influence

---

20. Wandruszka, "Österreichs politische Struktur," 291–300.
21. *AZ,* July 11, 1930.

in intellectual affairs during the First Republic. It had a dues-paying membership of 2,500 members with two-thirds in the Vienna branch. Several hundred of these members were full university professors. Writers and independent scholars, journalists and social reformers, priests and politicians all participated in meetings. Dozens of lectures and courses were offered every year, which attracted audiences that numbered in the hundreds. This significant organization has attracted only limited scholarly attention, however.[22] A closer look at the society's historical development demonstrates the sustained popularity of conservative thought in Vienna at the beginning of the twentieth century, the increasing politicization of its scholarly organizations, and the convergence of German nationalist and Catholic conservatism after the Great War.

The Leo-Gesellschaft was founded in 1892 by a group of six scholars led by Franz Schindler, a professor of theology at the University of Vienna and one of the leading ideologues in the Christian Social party. The group was named after Pope Leo XIII, and its founders wanted to establish an Austrian society for Catholic scholars that followed the example of the German Görres-Gesellschaft. In addition to demanding that the society be Austrian and scientific, they also stressed the importance of Catholic faith: "The task of the Leo-Gesellschaft is . . . the advancement and elucidation of science in a Christian spirit in all disciplines based on its own, autonomous research."[23] Scholars could pursue their own research interests as long as they were in keeping with the ethical foundations of the church, especially as laid out in the papal encyclical "Rerum Novarum." Catholic doctrine did not dictate the objects of investigation; it simply provided the ethical foundation and "Christian spirit" for research.

The society had an initial membership of eight hundred, subdivided into five sections: historical, headed by Professor Heinrich Srbik, an ardent German nationalist; social, led by followers of Karl Vogelsang, a Catholic social theorist and father of the radical corporatist visions of *Sozialreform*;[24] legal; literary and philological; and philosophical and theological. Most leading members resided in Vienna and were full university professors.[25] Despite professions of political neutrality, such claims had little basis in reality.

---

22. One book examines the Leo-Gesellschaft at length: Beniston, *Welttheater*, chap. 4. See also Weiß, *Rechtskatholizismus*, 42–63.

23. Schindler, *Leo-Gesellschaft*, 13.

24. Diamant, *Austrian Catholics*, 42–48. *Sozialreform* advocated an immediate return to the "organic" social order of the Middle Ages. Its antithesis was *Sozialpolitik*, the quest for the realization of a Christian order through gradual change.

25. Schindler, *Leo-Gesellschaft*, 13–20.

Schindler was one of many Leo-Gesellschaft members closely affiliated with Karl Lueger's Christian Social movement. More than a dozen members were in the conservative Austrian Herrenhaus. The Emperor and Archduke Franz Ferdinand were also contributors.[26]

The powerful position of the Christian Social movement in Vienna from the 1890s until the Great War contributed significantly to the Leo-Gesellschaft's early success. Representing a "politics in a new key," Karl Lueger's populist blend of anti-Semitism, anticapitalism, and municipal Christian socialism gathered momentum in the late 1880s and early 1890s.[27] Attracting members from across the middle classes—public officials, businessmen, white-collar employees, independent property owners, and educated professionals—the party won control of Vienna in 1895 (though the Emperor did not appoint Lueger mayor until 1897). Over the next decade, Lueger and his close associates Alfred Gessmann and Franz Schindler built a network of patronage in education and municipal government agencies, attracting educators, intellectuals, and technical experts.[28] Schindler, the party's key ideologue, cultivated the support of intellectuals through the Christian student association, the Cartellverband (CV), the newspaper the *Reichspost,* the Volksbund, and the Leo-Gesellschaft.[29] For the next two decades, the Christian Social Party dominated Viennese city politics and intellectual life.[30]

The Leo-Gesellschaft sustained substantial growth during the period of Christian Social ascendancy, making it the largest academic organization in Austria. Membership quadrupled to over three thousand. Over two hundred professors contributed, as did dozens of Catholic theologians and writers. Subsections in the arts and humanities were added. The society published eighty-seven volumes on a wide variety of subjects, with a concentration on Catholic social theory and medieval German culture. It distributed nine scholarly journals. Among many luminaries, future chancellors, ministers, and university rectors stood out. This was not solely a Catholic or Christian Social organization, however. Many individuals who figured prominently in German nationalist fraternities and associations, such as Srbik, Max Hussarek, Anton Orel, and Othmar Spann, also played leading roles in the

---

26. The society's *Jahrbuch,* later *Die Kultur,* published a full member list until the Great War. Members of the aristocracy made up around 25 percent of the society. Ten percent had university titles.

27. Schorske, *Fin-de-Siecle Vienna,* 116–80.

28. See Boyer, *Political Radicalism.*

29. Boyer, *Culture and Political Crisis,* 169, 298–30.

30. Ibid., especially 1–59, 446–52.

organization.[31] The society's popularity dwarfed that of progressive alternatives. As of 1912–13, the Viennese *Volkshochschulen,* the lynchpin of liberal and socialist education, boasted about 40 regular teachers (*Lehrer*), including 16 with university titles, 385 participants in its discussion groups, and 2,875 total students. Conservative intellectuals clearly predominated in imperial Vienna.[32]

In the decade before the Great War, the Christian Social movement developed from a more ecumenical organization into a decidedly Catholic one, and the Leo-Gesellschaft was at the center of those changes.[33] The decisive figure was Richard Kralik. Kralik first took a leading ideological role in 1903, spurring an "integralist" turn in Austrian conservatism that joined counterrevolutionary and antimodernist social goals, German nationalism, Catholicism, and anti-Semitism.[34] As Max Hussarek recalled, "He [Kralik] challenged atheist conceptions in the realms of philosophy, natural science, history, pedagogy, moral and political theory, and finally the arts. He showed that in all periods positive forces win out and that the advance of culture is based not on a series of revolutionary heretical appearances [*revolutionärer Ketzererscheinungen*] but on the enduring work of those who overcame heresies."[35] Kralik believed that Catholics were the defenders of the one true worldview and that they must combat the apostasies of socialism, democracy, and capitalism. Through this *Kulturkampf,* the threefold mission of the Catholic intellectual worldview—unity of science, the realization of moral enlightenment, and the attainment of aesthetic perfection—would be achieved. This conflict of worldviews was more than cultural; it was political: "All past revolutions in the areas of politics and culture have been victoriously overcome [by the church] and after all the culture wars, nothing is better equipped for the future than faith and the church."[36] Kralik argued that political, social, and cultural issues could no longer be considered independently; they had to be integrated into a single project. He urged Catholics, ethnic Germans, and conservatives to enter the fray. The society embraced this radical and political turn.[37]

The significance of this call to arms was due to Kralik's stature in the Catholic community. As Judith Beniston argues, Kralik was the most important

---

31. See Schindler, *Leo-Gesellschaft,* and Beniston, *Welttheater,* 89–93.
32. Kutalek and Fellinger, *Zur Wiener Volksbildung,* 173–76. Of these students, 43 percent were bureaucrats and civil servants.
33. Boyer, *Culture and Political Crisis,* 328.
34. Beniston, *Welttheater,* 89–93.
35. Max Hussarek, "Katholizismus und modernes Geistesleben," *NR* 4 (1923–24): 15.
36. Ibid.
37. Beniston, *Welttheater,* 91.

intellectual in Catholic Vienna from the 1890s until his death in 1934.[38] Born in 1852 in Bohemia and raised in Linz, he matriculated at the University of Vienna and received his J.D. in 1876. After he completed his exams, his father died, leaving him a small fortune that freed him from financial constraints and allowed him to work as an independent scholar. In 1877, he joined the Pernerstorfer circle, associating with Victor Adler, Gustav Mahler, Heinrich Friedjung, and Hugo Wolf. Therein he developed strong German nationalist feelings.[39] Influenced by Wagner and Nietzsche, Kralik wrote theater pieces and literary works designed to enact a German spiritual rebirth. His works rehashed religious and historical themes from the Austrian, German, and Christian past. His antimodernist preferences and his calls for *völkisch* rebirth resonated with Catholic elites and the uneducated masses alike.[40] Kralik hosted the largest weekly salon in Vienna, which welcomed over one hundred participants, including writers, academics, and politicians. He even enjoyed the endorsement of Karl Lueger.[41]

Intensifying battles between conservatives and Viennese socialists and liberals in the *Freie Schule* movement over educational reform and academic freedom reinforced Kralik's ideological push. Conservatives realized that political, religious, and ideological issues were interrelated. The Wahrmund affair of 1908 brought these concerns to a head. Ludwig Wahrmund, a professor of canon law and ecclesiastical history at the University of Innsbruck, angered many Catholics with his liberal theology and polemical attacks on modern Catholicism. Attempts to force him from his faculty position nearly split the Christian Social party and drove a wedge into the parliamentary coalition of bourgeois parties in imperial Austria. No longer could the Christian Socials allow religious matters to take a back seat to political exigencies; like the Austro-Marxists, they sought a closed community with a shared worldview (*Weltanschauungsgemeinschaft*).[42] A younger generation of scholars, trained in the Leo-Gesellschaft and Katholischer Volksbund and raised on Kralik's ideas, rose to prominence in conservative circles, including the Christian Social Party.[43] They emphasized the importance of social, economic, and political theory in transforming the world. The Leo-Gesellschaft reflected this new focus. Until 1910, its subsections held roughly the same

---

38. Ibid., 3. On Kralik, see Geehr, *Aesthetics of Horror*.

39. Beniston, *Welttheater*, 60–61. On the Pernerstorfer circle, see McGrath, *Dionysian Art*.

40. Kralik argued that Catholic literature was the only true literary form. He challenged Catholic modernists on the subject, famously quarreling with Carl Muth, editor of *Hochland*. See Hanisch, 'Der katholische Literaturstreit," 125–60.

41. Beniston, *Welttheater*, 68–75, 125.

42. Boyer, *Culture and Political Crisis*, 191–211.

43. Ibid., 306–21.

number of lectures while the majority of publications came from the religious and historical sections. By 1914, the social scientific section became the defining subgroup. It conducted over half of the society's total lectures; membership reflected this interest.[44] The more measured tone of Schindler disappeared from the society as the conflict between the emergent conservative and socialist *Lager* intensified. The death of Lueger in 1910 and the eclipse of Gessmann's national party beginning in 1911 intensified these trends.

Radical political articulations became more frequent once the Great War commenced. The Leo-Gesellschaft underwent a politicization and radicalization of its ideological positions. In its flagship journal, Kralik authored an article on the significance of Austria for the past and future of Central Europe. Heinrich Lammasch, the final minister president of the Habsburg Empire, argued for the Catholic foundations of all state theory and the formation of a faith-based League of Nations. The author Hermann Bahr wrote a corrosive article about the "civilization" of Western Europe. The latter piece, titled "Reason and Science," highlights the increasingly antimodernist, anticosmopolitan, and chauvinistic attitudes of Austrian conservatism:

> Before the war the West claimed that its peoples had common traits. There was a Cosmopolis, the kingdom of good Europeans, the glittering world of millionaires, dilettantes and aesthetes, and the cosmopolitans [*vaterlandlose Existenzen*] in sleeper cars.... There was the proud republic of spirit in science and art. There was international law. There were Internationals.... They believed that in addition to these common purposes they had a common means: human reason.... The war robbed us of all of these commonalities.[45]

Bahr mocked the ideals of cosmopolitanism and the Enlightenment and wondered whether these values had long ago ceased to exist. Moreover, he cast the discussion of reason in starkly nationalistic terms. Unlike German reason, the Western variety smacked of utilitarianism and pragmatism. Bahr identified Western reason with coarse instrumentalism: "Truth is what serves my drives. And there are only two drives in Western men: the drive for power and for money."[46]

The views expressed by Bahr did not differ much from dozens of other proclamations made by intellectuals during the world war, yet they attest

---

44. Franz Martin Schindler, "Die Leo-Gesellschaft, 1892–1917," *Kultur*, 1917, 241–43.
45. Hermann Bahr, "Vernunft und Wissenschaft," *Kultur*, 1917, 34.
46. Ibid., 34–36. For more on Bahr, see Steinberg, *Austria as Theater*, 131–41.

to the transformation of the Leo-Gesellschaft and Austrian conservatism as their world crumbled. Before the war, the society specialized in theological and philosophical treatises. When the war did not unfold the way these intellectuals hoped, they were faced with an inhospitable political and social reality. In response to these changes, Austrian conservative thinkers radicalized and sought broader support from within the Black Viennese ideological milieu.

The Postwar Politicization of Black Vienna

The Austrian conservative intelligentsia found itself in a precarious position after the war, as exemplified by the status of the Leo-Gesellschaft. The group endured straitened circumstances during and immediately after the Great War. It lost half of its total membership and the majority of its members residing outside of the new Austrian Republic. It ceased publishing its book series and halted production of *Die Kultur.* No general sessions were held during the war, and the total number of yearly lectures fell from seventy to thirty. Its revenues dropped precipitously with the loss of royal and aristocratic support, the suspension of dues collection, and inflation.[47]

Growing anxiety about the viability of the conservative worldview manifested itself in a turn to politics and a radicalization of rhetoric. As seen in the Hermann Bahr essay, the Leo-Gesellschaft announced itself as adamantly conservative, explicitly German, and anti-Enlightenment as early as 1917. When *Das Jahrbuch,* the successor to *Die Kultur,* began to appear in 1924, these tendencies were more pronounced. Whereas previously religious, historical, and philosophical essays predominated, now political discussions took center stage. The lead article in the first edition, written by Friedrich Schreyvogl—a future drama professor at the University of Vienna, German nationalist, and eventual Nazi supporter—aligned the society with the radical wing of the Christian Social party. He argued that only the Christian Socials understood the "facts" of the contemporary political world. He lauded them for their Catholic values. He condemned the Social Democrats as a party of mass violence and materialism and suggested that they be actively resisted. Finally, he argued for the termination of the current political system: "The renunciation of parliamentarianism, the derision of all intellectual tendencies based on the pure reason of the second-best, that reason developed by the mass movements—all of these are reminders that only a thoroughly spiritual

---

47. Theodor Innitzer, "Die Leo-Gesellschaft 1916–17," *Kultur,* 1918, 241–43.

revolution will bring an end to the political revolutions."[48] With this statement of elitist, antidemocratic, and counterrevolutionary fervor, the Leo-
Gesellschaft announced its turn away from strictly scholarly concerns toward
political and social activism.

Participation by leading Christian Social politicians enhanced the group's
prestige and contributed to its politicization. Most of these participants came
from the younger generation of religious radicals who emerged after Karl
Lueger's death in 1910. Ignaz Seipel, a theology professor and two-time
chancellor of Austria, made the connection between conservative politics,
the Catholic Church, and the society explicit. In an obituary for Franz
Schindler, Seipel could have focused on the scholarly achievements of his
mentor; instead, he stressed Schindler's political accomplishments. Not only
was Schindler's name synonymous with the Leo-Gesellschaft, Seipel suggested, but he was also the leading ideologue of the Christian Social Party.
Involved from its inception, the party owed its current political orientation
to him. Seipel portrayed Schindler as a political figure first and a scholar
second, a characterization that applied more to Seipel than to Schindler. This
reflected the ideological priorities of Austrian conservatism in the 1920s.
Seipel contributed articles and lectures to the society until the end of his life,
as did at least ten former and future chancellors, ten rectors of the University
of Vienna,[49] a half dozen education ministers,[50] archbishops, and the majority
of the Austrian Academy of Sciences.

The politicization of conservative intellectuals represented more than a
simple identification with the Christian Social party, however; it signified a
commitment to a German nationalism based on ideas of a pan-German Reich
in Central Europe.[51] The Leo-Gesellschaft provided a forum for Catholic
intellectuals of different stripes to voice their views, including those associated with the German national *Lager*. Catholics in the society, led by Richard
Weiskirchner, Leopold Kunschak, and Richard Kralik, reached beyond the
"Lueger coalition" to combat the Social Democrats and the First Republic.[52]
Along with the aforementioned Schreyvogl, Hans Eibl, a scholar of patristics
and early Christianity, was a leading exemplar of this Catholic-nationalist

---

48. Ibid., 16.
49. In chronological order: Heinrich Swoboda, Adolf Menzel, Alfons Dopsch, Johannes Döller,
Hans Sperl, Theodor Innitzer (who was also archbishop of Vienna), Wenzel Gleispach, Othenio Abel,
Ernst Tomek, and Oswald Menghin.
50. Josef Resch, Anton Rintelen, Emmerich Czermak, Heinrich Srbik (also the president of the
Academy of Sciences), Kurt Schuschnigg, Hans Pertner, and Oswald Menghin.
51. On *Reichsgedanken* in Austria, see Breuning, *Vision des Reiches* and Seefried, *Reich und Stände*.
52. This confirms and reinforces John Boyer's argument about Christian Socials and German
nationals in the late imperial period. See Boyer, *Culture and Political Crisis,* 448.

synthesis. In his work, he addressed two recurring themes for postwar conservatives: the travesty of the Paris Peace Accords and the historical mission of the German Reich. Eibl became one of the most popular Black Viennese intellectuals as a result of these writings. He excoriated the peace treaty, calling it "the greatest violation of human rights in history."[53] He argued that the *Diktat* foisted on the Central Powers violated the preliminary peace agreement of autumn 1918. Criticisms that compared the punitive terms of the Brest-Litovsk treaty to those of the Treaty of Versailles were groundless since "Russia did not lose an inch of true Russian soil [*echt russischem Boden*]."[54] Eibl did not clarify what qualified as "true soil," but his subsequent advocacy of German *Lebensraum* and his use of *Blut und Boden* rhetoric suggest he conceived of most of Central Europe as German land. His *völkisch* understanding of national belonging enjoyed a positive reception by conservatives across the political spectrum.

Not content with a juridical argument, Eibl also argued for the Central Powers' blamelessness during the crisis of July 1914 and for the humanitarian efforts of their armies in liberating Eastern Europe from barbarian Russia. In an unironic statement of revisionist history, Eibl contended that one group in particular owed Germans a debt of gratitude: the Jews. "Jews from around the world should thank the German people, since they led eastern Jews out of the ghetto through their victory over the armies of the Czar....We Germans from Austria can likewise enjoy the honor in the claim that the German people were the greatest liberators in this war."[55] Jews, Poles, and the whole of Central Europe owed their freedom more to the Germans than to Wilson or the Entente, since it was the Central Powers that removed Russian czarism from the map. As a reward for this "liberation," Eibl advocated for the immediate *Anschluss* of Germany and Austria and the reestablishment of a German-dominated "Third Reich" in Central Europe to rehabilitate and reanimate the German and Austrian "ideas." His historical argument drew on Richard Kralik's monumental histories of the Habsburg Empire and Joseph Eberle's and Heinrich Srbik's revisionist Austro-centric German histories. While these writers acknowledged and celebrated the multiethnic character of *Mitteleuropa,* they argued that German tradition represented the highest form of culture in the region; all others were subordinate. Eibl's contribution offered the first presentation to the society of

---

53. Hans Eibl, "Die Stellung der Nation," *JÖLG,* 1924, 28.
54. Ibid.
55. Ibid., 30.

conservative Austria's political mission. It also highlighted the dangers of the collapse of conservative values in the postwar period.

Contrary to the pessimistic pronouncements made by Black Viennese intellectuals in the first years of the Republic, conservative ideology enjoyed a healthy resurgence. By 1924, the Leo-Gesellschaft had stabilized its finances and began to recoup its membership losses. Membership increased from 1,600 in 1916 to 2,000 in 1923. By 1928, there were 2,500 members, a number that remained constant until 1938. Of these, 1,700 were involved in the Vienna main branch. The most important section remained the social scientific one. This section boasted contributions from over a hundred Viennese professors, as well as others ranging from pro-fascist German nationalists like Othmar Spann, Alois Hudal, Oswald Menghin, and Joseph Nadler to conservative academics like Alfred Verdross and Eric Voegelin. In assessing the relative popularity of Viennese conservatism, a comparison with the *Volkshochschulen* is instructive. In the postwar years, the number of active participants in the latter's discussion groups *(Fachgruppen)* increased to 1,100 members. Twenty instructors possessed university titles. Student enrollment increased from around 3,000 before the war to about 9,000 in 1931, yet these numbers were still smaller than those of the conservative, German nationalist-dominated University of Vienna.[56] These numbers further reveal that although progressives and socialists were making advances in higher education thanks to the Red Viennese city government, they had not supplanted conservatives.

Although the Leo-Gesellschaft was at the center of the reformulation of Black Viennese ideology, it lacked a broader public. The group published three thousand copies of its *Jahrbuch,* which indicated that its readership did not extend beyond its core membership into the ranks of the educated middle class, the *Bildungsbürgertum.* Moreover, despite its political turn, the Leo-Gesellschaft continued to devote much of its energy to scholarly research. Discussions within the society rarely referred explicitly to economic or political events, couching their arguments in theoretical terms. The group remained at a slight remove from the political fray. Nevertheless, Black Viennese conservatives had no intention of confining themselves to abstract discussions or veiled political statements. They recognized the need for public vehicles that could attract government officials, white-collar workers, and educated professionals. Joseph Eberle stepped into this breach with his journal, *Das neue Reich.* Members of the Leo-Gesellschaft flocked to the journal and provided

---

56. Kutalek and Fellinger, *Zur Wiener Volksbildung,* 185–207. On the University of Vienna, see Posch, Ingrisch, and Dressel, *"Anschluss" und Ausschluss,* 61–64. See also Weinzierl, *Universität und Politik.*

it with radical conservative content, building it into one of the largest and most influential intellectual publications in Central Europe.

Joseph Eberle and the Ideology of *Das neue Reich*

In October 1918, one month before the armistice ending the Great War and the November revolution that ended the Habsburg monarchy, Joseph Eberle published the first edition of a new weekly, *Die Monarchie*. Committed to the Habsburg Empire and the status quo, *Die Monarchie* quickly found its position untenable with the fragmentation of the Austro-Hungarian state, the abdication of Emperor Karl, and the revolutionary events of late 1918 across Central Europe. Eberle renamed the journal *Das neue Reich* and began advocating for the restoration of the monarch. He enlisted the services of his friend Kralik and members of the latter's large intellectual circle for this project. More than a mere monarchist mouthpiece or a reactionary outlet, the publication, in Eberle's vision, would provide a new, muscular version of German Catholicism, ready to do battle with the negative forces of the modern world.

Eberle was well-situated to build a new ideological movement in Vienna. He had spent most of his life in journalism and had developed excellent connections within Central European conservative circles. He was born in Ailingen (present-day Friedrichshafen) in Germany in 1884. After completing high school, he attended courses at several universities, receiving a Ph.D. in theology at Strasbourg. Because of a laryngeal malady that made it difficult for him to speak, Eberle was unable to pursue an academic career. Thereupon he became a journalist and polemicist. His first book, *Großmacht Presse,* a philippic against liberal Jewish media and plutocratic forces of capitalism, garnered him some attention, though the book was hardly a bestseller.[57] He received his break in 1913 when he became an editor at the *Reichspost.* Eberle met leading politicians and intellectuals; most important, he established a close working relationship with the *Reichspost* editor-in-chief, Friedrich Funder, and with Richard Kralik. Kralik and Eberle carried on a regular correspondence until Kralik's death in 1934.[58]

Eberle made his reputation writing jingoistic articles during the Great War. His main essays from the war years appeared in two popular 1918 books,

---

57. The book went through two editions by 1913, with a total printing of four thousand copies. These did not sell out until 1918, when a new five thousand-copy edition was released.

58. Hofer, "Joseph Eberle." On the Kralik-Eberle friendship, see Anita Ziegerhofer-Prettenthaler, '*Schönere Zukunft. Die führende Wochenschrift der (österreichischen) Ersten Republik (1925–1938)*," in Grunewald and Puschner, *Das katholische Intellektuellenmilieu,* 395–98.

Zertrummert die Götzen! (Destroy the Idols!) and *Die Überwindung der Plutokratie* (Overcoming Plutocracy). Eberle condemned liberalism and socialism as products of the spiritually bankrupt Enlightenment. Jewish journalists and entrepreneurs received special opprobrium as the main atheistic and materialistic forces in the world. He advocated an end to capitalism and a return to a German Catholic corporate existence modeled on the Holy Roman Empire. On the heels of his new popularity, Eberle cemented his status as a leading voice for Central European conservatism with a searing critique of the Paris Peace Accords, *De Profundis.*

Das neue Reich—edited by Eberle, endorsed by the *Reichspost,* and bolstered by contributions from Kralik's circle—immediately gained traction. Its circulation reached ten thousand by April 1921. In December 1924, the journal reached an all-time high of fifteen thousand copies. Its popularity owed as much to its intellectual content and the caliber of its writers as it did to Eberle's reputation. It established a clear sense of what it meant to be an Austrian German in the perilous conditions of postwar Central Europe. The journal tapped into various conservative strands and provided a forum for debate. Despite some ideological divergences, Eberle and *Das neue Reich* distilled these views into a relatively unified ideology of Austrian conservatism, one that was Catholic, (Austro-)German nationalist, antisocialist, antidemocratic, and anti-Semitic. These views, often couched in scientific and cultural terms rather than "political" ones, were more radical than those espoused by members of the Christian Social party or the Greater German People's Party. In fact, the early history of *Das neue Reich* demonstrates a growing distance between the antidemocratic Black Viennese intellectuals and Christian Social politicians. The political parties would have to catch up with Viennese intellectuals if they hoped to gain their support. This would not occur until the late 1920s, as Austrian politics took an authoritarian turn.

In the earliest editions of the journal, radicalized Christian Social authors took the lead in discussing the postwar order, opposing socialism and democracy and endorsing conservative unity. Alois von Liechtenstein, a close political ally of Karl Lueger, advocated for a bourgeois coalition of Catholic conservatives and German nationals in Austria in order to prevent socialist domination. Liechtenstein accused Otto Bauer, leader of the Social Democrats, of being a crypto-Bolshevik because of his "close friendship" with Leon Trotsky.[59] Aemilian Schoepfer, the publisher of the journal and chairman of the Tyrolean branch of the Christian Social party, leveled a scathing

---

59. Alois Liechtenstein, "Gedanken über die Koalitionsregierung Deutsch-Österreichs," *NR* 1 (1918–19): 241–43.

criticism against the republican ideas of the socialists, saying they derived from the atheistic Freemasons. Schoepfer argued that all post-French Revolution republics were the work of the Masons and that Germans must resist such abominations. This was the first in a series of antimodern attacks that employed anti-Masonic and anti-Semitic tropes.

In his first contribution, Richard Kralik tried to bridge the gap that had traditionally separated Catholic conservatives from their secular German rationalist brethren with an essay on a shared German mission. Kralik pointed to the common goals of Austrian Catholics and German nationalists, while demonizing Jews and socialists. Kralik equated Austrianness with Germanness, since it was the Austrians who had always defended the German and Christian imperial past, understood as the Holy Roman Empire: "Whoever is a good Catholic is also a good German, because Catholicism bestowed the highest honor upon German Catholics: the ideal, organic league of nations that was the Holy Roman Empire of the German nation. This holds true for Austrians, as well." Kralik rejected the Wilsonian League of Nations as an artificial liberal construct; the German Habsburgs could provide a better, organic version. Having established Germans and Catholics as the forces of good, Kralik then attacked Karl Marx and Ferdinand Lassalle as two "German" Jews who assailed the German state on behalf of their race. They had learned their materialism from the Jewish faith, turning it into a pseudoreligion. Their heretical ideas had to be eradicated once and for all. This blending of Catholic anti-Judaism with modern racial discourse would feature prominently in *Das neue Reich* and Black Vienna through World War II.[60]

Subsequent editions reinforced this antisocialist, antidemocratic, and anti-Semitic agenda. Ernst Karl Winter, the future founder of the Österreichische Aktion, composed an essay discussing the "Jewish" nineteenth century, which attributed Prussia's victory over France to the "Jewified" (*verjudete*) nature of the latter. Winter drew extensively upon the anti-Semitic ideas of Houston Chamberlain, Edouard Drumont, and Alfred Dühring. He also made his first attempt to create a credible authoritarian ideology in the spirit of the Action Française.[61] Anton Orel, a Christian Social politician, editor of the nationalist journal *Das neue Volk,* and founding member of the social organization the Austrian Antisemitenbund, offered several articles condemning "the wandering Jew" and his pernicious impact on European society. He also attacked Marx on anti-Semitic lines, mixing in the Catholic social theory of Karl

60. Richard Kralik, "Kulturpolitische Exkurse," *NR* 1 (1918–19): 249–50.
61. Ernst Karl Winter, "Das jüdische 19. Jahrhundert," *NR* 1 (1918–19): 273.

Vogelsang to defend corporatism against socialism.[62] Finally, Liechtenstein offered an antisocialist piece that advocated violence against the "Bolshevik" Social Democrats.

Kralik synthesized these ideas in a series of essays criticizing democracy. In the first piece, he presented a cosmological (re)vision of the war: "However one may interpret the decisions in the world war, the true victor is God, divine justice, the spirit, the holy spirit. I feel myself a co-victor because I stand on God's side. This world war is also a poem of God's; it is a tragedy in which the hero does not always win decisively against his enemies. It is a drama whose fifth act is not yet completed."[63] Karl Kraus's reaction to Kralik appears more comprehensible in this light. Kralik demonstrated a wholesale lack of sympathy for the millions of war dead, who were merely characters in some divine poem. He reinterpreted the war as a victory for German Catholicism and absolved its political representatives of any blame. Finally, he implicitly endorsed a violent "fifth act" that would overturn the new republican order of postwar Europe.

In a piece on republican virtue and democratic government, Kralik argued there could be no compromise with the new state if you were a true conservative. Democracy was a historical nullity. Writing in Aesopian terms about classical history, he suggested that Athenian greatness derived not from democracy but from its hierarchical society and slave system. He then asserted that Roman culture stemmed solely from the Empire, not the Republic. In other words, the classical tradition taught antidemocratic, militaristic, and imperialist lessons. Society was predicated on violence and inequality. Finally, Kralik advocated for a new, "true" democracy that would replace "sham democracy" (*Mauldemokratie*) by starting from völkisch premises rather than individualist ones:

> True democracy... comprises the whole people and all its social groups [*Ständen*] with the monarch as the head of the social body.... All true culture is *Volkskultur*. National culture is based on this. The true people, the culture carriers are not the Jewish-organized followers of Jewish power interests under the deceptive name of Social Democracy. The true people and true democracy are really its opposite. Everything for the people, everything from the people! The *Volk* is not a class with class prejudices and class hatred; rather, the *Volk* is everything—nation, government, intellectuals, nobility, army, king.[64]

---

62. Anton Orel, "Vogelsang und Marx," *NR* 5 (1922–23): 132–33.
63. Richard Kralik, "Überschau," *NR* 1 (1918–19): 291.
64. Ibid., 304.

Kralik's invocation of "true democracy" prefigured by ten years Chancellor Seipel's call for the same, when the latter turned away from republicanism and towards fascism.[65] Kralik's democracy combined nostalgia for the Holy Roman Empire with *völkisch* nationalism and authoritarian leadership. Only a führer could represent the interests of the people and thereby serve democratic needs.[66] This amalgam of traditional Catholic conservatism and German nationalism typified *Das neue Reich* and interwar Black Viennese ideology.

In a 1919 article Joseph Eberle provided a coda to *Das neue Reich*'s initial statement of purpose, characterizing the Austrian conservative intelligentsia as embattled by the forces of Judaism and the Enlightenment. He listed all 150 professors and lecturers at the University of Vienna with Jewish names. Eberle declared that 50 to 80 percent of all academic instructors were Jews.[67] "Non-German Jews" had overrun the university, putting conservatives to flight. Something must be done to salvage German culture and education. This piece served as a rallying cry for "besieged" Catholic and German intelligentsia. Eberle deployed the feelings of insecurity and marginalization of the conservative bloc effectively in growing his journal. In the early years of the Republic, *Das neue Reich* benefited from two kinds of popularity, both of which attested to the strength of conservative thought in Vienna: broad readership and influential contributors. By 1925 Eberle presided over the largest German language journal—as well as the largest Catholic one—in Europe. He established sizable audiences in Austria and Germany and smaller ones in Hungary, Italy, and Switzerland.[68] As impressive as the readership numbers were, the journal's contributors were even more so. Dozens of professors, writers, technical experts, politicians, and religious leaders engaged with the publication. Although some writers came from Germany or the rest of Austria, most were Viennese. In their professional capacities the writers for *Das neue Reich*—as opposed to the "Jewish" teachers ridiculed by Eberle—actually wielded the instruments of power within the Austrian intellectual establishment. Ironically, these intellectuals

---

65. Diamant, *Austrian Catholics*, 91–92.

66. See Stern, *Cultural Despair;* Mosse, *German Ideology;* and Mohler, *Die konservative Revolution.*

67. Joseph Eberle, "Juden als Universitätslehrer," *NR* 1 (1918–19): 311–12. He drew no distinction between professors and lecturers; few Jews were actual professors, given the anti-Semitism within the Austrian academy.

68. Ziegerhofer-Prettenthaler, *Schönere Zukunft,* 395–96, 405.

were highly critical of the very state that provided them with their livelihood and their prominence.[69]

A Sociology of Black Viennese Knowledge

Karl Mannheim, who spent parts of 1919 and 1920 in a Viennese refugee camp after fleeing Miklos Horthy's Hungary, argued in an early work on the sociology of knowledge that thought must be understood through an examination of its social origins. This requires not only an investigation of discrete ideas and thinkers but also a phenomenological inquiry into language, contextualization within the "historical-social situation," and an assessment of the ties between thought and (political) action.[70] Mannheim's first use of this method was a case study devoted to nineteenth-century German conservatism.[71] He traced its origins to the post-1789 world, when a group of thinkers rejected the liberal ideas of the Enlightenment, particularly its universalism. Conservatives offered a system of knowledge based on organic unity grounded in past, lived experience. Mannheim connected these elements of conservative ideology to a series of intellectual movements, demonstrating how historical events shaped the evolution of "old conservatism." He saw one example of this evolution in the growth of anticapitalist, Romantic rhetoric that flourished after 1815.[72] Both Mannheim's methodological approach and his discrete findings on German conservatism can inform a rich sociology of Black Viennese knowledge.

Whereas Mannheim restricted his inquiry to *altkonservativ* thought in the early nineteenth century, his argument about German nationalists and Romantic conservatives can be extended to Black Viennese *Neukonservativismus*. This Viennese tradition was steeped in one of the intellectual movements addressed by Mannheim: the Catholic social theory of the mid-nineteenth century. Like their antecedents, Viennese conservatives were loosely arrayed in the immediate postwar years in a number of different political, cultural, and intellectual organizations. In lectures at the Leo-Gesellschaft, in seminars with Richard Kralik or Othmar Spann, and especially in the pages of *Das neue Reich*, intellectuals grappled with the uncertainties of the postwar Central Europe and attempted to find a way out of the modern morass. Their ideas about state, society, and order evolved with the historical-social situation, reflecting

---

69. For findings on the conservatism of interwar German-speaking universities, see Ringer, *German Mandarins;* Weinzierl and Schulmeister, *Prüfstand;* and Weinzierl, *Universität und Politik.*

70. Mannheim, *Ideology and Utopia,* 3–5.

71. Mannheim, *Conservatism.*

72. Ibid., 31–71.

concerns about democracy, capitalism, socialism, and Judaism. After several years of intense debate between individuals across the sociopolitical spectrum—from democrats to fascists—a "new conservative" consensus emerged by the mid-1920s that rejected the Republic, advocated authoritarianism, and yearned for a greater German *Reich*. Black Viennese ideologues imagined a new social organization directed by an elite composed of intellectuals. To expand their audience, they involved themselves in more than intellectual discussion by joining the flourishing civic associations of the First Republic. Their duty was to persuade the educated classes and social elites of the need for conservative change. As the pages of *Das neue Reich* show, Black Viennese intellectuals developed an ideology meant to appeal to a broad intelligentsia consisting of professors, clerics, journalists, civil servants, technical experts, and white-collar workers. This social stratum was to be the vanguard of a new Right equipped with a muscular ideology capable of responding to worsening historical-social conditions with radical solutions.

Outrage over political events in postwar Austria profoundly shaped the output of Black Viennese authors, impelling them to seek a forward-looking transformation of historical conditions in Central Europe rather than just restoration. After the November revolutions in 1918, the former Habsburg Empire had dissolved into a series of new nation-states. Austria was separated from its traditional crown lands, losing access to the agricultural abundance of the Hungarian kingdom, the industrial centers in Bohemia and Moravia, and the natural resources of Galicia. Previously a multiethnic empire of 60 million people, the new state had a population of 6.5 million, with almost one-third of them residing in the capital. The emergence of the Social Democrats as the strongest party in the Austrian parliament in 1919, coupled with Communist successes in Russia, Hungary, and Bavaria, terrified conservatives. Inflation threatened the salaries of thousands of civil servants; unemployment loomed with the contraction of the Austrian state.

Initially these developments drove intellectuals to the bourgeois parties—primarily the Christian Socials but also the Greater German People's Party. Christian Social politicians such as Aemilian Schoepfer, Max Hussarek, and Alois Liechtenstein encouraged frightened readers to side with the party. In an effort to reach out to the anxious *Mittelstand* that feared for its status, Black Viennese authors invoked anti-Semitic conspiracy theories to account for the postwar tumult. Liechtenstein blamed the continued social unrest of 1919 on Jewish journalists, industrialists, and socialists. Liechtenstein saw anti-Semitism as part of a larger social question that appeared wherever "social mischief [*Übelstände*] overwhelmingly benefits people of Jewish origin and is energetically defended by them." This variant on the "stab in the back" myth, while never as popular in Austria as in Germany, nevertheless appealed to anxious Austrians.[73] Anti-Semitic actions should come as no surprise, Liechtenstein argued, since Austrians rightfully opposed "people who boast of no patriotic service and are mere specialists in distasteful profits." Liechtenstein argued that Jews were disliked because of their "obvious externals traits [*augenfällige äußere Merkmale*] that strongly differentiate them from our people." Anti-Semitism, a sociological and economic reality, would not disappear until Christian society was restored. Until then, Germans "live under the harsh domination of an Oriental company; our people however are not impotent [*schlaff*] like Hindus who just silently abide!"[74] This version of racist, Orientalist anti-Semitism characterized the output of Black Viennese writers. Anti-Semitic social reformers like Anton Orel and German nationalist professors and priests like Oswald Menghin, Hans Eibl, Karl Hugelmann, and Alois Hudal offered similar professions. For them, the audience for their work was ethnically German, Catholic, anti-Semitic, and socially déclassé.

Despite the existence of parliamentary parties capable of withstanding socialist advances on the national level, Black Viennese conservatives increasingly rejected the Republic and its political parties. Partly this stemmed from disappointment with the Christian Social party, which collaborated with the Social Democrats in the first Austrian parliamentary coalition. Intellectuals detested the moderation and need for compromise that characterized parliamentary democracy. They therefore pressed their readers to seek extralegal solutions. Eberle characterized the Social Democrats as terrorists and slandered the party's leaders as "a former librarian, a pair of half-educated high school teachers, a horde of illiterates, and a heap of invasive, impudent, wandering [*ahasverischer*] Jews." Compromise with those criminals was anathema, so Eberle refused support to the Christian Social Party, for he saw too many "ignoramuses" and opportunists in its ranks. Placing such people in leadership positions in a time of upheaval was tantamount to criminal behavior.[75] Eberle drew intellectual support for these views from Othmar Spann and his circle, the Basel priest Robert Mäder, the Swiss historian Gonzague de Reynold, the British Catholic Hilaire Belloc, and a Viennese monarchist, Hans Zessner-Spitzenberg.

As the international list of contributors mentioned above demonstrates, Black Viennese conservatives drew upon the ideas of radical conservatism

---

73. Patrick Houlihan, "Was There an Austrian Stab-in-the-Back Myth?" in Bischof, Plasser, and Berger, *From Empire to Republic,* 69–83.

74. Alois Liechtenstein, "Antisemitismus," *NR* 2 (1919–20): 679–80.

75. Joseph Eberle, "Zeitfragen," *NR* 2 (1919–20): 743–45.

from all over Europe, applying them to deteriorating conditions in Austria. Ongoing problems of food shortages, epidemics, and inflation plagued the fledgling nation.[76] Questions about the legitimacy of democratic states and forms of authority featured in conservative discourse. Intellectuals, coming primarily from the professoriat and religious elite, denounced the republican system and demanded a new authoritarianism to combat the dissolution of contemporary society. Johannes Messner—future editor-in-chief of *Das neue Reich,* a future professor of ethics in Vienna, and an adviser to Engelbert Dollfuss—traced the decline of Western philosophy and values, beginning with Luther, Hobbes, Locke, and Hume; continuing with the "Freemasons" Rousseau and Condillac; and culminating in Marx and Engels. Messner identified an incipient revolutionary undercurrent in modern philosophy that spelled doom for civilization. To counteract these forces, he offered a *cri de guerre:* "Back to Authoritarian Ideas! [*Zurück zum Autoritätsgedanken!*]." While he preferred the return of the Habsburg Emperor, he asserted that a dictatorship would also be better than the First Republic. Employing the social analyses of Spann, Houston Chamberlain, and Oswald Spengler, Messner, one of the more moderate members of the Black Viennese milieu, nevertheless addressed himself to the indignation of radicalizing conservatives in a "fatherless society."[77]

To turn the country and Europe around, Messner, Eberle, and the *Neues Reich* coterie stressed the importance of attracting the intelligentsia to conservatism. They lamented the inability of the bourgeois parties to win these "intellectual workers," since they represented the backbone of any successful top-down reconstruction project. Black Viennese ideologues construed "intellectuals" broadly, including not only academics and "creative" (*schöpfend*) individuals like writers, clerics, and philosophers, but anyone from the educated middle class (*Bildungsbürgertum*). They remained perpetually unsatisfied with the support engendered by radical conservatives from the ranks of intellectuals. Despite substantial gains in the 1920 elections, Eberle criticized the Christian Socials for their continued inability to win the intelligentsia. He chided them for their underestimation of intellect and their inattention to the importance of intellectuals: "It is odd, the Jews, the strongest representatives of materialism, nevertheless know that the world is ultimately ruled through intellect [*Geist*]. For this reason they strive after the intelligentsia [*Intelligenz*] in their press and literature, they try to buy each

76. On conditions at the end of the Great War, see Healy, *Vienna,* 258–312.

77. Johannes Messner, "Vorbereitung der Revolution durch die Philosophie," *NR* 1 (1918–19): 546–48. See also Healy, *Vienna,* chap. 6, on the collapse of paternal authority.

emerging talent at any price. . . . This is how they will win and rule . . . thanks alone to those intellectuals."[78] Eberle complained that Catholics, the "natural representatives of intellect," foolishly condemned it, valuing honorific titles of nobility over *Privatdozenten,* professors, and creative writers. He endorsed a new conservatism that emphasized radical ideas and intellectual merit over aristocratic tradition.

Several academics and clerics developed Eberle's criticism of Austrian intellectual culture, evincing an almost pathological anxiety about the landscape of Austrian science and higher education. This nervousness derived from a number of sources. First, Catholic scientists felt themselves to be at risk. With the development of the theories of evolution, thermodynamics and relativity, Catholic scholars believed that their breed of science had lost credibility. Moreover, Marxist "scientific socialism" exacerbated concerns, as the humanities and social sciences became a battleground. Catholic academics worried that their economic and social theories, richly developed in the late nineteenth century, would disappear from academic and policy discussions. There were also sociological and ethnic issues. Catholic scientists believed that the practitioners of the modern science were liberals, socialists, Freemasons, and Jews. The disproportionate number of Jews in Austrian institutions of higher education caused great distress, and many scholars felt called upon to defend the university.[79] Finally, the educational reform measures of the *Freie Schule* movement sparked a firestorm of controversy.[80]

Black Viennese authors addressed educators and social reformers with their views on the collapse of Austrian *Geist* and the destruction of the university. Richard Schaukal, an important fin-de-siècle writer, blamed "Jewified" schools for the emergence of socialism and identified Jews with anarchism and communism.[81] Sigismund Waitz, the future archbishop of Salzburg, called the republican government "the rule of Satan." He called the modern university a "center of moral decay," "pioneer of unbelief," and "teacher of hatred for authority." Waitz condemned freethinking, monism, and secularism, asserting that the practitioners of science had separated God from morality and morality from science. He demanded the re-Christianization of the university through an intellectual counterreformation. He stressed that metaphysics must once again find a place in scientific discussions, as the values inculcated by such systems counteracted the nihilistic impulses of

78. Joseph Eberle, "Zeitfragen," *NR* 2 (1919–20): 745.
79. Beller, *Vienna and the Jews,* part 1, demonstrates the preponderance of Jews in *Gymnasien* and the free professions.
80. Boyer, *Culture and Political Crisis,* 174–86.
81. Richard Schaukal, "Über Sozialismus," *NR* 3 (1920–21): 19.

individualism, positivism, liberalism, and materialism. He expected the state to establish a Catholic university in Austria and hire more German Catholics at all institutes of higher education.[82]

The educational reforms promulgated by the Austrian education minister (later, president of the Viennese municipal school council) Otto Glöckel vexed Viennese conservatives no end, since they suggested that the socialists wished to eradicate Catholic influence from the public sphere.[83] In response to Glöckel's attempts to broaden educational opportunities for the lower classes and remove religious instruction from elementary school curricula, one anonymous professor declaimed:

> No! We will not permit godless pseudoscience to reach the people but rather will drive it out of the universities!
>
> Yes, we want truth and science to reach the people. We want people's universities, people's education and enlightenment of the people [*Volkshochschulen, Volksbildung, Volksaufklärung*] in a comprehensive sense. The Catholic Church founded and developed the entire educational system. . . . Now the degenerate daughter has turned against her own mother, in order to persecute her and, if possible, kill her. We want enlightenment [*Volksaufklärung*]. The whole people should know what a massive swindle lurks behind faithless science.[84]

The author presented himself as a defender of science and enlightenment. In doing so, however, he redefined the terms of the debate in a Catholic and *völkisch* direction that rendered impossible any fruitful discussion between conservative and socialist ideological blocs. Intellectuals faced a Manichaean choice—between Christian science and nihilistic apostasy. Other authors who enlisted in this fight over science and education were Kralik, Hudal, the classicist Joseph August Lux, and the noted Catholic ethnologist and racial theorist Wilhelm Schmidt. Their intended audience was the Catholic and German *Mittelstand,* since this broad social group stood at the center of any program of *Volksaufklärung.*[85]

---

82. Waitz published more than a dozen articles on these themes in *Das neue Reich* in the first five years of the Republic.

83. For more on the Glöckel reforms, see Weidenholzer, *"Neuen Menschen."* For conservative views, cf. Zulehner, *Kirche,* 45–54.

84. Sigismund Waitz, "Bankerott der modernen Universitätswissenschaft," *NR* 2 (1919–20): 254.

85. See Richard Kralik, "Gralkultur und Philisterkultur,"*NR* 2 (1919–20): 538; Alois Hudal, "Aufgaben der katholischen Wissenschaft,"*NR* 2 (1919–20): 607; Josef August Lux, "Heutige

In response to the tumultuous conditions of the early 1920s, Black Viennese intellectuals became increasingly critical of the Republic and pressed their readers to embrace dictatorship. Eberle in particular remained implacable: "Now is the point, where we absolutely must begin to doubt, whether democracy and parliament, whether a ruling form built above all on the will of the masses is capable of leading a people out of the direst emergency and disorganization to order and achievement. We do not believe so. We do not believe in democracy."[86] Eberle questioned the intelligence of the masses and lamented the weakness of a democratically elected government. He implored conservatives to set up a dictatorship: "Parliaments and accommodating parliamentary committees have never saved the day in extraordinary times, in times of emergency, chaos and revolution. Only strong self-willed individuals have done it and led the people to new heights. Moses was a dictator—Caesar was a dictator." Drawing on the language of Carl Schmitt, Eberle argued for a strong führer in times of emergency. Black Viennese conservatives pined for new leaders who would do away with democracy.[87]

Besides drawing on classical models and German critics of democracy, Black Viennese intellectuals also looked to other European ideologues for positive models to emulate. Eberle, Messner, and others lent early support to European authoritarian and fascist movements while soliciting contributions from leading figures in those movements. In particular, the governments of Miklós Horthy and Benito Mussolini epitomized their dreams of overcoming democracy and socialism and creating authoritarian states. Hungary received early attention because of its former ties to the Habsburg Empire and the similar struggles it faced in the early postwar years. The first sustained international coverage in *Das neue Reich* focused on the rise and fall of the Communist Béla Kun regime and Admiral Horthy's successful establishment of an authoritarian state. Kaspar Inthal, former editor of the influential Catholic newspaper *Das Vaterland,* wrote several installments extolling Horthy's regime for overthrowing the Bolsheviks.[88] Inthal defended authoritarianism by arguing that liberalism and communism were equally evil, since they sapped the strength of the *Volk*. He stated there was "hardly anything to separate" the liberal coalition government of Mihály

Geistesmächte," *NR* 4 (1921–22): 737; Wilhelm Schmidt, "Katholizismus und Intelligenz," *NR* 5 (1922–23): 1012.

86. Joseph Eberle, "Nach der Wahlen," *NR* 3 (1920–21): 86.

87. Ibid. See also Eberle, "Grundsätzliche Erwägungen," *NR* 3 (1920–21): 85–86. See Schmitt, *Concept of the Political. Das neue Reich* reviewed Schmitt's publications positively.

88. Kaspar Inthal, "Die Wiedererhebung Ungarns," *NR* 2 (1919–20): 3–4; Inthal, "Chronik," *NR* 2 (1919–20):45, 92, 157.

Károlyi of November 1918 and the Communist government of 1919. He upbraided Hungarian leaders for seeking independence from Austria, arguing that anarchy was the just reward for their rejection of monarchy and embrace of "parliamentary strategy and modern demagogy."[89]

Hungarian Catholic conservatives wrote in *Das neue Reich* to share their experiences of Hungary's rebirth and to advance a positive program of anti-Semitism, *völkisch* nationalism, Christianity, and authoritarianism. Bishop Ottokár Prohászka of Székesfehérvár, a noted nationalist, anti-Semite, and representative of Hungary's new Right, offered essays about the dual threats of Judaism and Bolshevism to Christian Europe.[90] "The Jewish essence makes itself broadly felt in Budapest: lurking behind the mask of Magyarism are the grimaces of negation of all that is Christian-national."[91] The middle classes and intellectuals, the main audience for Prohászka's brand of Christian nationalism, seemingly cowered before these heretics, spelling doom for the Hungarian *Volk*. "Weak in character and without masculine courage or fortitude, they [the intelligentsia] become the plaything of the Bolsheviks."[92] Only a commitment to re-Christianization and authoritarianism would reverse Hungary's decline. Prohászka called for an end to all trappings of Western democracy and for reforms like a *numerus clausus* in the universities and free professions as a step toward "Hungarism," the ultranationalist and fascistic program of the new Right designed as a "necessary defense for the Hungarian race."[93] He applauded the new conservative measures undertaken in the first years of the Horthy regime and broadcast these successes to neighboring Austria.[94]

Kaspar Inthal, an early apologist for Horthy's regime, demonstrated the initial ambivalence of more moderate Viennese conservatives toward Mussolini's Italy. Nonetheless, he sided with Fascist ends—authoritarianism, an ethnonational state, and the destruction of liberal democratic institutions—if not their means. He questioned the Fascist terror tactics and Machiavellian politics of the Italian state, which was prepared to extend its power "with, without, or against parliament, with, without, or against the king, and with, without, or against the pope."[95] He criticized the chauvinist nationalism

89. Inthal, "Wiedererhebung," 3.

90. Hanebrink, *Christian Hungary,* 27, 56–57.

91. Ottokár Prohászka, "Das Schicksal Ungarns," *NR* 2 (1919–20): 115.

92. Ibid., 117.

93. Ottokár Prohászka, "Der Numerus Clausus," *NR* 3 (1920–21): 213. For more on Prohászka, see Hanebrink, *Christian Hungary.*

94. In addition to Prohászka and Inthal, Valentin Holzer and Béla Bangha, the Jesuit publicist, contributed to these discussions.

95. Kaspar Inthal, "Das neue Regime," *NR* 4 (1921–22): 979.

of Mussolini and his will to power; however, he believed Mussolini would learn to be a proper authoritarian. The key for Fascism would be reconciliation with the church. Once Mussolini learned to cooperate with the pope on the "Rome question" and built a bridge to Catholicism, Fascism would enjoy the popularity it deserved.[96] These ambivalences about "true" authoritarianism and fascism persisted in Black Viennese circles until the end of the *Ständestaat*. Nevertheless, it was clear by the early 1920s that the vast majority of Austrian conservative intellectuals rejected republicanism entirely and embraced authoritarian and fascistic reforms.

Black Viennese intellectuals came around to Italian Fascism once it consolidated power and reached a concordat with the Vatican. The arrival of Mussolini met with mixed feelings—Viennese conservatives approved of his revolution within Italy, yet they wanted an equitable resolution to territorial matters regarding the former Habsburg lands Trieste and the Tirol. In an August 1922 essay, the *Realschulenprofessor* Valentin Holzer offered a positive assessment of the Fascists, since they "confronted the violence of the socialists, a true plague on the land, with equal ferocity." Still, he hoped that the Catholic Partito Popolare Italiano—not Mussolini—could rally the forces of Christian Italy.[97] After the March on Rome in October 1922, the Fascists demonstrated that they "support Italy's separation from the plutocratic nations of the West and union with former enemies Austria, Germany, Hungary, Bulgaria and Turkey."[98] The Innsbruck professor Hans Malsatti detailed how the Fascists were rebuilding Italy and how they could serve as a model for Austrian leaders. He applauded the Fascists for the revolutionary change to Italian and European politics they had wrought: "Half measures are always exacted when whole steps are necessary. . . . Now these [Fascist] changes alone correspond to a true recovery: the reintroduction of a strong, stable, conservative authority over parliament. . . . Now can the education of the *Volk* begin."[99] Malsatti asserted that Austrian leaders had to identify the ailments of contemporary society "clinically" and root them out, as Mussolini had. If this meant the "euthanasia" of the modern state, so be it.

Discussions within Black Viennese circles about authoritarianism and fascism signaled a radicalization of the bloc by 1923. While the initial postwar years saw conservative intellectuals offering a variety of social and political solutions to contemporary problems, extreme answers gained in appeal as

---

96. Ibid., 980.
97. Valentin Holzer, "Italienische Vorgänge," *NR* 4 (1921–22): 920–22.
98. Ibid., 922.
99. Hans Malsatti, "Parlamentarisches System und—Wiederaufbau," *NR* 5 (1922–23): 615.

the First Republic foundered. The economic collapse and hyperinflation of 1922 led the Christian Social chancellor, Ignaz Seipel, to accept austerity measures in return for new Western loans as part of the Geneva Protocols. The state cutbacks eliminated the jobs of about one hundred thousand civil servants and bureaucrats—the key groups in the intellectual class. Hundreds of thousands of others endured pay cuts and early retirements, even as inflation decimated the economy. Consequently, Austrian intellectuals tired of the half measures of parliamentary governments. The examples of Horthy, Mussolini, Primo de Rivera in Spain, and even Adolf Hitler shone as beacons for a more beautiful future.

In the 1923 national election that followed the massive economic restructuring efforts of the Christian Socials, the Social Democrats picked up votes while the German nationalist parties suffered heavy losses. Remarkably, however, the socialists failed to increase their representation among intellectual workers, signaling to Black Viennese thinkers a changing tide among the Austrian educated classes. Eberle attributed this development to growing disaffection with the state and a desire for radical alternatives: "Doesn't everyone know that for three or five decades real intellectuals of all peoples have cursed democracy as a cult of incompetence, and a poisoner of the people.... Haven't Mussolini and Primo de Rivera, the conquerors of parliaments, been celebrated? Doesn't Hitler, the hater of parliamentarianism, receive hosannas from the masses?"[100] Independent-minded intellectuals with their *völkisch* pretensions set the tone for the masses; both groups demanded populist dictatorships. Eberle recognized that intellectuals across Europe were already moving toward fascist solutions, and he implored regular Austrians to join the cause. The invocation of Hitler's name, shortly after the failed Beer Hall Putsch, indicated Eberle's hope for a German Mussolini.

The Black Viennese belief system also featured a positive "new imperial" vision, grounded in Catholic theory and pan-German thought. Writers appealed to the "caste pride" of German intellectuals, highlighting their leadership role in a restored German Reich. The very title *of Das neue Reich* alluded to that promise, as Kralik explained: "It is the knowledge that the True, Good and Beautiful are one in God, that, because of this, science, politics, and art must also be one... that the more that true science departs from the True, true politics from the Good, and true art from the Beautiful, the more that all of these depart from God."[101] Kralik called this spirit "Grail culture," in reference to the Gralbund he had established in

100. Joseph Eberle, "Grundsätzliche Erwägungen," *NR* 6 (1923–24): 87.
101. Richard Kralik, "Gralkultur und Philisterkultur," *NR* 2 (1919–20): 538.

1904. Kralik wanted to reanimate German Christian belief through creative work in German Catholic literature, philosophy, science, and history.[102] A major component of this scientific discussion revolved around the radical, corporatist *Sozialreform* project of Viennese Catholics, which will be discussed at length in chapter 5.

The other main component of this vision was German nationalism. After the tumult of the early postwar years, there was an obvious need for ethnic Germans to find a positive historical tradition. While visions of a German Reich varied, Black Viennese intellectuals imagined Austria as the fulcrum for Central European affairs and the center of any future German state. The foundation for this argument rested on the historical importance of the Holy Roman Empire and the Habsburg dynasty in German history. The Graz historian Raimund Kaindl ignited these discussions with articles and books on *Anschluss*. Kralik, Ernst Karl Winter, and Andreas Posch elaborated these points in debates about the key elements in German history. They sought to reconcile Prussian and Austrian traditions in order to create a usable "German" past. These thinkers, in their efforts to attract German nationalists to the fold, also considered how to create a pan-German union that avoided the failures of the Second Reich. Even Heinrich von Srbik, the founding member of the Leo-Gesellschaft and frequent critic of *Das neue Reich,* joined in the defense of Austria's central role in past and future Germany unity.[103] This vision of a transcendent conservative Austrian "cosmopolitanism" was actually still German nationalist, Catholic, and exclusionary, serving to bridge the gap between conservatism and fascism.[104] While some conservatives advocated a restoration of the Habsburg monarchy, many turned their attention to a potential confederation of German and/or Habsburg states achieved through *Anschluss*. This did not entail a simple annexation of Austria to Germany; rather, it meant a "Greater Germany" that included all German territories in Central Europe and grouped them in a federated state under the symbolic leadership of Austria, not Prussia.[105] Although Black Viennese intellectuals did not reach a consensus on the contours of a German Reich, the Reich discourse itself illustrates the ubiquity of national thinking in interwar Austria and its ability to transcend *Lager* boundaries.[106]

Black Viennese intellectuals drew on international developments for ideological support and also contributed to transnational discussions of radical

---

102. The foremost fiction contributors were Kralik, Schaukal, Bahr, and Erika Handel-Mazzetti.
103. In particular, see Srbik, *Deutsche Einheit.*
104. Steinberg, *Austria as Theater,* x–xiii, xix.
105. On Austrian "cosmopolitanism" see Hacohen, "Kosmopoliten."
106. Seefried, *Reich und Stände,* and Thorpe, *Pan-Germanism.*

conservatism. Sharing the goals of authoritarianism and German nationalism, they created a relatively unified, conservative field that drew ever closer
as economic and political conditions worsened. Their views, combining a
positive "Austrian ideology" and a "Greater German vision" with a rejection
of Enlightenment ideas and an espousal of modern racism, offered intellectual sustenance for disaffected intellectuals in Vienna, Austria and Central Europe. After a few years, *Das neue Reich* reigned supreme in Viennese
intellectual circles, achieving a circulation and prominence that dwarfed all
other publications, including Kraus's *Die Fackel* and the Austro-Marxists' *Der
Kampf.* Ultimately, it took a new Eberle publication to supplant *Das neue
Reich,* one with an even more radical mission.

The Rise of *Die Schönere Zukunft*

In a surprise article in September 1925, Joseph Eberle announced that he was
leaving *Das neue Reich* to start a new journal. Citing intellectual fatigue and
the desire for a fresh start, he stated it was time for him to pursue a "greater
mission."[107] This must have perplexed subscribers, for *Das neue Reich* was
riding a wave of success. In seven years, the journal had expanded its weekly
output by 33 percent and increased its readership by 300 percent. Why start
over at a new journal? Otto Weiß speculates that Eberle left because his colleagues did not agree with his radical views.[108] This seems unlikely, since most
contributors followed him to his new publication, *Die schönere Zukunft.* There
does seem to have been tension between Eberle and his publisher, the Christian Social Aemilian Schoepfer.[109] Ironically, Eberle claimed that the political
tone of *Das neue Reich* itself had prompted this resignation. He wanted his
new paper to return to cultural matters. Nevertheless, *Die schönere Zukunft*
became not less political but extrapolitical, seeking transformative political
solutions outside of the existing system. Eberle and his Black Viennese associates distanced themselves from Austrian political parties, since they did not
correspond to ideological demands of radical conservatism. They abandoned
the Christian Social cause and the social activism of the Catholic Action
movement for fascistic political dreams and utopian social reforms. As chapter
7 will elaborate, this schism within Black Vienna developed slowly during the
1920s, though most intellectuals moved away from moderate solutions involving parliamentarianism or republicanism. Eventually the more radical *Schönere*

107. Joseph Eberle, "Mein Ausscheiden aus dem 'Neuen Reich,'" *NR* 7 (1924–25): 1189–90.
108. Weiß, *Rechtskatholizismus,* 17.
109. Hofer, "Joseph Eberle," 116–23; Eppel, *Zwischen Kreuz und Hakenkreuz,* 18.

Zukunft displaced *Das neue Reich* as Central Europe's conservative journal of choice. Thereupon, Black Viennese intellectuals used Eberle's paper to set the tone for the radicalization and fascistization of Austrian politics, from the late 1920s through the *Anschluss.*

Analyzing the origins and development of the Black Viennese movement through its scholarly associations, journals, books, and gatherings reveals an image of the Austrian conservative intellectual field in the early 1920s that diverges both from its mid-1930s incarnation and from retrospective interpretations of it. Instead of Catholic conservative and German national *Lager* vying with one another for bourgeois support, a relatively unified, "black" bloc existed, spearheaded by radical Viennese thinkers. This description is doubly appropriate, since it evokes the Christian Social movement and political Catholicism and the fascist wave set off by Mussolini and the Blackshirts. Like the ideologues of the Italian movement, Black Viennese intellectuals endeavored to create a new conservatism that drew on Austrian traditions, German nationalism and modern critiques of parliamentary democracy and capitalism.

Despite its fame as the socialist fortress of Red Vienna, interwar Vienna was a battleground between competing worldviews, between reds and blacks and moderates and radicals.[110] While scholars have noted the nationalist and conservative tendencies of the Austrian academy,[111] the broader impact of Viennese conservative ideology has received less attention. Black Viennese intellectuals and their ideas more than held their own in the public sphere of ideological collaboration and combat because of their commanding academic, religious, and political positions and the appeal of their ideas to a broadly construed class of intellectual workers. Their ideology represented a new phenomenon, one visible elsewhere in Europe, which wedded traditional values with new conceptions of nationalism, racism, and militancy. By the mid-1920s, the intellectuals of Black Vienna rejected the party politics of the Christian Socials and German nationalists as insufficiently extreme as they waged a *Weltanschauungskampf* on Red Vienna, the First Republic, and modernity more generally. As future chapters show, they increasingly won over moderates while also repelling their red opponents in the struggle for intellectual Vienna.

---

110. Diamant, *Austrian Catholics,* 93–94.
111. See Weinzierl and Schulmeister, *Prüfstand,* and Wimmer and Fischer, *Der geistige Anschluß.*

CHAPTER 2

The Austro-Marxist Struggle for "Intellectual Workers"

In the lead-up to the national elections of April 1927, the Austrian Social Democrats splashed an "Announcement of Intellectual Vienna" on the front page of their daily newspaper, the *Arbeiter-Zeitung,* which endorsed the socialist cause in strong terms. "The essence of Spirit [*Geist*] is above all *Freedom, which is now endangered and we feel obligated to protect it.* The struggle for a higher humanity and the battle against indolence [*Trägheit*] and sclerosis [*Verödung*] will always find us ready. Today, it also finds us prepared for battle."[1] Given the fervor of the sentiments and the celebrity of the letter's signatories, it made perfect sense that the socialists featured this letter. The three greatest psychologists in Austria—Sigmund Freud, Alfred Adler, and Karl Bühler—signed. The father of the Austrian constitution, Hans Kelsen, offered his support. The authors Robert Musil and Franz Werfel also appended their names. The modernist composers Anton Webern and Egon Wellesz added their signatures, as did the painters and architects Leo Delitz, Josef Dobrowsky, and Ernst Lichtblau. Two leading feminists, Fanina Halle and Daisy Minor, were endorsers, as was Alma Mahler. The list of signatories read like a who's who of interwar Viennese cultural life and seemed to signify a high point in the relations between the Austro-Marxists and Viennese intellectuals.

---

1. "Die Kundgebung des geistigen Wien," *AZ*, April 20, 1927, 1. Emphasis in the original.

Naturally the conservative press mocked the socialists for desperately pandering to "bourgeois intellectuals" and the intellectuals for their naive political convictions, arguing that true intellectuals saw through the "tax bolshevism" of the Austro-Marxists. In the *Reichspost,* editor Friedrich Funder argued that these intellectuals, who professed to stand "between and above all classes," should be classified alongside acrobats and contortionists, given their ability to occupy two distinct spatial positions at the same time. Their willingness to defend Enlightenment values while also endorsing the program of a "class dictatorship" showed their hypocrisy. Funder lamented the folly of those thinkers and suggested that they had offered themselves up as victims to a Marxist sacrifice while true intellectuals—that is, the Catholic German readers of the *Reichspost*—saw through the lies.[2]

When the socialists pulled off their most successful electoral result of the First Republic—garnering 42 percent of the vote and closing within two seats of the Christian Socials in the parliament—both conservatives and socialists pointed to intellectuals as a key determinant. Joseph August Lux, a student of the philosopher Othmar Spann and founder of the Richard Kralik Gesellschaft, criticized the Christian Social party for failing to engage the intelligentsia (*Intelligenz*) while commending the socialists for their outreach. Although he denied that the signers of the manifesto were "true" Austrian intellectuals—he called them "miserable refuse" (*kläglicher Abhub*)—he recognized that the Austro-Marxists were correct in recruiting the educated classes. Lux acknowledged that socialist pro-intellectual propaganda had contributed to their success.[3] Meanwhile, the socialist Robert Danneberg noted increased support from educated professionals in his statistical breakdown of the election.[4]

A closer analysis of the discourse about intellectuals during the Austrian First Republic nonetheless reveals the continued success of the Black Viennese establishment and the shortcomings of the Austro-Marxist–intellectual synthesis. The very concept of "intellectual" was much contested during the period. If one employs the term "intellectual" or "intellectual worker" as understood by the Austro-Marxists (and many Black Viennese ideologues), the evidence suggests that 1927 was really a setback. Their broad sociological classification comprised not only professors, writers, and artists but also bureaucrats and civil servants, military officers and priests, lawyers and accountants, engineers and middle managers. By these definitions, the

2. "Geist, Spiritus, und Bubikopf," *RP,* April 21, 1927, 1–2.
3. Joseph Lux, "Wird Österreich Leben?" *SZ* 2 (1926–27): 907–9.
4. Robert Danneberg, "Wahlergebnis 1927," *K* 20 (1927): 215.

Austro-Marxists never approached the level of intellectual hegemony for which they hoped or that they claimed. This was revealed in the same 1927 electoral analyses: the number of intellectual workers who voted against the socialists actually grew by more than ten thousand from the 1923 elections.[5] Nineteen twenty-three, not 1927, proved to be the high point and the moment of truth for socialist-intellectual relations. Around that time, the socialists concluded internal debates about the role and importance of intellectuals in their movement, yet they offered little support to the tens of thousands of them who lost their jobs in the wake of the Austrian hyperinflation and Chancellor Ignaz Seipel's austerity measures. Intellectuals felt abandoned and began to seek radical alternatives. Although the Austro-Marxists actively recruited scientists, social reformers, and modernist artists, they made little headway elsewhere. These "other" intellectuals possessed a middle-class suspicion of the working class (and "Jewish") socialist movement and remained committed to nationalism and conservatism. Although they did not support the Christian Socials unequivocally in 1927, this was largely because they were moving toward fascist groups like the Heimwehr and the Nazis.[6]

Scholars of interwar Austria have nevertheless preferred to view this moment as the pinnacle of Austrian socialism, when Austro-Marxists exerted their greatest political *and* cultural influence.[7] A closer look at what Stefan Collini has called the "question of intellectuals" belies this characterization.[8] In the 1910s and intensifying in the 1920s, Austrian thinkers wrestled with the concept of the intellectual and his or her role in political affairs.[9] Inspired by and contributing to debates in European Marxist circles, the Austro-Marxists broadly construed intellectual work as the labor performed by educated individuals in the bureaucracy, academy, business, and the free professions, as well as the arts. In key respects their analysis and proposed strategy mirrored Antonio Gramsci's, emphasizing the sociological position of intellectuals in the ideological struggle in modern societies. It was

---

5. Ibid., 215–16. These figures increased again in the 1930 and 1932 elections. Moreover, since the percentage of the working classes that voted socialist increased and the overall number of socialist voters stagnated and then retreated, bourgeois voters, including intellectuals, were clearly leaving the socialists and choosing other parties.

6 Pauley, *Hitler and the Forgotten Nazis,* 5–7.

7 Gulick, *Austria,* 709–13, 770–71, and Rabinbach, *Crisis,* introduction. Glaser, *Austromarximus,* reproduces the Announcement in its introduction.

8. Collini, *Absent Minds,* 1–3. See also the thought-provoking discussion of this work in the *Journal of the History of Ideas* 68, no. 3 (July 2007): 363–405.

9. The issue of the term's gendering is an intriguing one. In Austrian discussions, "intellectual" did not necessarily connote masculinity, as the favored term in Austro-Marxist circles (*geistige Arbeiter(innen)*) appeared in both masculine and feminine forms.

necessary that organic Marxist intellectuals win the battle against traditional intellectuals while recruiting the educated classes for the construction of a new ideational order.[10] To accomplish this, the socialists established research institutes, expanded the people's university system, and invited contributions from nonparty intellectuals. This resulted in many of the successes associated with Red Vienna.

That said, the Austro-Marxists' definition of intellectual worker became muddled in practice. In much of their theoretical work, they broadly construed intellectuals as a sociological class; however, the category as applied was often reduced to university-educated and bourgeois strata. Elsewhere, an intellectual seemed to be little more than an academic, writer, or "autonomous intellectual." This conceptual slippage had practical consequences, weakening the socialists' position in the rivalry for intellectual hegemony, since they neglected the larger sociological group at crucial moments, most notably in the economic crises of 1922–23. This chapter examines the various ways in which socialists defined intellectuals—using both sociological and cultural terms and including groups that ranged from the educated classes (*gebildete Stände*) to the free professions (*freie Berufe*)—and enumerates the problems that arose from these inconsistencies. While there is some question how much a working-class and internationalist party grounded in rhetoric of class struggle, secular statehood, and antibourgeois sentiment could have appealed to nationalist Austrian citizens, the Austro-Marxists did not do themselves any favors with their definition of intellectuals or their particular policy decisions.

This lack of success was not solely the fault of the socialists. At times, especially early in the Republic, the Austro-Marxists fought hard for intellectual support; however, conservative politicians and intellectuals stymied these efforts. Austro-Marxist ideas never gained a dominant position in Viennese institutions of knowledge and culture. In this respect the Austrian academy resembled that of Germany, where an entrenched "mandarinate" resisted modernizing tendencies and stood against progressive reform. Unlike the German mandarins, those in Austria maintained their status and influence into the 1930s.[11] The success of Black Viennese intellectuals derived from their successful deployment of ideas on nationality, ethnicity, religion, and history, yet it was also aided by Austro-Marxist ambivalence about the role of this group in the socialist struggle. Moreover, the focus on intellectuals in the capital blinded the socialist leadership to the overwhelming failures of their

---

10. Gramsci, *Prison Notebooks*, 5–16.
11. Ringer, *German Mandarins*, 1–13.

ideological struggle in the provinces.[12] As the years advanced, the triumphant optimism of the socialists gave way to resignation: despite the vibrancy of Red Vienna and the celebrity of its leading intellectual supporters, intellectually Vienna remained predominantly black.

The Austro-Marxist theoretical journal *Der Kampf* and the Eberle-run weeklies *Das neue Reich* and *Die schönere Zukunft* were at the center of this rivalry for intellectuals. Focusing on the former publication, this chapter investigates the interactions between the socialist movement and intellectuals beginning in the prewar period and continuing into the First Republic, arguing that the Marxists successfully attracted and radicalized a group of progressive intellectuals. The Austro-Marxist stress on empirical scientific work and humanist social goals appealed to those scholars and played an important role in the recruitment of Freud, Kelsen, Musil, and the other signers of the "Announcement." Nevertheless, the rhetoric of class and cultural warfare and the inability to offer solutions for middle-class socioeconomic concerns proved less effective than conservative calls for a "true state," "new Reich," or "more beautiful future." The "Announcement of Intellectual Vienna" and the 1927 election ironically demonstrate the continued strength of Austrian conservatism and the limits of the Austro-Marxist understanding of intellectual life.

Der Kampf and the Prewar Interactions between Austro-Marxists and Intellectuals

The Marxist-intellectual synthesis of the First Republic did not emerge spontaneously in the aftermath of the Great War. There were important precedents in the late nineteenth century, owing to the intellectual openness of the Austro-Marxists and ongoing debates in European Marxism about the importance of intellectuals for socialism. Shortly after the unification of the Austrian Social Democrats under Victor Adler at the party congress at Hainfeld in 1889, the party began to publish a theoretical journal, *Gleichheit,* in which Karl Kautsky and Carl Grünberg set the ideological tone. The Austro-Marxists also established intellectual associations like Veritas, der heilige Leopold, and the socialist student organization the Freie Vereinigung Sozialistischer Studenten und Akademiker. The socialist organizations attracted liberal democrats, who shared the socialists' desire for electoral and educational reform.[13] By the turn of the century, the progressive Freie Schule

---

12. Lewis, *Fascism*, vii–viii, 8–13. See also Jeffery, *Social Democracy*.

13. Bottomore and Goode, *Austro-Marxism*, 8–10. See also Kaufmann, *Sozialdemokratie in Österreich,* and Knapp, *Austrian Social Democracy*.

movement for secular education had been almost completely taken over by the Austro-Marxists.[14]

When the revisionist controversy surrounding Eduard Bernstein broke out in Marxist circles in 1899 over the collapse of capitalism and the role of revolution in socialist thought, the Austro-Marxists played a central role, engaging Marxists, reformers, and social scientists alike. Like Bernstein, they felt that Marxist science required reevaluation given the new economic developments of the previous three decades. However, they were not prepared to abandon the revolutionary message of Marxism for a reformist social democratic politics grounded in parliamentary action. On questions of political strategy, they charted a "third way" between the revolutionary stance of Lenin and Luxemburg and the mechanical, quasi-determinist materialism of orthodox Marxists. They acknowledged the importance of individual, voluntarist action for the socialist revolution, yet they refused to abandon the economic imperatives of traditional historical materialism. The Austro-Marxists responded not only to other Marxists but also to scholarly movements in their own country as they reformulated Marxist theory: the empiricism of Ernst Mach and the marginal utility school of economics of Karl Menger and Ernst Böhm-Bawerk. They sought to establish their socialism on firm scientific grounds, which required engaging contemporary natural and social scientific findings. The philosopher Max Adler and economist Rudolf Hilferding founded *Marx-Studien* in 1904 to provide a forum for such inquiries. This journal established Austro-Marxism as an independent current in European socialism, thanks primarily to Hilferding's seminal economic treatise *Finance Capital* and Otto Bauer's study on nationalism. These monographs evinced the Austro-Marxist commitment to blending empirical research with Marxist theoretical concerns.[15]

After the 1907 elections, when the Social Democrats made their first major parliamentary gains, the Austro-Marxists founded the monthly *Der Kampf* to discuss current events and theoretical concerns.[16] The editors stressed their commitment to social struggle and the betterment of humanity through increased scientific knowledge. The first lines of the new journal demonstrated the debt socialism owed to scientific thought: "Struggle is the developmental law [*Entwicklungsgesetz*] of Nature and humanity. From the dictum of Heraclitus that war is the father of things, through the struggle

14. Boyer, *Culture and Political Crisis,* 174–86.

15. Bottomore and Goode, *Austro-Marxism,* 12–14. See also Albers, *Otto Bauer;* Loew, "Austro-Marxism"; Leser, *Zwischen Reformismus und Bolschewismus.*

16. Glaser, *Austromarxismus,* 24–25. See also Viktor Adler, "Neue Aufgaben," *K* 1 (1907–8): 6–9.

for existence of Darwin up to the class struggle of Marx, this insight has grown in humans about the mysterious laws of man and his environment."[17] Though Marx, Engels, and Lassalle had also written about these men, the Austro-Marxists privileged scientific inquiry even more highly. Empirical science would be a cornerstone of all Austro-Marxist policy going forward. The editors called for the use of all available intellectual forces (*alle geistigen Kräfte*) to help unify and advance the socialist cause.

From *Der Kampf*'s inception, the Austro-Marxists acknowledged that the struggle for a classless society necessarily included cultural politics. They therefore devoted particular attention to the arts and sciences. In the first issue Engelbert Pernerstorfer expressed the need for proletarian poetry.[18] In the second, an engineer offered an overview of contemporary aeronautical technology. The author stressed the redemptive and humanitarian power of science and pointed to the necessary contributions of scientists to the realiza- tion of the "social idea."[19] As early as the third issue, the book review section primarily considered essays on science and literature. The editors understood *Der Kampf* had to harness new developments across all scholarly disciplines to improve the lives of the masses. They also knew this required the involve- ment of progressive thinkers in a variety of disciplines.

The first connections that *Der Kampf* established with nonsocialist schol- arly movements were with members of Freud's inner circle, particularly the psychologist Alfred Adler. In December 1907, Josef Strasser published a pos- itive essay on Adler's research into the inferiority complex and its importance for the class struggle. He believed that Adler's findings had sociological as well as biological implications. Strasser lauded Adler's theory of organ inferiority, which stated that underdeveloped or inferior organs often performed better because of a compensation mechanism. He related Adler's theory to the pro- letariat and Marxism: "Satisfaction of its needs is denied to the proletariat by external factors. It must invent satisfaction in its fantasy and live in the future, since the present does not offer anything. Thus emerges the worldview of the proletariat. . . . Workers demand scientific sense, critical spirit and creative fantasy; in short, spiritual superiority [*seelische Überwertigkeit*], which requires in turn a successful struggle against the bourgeoisie."[20] Strasser called for the proletariat to adapt psychically to overcome their economic inferiority. Adler and his students welcomed this allegiance, foreshadowing the collaboration

---

17. "Der Kampf," *K* 1 (1907–8): 1.
18. McGrath, *Dionysian Art*, details Pernerstorfer's intellectual predilections.
19. A. Bn., "Der Kampf in den Lüften," *K* 1 (1907–8): 93.
20. Josef Strasser, "Schwäche als Entwicklungsfaktor," *K* 1 (1907–8): 138.

between the Viennese municipal government and Adler in child psychology centers during the First Republic. They began to publish in socialist journals and advised the socialists on their youth policies.[21]

The prewar bonds forged by the Austro-Marxists with Ernst Mach's school of philosophy were even firmer than those with the psychological community, reinforcing the compatibility of Austro-Marxism and empiricism. David Josef Bach, later a leading cultural figure in interwar Vienna, studied under Mach.[22] Friedrich Adler, Victor Adler's son, was also a Mach student, remaining in close contact with Mach until the latter's death.[23] He recognized Mach as a revolutionary because his work caused "older conceptions about science as a model centered on constant, unchanging substantial elements" to collapse. This changeability was essential for any reformers—scientific, social, or political—wishing to alter the status quo, Adler argued. A Machian scientific understanding was integral for any Marxist epistemological system.[24]

The Austro-Marxists' appreciation for Mach's ideas increased with time and they defended his theories in international debates. Over the years, more than a half dozen articles appeared in *Der Kampf* supporting Mach's theories. The Austro-Marxists became Mach's leading defenders in the socialist arguments about empiricism instigated by Lenin. In *Materialism and Empirio-Criticism*, Lenin argued that Mach's empiricism amounted to a dangerous and reactionary solipsism, a subjective idealism that looked askance at socioeconomic conditions. Lenin saw Mach's focus on the perception of sensations as part of a broader philosophical effort to refute materialism and Marxism in the name of idealism.[25] The Austro-Marxists responded with an endorsement of Mach and the transformative power of individual perceptions and actions for the socialist cause. *Der Kampf* became known in Marxist circles as the journal that supported modern science and philosophy against dogmatic assaults from both the Left and the Right. Mach himself developed a close friendship with Victor Adler and eventually left part of his estate to the Social Democrats. This affiliation with Mach encouraged other scholars, including members of the Monist League, the Freethinkers, and the Ethical Society, to work with the socialists.[26]

---

21. On Adler, see Stepansky, *In Freud's Shadow.*
22. See Beniston and Vilain, *Red Vienna.*
23. Glaser, *Austromarxismus,* 52–53. Their correspondence is held at the Verein für die Geschichte der Arbeiterbewegung.
24. Friedrich Adler, "Die Entdeckung der Weltelemente," *K* 1 (1907–8): 239.
25. Lenin, *Empirio-Criticism,* 53–66.
26. Glaser, *Austromarxismus,* 66, 78–80.

The Austro-Marxists also approached women's rights advocates and school reformers in the late Habsburg era. The Social Democrats long advocated for full gender equality. Therese Schlesinger, an active socialist and feminist, exhorted women to fight for their rights. Schlesinger drew attention to inequality in educational, professional, and political opportunities and demanded immediate change.[27] Adelheid Popp highlighted the disgraceful treatment of female industrial workers—lower wages than their male counterparts, overwork, and gender discrimination. Popp insisted on the need for new labor legislation to protect female workers.[28] Sophie Lazarsfeld, a leading Adlerian psychologist, the mother of the sociologist Paul, and organizer of an important intellectual salon, argued for the alliance of modern psychology, feminism, and socialism. She also pressed for improved sex education and hygiene programs.[29] These feminists made gender inequality a significant issue for the socialists.[30]

The Social Democrats also lent support to Emmy Freundlich's *Kinderfreunde* and the "free school" movement, which advocated for secular education and pedagogical reform. Karl Seitz, the future mayor of Vienna, passionately endorsed the efforts of the reformers, identifying education as a key front in the battle against clericalism and conservatism. He hoped to awaken intellectuals to the necessity of a new *Kulturkampf*. The free schools were "a possible fighting league of anticlerical elements drawn from all classes and parties. . . . They [the intellectuals] have their place alongside us and they can lead this century's impending *Kulturkampf* against clericalism only if they join . . . the ranks of social democracy."[31] Through the invocation of a *Kulturkampf*, Seitz drew dividing lines between the socialists and the educated bourgeoisie on one side and the conservative aristocracy and church on the other. Seitz and his fellow Austro-Marxists calculated that these intellectuals likely distrusted the Catholic establishment more than the proletariat. Given that many leading Austro-Marxist theoreticians shared a liberal or Jewish background with these reformers, this was a reasonable assumption.[32]

Despite these affinities and collaborations, some Austro-Marxists still harbored doubts about the class prejudices among intellectuals deriving from their socioeconomic backgrounds. Intellectuals, according to Marxist

---

27. Therese Schlesinger, "Frauenarbeit und Politik," *K* 1 (1907–8): 313.

28. Adelheid Popp, "Frauenarbeit und Arbeiterinnenschutz," *K* 1 (1907–8): 313–17.

29. On Lazarsfeld, see McEwen, *Sexual Knowledge,* 96–98, 110–13.

30. On bourgeois feminist reformers, see Anderson, *Utopian Feminism.*

31. Karl Seitz, "Freie Schule und Sozialdemokratie," *K* 1 (1907–8), 355–56.

32. Beller, *Vienna and the Jews,* makes this argument. Hacohen, *Karl Popper,* also stresses the Jewish foundations of Viennese progressivism.

sociological analysis, typically came from upper-middle-class families of bankers and industrialists. The socialists feared the continued connection of the educated classes to either Catholic or capitalist worldviews. Karl Renner best encapsulated these concerns. He offered one of the first comprehensive Austro-Marxist discussions of the relation of intellectuals to the proletariat. Renner's analysis also responded to ongoing debates among European socialists. His article appeared during the debates provoked by Lenin's *What Is to Be Done?* and Trotsky's *Results and Prospects,* shortly after the Bolsheviks and Mensheviks split over the role of vanguard intellectuals in the socialist revolution. Renner believed that the very term "intellectual" [*Intellektuell*] was a bourgeois creation designed to separate the educated from the working classes and instill class enmity where brotherhood should exist: "Today students build a class stratum in bourgeois society, which is characterized as a 'scholarly vocation' [*gelehrte Berufe*]. They have been named 'intellectual workers' [*geistige Arbeiter*] in order to compare them favorably to the masses and branded 'educated' to contrast the two."[33] Renner linked the broader intellectual caste with the privileges of the church and the nationalism of German Catholic conservatives, questioning their inclusion in the socialist movement. He beseeched intellectuals to reconsider their anachronistic and self-aggrandizing ideas. He wanted to end the "subalternization of intellectuals," yet he feared that intellectuals would be dilatory in joining the cause: "Intellectuals must still follow their wayward path with the bourgeois parties for a while, until they overcome their caste pride [*Kastenstolz*] vis-à-vis workers, until they grasp that science and the proletariat, intellectual work and wage work belong together."[34] Renner did not call for a struggle for ideological hegemony à la Gramsci; rather, he advocated patience. He expressed the ambivalence that socialists felt toward the intellectual classes: they were potential allies in the class struggle because of their declining socioeconomic status, yet they were also unlikely to participate because of their conservative cultural prejudices.

Max Adler also addressed the subject of intellectual work, expressing a more positive attitude than Renner. He viewed this sociological group, originally drawn from the upper and middle classes, as part of an expanded proletarian class.[35] His focus was on how to employ their scientific findings for socialism. He believed progressive ideas would help to fashion the *neue Menschen* the socialists wished to create. As long as science was committed to

---

33. Hacohen, *Karl Popper,* 434.
34. Karl Renner, "Der Streik der Studenten," *K* 1 (1908–9): 433–39.
35. Adler, *Sozialismus.* See also Hanisch, *Der große Illusionist,* 105–16.

solving practical problems, it was an important tool for socialism. Renner's and Adler's positions helped account for the affiliation between the Austro-Marxists and the burgeoning social sciences in Austria, though they had not yet considered how to reach beyond a small group of liberal, often Jewish, intellectuals.[36] As Robert Danneberg's 1914 analysis of Viennese party members showed, only 259 out of 47,119 party members were academics; 88 percent came from the working classes.[37] Despite their affiliation with progressive intellectuals, socialists had almost no presence within the academic community. With the tumult of the Great War, however, intellectuals began to look more closely at the socialist movement, forcing the Austro-Marxists to reconsider not only what intellectual workers could do for them but also what they could offer in return. This involved broadening their understanding of the concept of the intellectual and searching for ways to integrate these workers into the socialist movement.

What Is An Intellectual? The Struggle over Intellectual Work(ers)

The aftermath of the First World War and the collapse of the Habsburg monarchy brought new opportunities for the Social Democrats. Austria had undergone a relatively peaceful revolution, becoming a democratic republic in November 1918. In the first elections the socialists became the largest party in the country.[38] However, there were myriad problems in the new state: food shortages, an influenza epidemic, and economic upheaval.[39] Moreover, the socialists did not rule alone; they operated a coalition government with the Christian Socials. The socialists still hoped to push through major social and economic reforms. To accomplish their aims, they knew they had to bring intellectual workers into their camp. The timing for such recruitment seemed propitious since many bureaucrats and state employees faced the prospect of unemployment due to the decreased demand for bureaucrats in a state of six million rather than an empire of fifty-three million.

36. Fleck, *Rund Um "Marienthal,"* 14–53.
37. Robert Danneberg, "Ein Blick," *K* 7 (1914): 396. Quoted in Hanisch, *Der große Illusionist,* 116.
38. The Social Democrats received 41 percent of the vote and seventy-two mandates, the Christian Social party 36 percent and sixty-nine mandates, and the German National Party 6 percent and eight mandates.
39. On the end of the war and the Austrian Revolution, see Healy, *Vienna;* Boyer, "Silent War"; and Bauer, *Die österreichische Revolution.*

Electoral gains emboldened the Austro-Marxists to confront Austrian conservatives more directly. In May 1919, *Der Kampf* became a weekly to address political and social developments better. The journal's leadership also changed hands; Friedrich Adler became editor-in-chief. This was a momentous choice since it showed the Austro-Marxists' newfound confidence, radicalization, and increased commitment to scientific collaboration. Adler was a controversial figure in Austrian society. In 1916, he had assassinated the Austrian minister-president Karl Graf Stürgkh as a protest against the government's war actions. He spent the remaining war years in prison. Adler was pardoned and released after the Austrian Revolution. His selection as editor implied a radicalization of socialist purpose. Adler had always stood on the left of the Austro-Marxist spectrum, opposing the prowar and conciliatory tendencies of Karl Renner. His selection as editor was a provocation of Austrian conservatives, who viewed him as a murderer and terrorist.

Adler's appointment also carried geopolitical and intellectual significance. Of all the important Austro-Marxists, he was perhaps the most committed to international cooperation. He had spent the previous decade in Switzerland developing socialist connections. He was also a surrogate son to Karl Kautsky and a close affiliate of the German movement. He read widely on French and British socialism and was the driving force behind the formation in 1921 of the International Workers' Union of Socialist Parties, the so-called Two and a Half or Vienna International. Rejecting both the Second International, whose nationalist and reformist tendencies led European socialist parties to support involvement in the First World War, and the Soviet Union-dominated Third International, Adler's organization tried to offer a coherent third way. Adler's internationalism and anti-Bolshevism indicated his desired goals for the Austro-Marxist movement: a radically democratic yet socialist political and economic force.[40]

Adler embraced pluralism in the realm of ideas, which shaped the direction of *Der Kampf* in the early years of the Republic in a more heterodox and radical direction. This represented a shift in the relationship between socialism and science. Despite the relative open-mindedness of prewar Austro-Marxists, they nevertheless had a dogmatism of their own. The party and its ideology were supposed to be unified; any differences were to be handled behind closed doors to avoid shows of weakness. Friedrich Adler (and to a lesser extent Otto Bauer) preferred to have open debate and lively

---

40. Braunthal, *History of the International,* 2: 264–70.

discourse.[41] In his book on Ernst Mach, Adler attempted a reconciliation of empiricism and Marxist historical materialism that allowed for Machian science to remain independent within the socialist epistemological universe. He commended Mach's nondogmatic approach to science and advocated a similar methodology for socialism. Adler invoked a critical struggle for knowledge, arguing that good science is autonomous, intersubjective, and corrigible: "Nothing contradicts the Machian spirit more than a dogmatic conception [*Auffassung*] of his theories. Only in critical struggles with his theories can they be accepted and become fruitful."[42] Adler linked Machian attitudes with Austro-Marxist demands for social and political change.[43] The treatise can be viewed as an intellectual mission statement for the postwar *Kampf*: it would be a journal of open debate that recruited individuals from diverse positions for the class struggle without forcing ideological compromise on the part of intellectuals. Adler's prominence encouraged heterodox progressives like Karl Popper to join the fold.[44]

Austrian conservatives such as the writers Richard Kralik and Hermann Bahr and the future archbishop of Salzburg, Sigmund Waitz, viewed these Austro-Marxist provocations as a threat to the Austrian people. In particular, they feared the loss of intellectual institutions to the socialists and the conversion of intellectuals to Marxism. They bemoaned the "Bolshevization" and "Jewification" of the academy and called on intellectuals to rally to the side of God, Austria, and German culture. This was a common lament among conservatives: the universities were becoming bastions of moral relativism and political nihilism. "True" intellectuals faced persecution for their views. They viewed the battle for intellectual hegemony as central to Austrian politics. They sought intellectuals for their cause in a broad variety of vocations. After all, one could employ *Geist* and *Bildung* in any profession, provided one possessed the requisite commitment to German (ethnic), Austrian (national), and Catholic (religious) *Kultur*.[45] Black Viennese intellectuals feared that the Austro-Marxists, particularly Bauer and Adler, better grasped the struggle for intellectual hegemony in postwar Austria.

Rhetorically, the conservative understanding of intellectuals differed from the formulations of the Austro-Marxists. Black Viennese thinkers focused on the cultural characteristics of intellectuals. On the other hand,

---

41. This attitude changed in the latter stages of the Republic; at that stage, Adler endorsed party unity against the Left opposition. See Rabinbach, *Crisis,* chaps. 2–3, 5.

42. Adler, *Machs Überwindung,* 11.

43. Ibid., 22–7.

44. Hacohen, *Karl Popper,* 299–300.

45. This definition of *Kultur* draws on Ringer, *German Mandarins,* 83–102.

Austro-Marxists, like Marxists across the continent, wrestled with the sociological categories of "intellectual" and "intellectual work." In the first years
of the Republic, Vienna served as a breeding ground for Marxist thinking
on the subject. Georg Lukács developed his ideas on class consciousness
as an exile in the Austrian capital. He explicitly responded to Max Adler's
"bourgeois" social philosophy, Mach's atomistic empiricism, and the general
complacency of Austrian and German social democrats in developing a neo-
Hegelian understanding of dialectical materialism. His work highlighted
the subjective and spiritual role of the proletariat in overcoming capitalism.
Intellectuals participated in the socialist revolution by helping to awaken
proletarian consciousness.[46] Karl Mannheim, who spent the period after the
overthrow of the Kun regime in Vienna, responded to Lukács' formulations
in *Ideology and Utopia,* finding an enthusiastic supporter in the socialist and
logical empiricist Otto Neurath.[47] Both men stressed the importance of
institutional and political support for the development and dissemination of
new knowledge. Antonio Gramsci spent an extended period in Austria in the
early 1920s as he devised ideas on hegemony and the position of intellectuals
in the class struggle. These men emphasized that intellectuals represented a
sociological category and that, even though all work required some intellect,
certain individuals performed social functions associated with intellectual
activity. They observed the conservative character of the dominant ideas and
knowledge systems and demanded challenges to the status quo through the
use of critical intellect and Marxist theory. These seminal ideas on intellectuals and ideology, which profoundly shaped Western Marxism, the sociology
of knowledge, and intellectual history, developed out of the hothouse culture
of postwar Vienna and Central Europe.

Austro-Marxist theories on intellectual work did not reach the sophisticated heights of the theories of Lukács, Gramsci, or Mannheim; however,
they were crucial to evolving Austrian political discourse. Friedrich Adler
in particular felt an unease and displeasure with prewar Austro-Marxist
attitudes. Like Gramsci, Adler contended that intellectual life could not
be dismissed as a mere superstructural byproduct of economic conditions:
ideas informed the way that the economic substructure was conceived and
constructed. Intellectuals were instrumental in remaking social and economic conditions: "The natural sciences in particular do not belong to
the superstructure of class relations but to the base, the technical relations

---

46. Lukács, *History and Class Consciousness,* 5–13, 36–38, 46–55.
47. Otto Neurath, "Bürgerlicher Marxismus," *K* 23 (1930): 231–33. On Hungarian exiles in
Vienna, see Congdon, *Exile and Social Thought.*

themselves. Natural science is no reflex or ideology of class relations, as parts of philosophy are. Its foundations are more solid, they do not change with class relations but only as part of the entirety of technical conditions of production."[48] Adler viewed intellectuals as the technicians of society, committed to applying scientific knowledge to social and economic problems. Scientific experts would help reconstruct production relations and thus also class relations. A flexible epistemology and a predilection for the natural and social sciences characterized the postwar Austro-Marxist understanding of intellectual work.

Oskar Trebitsch argued for a reconsideration of Renner's overall suspicion about the readiness of intellectuals to become socialists, thereby advancing Adler's position. To earn the support of intellectuals, he wanted to demonstrate the socialist commitment to intellectual work by creating unions for the universities, bureaucracy, and free professions. Only if intellectuals felt included in the socialist fight for better conditions would the intelligentsia abandon their traditional allegiances. Intellectuals must be granted a distinct status in the movement; their work must be encouraged and disseminated. Vienna was at the center of the strategy, Trebitsch argued: "In Vienna it indeed sometimes appears as if we already have enough strength at our disposal to provide the masses general and socialist education without having to venture beyond the ranks of the workers. This appearance deceives, however.... In Vienna we need many more intellectual workers yet—not as political leaders—but as intellectual colleagues."[49] Educating the educators must remain a priority. Trebitsch recognized that the socialists still occupied a weak position among intellectuals in the Austrian capital. Winning the city would allow socialists to begin to transform Austrian society. From a consolidated Red Vienna, intellectuals would travel into the provinces, spreading the socialist message. Trebitsch viewed education as the front line in a Gramscian war of position against conservatives and demanded that the socialists engage in a *Kulturkampf* for the hearts and minds of Viennese intellectuals.

Not everyone agreed with Trebitsch. Alfred Engel dismissed the category of intellectual worker altogether. "I reject the constitution of a special group.... Intellectual work cannot be recognizably delimited from bodily labor.... We have no organization for 'bodily workers' [*körperlichen Arbeiter*], so why one for intellectuals?"[50] Engel employed a cultural definition of the word. "Intellectual" operated as a subjective descriptor rather than a

48. Adler, *Machs Überwindung*, 184.
49. Ibid.
50. Alfred Engel, "Die Rolle der geistigen Arbeiter," *K* 12 (1919): 568.

sociological category. For Engel, socialists must advance their general program without developing a special course for intellectuals. Socialist focus
must remain on the unions and party apparatus, not on seeking potential
ideological allies.

These two positions delimit the Austro-Marxist intellectual discourse. For
Adler and Trebitsch, intellectuals were a distinct class, largely drawn from the
sciences. They represented a portion of a broader sociological group, the *Bildungsbürgertum*. They required targeted programs and patronage to engender
support. For Engel, like Karl Renner before him, intellectuals did not represent a distinct social group and did not deserve any special consideration.
The socialists never entirely overcame this tension, though some sought compromise. Richard Kassel offered a middle position, endorsing the inclusion of
intellectuals in the socialist movement while downplaying their special status.
Like it or not, he argued, intellectuals were now a concern for socialists and
must be integrated, for many had supported the party in elections. "In their
[Trebitsch's and Engel's] fundamental concept they are agreed: the intellectual
worker is an inorganic outgrowth of the party. We indeed called them and
they came. God knows what drove them to appear so promptly. So now they
are here, good—of what use can they be to the party?"[51] Kassel exhorted fellow Marxists to capitalize on the current socialist-intellectual alliance because
the opportunity was the product of unique historical conditions that might
not reoccur. Intellectuals had voted socialist in surprising numbers in 1919, yet
this was not necessarily because of ideological affinity but rather because of
"anger over the events of the war on the front and at home, desperation over
inflation and the impossibility of maintaining their accustomed standard of
living... and finally a bourgeois-republican revolutionary desire whose ful-
fillment seemed most likely with a radical party."[52] Like Mannheim, Kassel
recognized the role of historical and social circumstances in shaping ideologies and intellectual affiliations. He did not wish to limit the recruitment
of intellectuals to doctors, lawyers, engineers, and professors; there were also
bank tellers, accountants, technicians, chemists, teachers, state officials, and
others. He saw the entire sociological class of educated people as potential
targets in these trying times.[53] He acknowledged that these were not individuals raised in the movement, so they must be monitored and courted.
Otherwise, they could just as easily turn to other political alternatives. Like

---

51. Richard Kassel, "Zum Problem der geistigen Arbeiter," *K* 12 (1919): 814.
52. Ibid., 817.
53. Ibid., 815–16.

Gramsci, Kassel understood the dynamics of hegemonic struggle and pleaded that socialists engage decisively in the ideological battle.

These discussions prompted the leading philosopher of Austro-Marxism, Max Adler, to weigh in with a strategy for intellectuals. Adler revised his earlier position, arguing it was time for socialist leaders to draw intellectuals into the proletarian movement. Socialists must demonstrate that intellectuals were now members of the working class and that Marxism best represented their interests. The war should have shattered any remaining bourgeois pretensions that intellectuals harbored. Adler lamented that intellectuals still allowed petty vanities to cloud the truth: "While before it was arrogance and ignorance that kept intellectual workers at a distance from manual ones, now it appears to be envy and distrust. Intellectuals have never learned to understand themselves as one with the proletariat...and to find in socialism—in its struggle against the bourgeois state and for the overcoming of the capitalist economic order—its real task and the sole means for liberation."[54] This passage revealed Adler's ambivalence. He maintained that intellectuals possessed latent radical urges that the Austro-Marxists must awaken, yet he was not convinced they were ready. Nevertheless, the essay introduced an important—nearly Lukácsian—element into the Austro-Marxist definition of intellectuals. With a little education in class struggle and contemporary objective conditions, intellectuals would come to consciousness. Adler ventured a concrete plan on intellectuals that shaped Austro-Marxist policy for the coming years. He focused on three subgroups: white-collar employees in the private sector (*Privatangestellten*), public officials (*öffentlichen Beamten*), and free, autonomous workers (*freie, selbständig Berufstätigen*). Adler treated the first and third groups summarily, saying their problems did not stem from the nature of intellectual work but rather from socioeconomic forces. In this time of economic crisis, the number of bankers, lawyers, and managers simply exceeded the needs of the Austrian state. Many of them would simply have to leave Austria in search of opportunity. The same could be said of doctors, scholars, and artists—members of the third group. Only as the country's economic fortunes recovered would the domestic situation for these strata improve.[55] Public officials, on the other hand, served vital roles in the body politic. They stood outside the capitalist system and therefore received little consideration from the exploiting classes. Adler believed that if the socialists could reorient them toward the future (socialism) rather than the past (patronage—*Mäzenatentum*), the battle for intellectual workers could be won.[56]

---

54. Max Adler, "Der Kampf der geistigen Arbeiter," *K* 13 (1920): 61.
55. Ibid., 65–66.
56. Ibid.

Early 1920s theoretical discussions of intellectuals by the socialists thus focused on sectors of the educated classes beyond the traditional group of culture carriers. This did not mean that they disregarded or discounted writers, artists, scientists, and scholars; rather, it demonstrated a new awareness about Austrian society. Teachers, lawyers, and public officials were more numerous and more vital to the future of the Austrian state. Austro-Marxists recognized they had to reach these sectors if they hoped to reshape Austrian society. They attempted this feat through higher education reform and new vocational opportunities for the educated classes. For example, the adult education centers (*Volkshochschulen*) employed twice as many instructors in 1923 as in 1913 and had three times as many regular participants and nearly three times the enrollment. Moreover, new employment opportunities in the municipal government and at social scientific institutes temporarily helped to stabilize the employment of public officials.[57] Ironically, contrary to Adler's statements, Austro-Marxist policy resembled a new system of patronage more than a reorientation of cultural life to the socialist future.

Paralleling and counteracting these efforts by the socialists, conservative organizations actually gained strength in the early 1920s. As we saw in the previous chapter, the Catholic academic society the Leo-Gesellschaft recovered its prominent position in Viennese society by the early 1920s. Joseph Eberle's weekly *Das neue Reich* boasted the highest circulation of any intellectual publication and drew contributions from Austrian professors, public officials, and businessmen. These societies and journals catered to intellectuals as cultural and spiritual leaders of the people, an aristocracy of the mind that contributed to German, Catholic, and Austrian greatness. Black Viennese writers complained bitterly that clerics and academics, especially young scholars and *Privatdozenten,* now suffered the indignity of working for the same wages as workers. They wanted a program of de-proletarianization to lift up Austrian intellectuals.[58] They rejected mass democracy, where votes "are counted rather than weighed," demanding a new oligarchy of "scholars, bishops, and entrepreneurs."[59] For them, intellectual was not a mere sociological category; it was a subjective, Romantic concept, imbued with classical, medieval, and national heritage. Intellectuals were culture carriers and must be mobilized for a conservative rebirth.

---

57. Danneberg, "Wahlergebnis," 215–16.

58. Ernst Nießner, "Die niedergetretene Intelligenz. Die Besoldung von Klerus, Akademiker-, und Arbeiterschaft in Österreich," *NR* 4 (1921–22): 368–70.

59. Joseph Eberle, "Gründsätzliche Erwägungen," *NR* 6 (1923–4): 87.

The Austro-Marxists had to contend with these impulses even as they posited an alternate relationship between intellectuals and society. Pitted against a recalcitrant ideological foe, they provided a distinct, compelling vision that appealed to many intellectual workers. Their understanding had some severe shortcomings nonetheless. The emphasis on the sciences and the relative discounting of history and literature posed one problem. The preference for cosmopolitanism and Viennese culture over nationalism and the Habsburg Empire contributed to this. Their apparent willingness, characterized by Max Adler's essays, to sacrifice intellectuals to the dictates of economic necessity signaled to many that the socialist movement did not have their interests at heart. There was also a problematic conceptual slippage between sociological and cultural understandings of intellectual work that made Austro-Marxist strategy incoherent. Even as they devised policies to reach out to scientists and artists, they overlooked the officials and bureaucrats who had expressed a partial willingness to work with the socialists in the postwar years. Adler's and Kassel's attempts to broaden socialist understandings of intellectual work foundered, as the Austro-Marxists followed the conservatives in conceiving of intellectuals primarily as culture carriers.

Intellectual Workers of the World Unite?

After years of internal debates, the Austro-Marxists decided that intellectuals and their work merited special attention. They adopted concrete policies, like the unionization of white-collar professions and the establishment of new intellectual institutes, as part of their new strategy. Economics, psychology, and sociology all garnered greater support. Even though the socialists offered intellectuals new institutional opportunities, they never developed a comprehensive program that convinced most intellectuals of their place in a socialist future. As a result of their lack of success beyond scientists and avant-garde artists, their general neglect of intellectuals outside the capital, and their inability to provide an adequate response to the economic crisis years of 1922–23, the Austro-Marxists saw their broader ambitions for intellectuals dry up by the mid-1920s.

In the early 1920s, the Austro-Marxists proposed new policies to unionize doctors, lawyers, and bureaucrats in an effort to build greater class solidarity between the working class and intellectual workers. In these proposals, the socialists showed little sympathy for the declining social status of this group, however. When they appealed to private and state employees (*Privat- und Staatsangestellten*), they stressed that a state of six million people would never provide enough jobs for all former imperial officials and that these new proletarians should accept their new, lower status.[60] In discussions about the socialization of the medical profession, Karl Kautsky, Jr. and Arnim Holitscher urged doctors to put themselves at the service of society and mocked outdated "bourgeois" notions about house calls and private practice. Doctors must become medical administrators in the socialist state, developing prophylactic programs rather than merely treating individuals.[61] This reflected the general Austro-Marxist preference for expert-driven, top-down solutions to problems.[62] While hesitant to transform lawyers en masse into state officials, they still aimed to turn them into technocrats.[63] Overall, the Austro-Marxist program for professionals offered little to justify a conversion to socialism. Intellectuals, who had long been leery of the socialist movement and were more concerned about pauperization than exploitation, did not see the value of technocratic solutions.

After the national election of 1923, the tone of discussion about intellectual workers changed markedly, for the Austro-Marxists realized they were making little progress with the group. The Social Democrats had campaigned against the austerity measures enacted by the Christian Socials during the hyperinflation years, arguing that austerity hurt workers, officials, and intellectuals. They condemned Ignaz Seipel's economic program of *Sanierung,* its attendant job losses, and its deflationary impact. While the Social Democrats picked up votes, they still lagged nearly 5 percent behind the Christian Socials. They failed to increase their share of the educated population and lost ground in the provinces.[64] For Black Viennese leaders, this signaled the bankruptcy of social democracy and the antidemocratic preferences of the educated classes. As Joseph Eberle triumphantly proclaimed in an election postmortem, "Doesn't everyone know that for three or five decades real intellectuals [*wahrhafte Intellektuellen*] of all peoples have cursed democracy as a cult of incompetence, and a poisoner of the people?"[65] Eberle recognized that intellectuals across Europe and particularly in Austria were already moving toward fascist solutions by 1923—two cases in point were Mussolini's Italy and the Spanish dictatorship of Primo de Rivera. The Austro-Marxist

60. Ernst Bacher, "Die Privatangestellten im neuen Deutschösterreich," *K* 12 (1919): 35–42; Karl Appel, "Beamte und Sozialismus," *K* 14 (1921): 122–24.

61. Arnim Hollitscher, "Die Sozialisierung des Aerztestandes"; Karl Kautsky, "Die Uebernahme der Aerzte durch die Gesellschaft"; Josef Friedjung, "Die Vergesellschaftung der ärztlichen Tätigkeit," *K* 1 (1919): 323–27, 621–24, 735–40, respectively.

62. On "clinic culture," see McEwen, *Sexual Knowledge,* chap. 4.

63. Engländer, "Zur Frage der Sozialisierung der Rechtsanwaltschaft," *K* 12 (1919): 555–59; Oskar Trebitsch, "Das Problem der Richterbestellung," *K* 18 (1925): 425–31.

64. Hacohen, *Karl Popper,* 293–5.

65. Eberle, "Grundsätzliche Erwägungen," 87.

leadership also saw this, deciding that the key to future elections would be not intellectuals but farmers and peasants.[66]

This does not deny that there was a vibrant cross-pollination at work between socialism, science, and empirical philosophy during the First Republic. However, almost all of these intellectuals belonged to a small subset of intellectual workers. Many of them came from liberal, Jewish backgrounds and remained outside the traditional institutions of knowledge—the bureaucracy, the universities, and government. Jews, Protestants, and non-Germans had no viable alternatives to Red Vienna since assimilation was denied them by other groups.[67]

The collaboration of Marxists and progressives merits closer attention, since it produced an efflorescence of intellectual life in the Austrian capital. In debates about economic socialization, *Der Kampf* opened the discussion up to a broad array of thinkers. In addition to Austro-Marxists like Helene Bauer and Käthe Pick (later Käthe Leichter), who argued for centralized, state-run socialization, the sociologist Rudolf Goldscheid and philosopher Otto Neurath contributed their theories. Goldscheid, a professor in Vienna and president of the Monist League, offered his vision of corporate guild socialism. Neurath's program imagined a moneyless economy built on coordinating boards similar to those established during the Great War.[68] The Austro-Marxists also provided outlets for criticizing the so-called Austrian School of economics. When Helene Bauer attacked the school, she drew on the work of Joseph Schumpeter, who had collaborated with the socialists in their initial cabinet. Schumpeter had argued that the Austrian School had devoted insufficient attention to the empirical and social foundations upon which subjective economic decisions were based. Bauer claimed this reinforced Marxist economic theory.[69] The Austro-Marxists endorsed economic trends that challenged neoclassical orthodoxy. They followed John Maynard Keynes's work with keen interest and endorsed Karl Polanyi's findings, which combined economic and social analyses. Polanyi subsequently became a regular contributor to socialist journals.

---

66. Gulick, *Austria*, 689–95, 1380–81.

67. Hacohen, *Karl Popper*, 299–309, addresses the difficulties of Jewish assimilation in interwar Vienna and the ambivalence of Austro-Marxism with regard to Judaism. Gruber, "Jewish Question," offers a critical reading of the relationship between Austro-Marxism and Viennese Jews.

68. Rudolf Goldscheid, "Goldscheids 'Naturalabgabe,'" *K* 12 (1919): 336–40, and Otto Neurath, "Wirtschaftsplan, Planwirtschaft, Landesverfassung und Völkerordnung," *K* 13 (1920): 224–27.

69. Helene Bauer, "Bankerott der Grenzwerttheorie," *K* 17 (1924): 105–13.

The most successful outreach by the Austro-Marxists was in psychology. Following the traumas of the war era, psychologists in Vienna recognized the need for social reform. Prompted by the physicians Julius Tandler and Josef Friedjung, the municipal government invested substantial resources in social welfare programs, psychological clinics, and child welfare centers.[70] Alfred Adler was the inspiration behind the child psychology sites, which were set up in every district of the city. With the arrival of Karl and Charlotte Bühler in 1922 and the founding of the Psychological Institute, there were three major groups of psychologists in the city. All of them received support from the Austro-Marxists.[71] Many of the scientists involved had socialist upbringings, so bridging science and politics was relatively straightforward.[72] While the Adler and Bühler circles were significant for Viennese social reform efforts, the attraction of the Freud circle was a major postwar coup for the Austro-Marxists. Close associates of Freud's such as Helene Deutsch, Siegfried Bernfeld, and Friedjung wrote articles in *Der Kampf* that deployed Freudian theories. Otto Jenssen and even Otto Bauer incorporated Freud's ideas into their analyses of radicalism and the proletariat.[73]

As chapter 4 explores in depth, the connections between the Vienna Circle of logical empiricism and Austro-Marxism were strong. Hans Hahn, Otto Neurath, and Edgar Zilsel all wrote in *Der Kampf*. Austro-Marxism and logical empiricism were literally fraternal: Josef Frank was the key architect of the Vienna public housing movement and his brother Philipp was a member of the Wiener Kreis. The Social Democrats provided the logical empiricists with places to teach (*Volkshochschulen*) and work (the Social and Economic Museum, founded and directed by Neurath), while the Vienna Circle provided the Austro-Marxists with broader intellectual credibility. Josef Frank and Otto Bauer used the Verein Ernst Mach, the public face of the Vienna Circle in the late 1920s and early 1930s, as a forum for theoretical discussions that introduced their ideas to a broader intellectual audience.

---

70. Tandler has been a frequent subject of recent scholarship. See Logan, *Hormones, Heredity, and Race;* McEwen, *Sexual Knowledge;* Paul Weindling, "A City Regenerated: Eugenics, Race, and Welfare in Interwar Vienna," in Holmes and Silverman, *Interwar Vienna,* 89–113, and Baader, Hofer, and Mayer, *Eugenik in Österreich.*

71. On Freud, see Danto, *Freud's Free Clinics,* 1–33. On Adler, see Stepansky, *In Freud's Shadow.* Benetka, *Psychologie in Wien,* and Mitchell Ash, "Psychology and Politics," in Ash and Woodward, *Psychology,* 143–64, treat the Psychological Institute.

72. Fleck, *Rund um "Marienthal,"* 122–67.

73. Siegfried Bernfeld, "Sozialismus und Psychoanalyse," *K* 19 (1926): 385–88; Otto Jenssen, "Zur Psychologie des Radikalismus," *K* 16 (1923): 272–78; Otto Bauer, "Buch des Bundespräsidenten," *K* 17 (1924): 209–16.

Despite these successful interactions, a resurgence of conservatism high-lighted the mid-1920s, spurred by growing discontent with the government and the economy. This contributed to the radicalization and fascistization of Austrian interwar culture. In this period *Das neue Reich* underwent its greatest expansion, and the Othmar Spann and Richard Kralik circles came to prominence. For example, in 1923 the circulation figures of *Das neue Reich* jumped from eleven thousand to fifteen thousand. Eberle's second weekly, *Die schönere Zukunft,* premiered in late 1925 and quickly reached a circulation of twenty-five thousand. Its contributors came not only from the professoriat and conservative literary circles but also from the professional classes. The growing appeal of Black Viennese ideas—which supported German and Catholic rebirth and rejected democracy and capitalism—attested to the limits of Austro-Marxist intellectual policies.[74]

Othmar Spann, appointed a professor in the law faculty in Vienna in 1919, achieved a national reputation as a conservative leader with his book *Der wahre Staat.* Spann categorically rejected democracy and socialism and argued for an authoritarian, corporatist state, ruled by men of intellect. In his vision of the true state, the two highest status groups were "creative intellectuals" (*schöpferische geistige Arbeiter*) and "state leaders" (*Staatsführer*), a group that included not just state authorities but also generals, high priests (*Priesterstand*), educators (*Erzieherstand*), and other wise men (*Weisen*).[75] As the next chapter shows, this conservative elaboration of Plato's political theory, combined with denunciations of socialism, democracy, and capitalism, gained widespread support. His texts on economics and sociology were best-sellers; his lectures attracted hundreds of students. He contributed substantially to the political and intellectual discourse of the Republic and helped drive the fascist turn in Central Europe.

With this growth in popularity of radical conservative ideologies, the Austro-Marxists feared that intellectuals were slipping away. The Austro-Marxists turned away from discussions of the broader sociological class of intellectuals to cultural definitions. Their earlier mistrust of the broader intellectual class reemerged. They assailed bourgeois intellectuals and criticized the ringleaders of Black Vienna. The socialists abandoned policy suggestions for the alleviation of economic conditions, preferring to denounce Kralik,

---

74. Lewis, *Fascism,* introduction. Lewis notes that the Vienna-centric strategy of the Austro-Marxists also left provincial socialists in a precarious position, allowing conservatives to control much of the country.

75. Spann, *Der wahre Staat,* 232–45.

Spann, and their benighted followers.[76] *Der Kampf* devoted several articles to the critical deficiencies of Spann's work. Helene Bauer rejected Spann's economic theory, stating that his attempt to build an economic science without relying on either causal laws or empirical economic research resulted in a purely metaphysical, unverifiable system. Max Adler, who sparred with Spann at the Fifth German Sociological Conference in 1926, argued that his confusion of physical causality (mechanical, natural laws) and psychological causality (processes in the social world that occur through conscious activity) prevented Spann from constructing a viable social scientific system.[77]

Although Spann's views were initially rejected for their intellectual deficiencies, later articles concentrated on his pernicious influence on students and officials. Otto Leichter used the inclusion of a Spann article on imperialism in the *Handwörterbuch der Staatswissenschaften*—the definitive German dictionary for political science—as an opportunity to attack the conservatism of German (and Austrian) intellectuals. The inclusion of an article by a nonspecialist and conservative ideologue in the discipline's most important reference text, when the works of Rudolf Hilferding, Joseph Schumpeter, and Rosa Luxemburg were available, demonstrated how far the intellectuals of the day were from the revolutionary French *encyclopédists*:

> These encyclopedists were unified in their intellectual preparation for the French Revolution and thereby created a monument to pre-Revolution intellectual trends and an eternal monument to the intellectual class that emerged from the aristocracy, who paved the way for the Revolution with the persuasive power [*Werbekraft*] of their ideas.... Admittedly none (or very few) of today's intellectuals... have the ambition to understand the signs of the times and fewer still are prepared to engage in daily political and economic struggles.... Thus the comparison of the spirit [*Geist*] that filled the encyclopedists of the French Revolution with the evil spirit [*Ungeist*] of today's German professors is endlessly sad.[78]

The selection of "our" Viennese professor, as Leichter dubbed Spann, drove home the point that intellectuals were now radical conservatives. Leichter criticized the German professoriat for its willingness to cast its lot with the

---

76. See Jacques Hannak, "Der Theoretiker des Neoklerikalismus," and H. Johann, "Der Vaterländische Dichter als Denker," *K* 18 (1925): 148–55 and 211–19, respectively.

77. Helene Bauer, "Othmar Spanns Tischlein-deck-dich," *K* 15 (1922): 178–82, and Max Adler, "Zur Kritik der Soziologie Othmar Spanns," *K* 20 (1927): 265–70.

78. Otto Leichter, "Enzyklopädisten von heute," *K* 15 (1922): 372–73.

capitalist classes. Intellectuals were now conservative mandarins, incapable of using their reason for social good.[79]

These appeals failed to counter Spann's rise. His universalist philosophy offered a conservative alternative to the Austro-Marxist attempts to curry favor with traditional intellectuals. It also sought to integrate intellectual workers into the nation, but it offered them a position of leadership in the future "true state."[80] This utopian vision was quite popular with intellectuals who longed for a restoration of their social status. Through his institutional influence at the university, in the fraternity the Deutsche Studentenschaft, and in the Leo-Gesellschaft, he managed to place over half a dozen students in professorships across Austria while thwarting the efforts of other academics who did not share his political views. Spann's influence was a symptom of a larger problem: the conservatism of the university system and the constant interference of the state in scientific matters. The professors Ludo Hartmann and Hans Hahn spoke out vehemently against this meddlesomeness and exposed the political favoritism and cliquishness of the professoriat to scrutiny.[81] Despite their complaints about the politicization of academic culture, the socialists never succeeded in making this subject a major issue with the government or the broader intellectual class.

Although they were unprepared to abandon their efforts, the tone of subsequent articles by Austro-Marxists about intellectuals demonstrated resentment and anger. The socialists railed at the reactionary nature of the intelligentsia and ceased arguing for their inclusion in the socialist movement. In an article on the Viennese intellectual landscape, Therese Schlesinger chose to neglect the contributions of all nonparty members to socialist knowledge. This was a startling reversal from her earlier pamphlets on the reciprocal relationship between intellectuals and socialism. She believed that the socialist movement had undergone fundamental structural changes in the last few years: the educational apparatus in place within the party could now produce large numbers of organic intellectuals. Consequently, only socialists and their supporters now qualified as intellectuals. There was no need for bourgeois intellectuals after all.[82] Another article focused on the cultural associations established by workers and the party's encouragement of *Bildung* for the

---

79. Ibid., 376–77.

80. In the 1926 edition of his *Haupttheorien der Volkswirtschaftslehre,* Spann added a section about the role of intellectuals in universalism.

81. Ludo Hartmann, "Grundlagen einer Universitätsreform," *K* 17 (1924), 142–45, and Hans Hahn, "Lehr- und Lernfreiheit an den Hochschulen," *K* 17 (1924): 170–75.

82. Therese Schlesinger, "Die Stellung der Intellektuellen in der Sozialdemokratie," *K* 16 (1923): 264–72.

masses. Intellectual work was no longer viewed as part of the struggle to reshape productive forces, as Friedrich Adler had argued; instead, it was a superstructural element that rounded out proletarian culture.[83] These articles show that the Austro-Marxists had largely ceded the intellectual battlefield to conservatives by 1924 yet trumpeted their limited successes as if they were the victories they had always sought.

In many ways, then, 1927 represented a last stand for Austro-Marxist efforts to recruit intellectual workers. Despite myriad setbacks, the Social Democrats believed they had a real chance to take control of the national government in 1927 and marshaled all their strength in the campaign. They toned down their secular, anti-Catholic message and focused on the positive achievements of the Viennese government as evidence of their readiness to govern. Despite the renewed efforts, they did not have much new success with intellectual workers. This was evident in the pages of *Der Kampf* and the manifesto of Viennese intellectuals, where past achievements were celebrated and future goals eschewed. Intellectual Vienna—previously a broad substratum of Viennese society—was now synonymous with modernist artists and liberal social reformers. Going forward, conservative movements benefited more from the involvement of intellectuals than did the Austro-Marxists. In addition to growing the Black Viennese ideological field, bureaucrats and civil servants turned to the Austrian Nazis in large numbers, abandoning all other parties.[84] The moderate conservative political theorist Alfred Verdross publicly endorsed the authoritarian constitutional amendments of 1929. Othmar Spann's pupils wrote the antidemocratic oath of the Heimwehr, and his ideas helped shape the 1934 Austrofascist constitution. Eric Voegelin, Johannes Messner, and other professors wrote encomia in favor of the *Ständestaat* and rose to fill governmental posts. Thanks to the debates about intellectual work in the First Republic, initiated by the Austro-Marxists but conducted across the cultural landscape, intellectuals engaged in political affairs to a degree far greater than ever before. Unfortunately for the socialists, most intellectuals preferred other options.

The "Announcement of Intellectual Vienna" was therefore the culmination of a lengthy rivalry over intellectuals, intellectual work, and modern radicalism between red and black thinkers. In the immediate postwar days, Austro-Marxists believed intellectuals would join the proletariat in crafting a new order. They endeavored to incorporate these men and women by offering them a role in the socialist cause. Some joined. However, inflexibility on

83. J. Zach, "Zur Frage des geistigen Lebens in unserer Partei," *K* 18 (1925): 470–74.
84. Pauley, *Forgotten Nazis,* 93–95; Hacohen, *Karl Popper,* 296–97.

economic and cultural policy led to an inability to attract public officials, university professors, and middle-class professionals. The Announcement highlights the ambiguity of the Viennese and Austrian intellectual land-scapes: despite the apparent success of the Austro-Marxists in recruiting internationally recognized figures, they could not stem the tide of radical conservatism among traditional intellectuals. Socialist denigration of non-scientific work and lack of interest in recruiting intellectuals beyond the capital excluded many potential converts. Coupled with the resurgent popu-larity of Black Viennese ideology and a lack of political decisiveness,[85] the Austro-Marxists were engaged in a losing battle. This unsuccessful ideologi-cal contest had dire consequences as intellectuals provided the foundations for Austrofascism and the *Anschluss*.

---

85. Hanisch, *Der große Illusionist,* 273–77, and Rabinbach, *Crisis.*

CHAPTER 3

The Spannkreis and the Battle for Hegemony in Central Europe

In 1936 the philosopher Othmar Spann found himself defending his philosophy against an unlikely enemy: the Nazis. Long a supporter of the movement and a member of the party even when it was illegal in Austria, Spann felt compelled to defend the intellectual and political position of his circle of universalist philosophers and its compatibility with National Socialism. In fact, his school faced criticism from all sides: the Nazis rejected its work as insufficiently *völkisch;* the Austrofascist state, established in 1934, viewed it as unpatriotic; socialists saw it as antiproletarian and fascist; and social scientists castigated it as unobjective, metaphysical, and politically partisan. Even with liberals and socialists largely suppressed in German lands and his own desires for a greater German state close at hand, Spann saw the Nazis turning his own ideological weapons against his desires.

Spann began his defense with a short biographical sketch, designed to demonstrate his German nationalist credentials. He recounted his frequent confrontations with ideological opponents during the course of his thirty-year academic career. He had argued with the Historical School of German economics as a young professor. He had incurred the wrath of the Social Democratic majority in Vienna with his antidemocratic, anti-Marxist, and anti-Semitic book *Der wahre Staat* in the early 1920s. He had waged battle against the sociology establishment in the mid-1920s, engaging in a pointed exchange with the bourgeois intellectuals Max Adler, Werner Sombart, and

Ferdinand Tönnies. Even the Austrofascist state had recently begun suppressing his publications. It was only the Nazi accusation of insufficient commitment to the German people and race that truly disturbed him. He argued that the other movements had been correct to view his *Ganzheitsphilosophie* as a threat: "My Marxist, liberal, Freemason and centrist opponents have not misunderstood me and have good reason to combat me. It follows that my *völkisch* opponents misunderstand me and have unjustly attacked my theories."[1] Spann made it clear that he had political and ideological enemies; however, the Nazis were not among them. He maintained that his philosophy actually served as a political weapon against Marxist, liberal, and democratic forces. Anyone who followed Spann's work would see he was a radical conservative and *völkisch* nationalist.

In the same piece, Spann suggested that his philosophy should serve as the scientific foundation of National Socialist ideology. He was not a politician, but his ideas could serve the political purposes of others: "Since I am no practical politician, they [politicians] should not confront me in the arena of political combat. They cannot oppose me as a politician, only as a bearer of an idea."[2] Spann insisted that all political systems of world-historical significance, such as Hitler's, required supporting ideological rationales to endure—his philosophy would serve the Nazis ably. He hoped to sidestep criticism from Nazi circles that his philosophy was insufficiently Nazi through his invocation of disinterested scientific thinking. His philosophy, unlike that of Alfred Rosenberg or Robert Ley, objectively demonstrated the uniqueness of the German race and provided a credible justification for the Nazi state and its vision of the *Volksgemeinschaft*. Nevertheless, this effort at clarification failed, as his rivalry with Rosenberg, the chief Nazi ideologue, only increased. His failure to accept racial theory as the sole explication of the historical process made his views unacceptable to Nazi ideologues. Ultimately, Spann and his students faced persecution from the Nazis despite their unswerving support for Hitler.

The essay captures the ambiguous position of Spann and his circle in the 1930s and sheds light on the precarious position of radical conservatism in interwar Central Europe. For Spann—as for his most famous acolytes Konrad Henlein, the leader of the Sudetendeutsche Partei, and Heinz Rutha, a Sudeten Wandervogel leader—interactions with the Nazi leadership

---

1. Othmar Spann, "Leidlicher Austrag unleidlicher Dinge. Eine Erwiderung auf überwitzige Angriffe," *SL,* 1936, 123.
2. Ibid., 125.

were fraught with contradictions and conflicts despite many common aims.[3] Fighters against all things Enlightenment and modern, the Spannkreis supported nearly every authoritarian, radical conservative, and fascist movement in interwar Europe at some point—first among those were the Nazis. The group—composed primarily of university colleagues, students, youth association members, and journalists—sought to form the scientific and ideological basis of these political movements. They struggled to gain international influence and frequently fell out of favor with the political groups they endorsed, since they refused to compromise their philosophical views. This resulted in the curious circumstance that leading members of the Spannkreis were Nazi members or sympathizers yet were arrested as political enemies in the Sudetenland and Austria.[4]

Ironically, Spann's defenders after the war cited this politically charged 1936 article as proof of the philosopher's purely intellectual interests and anti-Nazi bona fides.[5] These apologists asserted that when one combined Spann's apolitical assertions, his equivocal position on racial theory, and his arrest by the Nazis, "Othmar Spann was... a *großdeutsch* patriot but at no time was he a Nazi."[6] Despite these protestations, the Spannkreis's fascist bona fides seem beyond dispute. For example, Spann received a full Nazi Party membership in 1933, and he supported the National Socialist Party (NSDAP) unstintingly from its inception in 1920.[7] His closest associate, Walter Heinrich, played a pivotal role as a propagandist in the Sudetenland among the Rutha and Henlein circles. He also lectured to Italian Fascist groups in the late 1920s and Nazi organizations in the mid-1930s. Heinrich and Walter Riehl served as the ideological inspiration behind the radical wing of the Austrian Heimwehr in 1929 and 1930. Their universalist philosophy even influenced the construction of the Austrofascist constitution in 1934. In other words, arguably the most influential intellectual group in interwar Vienna was also its most radical, enjoying an impact well beyond the academic sphere. This chapter explores these affinities.

Against the rehabilitation of the Spannkreis as an apolitical scientific group, this chapter takes a closer look at the intellectual output and political activities of Spann and his circle, accounting for their popularity and the consequences of their notoriety. It situates the Spannkreis at the center of

---

3. On Spann's influence in the Sudetenland, see Haag, "'Knights of the Spirit.'"

4. On the fate of Henlein and Rutha, see Cornwall, *Devil's Wall.*

5. Pichler, *Othmar Spann,* 18.

6. Ernst Kaltenbrunner, "Othmar Spann," *Mut* 225 (May 1986): 46, cited in Pichler, *Othmar Spann,* 51.

7. Siegfried, *Universalismus und Faschismus,* 152–56.

the movement culture of Black Vienna, where the group provided intellectual stimulation for many and a challenge for some. As the previous chapter demonstrated, the Austro-Marxists acknowledged that the Spannkreis was the most influential intellectual group in interwar Vienna, one that must be combated. Spann's popularity was tangible: his lectures attracted hundreds of people, his students met with academic success, and his ideas circulated among the political elites of Central Europe. He was a lightning rod for controversy and rarely found himself excluded from the major social, political, and intellectual discussions across Central Europe. As the title of a 1934 book, *Kämpfende Wissenschaft,* suggests, Spann believed his theory was a "fighting science," designed to crush opposing social, political, and intellectual movements. His students lumped their enemies together under the banner of "individualism"—democracy, liberalism, capitalism, socialism, and empiricism. They advocated ruthless measures against those ideas and hoped for a radically conservative, even fascist revolution that would crush them all. The Spannians waged war in lectures and pamphlets, in scholarly congresses and university classrooms, behind closed doors in the government, and at political rallies. Like the philosophers of the Vienna Circle and the Austro-Marxists whom they opposed, the Spannkreis engaged radically in the affairs of interwar Europe. Despite the historiographical emphasis on the successes of red groups, the Spannkreis won the battle for philosophical and scientific hegemony in Vienna, impacting Central European historical developments profoundly.

It is essential to recognize the centrality of politics to Spannian (and Black Viennese) thought and conversely the centrality of Black Vienna to Austrian and Central European politics. Spann's political convictions derived from his philosophy, not vice versa. This made the Spannkreis a heterodox advocate for the political organizations it endorsed. It sought to realize its idiosyncratic political and scientific ideals in the world and pursued ideological alliances based on perceived intellectual affinity. Nevertheless, apolitical or objective science was the furthest thing from Spann's imagination. Practical political activity was an indispensable part of the circle's philosophical worldview: thought came first, yet thought and action formed part of a larger unity. This makes it impossible to separate his theoretical works from his political activities or to make claims of political naïveté or strict scientific engagement, as some later writers have argued.[8] His works, most notably the political tract *Der wahre Staat* and his philosophical opus *Die Kategorienlehre,* form a whole that advances a distinctive worldview, which deserves closer scrutiny.

---

8. In particular, see Johnston, *Austrian Mind,* 311–15.

The efforts of his comrades in the universalist journal *Ständisches Leben* and Joseph Eberle's publications contributed to popularization of anti-Semitic, antiliberal, antidemocratic, ultranationalist, conservative, and fascist discourse.

With the restoration of a conservative academy after the war,[9] the political and ideological impact of the Spannkreis received less attention than befitting a group of this significance. This was particularly true of its intellectual influence and its centrality to Viennese conservatism. As chapter 1 showed, Spann was hardly alone in his views. Many thinkers drew on his seminal postwar treatises in their own efforts. The case of the Spannkreis can therefore shed light on the broader experience of Black Viennese cultural life. Like the Spannians, most Black Viennese intellectuals did not unequivocally endorse fascism or the Nazis, yet they nevertheless encouraged and justified their rise with their work and actions. They endeavored to subvert the present order and establish a more German, Christian, and authoritarian future through cultural and political organizations. The exploration of Spann and his philosophy thus casts in stark relief the battle lines in interwar Vienna. Its most influential intellectual group was also its most radical and politically impactful. This means that Red Vienna was not the Marxist fortress portrayed by supporters and detractors alike. In the battle for science, as in the political struggle, Spann's fighting science won a decisive victory in Vienna—with tragic consequences for Central European history, science, and philosophy.

Othmar Spann, the Origins of Universalism, and *Der wahre Staat*

Othmar Spann's early years convinced him of the need to find solutions to social and political problems through theoretical speculation and practical investigation. Spann was born in 1878 in a suburb of Vienna. After completing high school, he attended several universities, graduating with his doctorate in political science in 1903 from the University of Tübingen. From 1904 to 1907 he lived in Frankfurt, conducting empirical research on the birthrates of illegitimate children. In 1907, he finished his *Habilitation* thesis in economics in Brünn (Brno) and began work as a *Privatdozent,* publishing a best-selling economics textbook. Spann remained in Brno until 1919, becoming a full professor in 1911. He fought on the eastern front during World War I and suffered injuries in Ukraine in 1914. He spent most of the war back in Vienna.[10]

---

9. See Fleck, "Restoration."

10. Hausmann, *Othmar Spann,* 4–10; Resele, *Othmar Spanns Ständestaatskonzeption,* 4–14.

His earliest work argued that complex issues in the contemporary world required holistic answers that employed economic, sociological, and cultural analyses. By the time the University of Vienna appointed Spann a professor of economics and sociology (*Nationalökonomie und Gesellschaftslehre*) in the Law Faculty in 1919, he had already made a reputation for himself as a social theorist. His first two major works, *Die Volkswirtschaftslehre* (1911) and *Die Gesellschaftslehre* (1914), were recognized for their contributions to the burgeoning fields of economics and sociology.[11] Spann introduced the concepts for which he would become famous: universalism and the philosophy of totality (*Ganzheitsphilosophie*). He used the German Historical School of economics as a departure point. Although he embraced the school's emphasis on ethical concerns, he found its statistical approach and reformist agenda inadequate.[12] He argued instead for a comprehensive understanding of the hierarchical structures in society that allowed for social, economic, and political strength and stability. This involved theoretical speculation in addition to empirical observation; in contrast to the historicists, he privileged the former over the latter.

Spann provided the basics of his new "universalist" philosophy in epigrams, one of which was the Aristotelian "whole comes before the parts." He argued this was the only way to understand the economy or society: starting from the whole (*das Ganze*) and working back to discrete components. For example, one could not assess the value of an economic good unless one knew what worth society as a whole assigned that item. Prices were thus not determined by supply and demand or by subjective calculations but by a society's norms and needs. This interpretation flew in the face of the economics theories of the Historical School and the marginalist school of Eugen Böhm-Bawerk and the young Ludwig Mises.[13] Spann extended his argument to include sociology, claiming that the understanding of society did not emerge from aggregating data about individuals. Rather, it came from identifying the animating ideas of the whole community and then looking at how well individuals adhered to those norms. Scientific understanding emerged as a consequence of a thorough knowledge of a given society's worldview. Bruce Caldwell has characterized this approach as "intuitive universalism,"[14] yet it was something more than that: it valued inductive research to the extent that it reinforced Spann's hierarchical and totalizing vision.

---

11. On their continuing impact in Weimar Germany, see Köster, *Wissenschaft der Außenseiter*, 180–92.

12. Caldwell, *Hayek's Challenge*, 40–42.

13. Ibid., 39–82.

14. Ibid., 138–40.

This hybrid methodological approach nevertheless rested on underlying assumptions about the centrality of authority and order, which placed Spann's philosophy firmly in conservative thought circles. The well-being of state and society as composite "wholes" took precedence over the individual and his or her concerns. Spann's models presupposed societies grounded in total obedience to authority. His preferred explanatory pairs reinforced this: teacher-student, general-infantryman, priest-flock and father-son. This style of totalizing thought found widespread support among conservative intellectuals across the Habsburg monarchy. His *Volkswirtschaftslehre* was one of the most popular economics texts of the 1910s and 1920s, appearing in twenty-eight editions during that span.[15] His books spurred his ascent to the top of the academic hierarchy as a full professor by the age of thirty-three. Nevertheless, he also wanted to develop a broader social and political following.

Spann's call to Vienna represented a crowning achievement for a Habsburg intellectual, though his arrival coincided with the end of World War I, the dissolution of the Habsburg Empire, and the November revolution that led to the formation of the Austrian Republic. Upheaval and uncertainty reigned in all spheres of life. After the Paris peace treaties, the Social Democrats established themselves as the strongest political party in the new state of Deutsch-Österreich and headed a coalition government. All adults, male and female, over the age of twenty gained the right to vote, and Austria had a representative democratic government for the first time.[16] These early democratic days were also a time of epidemic sickness, starvation, and economic instability. Many doubted whether a rump Austrian state could survive, and some hoped for its failure.[17] Spann expressed much of this insecurity, resentment, and anger in his early 1920s work and gained a following as a result.

The University of Vienna appointed Spann partly to serve as a counterweight to the legal theorist Hans Kelsen, the author of the new Austrian constitution.[18] Kelsen was a democrat, a liberal, a moderate supporter of the Austro-Marxists, and the founder of a positivist school of legal theory. He was also one of the most hated professors at the academy and a frequent target of anti-Semitic attacks.[19] Spann also balanced out Max Adler, the Austro-Marxist theorist. Like Kelsen, Adler was born a Jew who was harassed

---

15. Hausmann, *Othmar Spann*, 7–8 and Resele, *Othmar Spanns Ständestaaatskonzeption*, 14–15.

16. Boyer, "Silent War."

17. On Austrian viability, see Bruce Pauley, "Austria's *Lebensunfähigkeit*," in Rabinbach, *Austrian Socialist Experiment*.

18. Reinhold Knoll, "Die 'verdrängte' Soziologie: Othmar Spann," in M. Benedikt et al., *Totalitarismen*, 461.

19. Thomas Olechowski, "Hans Kelsen und die Universität Wien," in *Hans Kelsen und die Bundesverfassung*, 32–39.

by German nationalist students. Spann quickly became an indispensable force in the Law Faculty. University archives reveal that well over 90 percent of all law students during the First Republic took at least one course with Spann. This included most members of the monarchist Österreichische Aktion, the central figures of the Ludwig Mises economics seminar, the intellectual group the Geistkreis (including Friedrich Hayek, Oskar Morgenstern, Fritz Machlup, and Gottfried Haberler), and future conservative political theorists and professors Eric Voegelin and Johannes Sauter. Spann's course offerings frequently criticized democracy and socialism.[20] His courses enjoyed the largest enrollments and his teaching inspired the formation of seminars and discussion groups.

In the summer of 1920, Spann held a series of lectures titled *Der wahre Staat* that expanded his reach beyond the academy into popular and political circles. These lectures, published the following year, went through four editions during the First Republic. The book has been called "the Bible of Universalism."[21] It remained a fixture in discussions about state forms, government, and society for the remainder of the Republic. It was Spann's clearest attempt to turn his philosophical theories into political praxis. With *Der wahre Staat,* Spann established himself as a preeminent voice in the university and a hero to the nascent Black Viennese intellectual community. As he stated, he offered these lectures in response to recent events in Austria and Central Europe. He hoped to identify problems plaguing the region and offer solutions. Spann believed there was a fundamental crisis of thought under way. He criticized contemporary modes of thought as individualistic and hoped for an antipositivist and antimodern counterreformation.[22]

Spann exposed the unstable zeitgeist of the early Republic to scrutiny, calling for apolitical reflection from all members of the Austrian community. He spoke at length about his audience and his hopes for unifying diverse groups through scientific exploration of current affairs: "Among them could be found all directions of political thought and inclinations, from the extreme Right to the extreme Left. For this reason, there was a lot that divided us. But if we want to undertake together a common investigation, then we must focus on what binds us all: the search for truth [*Das Streben nach Wahrheit*]."[23] Spann attempted to veil his political intentions behind the cover of pure academic research while nevertheless supporting a political trajectory. He

---

20. Course information derives from the Archiv der Universität Wien, Rechtswissenschaftliche Fakultät, Juridische Personalakten.

21. Resele, *Othmar Spanns Ständestaatskonzeption,* 15.

22. Spann, *Der wahre Staat,* 3–4.

23. Ibid., 6.

pronounced himself to be above politics. As a corollary to his search for truth, he declared, "First, we are not conducting any party politics! Perhaps every thought and word that we express here today could also carry immediate party political significance, but we are not here concerned with these political effects, since we, as pure researchers and analysts, should not take a single step away from the aims of truth."[24] In this passage, Spann introduced a semantic distinction between "party political" and "political" discourses, a standard early twentieth-century differentiation and one he would continue to use to sidestep political criticism. The former term expressed the positions of particular parties and typically came from professional politicians. The latter, objective form offered political recipes independent of party affiliation. The ideas Spann advanced indeed fell into the latter category even as they represented a clear political and ideological intent.[25]

Der wahre Staat left little doubt that Spann had political aims that could be satisfied only by radical groups. The first section of the book, entitled "The Essence of Society," examined the two major approaches to social theory, the individualist and the universalist, arguing that only the second was viable. Individualist theory viewed society as the summation of discrete entities bound together by rationalist laws. Individualism therefore allowed for utilitarian but not social ethics. The consequences of such an approach were all negative: subordination and capitalist exploitation, plutocracy, and atomistic mass democracy or anarchy.[26] This left only one alternative: universalism. In this conception, society must be understood as composed of reciprocal relationships (*Gezweiung*) rather than atomistic points (*Entzweiung*). Since individuals could not be understood apart from their interpersonal relations, it was dangerous to start from the individual. He concluded that order, achieved through the rule of law and obedience to authority, must take precedence over freedom and liberty, since the latter were possible only *after* the establishment of the former. As he admitted, universalism required inequality rather than equality in the name of order. Drawing on historical examples of empires, he showed that the best states and societies upheld the "organic inequalities" of the community.[27]

In the second section of the book, Spann applied his theories, presenting a case against postwar political and ideological developments. If there were any questions about his political orientation, he dispelled them with an attack

---

24. Ibid., 6–7.

25. See Ringer, *German Mandarins,* for similar claims made by the conservative German professoriat during the interwar period.

26. Spann, *Der wahre Staat,* 19–27.

27. Ibid., 44–68.

on democrats and socialists: "Today it is not known what will come from the revolution, and those who believe that they know, the socialists or the democrats, actually have no clarity on the matter." He included "acolytes of the scientific method" in his condemnation of the postwar order, thereby establishing a conservative touchstone argument of the interwar era: modern science and progressive politics together destroyed the social fabric. For Spann, the search for scientific laws of society impeded better understanding of communal life since each community was unique and historically contingent. It was the responsibility of universalists to re-create Germanic modes of living rooted in tradition if Central European culture was to thrive again. It was high time for a period of "de-rationalization."[28]

Spann identified three "crises" that could be overcome with universalist solutions: a political crisis of democracy and liberalism; an intellectual, economic one of individualism and capitalism; and a crisis of socialism. Generally, Spann demanded a *völkisch* revolution by cultural Germans. "The German people have only tolerated the Enlightenment and liberalism for the last couple of centuries and only in this way have they taken part in it; it has never entirely taken root."[29] He argued for a counter-Renaissance steeped in German Christian values.[30] He ridiculed the "frivolousness" of mass democracy and asserted the necessity for the rule of a select few: "Democracy wants to vote about truth—that is not only unfeasible [*undurchführbar*]...but also frivolous, because setting the majority in the saddle means that the lower rule over the higher."[31] The solution to this crisis of democracy is simple: a führer state. "The will of the people as political will may be built only through the führer, before it can be expressed as such."[32] For Spann, the führer represented the people and its collective will, standing above contemporary problems. Spann called for a conservative revolution to cast off the yoke of individualist oppression and return German Central Europe to glory.[33] While Spann made no profession of political allegiance, the National Socialist Party, which was based on a *Führerprinzip* and also initially drew ties to the values of a conservative Catholicism, seemed a natural ally for this kind of thinking. Indeed, Spann affiliated with the NSDAP after its founding in 1920.[34]

---

28. Ibid., 79–96.
29. Ibid., 103.
30. Ibid., 97–110.
31. Ibid., 110.
32. Ibid., 111.
33. Siegfried, *Universalismus und Faschismus*, 152–53.
34. On the relationship between early Nazism and the Catholic Church, see Hastings, *Roots of Nazism*. On early Austrian Nazism, see Pauley, *Hitler and the Forgotten Nazis*, 16–35.

Even more than through his criticisms of capitalism and liberal democracy, Spann galvanized support through his critical deconstruction of Marxism. Unlike other Central European critics of socialism—most notably Mises— Spann had a thoroughgoing knowledge of Marxist theory. His economic textbook in fact devoted careful attention to the arguments of Marx, Engels, Bebel, and Kautsky. Nevertheless, his verdict on both the theory and the practice of contemporary Marxism was wholly negative. He viewed it as a bastardized combination of individualism and universalism that deceived people with its pseudoscientific theories and utopian social goals. He castigated Marxism as unobjective, ideological, nihilistic, and destructive. Marxism could provide no answers to present-day problems; its success jeopardized the traditional religious, philosophical, and communal values of the German *Volk*. Spann railed against the Bolsheviks and the Austro-Marxists. The former group represented the logical, terroristic outcome of Marx's thought while the latter were Marxists in word but not deed. He condemned particularly the actions of Otto Bauer, who rejected the centralizing tendencies of Marxism and advocated smaller, corporate-like councils.[35] According to Spann, Bauer's socialization program would establish a false corporate society based on equality and not hierarchy. Writing at the height of Austrian Social Democratic success, Spann feared the coming of a socialist state and wanted to warn his audience away from such measures. Even after the socialization debates of 1919–20 passed and the Austro-Marxists withdrew from the national government, Spann continued to attack the foreignness of Marxism, highlighting its "Semitic" qualities.[36] The rhetoric of anti-Semitism served as a major rallying point for Viennese conservatives. This drove Austrian socialists to respond to Spann and defend themselves against charges of philo-Semitism.

Spann's antimodernist screed situated him squarely within a growing group of "conservative revolutionaries," and he established ties to many of them.[37] For example, his correspondents Werner Sombart and Oswald Spengler also lamented the current state of affairs in Europe. Spann went beyond the typical cultural despair of the day, however, and advocated solutions.[38] With *Der wahre Staat,* he became an important contributor to European corporatist discussions in the early interwar years.[39] He also played a leading role in the debates about *Nationalökonomie* in the Weimar Republic.[40] The second

---

35. See Bauer, *Weg zum Sozialismus.*
36. Spann, *Der wahre Staat,* 163.
37. See Mohler, *Konservative Revolution.*
38. See Stern, *Cultural Despair.*
39. Seefried, *Reich und Stände,* 123–26. On corporatism, see Maier, *Recasting Bourgeois Europe.*
40. Köster, *Wissenschaft der Außenseiter,* 180–92.

major section of *Der wahre Staat* shifted from analysis (*prüfen*) to reconstruction (*aufbauen*), presenting Spann's vision of the true state. The epigram at the beginning of the section neatly captured his authoritarian and elitist stance: "Equality among equals. Subordination of the intellectually inferior under their intellectual betters—those are the constitutive laws of the true state."[41] Spann reprised his earlier theories of society and economics, reasserting that the community must come before the individual and that society must be viewed organically instead of mechanically. Society must be organized hierarchically rather than equitably. Spann advocated for a corporatist, decentralized state built around local, guild-like structures. The corporate entities (*Stände*) would operate as self-contained totalities, composed of smaller parts and constituting higher entities (*Urstände*). The intellectual estate was the highest *Stand* and therefore primary; it dictated what transpired below in acting (*handelnde*) *Stände*.[42]

At the heart of Spann's argument lay a fundamental desire for the salvation of the German people. He wanted to unite a fragmented *Volk* with a common mission. "The German *Volk* has tolerated pain and adversity and even dishonor; it has also recently gotten entangled in vile errors. It is now time to rectify the dishonor and to remove the boil, that is, democracy and Marxism, which has perpetrated all our suffering."[43] *Der wahre Staat* was a rallying cry for those disaffected by World War I and its aftermath. Spann challenged the new Central European order and incited his listeners to revolutionary action.

As we will see, criticisms of *Der wahre Staat* abounded in liberal and socialist circles, among politicians and academics, yet Spann's ideas resonated with the *Bildungsbürgertum,* nationalist students and conservative Catholic societies. *Der wahre Staat* placed Spann at the center of the Viennese and Central European intellectual universes. While he enjoyed success with politically minded students and activists, he found it more difficult to gain a following in social scientific circles. This only spurred the radicalism and activism of his burgeoning movement.

Spann's Struggle for Academic Acceptance

As its defenders have noted, focusing solely on the political activities of the Spannkreis distorts its image, for its members believed that the key to their success ultimately rested on the respectability of their intellectual output. Only if their ideas enjoyed esteem from a broad range of European

41. Spann, *Der wahre Staat,* 185.
42. Ibid., 187–208.
43. Ibid., 299.

intellectuals and politicians could universalism transform the world. Thus, for all their political pronouncements and partisan activism, they participated first and foremost in scholarly discussions. The success of the Spannkreis in Black Vienna owed not only to Spann's philosophical insight and his relentless propagandizing but also to a favorable political and ideological climate. Spann hoped to find broader acceptance in the German and European academic worlds, too. This led to conflicts with other scholars, culminating in a lively debate at the Fifth German Sociological Congress in Vienna in 1926. Despite his appeal in Austria and the Sudetenland, Spann met with limited academic success abroad. This drove the Spannians to redouble their political endeavors in Central Europe.

One of the Spannkreis's major accomplishments in the academic world was its rediscovery and promotion of Romantic philosophy. In 1922, Spann founded a book series, the *Herdflamme,* devoted to works of Romantic political theory. He published four volumes by the political theorist Adam Müller, two by Fichte, and one each by Schelling, Hegel, Franz von Baader, Friedrich List, and Freiherr vom Stein. Spann nearly single-handedly started a Müller renaissance, whose ideas enriched conservative discussions across Central Europe. Spann's colleagues Wilhelm Andreae and Jacob Baxa participated in this project, thereby lending it further academic credibility. These efforts enjoyed such success that Carl Schmitt addressed Spann and the Romantic renaissance in *Political Romanticism* and *Political Theology.* Schmitt criticized the Romantics for their muddled thinking and opportunism and argued that contemporary conservatives needed firmer foundations for their theories of sovereignty and legitimacy.[44] Hannah Arendt also critically assessed the "Adam Müller Renaissance" in Germany—its origins in the Spannkreis, its appeal to Catholic conservatives, and its dissemination into Nazi circles.[45]

With the publication of his philosophical summa in 1924, *Die Kategorienlehre,* Spann enjoyed critical attention from the broader German-speaking scholarly community. Viewed as a significant contribution to the methodology and philosophy of the social sciences, *Die Kategorienlehre* led the German sociological community to convene its congress in Vienna the following year. In the work, Spann combined the lessons from his previous studies on economics, politics, and society into a comprehensive system of knowledge. He endeavored to find the ontological and epistemological totalities that undergirded scientific speculation and phenomenal existence: "What

---

44. Schmitt, *Political Romanticism,* 21, 141.

45. Hannah Arendt, "Adam Müller—Renaissance?" *Kölnische Zeitung,* September 13, 1932, and September 17, 1932, Unterhaltungsblatt.

is clearly true for economics must also pertain for the entirety of sociology, since universalism demonstrates that society is a totality which is broken down into different parts (science, art, business, etc.)—this all proves to be a unity. That the concept of totality is furthermore not only for economics and society but for all intellectual matters... is no longer hard to discover."[46] Spann offered a universalist rejoinder to the *Wissenschaft* debates of the early twentieth century. His intervention in these debates, which received new life from Max Weber in a series of lectures in Vienna in the years after the Great War, gained universalism a hearing within the academic community. Universalism rejected the attempts to find mechanical laws in the human and social sciences, arguing that these disciplines were like physical science. Mechanical causality ran contrary to human experience, Spann said. This led to a dismissal of "value-free" or objective social science, since social science was contingent on the cultural heritage of its practitioners. Many social scientists greeted the book as a major contribution to the ongoing methodological discussions of their emerging disciplines. In particular, students of Dilthey's *Lebensphilosophie* and the sociologists Werner Sombart and Ferdinand Tönnies voiced positive verdicts.[47] Through this work Spann also reanimated idealist philosophy in Austria, a location that had not often provided fertile ground in the past.[48]

Despite this degree of intellectual acceptance, Spann had more adversaries than allies. His unwieldy prose, replete with neologisms and convoluted concepts, led many to dismiss universalism's metaphysical claims. Upon further examination of the ideas in *Die Kategorienlehre,* sociologists questioned the normative assumptions of its holistic epistemology. When the Fifth German Sociology Congress convened, tensions boiled over. The congress transformed into a debate that pitted Spann against several leading sociologists of the day: Sombart, Leopold von Wiese, Max Adler, Franz Oppenheimer, and Ferdinand Tönnies. As the discussion progressed, it became clear that this was more than just a methodological debate. Competing worldviews were at stake, ideas that would have a profound impact on Austrian and European affairs. If Spann had initially viewed this meeting as an opportunity to reach out to other social scientists, he was quickly disappointed. Instead, the Spannkreis ended up more isolated than before.

---

46. Spann, *Kategorienlehre,* 13.

47. On Dilthey, Tönnies, and Sombart, see Ringer, *German Mandarins,* 315–34, 352–66. Hughes, *Consciousness and Society,* remains the standard intellectual history of social scientific thought at the turn of the century.

48. Haller, "Österreichische Philosophie?" 173–81.

Werner Sombart convened the congress and laid out the topics of debate—largely drawn from *Die Kategorienlehre*—before calling on Spann to initiate discussion. He identified two major directions developing in contemporary sociology that seemed to be drifting apart: a "sociological" method that involved quantitative analysis and the development of mechanical, societal "laws" and an "empirical, historical" one that focused on the qualitative characteristics of social groups. He encouraged a wide-ranging discussion on the merits of each approach, enjoining his colleagues to find grounds for reconciliation.[49] Spann spoke first and elaborated the terms of debate by distancing his approach from its "scientistic" rivals. Although generally sympathetic to Sombart's views, Spann took umbrage at his dualistic interpretation of sociology.[50] He opposed not only the naturalizing tendencies of sociological approaches but also the individualism of the empirical method. In an attack on Sombart's categorizations, Spann rejected the equation of historical and empirical methods. With a critique of the natural scientific approach to social sciences, which would be taken up and elaborated by his student Eric Voegelin,[51] he argued that statistical and mathematical analyses of human phenomena could not produce causal laws and that empirical observation could not grasp the complexity of lived experience. He viewed sociology as the science of human coexistence, a human science (*Geisteswissenschaft*) that must be differentiated from natural sciences. He argued that society did not operate according to mechanistic, causal laws; it had to be examined through its unified spirit. What was needed was an idealist technique built on German foundations and steeped in historical tradition. To make the case for a "sociology of the spirit," Spann offered an alternate genealogy of sociology, according classical and conservative philosophers pride of place. Sociology began not with Auguste Comte, Karl Marx, or Herbert Spencer but with Plato, Aristotle, Augustine, and Thomas Aquinas.

Spann's lecture had an incendiary effect. Karl Dunkmann, a *Spann-Schüler*, observed that "Spann fatally wounded the pride of modern sociology, namely its basis in a natural scientific approach to experience, its pure empiricism.... Here came a small knight from the long-forgotten 'dark' Middle Ages, who defeated the entire colony of modern empirical science."[52] Spann provoked his fellow sociologists into violent responses and counterarguments. Leopold von Wiese, the founder of Germany's first sociology department in

---

49. Dunkmann, *Kampf,* 1–2.

50. Sombart and Spann carried on a decades-long correspondence. Sombart also contributed to Spann's journal, *Ständisches Leben.*

51. See Eric Voegelin, "The Origins of Scientism," *Social Research* 15, no. 4 (1948): 462–94.

52. Dunkmann, *Kampf,* 8.

Cologne, argued that sociology required empathic understanding (*Verstehen*) and empirical description (*Erklären*), individual psychology and general laws. The whole does not come before the parts, he argued; they are coeval (*gleichseitig*) and reciprocal. Spann's main concerns about *Geist* and totalities, Wiese argued, did not belong to sociology but to social philosophy, which must be strictly differentiated from scientific pursuits of knowledge. Mere speculation on society's origins did not satisfy the demands of scientific inquiry regardless of whether it was a *Natur-* or *Sozialwissenschaft*. To Wiese, Spann's approach was no *Wissenschaft;* it was a series of unverifiable, metaphysical claims.[53]

Max Adler, the Austro-Marxist social philosopher and Spann's frequent adversary at the University of Vienna, offered an epistemological and political critique of Spann's position. With their clear political differences in mind, there was more at stake than just intellectual supremacy in methodological matters. This was a struggle for preeminence in Viennese cultural affairs. Ironically, Adler offered mild support for Spann. He, too, rejected the attempt to turn sociology into a natural science, calling it a mystifying (*verblüffend*) endeavor. Socioeconomic conditions determined the horizons of human actions and understanding, so the belief in universal social laws was utopian. Adler maintained that societies could not be understood by looking solely at the experiences of individuals through statistical aggregation. A social a priori category existed that undermined "bourgeois" individualism: human experience must be understood through the recognition that the species is inherently social, which means that individuals must be understood through their social backgrounds. Given their common criticisms, Adler wondered why Spann did not refer to his work, or better yet to Marx's and Engels's. For Spann, sociology seemed to stop after Hegel, even though Marx developed sociology and empirical science to a higher level. Adler assailed Spann's "highly naive metaphysic," asking two fundamental questions: "What is this whole and above all where is it?...How can one start from the idea of a social whole, when this whole is really the problem and when there is initially nothing further to find than one consciousness that builds a 'whole' together with another consciousness?"[54] Adler wondered how one came to understand the whole *as such,* especially if it was composed of reciprocal relationships between individual beings. Only Marx's dialectic, which demonstrated the interplay of part and whole in human societies, could offer universalism a way out. As Dunkmann grudgingly acknowledged, Spann was unable to

---

53. Ibid., 13–16.
54. Ibid., 27–28.

offer a compelling rejoinder to Adler, resorting instead to foreboding interpretations of modern society and the impacts of Marxism.

Ferdinand Tönnies closed the proceedings with a moderate yet critical appraisal of Spann's work, a particularly frustrating setback for universalism, since Spann saw Tönnies as a conservative ally. In his contribution, Tönnies discussed the distinction between naturalism and supernaturalism. Although Spann never professed to be a "supernaturalist," Tönnies asserted, it seemed evident to him that Spann's positions had been based on a kind of revelation. Tönnies did not condemn Spann for this; he merely wondered how to reconcile social scientific research, grounded in the natural world, and Spannian metaphysical speculation. Spann had long viewed Tönnies's work in a favorable light and saw his own social critique as an extension of Tönnies's work on *Gemeinschaft* and *Gesellschaft*. Tönnies's repudiation of Spann's approach cut deeply.

The German Sociological Congress in Vienna revealed that Spann's ideas had not gained much acceptance in the German academic world. While some scholars saw merit in his philosophical speculations or his economic theories, almost no one believed his ideas could form a credible basis for scientific investigation.[55] Though Sombart, Wiese, and Tönnies may have sympathized with his conservative values, they agreed with the socialist Adler about the weaknesses of universalist theory as *Wissenschaft*. This intellectual contretemps forced Spann to consider other avenues to acceptance: the Austrian academy and radical conservative political organizations. These outlets proved more receptive to his work.

The Birth of the Spannkreis and Its Early Social and Political Activities

Despite his failed overtures to German social scientists, Spann enjoyed growing support in Austria and the Sudetenland. *Der wahre Staat* made him a sensation overnight. German nationalist and conservative Catholic students flocked to his lectures. He became a frequent guest of the nationalist student fraternity, the Deutsche Studentenschaft. He participated regularly in the Akademische Legion, a powerful organization of conservative instructors in higher education. He established himself as a central figure at the University of Vienna.[56] With widespread support from the faculty and a political

---

55. On Spann in Germany, see Köster, *Wissenschaft der Außenseiter,* 180–92.

56. Siegfried, *Universalismus und Faschismus,* 64–71. Spann's main allies were the historians Karl Hugelmann, Oswald Menghin, and Heinrich Srbik; the philosopher Hans Eibl; the jurist Hans Graf Gleispach; and the paleontologist Othenio Abel.

leadership generally receptive to his critiques of modern society, Spann established a circle of students who had little difficulty negotiating the politically charged waters of the Austrian academy. Whereas most professors struggled to get their students academic appointments, an inordinate number of Spann's students received them. Walter Heinrich, an economist and social theorist, graduated in 1925, finished his *Habilitation* thesis in 1928, and became a professor at the Hochschule für Welthandel in Vienna in 1933. Wilhelm Andreae, also an economist, habilitated in 1927 and became a professor in Graz; in 1930 he was promoted to full professor before moving to Gießen in Germany in 1933. Friedrich Westphalen habilitated in 1933 and became a professor in Vienna in 1938 at the Hochschule für Bodenkultur. Hans Riehl, a future leader in the Austrian fascist Heimwehr, graduated in Vienna in 1923 and habilitated in 1928 in Graz (under Andreae). Jacob Baxa, a sociologist, graduated in 1919, habilitated in 1923, and became a professor in Vienna in 1932. A comparison of placement success with the Vienna Circle of logical empiricists is telling. Spann managed to place four students into full professorships in Austria during the interwar period; Moritz Schlick did not manage to place a single one. Likewise, the psychologists Karl and Charlotte Bühler could not place anyone in German or Austrian universities.[57] Although members of Schlick's and Bühler's respective circles attracted international recognition for their work in philosophy and science, they could not find institutional security in interwar Austria. The converse was true for the members of Spannkreis: they dominated the Austrian intellectual landscape yet enjoyed little international success.

The importance of ideology in the Austrian academy can also be seen in the *Habilitation* process, which Spann and his Black Viennese colleagues exploited for their students and made exceedingly difficult for individuals with opposing views. Wilhelm Andreae had his *Habilitationsschrift,* a translation of Plato's *Republic,* rejected in Munich in the early 1920s. Spann published the translation in his book series and then permitted Andreae to use the same work for his *Habilitation* in economics in 1927, even though the work was not about economics, nor was Spann an expert in classics.[58] On the other hand, Edgar Zilsel, who studied under Schlick, Hans Kelsen and Heinrich Gomperz, had his *Habilitation* thesis rejected—it was a historical and sociological investigation (a Marxist *Ideologiegeschichte*) of the concept of genius. His activity in the Social Democratic party and the Viennese adult

57. Circle members Hans Hahn, Philipp Frank, Viktor Kraft, and Rudolf Carnap were professors during the interwar years. Hahn, Kraft, and Schlick all were established in their professions before founding the circle; Carnap and Frank had to leave Austria to receive professorships. See chapter 4.

58. Siegfried, *Universalismus und Faschismus,* 72.

education centers damaged his prospects. Zilsel did not receive a full university position until he came to the United States in the 1930s.[59] The Catholic sociologist Ernst Karl Winter, a founding member of the Österreichische Aktion and one of the unique intellectual figures of interwar Vienna, had his *Habilitation* thesis rejected by Spann when he refused to contribute to a pro-Nazi publication. He did not gain a teaching position and had to support himself through independent scholarship and tutoring.[60] The experiences of Andreae, Zilsel, and Winter show that politics played a vital role in academic success.

Spann's circle grew to impressive size by the 1930s. Both the group's publication record and its organizational activities bear this out. Using Spann's theoretical journal *Ständisches Leben* as an indicator of the most important contributors to the movement, we can count around fifty Viennese members of his group, the vast majority of whom were professors, *Privatdozenten,* and other scholars with Ph.D.'s. Another ten academics worked elsewhere in Austria, and twenty came from around the world (mostly Germany). These men and women constituted the core of Spann's Sunday morning seminar and his students at the university. Conservatively, the Spannkreis included several hundred active members in Vienna, most of whom were university-educated, often with advanced degrees. Through the enterprising work of Walter Heinrich and Spann's personal assistant, Walter Brand, the Kameradschaftsbund, a society for the creation of an intellectual elite committed to transforming Central Europe, came into existence in 1926. Its membership quickly reached several hundred. The organization was particularly powerful in the Sudetenland, where it infiltrated the most important German cultural organizations.[61]

Spann's popularity derived partly from his captivating lecture style and collegial demeanor. Ernst von Salomon, the Freikorps member and accomplice in the assassination of Walter Rathenau, participated in the Spannkreis in 1932 and 1933. He recounted it vividly:

> I seated myself in Spann's class in the largest lecture hall at the university on a damaged bench between an Austrian general and a young girl.... And I was from this moment on transfixed [*eingespannt*]. Greeted by a deafening, thunderous stamping, he read *Volkswirtschaftslehre.* ... Spann was a master of his art. I cannot deny that it gave me indescribable pleasure to see how he conjured the theories of economics

59. Stadler, *Vienna Circle,* 520–26.
60. Heinz and Winter, *Winter,* 136–69.
61. Haag, "Kameradschaftsbund," 133–41.

out of his bag of tricks like Santa Claus pulled bright, beautiful gifts from his sack.[62]

Spann amazed his students with his breadth of knowledge and his passion. He drove them hard and expected them to master more than just the required material. For these reasons, Salomon characterized Spann as both the most inspiring (*anregendste*) and exhausting (*anstrengendste*) person he knew. His exhortations included a call to action. Salomon explains: "In Spann's system and concepts lay the secret of the 'third power': how to find a solution, if possible, that went beyond all the other solutions of the day. . . . Didn't it all exist in the magnificent system of Spann's, what the parties dreamed of and hoped for, yet could not realize because another party worked to the contrary?"[63] Universalism provided his students with the hope that the tensions in postwar Europe could be overcome with a shift in worldview.

The seduction of universalist unreason also benefited from the ongoing tumult of the 1920s and 1930s, since it offered a solution to social, economic, and political crises with its call for a return to an organic totality. The inflation of the early 1920s and the Great Depression in the early 1930s both proved destructive to the intellectual classes. The continued parliamentary impasses in Germany and Austria and the rise of political movements like Italian Fascism suggested that the Spannians were onto something with their theories. The Spannkreis, which made no secret of its desire for political influence,[64] capitalized on the instability of the period, reaching out to antidemocratic and authoritarian forces across Europe. Members became involved with several fascist and radical conservative movements in the 1920s and early 1930s. First, they established ties to the NSDAP. Walter Riehl, the brother of the Spannian Hans, was the head of the Austrian NSDAP during the 1920s. In the mid-1920s, Walter Heinrich and Hans Riehl took on leadership positions in the fascist Heimwehr. In 1930, Heinrich helped author the oath of the organization along Spannian lines.[65] Although not all members of the highly fractious Heimwehr embraced Spann's message, the Korneuberg oath demonstrates the political radicalism of the Spannkreis:[66]

We demand from every comrade: undaunted faith in the Fatherland, tireless diligence, and passionate love of the homeland [*Heimat*]. We want to grab the power of state and reorganize the state and economy

---

62. Salomon, *Fragebogen*, 205–6.
63. Ibid., 208.
64. Haag, "Kameradschaftsbund," 138–39.
65. Richard Steidle was the putative author of the oath, yet he worked closely with Heinrich.
66. Siegfried, *Universalismus und Faschismus,* 72.

for the welfare of the entire *Volk*....We condemn Western democratic parliamentarianism and the party state! We want to establish the self-administration of the *Stände* in its place as well as a strong state leadership, not composed of party members, but of leading people of the great *Stände* and from the most capable and truest men from our movement. We fight against the decay of our *Volk* perpetrated by the Marxist class struggle and liberal-capitalistic economic form....Every comrade recognizes three powers: faith in God, his own hardened will, the word of the führer!

The Heimwehr intended this oath to respond to the Social Democratic *Linzer Programm* of 1926. In that statement, the socialists advocated violence in response to potential coup attempts by unconstitutional forces like the Heimwehr. The program was frequently misinterpreted as a call for Marxist revolution,[67] and Viennese conservatives like the Spannians viewed it as a goad to more radical action, especially after the street violence associated with the July 1927 Justizpalast fire. The Heimwehr consequently promoted the overthrow of the state and the destruction of democratic parliamentarianism in the name of the *Volk*. Even though Heinrich and Riehl would leave the Heimwehr, it was not because of a change in their political viewpoint; rather, it was due to the insufficient commitment to revolution within some segments of the organization.[68]

The Spannkreis also participated in fascist cultural and institutional associations, trying to gain a foothold in those movements. Starting in 1926 with the Kameradschaftsbund, Walter Heinrich, Walter Brand, and Konrad Henlein successively infiltrated several Sudeten German organizations, culminating in the formation of the German nationalist Sudetendeutsche Partei. After 1929, Spann, Heinrich, and others also belonged to Alfred Rosenberg's National Socialist Society for German Culture and the Fighting League. Rafael Spann, Othmar's son, made trips to Italy with the goal of gaining Fascist support for Spannian ideology. Both he and his father lectured to Fascist audiences at Italian universities. Othmar Spann also delivered speeches to the Hungarian Arrow Cross.[69] There was hardly a group of radical conservatives in Europe to which the Spannkreis did not reach out. Its commitment to the destruction of democracy and socialism and the creation of a fascist state served it well as the group strove to become a force in Vienna and beyond.

---

67. Hanisch, *Der große Illusionist,* 230–40.
68. Lauridsen, *Nazism,* 189–92.
69. Siegfried, *Universalimus und Faschismus,* 100–1, 133–9, 152–3.

This endeavor began and ended with Austrian affairs, particularly with the ongoing appeal to intellectual leaders in Black Vienna.

Circles Unite: Spann's Turn to the Catholic Intelligentsia

Throughout the process of recruitment of new members and reconciliation with other political radicals, the Spannkreis did not lose sight of the need for alliances with other intellectuals in the fight against Marxism, liberalism, and democracy. Intellectuals were the culture carriers of any society and would therefore be instrumental in any counterrevolutionary efforts. Starting in the mid-1920s, the universalists affiliated with the Black Viennese intelligentsia that centered on the Leo-Gesellschaft and the Joseph Eberle journals, *Das neue Reich* and *Die schönere Zukunft*. Spann's movement became a node in this intellectual community. Spann contributed to the integration of the German nationalist community into Viennese Catholic conservative discussions, thereby helping to overcome the traditional *Lager* mentality of Austrian politics and culture.

Spann's initial contacts with the Eberle circle took place in 1923 at the peak of postwar Austrian problems. The hyperinflation and ensuing Geneva Protocols sparked outrage about the failures of parliamentary solutions. They also increased calls for economic approaches that would replace capitalism. As a result, Spann's proposals for a true state received renewed attention in Black Vienna. Eberle published excerpts of *Der wahre Staat* in *Das neue Reich*. The prior of the Viennese Dominican convent applauded Spann's Romantic social theory, particularly his criticisms of modern society. The author worried about the insufficient attention that Spann devoted to Christian social teachings, stemming from Pope Leo XIII's encyclical "Rerum Novarum," which would become a recurrent criticism.[70] Nevertheless, he offered universalism his approval. In the social scientific section of the Leo-Gesellschaft, Josef Löwenthal stressed the importance of Spann's critique of contemporary society. Spannians subsequently engaged more in the organization; in particular, Jacob Baxa, Franz Zehentbauer, and Richard Kerschagl lectured regularly.

Spann's close personal ties with leading figures in these movements facilitated the intellectual convergence of German nationalists and Catholic conservatives. As discussed in chapter 1, Hans Eibl played a prominent role in Black Viennese society, as did fellow nationalist allies like Wenzel Gleispach, Oswald Menghin, Heinrich Srbik, and Eugen Kogon. The members of the

---

70. Hyazinth Amschl, "Der wahre Staat nach Prof. Dr. Othmar Spann," *NR* 5 (1922–3): 785–87.

monarchist movement the Österreichische Aktion came largely from Spann's circle. Spann played a formative role in the Deutsche Studentenschaft, created to bridge the differences between German nationalist and Catholic students.[71] After Eberle's departure from *Das neue Reich* to form *Die schönere Zukunft,* Spann and his allies followed Eberle. Universalism now served as a core idea in the radicalizing intellectual world of Black Vienna.

Conversely, universalists saw *Die schönere Zukunft* as the key to winning over Black Vienna to their brand of radicalism. Boasting a circulation of around twenty thousand and regular contributions from leading conservative professors, Catholic clergymen, and politicians, it was the most influential conservative intellectual journal in Central Europe.[72] Walter Heinrich wrote a series of articles extolling Italian Fascism along universalist lines. Jakob Baxa and Joseph August Lux contributed regular articles on Romantic political thought and culture. Overall, between 1925 and 1932, universalists published dozens of articles in the journal.

The culmination of this process came on 20 March 1932, when Spann published the lead article on the "day of reckoning for German Catholics." The article represented Spann's attempt to dictate the ideological terms of Black Vienna going forward. First, it intended to distill the tenets of universalism for the uninitiated and to advocate for its adoption by all Central European conservatives. Second, it targeted competing social views within the Catholic community and submitted them to withering criticism. The immediate occasion for the article was the publication of the papal encyclical "Quadragesimo Anno," which offered a reform program for contemporary society. Spann (and many Austrian conservatives) interpreted the encyclical as a call for radical social transformation. "If German Catholics are supposed to create a new life through this encyclical, then many must recognize that a fundamental inner reform is necessary. After all, which viewpoint about the state and economy have the leading German Catholics of the last few decades represented? Not a corporate one [*ständisch*] but an individualistic, liberal one!"[73] He directed these comments at the Catholic social theorists behind "Quadragesimo Anno," known as Solidarists, who wanted to build the corporate state upon a foundation of cooperative capitalism, one that used interest groups to reduce conflict. Solidarists also did not categorically reject parliamentary democracy, feeling that a corporate order could be compatible with it. This placed Solidarism in the moderate German Catholic tradition of *Sozialpolitik,* which traced its origins back to

71. Siegfried, *Universalismus und Faschismus,* 69–71.
72. Hofer, "Joseph Eberle," 103–9.
73. Othmar Spann, "Schicksalsstunde der deutschen Katholiken," *SZ* 7 (1932–33): 565.

Bishop von Ketteler. The radical opponents of this viewpoint, associated with the Viennese publicist Karl von Vogelsang, represented a countervailing trend called *Sozialreform*.[74] The majority of Black Viennese intellectuals derived their social views from the latter trend, whose critiques closely resembled Spann's.

Spann's attack on Solidarism focused on its dangerous combination of individualist and universalist tendencies. Like Marxist socialism, Solidarism represented a hybrid form of social organization. In fact, Solidarism rested between individualism and socialism, meaning it was even more pernicious than socialism. "Solidarism cannot make the illogical [i.e., individualism] logical, the incompatible compatible. For this reason, it remains everywhere lifeless [*flau*] and half-hearted. It is understandable in this light that the new proponents of Solidarism will also fail in their efforts to reconcile its contradictions."[75] With its willingness to compromise with democracy and capitalism, Solidarism promised only the continued descent of Western culture. For Spann, the encyclical

> can have a deeper effect only if a fundamental reform is achieved in certain German Catholics. Not through the advancement of Solidarism nor through a dull, weak disavowal of external democracy.... Only a decided reform through organic–universalistic thought will do justice to these religious ideas. The immediate practical demand that results from organic thought is a corporate order. This demand makes sense only if a fundamental break with all individualism, liberalism, and capitalism succeeds; in practical politics this includes a break with democracy and the party state.[76]

The resonances with the Korneuberg oath are unmistakable. Catholic intellectuals had to join in the fascist fight. As long as Catholics continued to base their aspirations on capitalism and democracy, it would be impossible for them to achieve their mission.

In the wake of the article, the Spannkreis engaged in a publicity blitz to elaborate its program and its compatibility with Catholic thought. Heinrich wrote articles depicting the economic structure of Spann's *Ständestaat*. Karl Pawel, a recent *Habilitant* in Innsbruck, reconciled scholastic philosophy with universalism. These intellectuals hoped to demonstrate that Spann's system had a more solid practical *and* theoretical base than Solidarism and that it was the only truly Catholic social order.

---

74. Diamant, *Austrian Catholics*, 16–22, 41–47.
75. Spann, "Schicksalsstunde," 566.
76. Ibid.

Unsurprisingly, the Spannians provoked a firestorm. As chapter 7 details, articles in support of Solidarism cropped up in *Die schönere Zukunft* and *Das neue Reich*. This did not result in a defense of democracy or the First Republic but was solely a different form of radical conservatism. After months of heated debate, Joseph Eberle himself felt compelled to weigh in. Eberle admitted that Spann had been too hard on Catholic social theorists, since most conservatives desired the same ends. Nevertheless, he tried to clarify and defend Spann's position. Eberle argued that Spann's anti-Enlightenment and Romantic notions of the state could be reconciled with the "Christian democracy" advocated by Solidarists. He excused Spann's strident tone as a product of the repeated attacks that Spann had already suffered. Eberle supported Spann's commitment to pure theory that refused to tolerate compromise with corrupt mixed forms. The editor lauded Spann as a warrior against Marxism, an ideologue and provocateur. Eberle complimented him as one of the most influential economists and social scientists of the day.[77] Spann's effort to dominate the educated Austrian and German Catholic community therefore met with ambiguous results. The Spannkreis gained new supporters in smaller Catholic circles, particularly in the Wiener Studienrunde katholischer Soziologen and the Kärntner Gruppe katholischer Soziologen.[78] It also attracted the attention of Christian Social politicians, who applied some of Spann's ideas in the Austrofascist regime. Though his students contributed articles to *Die schönere Zukunft* until 1938, Spann never again wrote for it. He also became the target of the Austrofascist weekly *Der christliche Ständestaat*. The rise in Germany between 1930 and 1932 of the Nazis, whose racial ultranationalism disgusted some Viennese Catholic thinkers, curbed the appeal of Spann's German nationalist and fascist ideas, which had more than a passing resemblance to Hitler's.

Ständisches Leben

Partially as a result of the Spannkreis's stagnating position within the Black Viennese intellectual constellation but mostly because of its desire to propagandize politically, Spann founded a new journal, *Das ständische Leben,* in early 1931. The journal appeared monthly for seven years during the height of the Depression and the crises of parliamentary democracy in Central Europe, serving as a vehicle for the most radical European conservative movements. Despite its publication in Berlin, *Ständisches Leben* was

---

77. Joseph Eberle, "Kontroverse um Othmar Spann," *SZ* 7 (1932–33), 785–86.
78. Siegfried, *Universalismus und Faschismus,* 133–34.

a Central European—more properly, Viennese—intellectual organ. Viennese authors initially comprised around half the total number of writers, and that ratio only increased over the years. Articles covered a vast array of subjects, yet economics, politics, philosophy, and sociology were the most frequent.

Spann provided the mission statement for the undertaking: developing a holistic social science and advancing policy applications. Such efforts must necessarily begin on the intellectual level: "This paper is dedicated to the elaboration of universalistic theoretical concepts in all social sciences. It will remain strictly in the realm of science and is determined to serve praxis in this manner. True thought must amount to action, since thought lights the way for all action. Thus, history is always decided on the level of intellectual life."[79] Spann again asserted the primacy of scientific thinking over partisan ideology and the leadership role of intellectuals in contemporary society. One should not take his claims of apolitical scientific investigation too seriously: "Overcoming individualist thought and its antecedent, Marxism, is the historical task that falls to universalist theory. To perform this task will require more than mere conceptual work. It requires a community that understands its responsibility, that it must wake its constructive strength through creative power."[80] Through a reanimated German *Volk,* strengthened by universalist theory, Europe would overthrow democracy and socialism and establish true authoritarian, corporate states under the leadership of strong führer.

A year into its existence, *Das ständische Leben* permanently shifted its focus from the scientific elaboration of universalist theory to overt political advocacy and propaganda. Several historical factors prompted this change. First, the attempted takeover of Black Viennese thought had foundered. The alliance with the Heimwehr had also collapsed. This meant the end of Spann's hope for a universalist-led Austrian fascist movement. It also left the Spannkreis at odds with the Christian Social party, which was radicalizing in its own right.[81] It was time to reach out to other viable political organizations, like the Italian Fascists. Walter Heinrich published an article designed to popularize Fascist ideology in German-speaking lands.[82] With the 1932 Nazi electoral breakthrough, the universalists turned their attention to appealing to Nazi sympathizers. The Nazis garnered 37 percent of the popular vote in the March presidential election, becoming the most popular party in Germany.

---

79. Othmar Spann, "Zum Geleit," *SL,* 1931, 1.
80. Ibid.
81. Siegfried, *Universalismus und Faschismus,* 142.
82. Walter Heinrich, "Faschistische und universalistische Staatslehre," *SL,* 1932, 101–5.

They also had a growing following in Austria, particularly in the Austrian academy. Consequently, the universalists wrote monthly about Fascism and Nazism. In April, an advertisement for the *Deutsche Volkswirtschaft,* a Nazi economics journal, appeared alongside Spann's article about the "inner history" of the German *Volk.* Spann began to devote himself to issues of race and national belonging. He identified a unique German *Geist* and a single racial lineage (*Abstammung*). All Germans must defend their blood from corrupting forces.[83] In May, an Italian professor named Renzetti celebrated the Fascist rebirth of Italy. Werner Sombart, Spann's academic foe yet political ally, made his first contribution the following month with a strident attack on capitalism and a defense of autarchy.[84] The culmination of this politicization came in January 1933, when Benito Mussolini provided the lead article.[85] If before 1932 it could perhaps be argued that the Spannkreis kept its political advocacy separate from its intellectual work, this was no longer the case. In the pages of *Das ständische Leben,* universalists explicitly connected the political efforts of Fascism and Nazism to the universalist program.

During the next three years, the pinnacle of the journal's success, the contributors extolled the virtues of these movements and provided ways that universalism could serve them. They also combated mounting criticism from ideologues within these movements, who viewed Spann's philosophy as a political threat. In a review of another Mussolini article, Spann enthusiastically embraced the European trend toward fascism, seeing it as a culmination of universalist teachings:

> One's first impression of the essay is amazement at the modesty of Mussolini. Anyone with the slightest understanding of Fascism and its historical significance knows that he not only saved Italy from the open revenge of Bolshevism, which threatened to devour it, but also the whole of Central—and perhaps all of—Europe. . . . If Fascism had not succeeded in Italy and had instead submitted to advancing Bolshevism, invariably Austria would have suffered collapse and then Germany could no longer have held out. And wouldn't the West have followed?[86]

Spann's hagiography of Mussolini embraced the führer principle as the saving grace for European civilization. Mussolini alone had saved Europe. Fascism's

---

83. Othmar Spann, "Innere Geschichte des deutschen Volkes," *SL,* 1932, 196.

84. Renzetti, "Wiederaufbau," *SL,* 1932, 234–35; Werner Sombart, "Die Zukunft der Weltwirtschaft," *SL,* 1932, 288–90.

85. Benito Mussolini, "Die Lehren des Faschismus," *SL,* 1932, 1–9. The editor received Mussolini's permission to publish the article.

86. Othmar Spann, "Instinkt und Bewusstheit in der Geschichte des Faschismus," *SL,* 1932, 10.

lone shortcoming was its lack of theory. He therefore recommended that Fascism adopt universalism. He also called for a German variant of Fascism. When the Nazis came to power, the universalists felt they had found their cause. Spann, Heinrich, Riehl, and others joined the NSDAP despite its illegal status in Austria.

Heinrich and Ilse Roloff, the new editor of *Ständisches Leben* in Berlin, went furthest in their overtures to the ascendant Nazis. Heinrich contributed three major articles in 1933, one that reprised his earlier work on Fascism and two about the reconstruction of German society in light of the Nazi "seizure of power" in January. The first essay was an expanded version of a lecture Heinrich had given before a Nazi provincial economic board (*Gauwirtschaftsrat*) in Düsseldorf on 26 March 1933.[87] This was a mere three days after passage of the Enabling Act, which granted the Nazis control of the state apparatus. Heinrich was already offering economic advice to Nazi business leaders within a week of their takeover. Heinrich's other article also derived from a speech—this one to a Nazi *Kampfbund* assembly in the Ruhr valley. The two articles saluted recent German developments and proclaimed the coming of a new corporate and fascist order. Heinrich reveled in the advance of authoritarian ideas across Europe. He quoted Hitler, proclaiming "The State has become a *Stand* again!" He argued for a comprehensive coordination (*Gleichschaltung*) at all levels of society. Heinrich boasted that Germany had entered a new Golden Age under Hitler.[88]

Roloff developed the ideological similarities between universalism and Nazism in the face of growing opposition from Nazi ideologues. She favorably compared several major features of Hitler's and Spann's respective thought—their views on objectivity and subjectivity, idealism and rationalism, and racial and social theory—and concluded that they embodied two vital contributions to the radical transformation of European society:

> The German spirit has produced men in the realms of politics and science who have conducted the same fight against the same poisons—of Jewish Marxism, international liberalism and Western, un-German state conceptions. It is in this light that a closer examination of *Mein Kampf* and Othmar Spann's so-called universalism or *Ganzheitslehre* shows truly striking agreement. Slight differences are produced only due to the different type of activity [*Tätigkeitsrichtung*] of a politician

---

87. Walter Heinrich, "Die Überwindung des Parlamentarismus in Reich, Land, und Gemeinde," *SL*, 1933, 191–95; "Die berufsständische Wirtschaft im neuen Staat," *SL*, 1933, 409–18.
88. Heinrich, "Überwindung," 191, 195, 418.

and a scholar. However, both see before them the task of building a singular spirit in the people.[89]

According to Roloff, Hitler and Spann both rejected Marxism, liberalism, and democracy. They espoused a fundamental anti-Semitism. They believed in a defense of the German spirit and the rebirth of the *Volk*. Although Hitler was primarily a statesman and Spann a philosopher, they pursued the same thing: the true state composed of members of the *Volksgemeinschaft*. Spann and Hitler were therefore brothers-in-arms.

Roloff's exploration of racial theory merits closer scrutiny since it contradicts later analyses by Spann apologists that claim he resisted the racialism of the Nazis. After World War II, Spannians—especially Heinrich—asserted that universalism and Nazi racial theory were antithetical. In 1933, Roloff flatly rejected this view. She cited numerous occasions when Spann had written positively about racial theory. Although no "racial materialist"—one who reduced all of humankind's intellectual accomplishments to biological nature—Spann agreed that the biological or racial was an "index" of intellectual potential: "The race I am indicates what intellectual values I can realize. Much as a pigeon does not have the qualities of a lion, nor a criminal those of a hero, one race cannot manifest the qualities of another."[90] Spann privileged spirit over bare biological fact. This was not a rejection of racial theory or eugenics, Roloff claimed. Spann merely demanded that the people receive a universalist education that would help the *Volk* realize its racial potential. The two principles—Hitler's biologism and Spann's idealism—could work together harmoniously. Roloff summarized Spann's racial views thus: "For Spann the foundation of racial purity was self-evident."[91]

The Roloff article not only revealed the pro-Nazi orientation of the Spannkreis but also hinted at the problems that plagued the group. The main justification for the article was a defense of universalism against ideological opponents within the Nazi Party. It was only secondarily a profession of sympathy with the Nazis since, as Roloff made clear, this was self-evident to circle members. Roloff responded at length to criticisms raised by Alfred Rosenberg and Robert Ley about Spann's "idealism." In the coming years, Spann and his associates devoted ever-greater time to combating the views of the Nazi intelligentsia as they tried to gain acceptance in the Third Reich.

---

89. Ilse Roloff, "Adolf Hitlers 'Mein Kampf' im Lichte der Gesellschaftswissenschaft," *SL, 1933*, 608.
90. Ibid., 611–12.
91. Ibid., 616.

The Spannians continued to court the Nazis with anti-Semitic and racialist articles with little success. Spann's lead essay in 1934 classified and attacked inferior, parasitical (*ausgelaugt*) peoples.[92] In another article about the importance of *völkisch* and racial science, Otto Dietrich demanded that all scientists support the Nazis: "Science runs into problems if it loses its living connection to the people and its national needs. Science is not self-justifying [*Selbstzweck*], it must serve the nation with both feet rooted in the people in order to fulfill its mission. The ideological root of the German people today is National Socialism and the Nazi state expects from German science and its intellectual community not lip service, but whole-hearted commitment."[93] The Spannkreis fully embraced a nationalist, exclusionary science. They also endorsed Nazi book burnings and *Gleichschaltung* legislation. In a May 1934 article the Spannians triumphantly claimed that Hitler had realized the goals of Spann's *Der wahre Staat* and began publishing monthly updates on Nazi activities.[94]

This focus on appealing to the Nazis caused the Spannkreis to miss a genuine opportunity for political acceptance in Austria, where universalism was still both popular and influential. Conspicuously absent from *Ständisches Leben* is any discussion of events in Austria. This is a striking omission considering the overwhelming number of Viennese contributing to the journal and the fact that Austrian conservatives had made major strides toward creating their own true state with the suspension of parliament in March 1933, a successfully waged civil war in February 1934, and the establishment of a corporate state in May. As contemporaries and subsequent scholars noted, there was actually a good deal of common ground between the *ständisch* visions of the Dollfuss regime and Spann's true state.[95] The Austrofascist state took "Quadragesimo Anno" as its starting point, yet it did not implement those ideas in a Solidarist fashion. It established corporate bodies in economics, culture, and politics that corresponded to the Spannian model, especially in their emphasis on hierarchical and authoritarian rule rather than decentralization.[96] Nevertheless, Spann rejected the *Ständestaat* categorically. In *Kämpfende Wissenschaft,* he dismissed any overlap between the two systems:

---

92. Othmar Spann, "Auslaugung und Anhäufung," *SL,* 1934, 1–8. According to the theory, some peoples, like the Czechs and Jews, were drawn to the higher values of others and ingratiated themselves to the superior group (Germans).

93. Otto Dietrich, "Wissenschaft in Nationalsozialismus," *SL,* 1934, 174–75.

94. Friedrich Völtzer, "Der Weg zur organischen Wirtschaftsorganisation," *SL,* 1934, 234.

95. See the SS report, *Der Spann-Kreis,* 22; Salomon, *Fragebogen,* 217–18; Kluge, *Der österreichische Ständestaat,* 49–50.

96. Helmut Wohnout, "A Chancellorial Dictatorship with a 'Corporate' Pretext: The Austrian Constitution between 1934 and 1938," in Bischof, Pelinka, and Lassner, *Dollfuss/Schuschnigg Era,*

[The new state] has made an eerie carnivalesque joke [*unheimliche Fast-nachtsscherz*] out of the corporate order. I raise forceful objection to the intellectual borrowings that the Austrian constitution has made from my lessons. People do not believe that they must understand thoughts in order to successfully borrow them. The May Constitution is a mix of the ideas of 1789 and contemporary corporate ones. I must complain bitterly against this corruption of corporatist ideas.[97]

Spann did not believe that the Austrofascists had gone far enough in rooting out the evils of liberalism, capitalism, and democracy and would not have his name associated with such an equivocal state. This rebuke closed the door on any possible reconciliation between the Austrofascist state and Spann. Although he was too powerful to be released from his teaching position, the Austrofascist regime closely monitored Spann and his followers until the *Anschluss*.[98] While it enjoyed continued influence until 1938 in the Sudetenland through Konrad Henlein's *Sudetendeutsche Partei,* the Spannkreis had reached the limits of its political and intellectual influence in Central Europe.

In 1936, the German SS commissioned a report on the influence and the threat of the Spannkreis to Nazism. "The Spannkreis avoids appearing openly to the world. Its members disguise their true political intentions behind claims of pure scientific interest and objective research. With this tactic they infiltrate different political groups, since these groups seek to find unions with science in order to support their claims with the help of scientific theories." Later in the same report, it detailed the successes of the circle, particularly in Austria: "In all areas of intellectual life in Austria, particularly in the sciences, the Spannkreis today plays a leading role. Naturally, the Austrian universities, which are densely populated with Spann supporters, provide a dangerous gateway to universalist thought."[99] This report reinforced the ambiguity of the universalist case in interwar Central Europe. It highlighted the intellectual influence of the Spannkreis and its political proselytizing. It noted that the Spannians cloaked their radical political activities in scholarly garb. It also evinced the hatred the Nazis harbored for universalism. Alfred Rosenberg and leading Nazi ideologues felt that Spann's philosophy did not emphasize racial

---

143–61. On the Austrofascist state, see Emmerich Tálos, "Das austrofaschistische Herrschaftssystem," in Tálos and Neugebauer, *"Austrofaschismus,"* 394–411.

97. Spann and Steffanides, *Kämpfende Wissenschaft,* 234.

98. Less prominent professors who shared Spann's ideological proclivities did not fare as well. Gleispach lost his job in 1933. Spann responded angrily, saying the "blind" Austrian "separatists" believed they could construct an authoritarian state without the *Volk.*

99. *Spann-Kreis,* 11, 22.

theory sufficiently. No matter how hard they tried to clarify their position, the universalists found themselves "caught between two stools"[100]—that is, Nazism and Austrofascism—rejected by the former and rejecting the latter.

This ambiguity led to the paradoxical circumstance that Othmar Spann, Walter Heinrich, and others could claim retrospectively to be opponents of the Nazis despite offering them passionate support. The events of the day of the *Anschluss* drive this point home. After the Nazis entered Austria, Spann allegedly gathered his family in Vienna, opened a bottle of champagne, and declared it to be the greatest day of his life. Two hours later the gestapo arrested him.[101] Heinrich followed his mentor into a concentration camp within days. They were among the first Austrian victims of Nazi persecution. Spann's influence died on the same day that many of his political dreams were realized.

The overwhelming popularity of Spann and his philosophy during the 1920s must lead to a reconsideration of the intellectual history of First Republic Vienna. For many years, the Spannkreis served as a linchpin of Viennese culture and Central European radical conservative politics. The most influential intellectual group in interwar Vienna was also its most conservative. It was also the most politically impactful. Red Vienna was therefore *not* a Marxist fortress. Nor were the dividing lines between German nationalists and Catholic conservatives so clearly drawn until *after* the Nazi ascendancy in Germany. Conservative forces worked in concert, controlling the academic commanding heights and dictating the intellectual climate of the period. Spann's fighting science won a decisive victory in interwar Vienna—with tragic consequences for Austrian history, science, and philosophy. As subsequent chapters will show, progressive intellectuals therefore had to create intellectual and cultural communities outside the traditional establishment if they hoped to gain a hearing. They produced a counterhegemonic space and discourse explicitly directed at challenging the Spannians and other Black Viennese groups on their own terms.

---

100. "Othmar Spann, der *Völkische Beobachter* und *der Christliche Ständestaat*—oder: *Der Wahre Staat* zwischen zwei Stühlen," *CS* 2 (1935): 413–14.

101. Salomon, *Fragebogen,* 218.

CHAPTER 4

The Verein Ernst Mach and the Politicization of Viennese Progressive Thought

On February 24, 1934, the Viennese police commissioner summoned Moritz Schlick, one of the founders of the Verein Ernst Mach, to police headquarters to answer questions about the group. The date here is significant, for the interrogation took place less than two weeks after the conclusion of the Austrian civil war. Hundreds of Austrians, mostly workers, had died in the streets. The workers' forces had been crushed, the Social Democratic Workers' Party (SDAP) outlawed, and trade unions disbanded. Socialist leaders had either fled the country or gone into hiding. The country was under martial law, and the army patrolled the streets of Vienna. Austria was a de facto one-party state, a reality confirmed with the promulgation of the corporatist, Austrofascist constitution in May. As the government consolidated power, it cracked down on organizations with potentially subversive leanings, like the Verein. This process had begun a year earlier with the outlawing of the Austrian Freethinkers and the Nazi Party, yet repressive measures accelerated after February 1934.[1] In this instance, the police wanted Schlick to demonstrate the political reliability of his society.

---

1. Wolfgang Neugebauer, "Repressionsapparat und –maßnahmen 1933–1938," in Tálos and Neugebauer, *Austrofaschismus,* 298–320.

They requested that he summarize the group's activities and political views, since government officials had deemed the society politically suspect.[2]

Schlick wrote three letters to state authorities between 2 March and 23 March, defending his society and its apolitical, scientific intent. He begged that they reverse their unfavorable ruling. Schlick suggested that the regime possessed an erroneous preconception of the group: "[It] could only have been that the society supported or performed activities against the state or regime. I hereby attest that this assumption is absolutely untrue and that the facts will completely refute the claim."[3] Schlick gave a brief history of the society, touting its scientific bona fides and political neutrality. It was named after the Austrian physicist Ernst Mach and had been founded with the purpose of supporting empirical research in the natural and social sciences. Since its inception, the society had remained true to this vision, conducting lectures and conferences that served the empiricist cause. In 1930, the society founded a journal, *Erkenntnis,* in collaboration with the Society for Empirical Philosophy in Berlin. The group's success inspired successor movements, like the Société Henri Poincaré in Paris. Schlick concluded, "The facts provided should suffice to prove that the society is absolutely unpolitical [*absolut unpolitisch*]."[4] Each of Schlick's letters employed this phrase.[5] The stridency of his tone was evident: no dispassionate observer, he claimed, could deny his factual assertions after a rational evaluation of the facts. He believed that the weight of objective arguments would triumph, even in an authoritarian state. The government was unswayed, however, and disbanded the society on March 6.

In justifying the "absolut unpolitisch" claim, Schlick employed the philosophical techniques he had developed in the Vienna Circle, particularly Ludwig Wittgenstein's notions of verification, first presented in the *Tractatus Logico-Philosophicus.*[6] Wittgenstein argued that the world consisted of facts—logically verifiable propositions—not of things. The determination of truth and falsity of facts was at the heart of philosophy and our understanding of the world. Once verified, these facts were universally true "while everything

2. Moritz Schlick to the Bundes-Polizei-Direktion, 3 March 1934, Moritz-Schlick-Nachlaß, Vienna Circle Foundation, Amsterdam.

3 Ibid.

4. Ibid. Emphasis added.

5. Schlick to Hofrat Ganz, 2 March 1934; Schlick to the Bundes-Polizei-Direktion, 3 March 1934; Schlick to the Sicherheitskommissär des Bundes für Wien, 23 March 1934, Moritz-Schlick-Nachlaß, Vienna Circle Foundation, Amsterdam.

6. Stadler, *Vienna Circle,* 195–218, 233–99, 422–41.

else remains the same."[7] In his letters, Schlick performed a Wittgensteinian analysis of the Verein: he restated the police's propositions and then verified (or refuted) them. The society was demonstrably committed to empirical, scientific research. Science must be objective and hence apolitical. There was no evidence of any party political activity by the Verein. Therefore, it must be *absolut unpolitisch*. In light of the veracity of these propositions, the society should be allowed to continue its work, Schlick argued.

Schlick dissembled when making this assessment, and his interrogators recognized it. His understanding of a value-free, objective science had come under intense scrutiny during the *Wissenschaft* debates of the previous decades. As previous chapters have shown, both the Austro-Marxists and their progressive allies in Red Vienna *and* the Black Viennese conservatives in the Eberle and Spann circles denied the reality of disinterested science. Part of Schlick's conviction was philosophically derived, but a lot of it was personal. He was largely unpolitical, engaging mostly in academic conferences devoted to philosophical debate. He was a good nineteenth-century liberal, and his conception of the Ernst Mach Society reflected the liberal belief in the personhood of civic associations. How could a collective entity like this one possess political convictions? he wondered.

Nevertheless, the Ernst Mach Society was not unpolitical. This chapter examines the group's origins, arguing that its members and closest associational affiliates shared radical social, cultural, and political agendas. Founded by members of the Austrian Monist Association, the Austrian Freethinkers' Association, and the Vienna Circle of logical empiricist philosophers in 1928, the society was committed to a scientific world-conception that militantly rejected metaphysics, religion, and nationalist pretensions. Such views left the members of the society at odds with the prevailing ideological trends in conservative Vienna. The natural ideological allies for the Machians were the Austro-Marxists, who also espoused antimetaphysical and empirical ideals. Even if the Verein Ernst Mach did not explicitly endorse socialism, many of its members did, and they used the society to develop those affinities. Schlick disingenuously argued that the commitment to empirical science and antimetaphysical philosophy were neutral politically and ideologically; however, those foundational tenets set his group at odds with Black Vienna and Austrofascism. In the authoritarian climate of 1934, the ideas were subversive of the new Central European order.

---

7. Wittgenstein, *Tractatus*, 5. Schlick's use of the *Tractatus* as an ideological tool is ironic and instructive. The *Tractatus* proves to be more than a treatise on logic and language but also more than an ethical text, as Janik and Toulmin maintain in *Wittgenstein's Vienna*.

Contemporary scholars have argued that late Enlightenment Viennese intellectuals—like those in the Ernst Mach Society, the Freethinkers' Association, and the adult education institutes—existed within a reform-based "socio-liberal cultural movement" that emerged out of late imperial liberal institutions.[8] However, Viennese intellectual and cultural life experienced an important break after the Great War, and the "retreat from politics" that scholars attribute to fin-de-siècle intellectuals did not carry over to the First Republic.[9] Science, culture, and education became increasingly political, and the advocates of change became more assertive in their claims. This took place on both sides of the ideological divide. A resurgent conservative bloc, intent on limiting the impact of Red Viennese measures, stood in the way of the dissemination of progressive ideas. In this climate, members of the Vienna Circle suffered persecution for their beliefs and were excluded from the corridors of knowledge and power. This drove them to alternative social, cultural, and political organizations to further their endeavors. In adult education institutes, monist and freethinking societies, and other Red Viennese organizations, circle members developed counterhegemonic currents. Socialist control of the Viennese municipal government provided opportunities for intellectuals to apply their innovative ideas in real-world situations. This fusion of theory and practice produced a volatile intellectual climate, one that made Vienna famous as a "socialist laboratory."[10] As the 1920s wore on, these groups only radicalized; the Verein was a product of these transformations. The history of the Verein and its members can serve as a case study for the new political character of Viennese intellectual life in the First Republic. The society was a product (and producer) of the radical sociopolitical field of Red Vienna.[11]

The Vienna Circle and Adult Education

The future core of the Ernst Mach Society largely came from the group of philosophers and scientists called the Vienna Circle of logical empiricists,

---

8. Stadler, *Vienna Circle*, 180. See also Stadler, "Spätaufklärung." The emphasis on the apolitical nature of the Vienna Circle first emerged in the postwar accounts written by Vienna Circle members like Viktor Kraft, Philipp Frank, Friedrich Waismann, and Herbert Feigl.

9. See Schorske, *Fin-de-Siècle Vienna.*

10. Gruber, *Red Vienna,* 12–44.

11. Bourdieu, *Cultural Production,* 29–73. Bourdieu's relational model of fields, with its emphasis on institutional and associational interactions and the importance of cultural capital, applies well to the interwar Viennese landscape. The intense relationality of the Viennese field does not permit a strict separation of social, cultural, and political organizations. Bourdieu's sociological model therefore allows for a more subtle, dialectical engagement with ideas and groups. See Timms, "Cultural Parameters," for an elaboration.

most of whom shared progressive social and political leanings that predated the war. The postwar ties the circle established with the socialist-run adult education centers reflected both these earlier commitments and the engaged intellectual culture of First Republic Vienna. Over a dozen intellectuals converged on the Austrian capital after the war as a result of an unlikely combination of personal decisions and historical events. Otto Neurath, incarcerated for his involvement with the failed Bavarian Soviet Republic, secured an early release from prison in Germany and returned to Vienna in 1919. The mathematician Hans Hahn and Schlick were appointed professors at the University of Vienna in 1921 and 1922, respectively. Hans Feigl came to study with Hahn; Friedrich Waismann joined Schlick. Viktor Kraft and Edgar Zilsel, both of whom had completed their doctoral work in the 1910s and taught in Vienna, also participated by the mid-1920s. The circle officially came into being around Schlick in the fall of 1924; the arrival of Rudolf Carnap in 1925 cemented the group's standing.

The circle's radical, nonconformist origins in the late imperial period laid the groundwork for the antiestablishment character of its postwar incarnation. The First Vienna Circle was not a conventional fin-de-siècle liberal group. In the first years of the new century, Neurath, Hahn, and Philipp Frank held regular meetings to discuss avant-garde scientific and philosophical developments. They examined Henri Poincaré's conventionalism and Pierre Duhem's instrumentalism, Ernst Mach's empiricism, Frege's symbolic logic, thermodynamics, and Einstein's theory of special relativity.[12] The discussions were theoretical in nature, yet there was a socially subversive undercurrent, since these ideas undercut the certainties of the scientific and physical worlds. Their commitment to relativistic, conventionalist, and antifoundationalist scientific approaches horrified members of the Austrian academic community. They did not restrict themselves to science either; they also engaged socially and politically. Neurath, the son of a liberal social reformer, advocated for economic socialization on scientific lines, arguing that a moneyless economy could correct the problems of capitalist society. He confronted the assumptions of economists from the marginalist Austrian and German historical schools. These actions culminated in his work on German planning boards during the Great War and the socialization committees after it.[13] Hahn was a leading member of the Vereinigung sozialistischer Hochschullehrer, a group that advocated secular education reform, nonpartisan academic appointments, and academic freedom. Philipp Frank also had close ties to the socialist

---

12. Rudolf Haller, "Der erste Wiener Kreis," and Uebel, *Forgotten Vienna Circle.*
13. On Neurath's socialization plans, see Nemeth, Heinrich, and Soulez, *Otto Neurath.*

cause: his brother Josef was a primary architect for the Red Vienna public settlement movement.[14] Through their activities before the war, the First Vienna Circle not only established some of the philosophical foundations of the later Vienna Circle but also set a precedent for social and political engagement.

At the turn of the century, Austria was one of the most culturally conservative nations in Europe. The advocacy of avant-garde scientific theories therefore put the First Vienna Circle—and its intellectual forbears—under pressure. Ultimately, it left them in marginal positions until several years after the Great War. In the wake of the Wahrmund affair, discussed in chapter 1, intellectuals advocating secularist, rationalist, or liberal views faced a hostile academic landscape.[15] Ernst Mach, for example, was an intellectual outsider at the University of Vienna from 1895 until his death in 1916. Always supportive of socialist causes, he left a portion of his estate to the Social Democrats in his last will and testament. His theories of sensationalism and radical empiricism were challenged on all sides, most notably by his successor Ludwig Boltzmann.[16] His students, among them David Josef Bach and Friedrich Adler, either had to leave the country to find appointments or give up academics altogether. Unable to find positions in Vienna, Frank moved to Prague and Neurath to Heidelberg. Hahn did not receive a position until after the war. The First Vienna Circle disbanded because of a lack of opportunity at home.

The postwar existence of the circle was also precarious as a result of the machinations of the conservative academy. Advocates of new directions in science and philosophy struggled for recognition. Schlick almost had his appointment to Mach's chair in inductive sciences rejected. The philosophical faculty objected that Schlick was not devoted to an idealist worldview. There were also concerns about his support of Einstein's theory of relativity. The faculty preferred Hans Eibl, the German nationalist philosopher with close ties to Joseph Eberle, Othmar Spann, and Richard Kralik. Without the strenuous lobbying of Hahn, it is unlikely that Schlick would have received the appointment. As scholarship on First Republic higher education has shown, the conservative politics of the university intensified after the Great

14. See Nemeth, Heinrich, and Soulez, *Otto Neurath,* and Neurath, Neurath, and Nemeth, *Otto Neurath, oder, Die Einheit von Wissenschaft.* See also Stadler, *Vienna Circle,* 508–17, 530–38, 631–36, 642–52.

15. Boyer, *Culture and Political Crisis,* 191–211.

16. See Haller and Stadler, *Ernst Mach,* and Blackmore, Itagaki, and Tanaka, *Ernst Mach's Vienna.*

War, making it even more difficult for individuals like Schlick to gain entry.[17] Given that Schlick's social and political views were less objectionable than those espoused by future members, it is clear that academic acceptance was unlikely in Austria. Nevertheless, this toehold in the academy provided a small yet important base for the development of scientific philosophy.

Relatively speaking, Schlick had it easy academically and stayed above the political fray. After the controversies surrounding his appointment, he looked askance at political squabbles. His aversion to confrontation and controversy probably accounted for Schlick's naive disregard of the political inclinations of his colleagues. Nevertheless, most other circle members faced significant obstacles to attaining stable positions in postwar Vienna because of their intellectual views, political convictions, religious origins, gender, or ethnicity. Neurath failed to secure an academic post and quickly began working for various socialist causes, including the settlement and adult education movements. He later founded the Vienna Social and Economic Museum with subventions from the Social Democrats. Friedrich Waismann, a Jew, was unable to find a university post and worked instead as a librarian alongside Schlick. Edgar Zilsel had his *Habilitation* thesis rejected. Viktor Kraft was passed over for a philosophy chair in favor of Eibl. The members of the Vienna Circle understood themselves as an embattled enclave with few options for academic advancement. They rarely enjoyed professional success commensurate with their international reputation.

As a result of this exclusion, members of the Vienna Circle sought alternative opportunities at adult education centers (*Volkshochschulen*), where a greater degree of academic freedom existed. The *Volkshochschulen* emerged during the late imperial period as a complement to the Free School movement. As we saw in chapter 2, the progressive founders of the latter movement found themselves drawn into the socialist fold because of the reactionary nature of the Viennese educational establishment.[18] The *Volkshochschulen* began as a part of a liberal attempt to offer scientific lectures and courses to a broader public with a central lecture hall at the Urania on the Danube Canal in Vienna's First District. These meetings, first convened in the 1880s, reached a new level of popularity between 1897 and 1910, the height of Christian Social power. While the Urania lectures remained nonpartisan, programs at branches in working-class districts were driven by progressives and socialists.

---

17. A selected list: Wimmer and Fischer, *Der geistige Anschluß;* Weinzierl, *Universität und Politik;* Erika Weinzierl, "Hochschulleben und Hochschulpolitik zwischen den Kriegen," in Leser, *Das geistige Leben Wiens,* 72–86; Heinz Fischer, "Universität zwischen Tradition und Fortschritt," in Achleitner, *Österreich,* 204–31.

18. Boyer, *Culture and Political Crisis,* 191–200.

Those centers focused on language instruction for non-Germans and vocational training for new industrial workers.[19] As the movement expanded in
the postwar era, thanks partially to Otto Glöckel's educational reforms, all
of the growth unfolded in Jewish and working-class districts such as Ottakring,
Leopoldstadt, Simmering, Landstrasse, and Brigittenau. Glöckel and progressive professors including Josef Friedjung, Ludo Hartmann, and Julius Tandler
played instrumental roles in the expansion of the *Volkshochschulen*.[20] Under
their leadership, the adult education centers cast their net far and wide for
talented instructors. The movement typically selected its teachers from the
ranks of those excluded from the university system—among socialists, democrats, Jews, and women. Slowly, a counterculture emerged that challenged the
conservative establishment.[21]

The positive interactions between socialist politicians, the school reform
movement, and progressive intellectuals had a twofold effect. First, it provided
intellectual credibility to the educational policies of the city government,
since many thinkers of international reputation participated.[22] Groundbreaking developments in math, physics, and philosophy were discussed in adult
education courses, providing opportunities that were scarcely available at the
University of Vienna. Second, the socialists' ecumenical embrace of diverse
intellectual methods brought liberals, democrats, and other excluded intellectuals into the socialist ranks. The socialist commitment to empirical science
for the transformation of existing socioeconomic conditions appealed to a
large segment of Red Viennese intellectuals. Spurned by the conventional
knowledge industry, progressives found this intellectual orientation inviting.[23]

A closer look at the activities of Vienna Circle members in adult education demonstrates both their diversity of thought and their increasing dedica-
tion to socialist projects. Five members—Herbert Feigl, Viktor Kraft, Otto
Neurath, Friedrich Waismann, and Edgar Zilsel—were regular instructors.
Practically everyone else offered lectures at one time or another. In all, Vienna
Circle members conducted hundreds of lectures and taught thousands of
pupils. Zilsel's work best exemplifies the growing affinity between logical empiricist philosophy and social democratic politics, which manifested

---

19. Wilhelm Filla, "Zwischen Arbeiterbewegung und Bürgertum," in Filla, Gruber, and Jug,
Erwachsenenbildung, 97–100; Kutalek and Fellinger, *Zur Wiener Volksbildung*, 129–39.

20. Kutalek and Fellinger, *Zur Wiener Volksbildung*, 141–6.

21. Weidenholzer, *Auf dem Weg*, 274–78. Not all the *Volkshochschulen* pursued this "new direction": see Böck, *Volksbildung oder Volk-Bildung*, 122–24. See also Achs and Krassnig, *Drillschule, Lehr-
schule, Arbeitsschule*.

22. This group included Karl Popper, Karl Polanyi, Anna Freud, and Alfred Adler; the social
scientists Karl and Charlotte Bühler, Paul Lazarsfeld, Maria Jahoda, and Hans Zeisel.

23. Glaser, *Austromarxismus*, 39–95.

itself concretely in the Ernst Mach Society.[24] Through his engagement with socialist-run institutes, Zilsel's scholarship moved from a liberal to Marxist position, and he encouraged his students to follow his lead.

Before we examine Zilsel's work, the activities of Feigl, Kraft, and Waismann merit attention, since these individuals are typically viewed as the apolitical "right wing" of the Vienna Circle. Their activities not only reflected the thinkers' scholarly interests but also demonstrate how previously unengaged intellectuals from liberal backgrounds came to support socialist projects.[25] Feigl lectured on freedom of the will, the origins of knowledge, and philosophy of nature. He also taught topics that occupied him professionally well into his American exile: contingency and law in nature and the philosophical foundations of inductive knowledge. Despite the appeal of theories of "uncertainty" to a small group in the Austrian academy, these courses had little chance of appearing at the university.[26] Feigl embraced the opportunity to flout the establishment and offer lectures on relativity and radical empiricism.[27] Kraft, who became a member of the adult education executive board, offered a variety of introductory courses on philosophy. He lectured on the basic concepts of historical worldviews, the meaning of life, and Chinese philosophy. Even with two other jobs, Kraft participated in adult education from 1910 to 1935; the number of courses he offered increased with time.

Waismann's courses likewise reflected his shifting intellectual commitments, including an advocacy of socialist educational reform. He used the adult education centers to teach politically unpalatable scientific theories. In the early years of the Republic, he taught the foundations of mathematics. With the arrival of Schlick in Vienna, Waismann instructed on relativity theory. As the Vienna Circle emerged, he turned to logical analysis and empirical philosophy. Like Kraft, he did not cease his involvement with adult education even when the Mach Society emerged as an alternate intellectual forum. The adult education centers became places where intellectuals could subvert the cultural politics of Black Vienna. While financial necessity and a lack of academic opportunity played some role in this involvement, these were not the sole factors. This is demonstrated by the unequivocal support in 1929 for the philosophical and political manifesto of the Vienna Circle, "The Scientific World-Conception," by these three writers. The rhetoric

---

24. For a list of courses by Vienna Circle members, see Kaller, "Wiener Kreis und Volksbildung."

25. These members each wrote about the circle later and all downplayed their previous sociopolitical involvement. See Herbert Feigl, "Wiener Kreis in America," in Fleming and Bailyn, *Intellectual Migration,* 630–40; Kraft, *Vienna Circle;* Waismann, *Wittgenstein.*

26. See Coen, *Vienna.*

27. Feigl, "Wiener Kreis." See also Stadler, *Vienna Circle,* 624–30.

of revolution and the recognition of the possibility of social transformation through improved educational opportunities expressed the ideological convictions of the left *and* right wings of the movement.[28]

While Feigl, Waismann, and Kraft remained more or less liberal in orientation, Neurath and Zilsel invested increasingly in the socialist cause in the 1920s. Neurath's résumé of lectures attested to his legendary energy and social activism. His interests also paralleled developments in Central Europe. In the early 1920s, he instructed on the planned economy and the settlement movement, as the German and Austrian governments wrestled with socialization measures and the Viennese authorities embarked on their public housing initiative. This led to discussions on urban design and architecture, as he advocated for Red Viennese housing projects. Eventually, he sent Feigl to Dessau to establish connections between the German Bauhaus and the logical empiricists.[29] By the mid-1920s, he frequently taught economics and political science. Neurath had developed this thinking in debates with the Austrian school of economics, which had been ongoing since before the war. In his lectures, he carried on the socialist calculation debate, which pitted Austrian economists against socialists, with the former arguing that a planned economy was wasteful and inefficient.[30]

In the lectures from the late 1920s, Neurath developed the ideas that animate his most Marxist monographs, *Life Formations and Class Warfare* and *Empirical Sociology*, which will be discussed in chapter 6. They argued for a close alliance of scientific philosophy, the social sciences, and Marxist scientific socialism. Neurath interpreted Marx as a predecessor of the Vienna Circle because of his commitment to empirical economic and sociological research. He made explicit the connections between class struggle and intellectual conflict. Neurath's newfound emphasis on struggle reflected the heightened political tensions in Austria and Central Europe after 1927. Austrian conservatives had embarked on an authoritarian course, allying with the fascist Heimwehr to suppress the workers' movement. They had also advanced a series of authoritarian constitutional amendments designed to strengthen the executive branch at the expense of the judiciary and the legislature and to undercut the autonomy of Vienna. It was clear that the stakes of

---

28. Stadler, *Vienna Circle*, 744–48. The designations "left" and "right" in the Vienna Circle did not refer to political orientation; they defined different philosophical agendas. Only Schlick demurred from wholesale support because of the stridency of the manifesto's tone.

29. Feigl, "Wiener Kreis," 637.

30. Ludwig Mises held Neurath in particularly low regard, calling his economic views "disruptive" and "nonsense." See Mises, *Memoirs,* 32. On the calculation debates, see Steele, *From Marx to Mises.*

ideological preeminence had risen. To achieve hegemony, Neurath argued, it was necessary to enlighten the masses and provide them empirical reasons to support socialism. He redoubled his socialist activities as a result. Long active in the settlement movement, he also opened the Social and Economic Museum of Vienna in 1925. He sought new ways of disseminating scientific information to the masses, which led to his groundbreaking work on pictorial statistics and picture language, the Isotype model.[31] His graphical representations of data appeared regularly in the *Arbeiter-Zeitung* from 1925 on, achieving such popularity that the conservative *Reichspost* began mimicking the approach in 1927.[32]

It was Edgar Zilsel who established the closest interactions between circle intellectuals and the adult education movement, however. He best exemplifies the intellectual and political radicalization that took place as a result of exclusion from the academy and immersion in Austro-Marxist cultural politics. After the rejection of his *Habilitation* in the mid-1920s, Zilsel could not find a university job. Consequently he returned to the adult education institutes, where he had worked from 1916 until 1919. He taught courses on the history of philosophy and science and lectured on the cult of personality. He instructed on the latest developments in physics, biology, and chemistry.[33] Zilsel also led philosophy discussion groups, often devoted to single texts. These discussions elucidate his radical ideas and intellectual orientation. They show Zilsel's conversion from a liberal intellectual to a full-fledged Marxist. In fact, he ended up on the left of the Austro-Marxist spectrum. In 1924 and 1925, he discussed the works of three of his university advisers, Moritz Schlick, Heinrich Gomperz and Hans Kelsen, all consummate liberals. He offered a Machian critique of the fields of his advisers—philosophy and jurisprudence—advocating inductive investigation into the origins of knowledge and the emergence of social and legal norms. These critiques shared much with his prewar psychohistorical meditations on genius. His first book, *Geniereligion,* had traced the development of the cult of genius through its various historical and psychological variations. He argued that the notion of genius was a metaphysical one promoted by half-educated literati and philosophical dilettantes. Zilsel dismissed the cult of genius and endeavored to quantify the success of those deemed great. He attacked metaphysical

31. Stöckler, "Wiener Bildstatistik."

32. See Cartwright, Cat, Fleck, and Uebel, *Otto Neurath;* Nemeth, *Otto Neurath;* Nemeth and Stadler, *Encyclopedia and Utopia;* and Nemeth, Heinrich, and Soulez, *Otto Neurath.* On the *Reichspost's* appropriation of Isotype, see the April 1927 editions of the journal.

33. Kaller, "Wiener Kreis und Volksbildung"; Paul Zilsel, "Über Edgar Zilsel," in Stadler, *Vertriebene Vernunft,* 2: 924–32. On Zilsel's relationship with the circle, see Zilsel, *Social Origins.*

obscurity, critiquing the culture of German education, which canonized its intellectual heroes and waxed rhapsodic about the genius of the German spirit.[34]

Zilsel's ideological and philosophical attitudes shifted substantially in 1926 as he engaged in Austro-Marxist debates. His reading group redirected its attentions from liberal texts to more radical works of contemporary social science and philosophy. This signaled Zilsel's turn away from abstract investigations to pointed social critique. He first discussed Otto Bauer's *Das Weltbild des Kapitalismus,* a critique of postwar capitalist society and its attendant conservative ideological impulses. The Bauer reading was accompanied by a discussion of Hegel's *Philosophy of History.* These two selections highlighted Zilsel's new interest in contemporary Marxism and his increasing politicization. In the 1920s, David Riazanov spearheaded the effort to create a complete edition of Marx and Engels's work. This undertaking unearthed works of the young Marx. This led Marxist theoreticians back to Hegel and the Left Hegelians. While in Vienna in the early 1920s, the Hungarian Georg Lukács had arrived at a similar focus in his *History and Class Consciousness.* Zilsel's embrace of Hegel was particularly innovative since German Idealist philosophy had never played a significant role in Austrian philosophy. At this juncture, Zilsel found himself on the cutting edge of interwar socialist debates.[35]

Zilsel saw Hegelian (and Marxist) philosophy as an important supplement to the monism he had learned from Schlick, allowing him to take logical empiricism in a radical direction. According to Zilsel, the dialectic, with its emphasis on the transcendence of negations in a higher unity, corresponded to Schlick's unitary vision, which Schlick described thus: "The result we have arrived at is to be welcomed in the interest of a unified, truly satisfactory worldview. For the dualistic world picture put forward by the supporters of interaction necessarily carries with it the renunciation of complete knowledge of the world."[36] For Schlick, dualistic notions of mind-body, life-afterlife, and subject-object did not hold. Zilsel argued that this monistic logic was compatible with Hegel's concept of *Aufhebung.* He also applied Schlick's analytic to the capitalist world, arguing that capitalism perpetuated a false, dualistic social organization of bourgeoisie-proletariat that had to be overcome through political action. Monism, when linked to Hegelian dialectics and Marxist materialism, was therefore attainable only in the socialist state, which had overcome class conflict and alienated labor. Zilsel drew these

---

34. Stadler, *Vienna Circle,* 755–56; Zilsel, *Geniereligion,* 5.
35. Haller, "Österreichische Philosophie," 173–81. See also Smith, *Austrian Philosophy,* 1–34.
36. Schlick, *General Theory,* 325–26.

conclusions from ideas explored at adult education institutes—conclusions that the liberal Schlick would never have imagined.

Zilsel's new views reached a peak in his second book on genius, which he dedicated to the *Volkshochschulen*. The title of the book is instructive: *The Emergence of the Concept of Genius: A Contribution to the History of Ideas of the Antique and Early Capitalism.* It was an economically grounded intellectual history, a Marxist *Ideologiekritik*. He eschewed the psychological method he had used previously and turned to economic explanations for the emergence of the concept of genius.[37] The target of his critique was no longer semieducated literati but the capitalist bourgeoisie. With the emergence of capitalist society and the decline of religiosity, he argued, the ascendant bourgeoisie needed substitutes for ideals of religious immortality. The modern concept of genius stemmed from the Renaissance period, as did a new "corporate pride" (*Standesstolz*) that honored middle-class knowledge and style. This led to sterility, conservatism, and close-mindedness, particularly in the arts and literature. Modern capitalist society produced a value vacuum, valorizing those idle wealthy whose creative output derived from the free time they gained through the exploitation of others. His analysis led Zilsel to reject contemporary society and its disdain for critical scientific thinking.[38]

Personal and historical experience played a substantial role in Zilsel's new intellectual and political orientation. His failed *Habilitation* had soured him on the academy. His involvement at the *Volkshochschulen* taught him how the hegemons of society suppressed the creative impulses of the working class and blocked the free development of thought. The growing power of Black Viennese ideas convinced him that radical change was needed. These experiences inculcated an appreciation of adult education and socialism, which actively thwarted the rising conservative wave. He openly expressed his gratitude to the adult education movement for nurturing interdisciplinary scientific research and allowing the discussion of pressing social issues. He argued that only workers' circles seriously attempted social and economic change. Zilsel saw the adult education and workers' movements as the home for modern science and antimetaphysical philosophy. It was only through these movements that the world could be transformed.[39]

Zilsel continued his radical development after 1926, contributing to Austro-Marxist theoretical debates. His next adult education courses also dealt with Marxist developments, as he examined the work of Max Stirner and the Left Hegelians. He also led working groups on "the philosophical

---

37. Zilsel, *Entstehung des Geniebegriffes*, 1–6.
38. Ibid., 324–26.
39. Ibid., ix–x.

problems of socialism." These likely focused on the work of the Austro-Marxist philosopher Max Adler, who had recently published *Kant and Marxism,* to which Zilsel objected strongly. Adler contended that Marx had discovered an epistemological category Kant had overlooked: the social a priori. Human beings were fundamentally social creatures and all thinking about individuals had to start from the interpersonal and societal relations that inscribed them. Zilsel rejected the unscientific, unverifiable, and metaphysical elements of Adler's Marxism, alternately seeking a connection between Marxism and empirical scientific research. Zilsel was developing a unique Marxist theory, one that combined law-like empirical research into economic conditions with a desire for a unification of knowledge inspired by Spinoza, Hegel, and Schlick. His disagreement with Adler showed that Zilsel had actually moved to an ideological position more radical than that of the Austro-Marxists. He rejected the quiescence of the Austro-Marxist leadership in the late 1920s and 1930s as political and economic conditions worsened in the region.

In summary, the involvement of Vienna Circle members in the adult education movement reveals several points about the engagement of progressive intellectuals during the interwar era. First, these thinkers resisted topics that predominated in the conservative academy, thereby establishing themselves as a counterhegemonic force. God, religion (except Eastern ones), and metaphysics received no attention. There were no discussions of Romantic philosophy. German and Austrian patriotic traditions came in for critical scrutiny. There was no talk of the Great War, the old monarchy, or the ills of constitutional democracy, subjects regularly addressed by professors at the University of Vienna and by the Spannkreis. With their silence, the Vienna Circle members spoke volumes. Second, the adult education system produced a vibrant interdisciplinary culture in Red Vienna. Circle members like Zilsel and Neurath incorporated new ideas—particularly in psychology, sociology, and history—into their own formulations, producing new critiques of the world around them.

Third and most important, there was a clear radicalization of the political convictions of Circle members. The adult education system, supported by the socialist government of Vienna and derided by conservatives, was a bastion for those excluded from traditional halls of learning. Feigl, Kraft, Neurath, Waismann, and Zilsel were all barred from the university system as a result of political or racial discrimination.[40] This exclusion prompted a realization for Circle intellectuals that their "apolitical" scientific views were not actually free

---

40. The connection between Jews and Red Viennese organizations has received ample attention. See in particular Beller, *Vienna and the Jews.*

from political considerations. Feigl and Waismann became socially engaged for the first time, while Neurath and Zilsel moved into the Austro-Marxist mainstream. Progressive intellectuals like these men, especially Jewish ones, accepted that they had to fight alongside the socialists.[41]

The relative scarcity of intellectuals like Schlick, who remained above the political fray, attests to the transformation of interwar Viennese intellectual life. Freud, another classic liberal, recognized the need for political commitment in a time of ideological conflict; his students flocked to the adult education centers.[42] Only Schlick could remain committed to airy ideals about the collective welfare of society in ways that his marginalized students Waismann and Zilsel could not. Theory and practice were irrevocably linked in interwar Vienna, a fact that Schlick realized too late. Schlick did not need to develop the implications of his worldview, for he possessed a secure social standing. His fellow Monists and Freethinkers did not have the same luxury, however, and they followed a path of politicization and radicalization similar to Zilsel's.

The Monists and Freethinkers

If one looks at the announcement of the founding of the Verein Ernst Mach, most of the names listed should be familiar: Schlick and Hahn were the chairmen; Neurath and Carnap were secretaries. Feigl, Zilsel, and Waismann were slated to lecture, as were Vienna Circle associates Philipp Frank and Karl Menger. There are several additional names, however, that demonstrate the associational connections that circle members had established within Red Vienna. Otto Bauer and Josef Frank showed up as lecturers, as did Josef Friedjung, the leading figure in the adult education movement. The other individuals on the broadsheet belonged to the Austrian Monist Association and the Austrian Freethinkers' Association.[43] These groups made crucial contributions to the makeup of the Ernst Mach Society, comprising the majority of members. The Monists provide a good sense of the strains on progressive Viennese intellectuals in the immediate postwar landscape. Their decline speaks volumes about the radicalization of interwar Vienna. Their

---

41. Hacohen, *Karl Popper,* chapter 7, highlights the lack of alternative groups for Jews to join other than socialists. As Lisa Silverman also notes, "Jewish difference" was a defining analytical category in interwar Vienna, preventing Jews from inclusion in emerging concepts of "Austrianness." See Silverman, *Becoming Austrians,* introduction.

42. Danto, *Freud's Free Clinics.*

43. Stadler, *Vienna Circle,* 332–33, 582–84. Wladimir Misar and Edgar Herbst were Monists; Josef Friedjung, Robert and Steffi Endres, and Carl Kundermann were Freethinkers.

moderate views remained relatively constant, so the eclipse of the Monists reveals the rapid politicization of knowledge after the war. The Freethinkers, on the other hand, rose on the back of their radicalization and became a legitimate cultural force. Many Monists joined them because of their similar ideological stances and the latter group's popularity, especially with the working class. A close examination of the Freethinkers' theoretical organ, *Der Freidenker*, demonstrates the turn toward politics that progressive organizations undertook in response to interwar crises.

The biologist Ernst Haeckel founded the German Monist Society in 1906 as an organization for combating unscientific *Weltanschauungen*.[44] The society was committed to the conquest of the world through natural science and technology. Its manifesto declared,

> The monumental advances in the natural sciences have displaced and disposed of antiquated dogmatic and mystical representations of the world and humanity, body and soul.... Monistic representations are increasingly replacing antiquated dualistic ones; those dissatisfied with *Weltanschauungen* sanctified by tradition now seek a scientifically grounded, unified *Weltanschauung*. This outlook rejects faith in antiquated, traditional dogma and revelation and sets in its place pure reason.[45]

The Monists advocated a scientific worldview (*wissenschaftliche Weltanschauung*) devoted to the rational exploration of the universe. These ideas carried a resonance into the coming years: Schlick's aforementioned *General Theory of Knowledge* paraphrases them explicitly. The Vienna Circle and the Ernst Mach Society also took up this call for a scientific worldview but changed the word "worldview" to "world-concept" (*Weltauffassung*) to avoid the metaphysical ballast of the former term.

Haeckel and the early Monists did not shy away from metaphysical tendencies, however. They evinced a positivist, almost scientistic, confidence in human reason. They felt that fin-de-siècle European society had reached a moment of spiritual crisis. Advances in science had not been matched by concomitant developments in society, politics, or the arts. The Monists believed that only science could combat false theological and philosophical ideas. They hoped their commitment to scientific research would lead to a

---

44. Haeckel announced his plan at the International Freethinker Congress in 1904, showing the connection between Monists and Freethinkers from the outset. See Volker Drehsen and Helmut Zander, "Rationale Weltveränderung," in Drehsen and Sparn, *Weltbildwandel zur Weltanschauungsanalyse*, 219–20.

45. Heinrich Schmidt, "Gründung des deutschen Monistenbundes," *Das monistische Jahrhundert* 1 (1912–13): 740.

renewal of society and the establishment of an ersatz religion of science.[46] Monism found its primary appeal among scientists and members of the *Bildungsbürgertum*. Their worldview was a positivist, materialist, and cosmopolitan one, putting them at odds with the emergent nationalist movements of the time and the religious establishment of Central Europe. Their views did not make them atheistic necessarily, as Haeckel himself demonstrated. "[W]e find God in the natural laws themselves. The will of God is found in falling raindrops and in growing crystals, in the smell of roses and the spirit of humankind."[47] Of course, Haeckel's views did not represent those of the entire association, and there were distinct divisions in the group from the outset. Nothing more than a minimal ideological consensus ever formed, and the Monist Society remained loosely organized.

The Austrian Monist Association, led by the positivist philosopher and adult education advocate Friedrich Jodl, adopted a more antimetaphysical and anticlerical position than the German branch, as was appropriate for the more conservative and Catholic Austria. Austrian Monists launched a campaign, the *Austrittsbewegung,* to get nonpracticing Catholics to leave the church. At its height, the movement encouraged thousands of people annually to leave the church. They joined forces with the social democrats in the Freie Schule and Kinderfreunde educational movements and lectured in the adult education institutions.[48] Jodl himself represented an important precursor to the Vienna Circle and the Verein Ernst Mach. One of the founders of the *Volkshochschulen,* Jodl made his name as a popularizer of the philosophies of Ludwig Feuerbach, August Comte, and David Hume. His commitment to empiricist epistemology and positivist philosophy made him a controversial figure in the Austrian academy. His work on ethics, which argued for a naturalistic and objective approach to human action, served as a basis for Schlick's. His willingness to resist the religious and metaphysical approaches of Austrian academicians made him a hero to the logical empiricists and Austro-Marxists, who named a street and apartment complex after him.[49]

After moderate successes during the fin-de-siècle, the Great War and its effects dashed the Monists' hopes, splintered the organization, and reduced its influence. Although the Austrian Monist Association emerged from the war under the able leadership of sociologist Rudolf Goldscheid, there were

---

46. Drehsen and Zander, "Rationale Weltveränderung," 217–9.
47. Haeckel, *Monismus,* 33.
48. Drehsen and Zander, "Rationale Weltveränderung," 221–25. Although there was an Austrian society, Austrian members were usually involved in the German Society.
49. Jodl died in 1914, and his student Wilhelm Börner succeeded him at the Ethical Society and the Monist Association. See Börner, *Friedrich Jodl,* and Glaser, *Austromarxismus,* 123–25.

never more than a few hundred members after the war. Neurath, Schlick, and Feigl participated, as did Wilhelm Börner, Paul Kammerer, and Edgar Herbst, who were also members of the Freethinkers' Association and the Austrian Ethical Society. These individuals increasingly sought other outlets for the expression of their intellectual positions as the Monist Association foundered. Although the Monists limped along until 1934 (when they were disbanded by the Austrofascists), disillusioned members typically turned to two outlets: the Social Democrats and the Freethinkers.[50]

The Freethinkers' Association was first founded in 1869 in Graz as a society for "humanity, enlightenment, and education."[51] In Vienna, the Free-thinkers emerged two years later out of the Society of Individuals without Denomination. The reactionary environment of the neoabsolutist era in Austria-Hungary precipitated their formation. Like the Monists, the Free-thinkers were opposed to theological and metaphysical concepts and advo-cated leaving the church. They also supported the Free School movement. Though this brought them in contact with the Social Democrats before the war, the alliance was not official. There was no clear overlap in members, and their respective theoretical organs never mentioned the efforts of the other group. Up until the war, the Freethinkers were primarily an anticlerical intel-lectual group composed of members of the *Bildungsbürgertum*.

Because of dissension over the war issue, the Freethinkers' Association splintered in 1914. It did not recover until 1921, when it reconstituted along radical lines. By this point, the initial optimism of the Austrian Revolu-tion had receded, and the promise of a social democratic state had faded. Socialists and progressives were on the defensive, and were largely confined to the capital and industrial cities. Ongoing food shortages, inflation, and unemployment wreaked havoc on the working population and signaled to the Freethinkers the need for social transformation. Within a decade, there were 310 local Freethinking groups, nine provincial organizations and nearly fifty thousand members. The journal *Der Freidenker* had a circulation of fifty thousand copies. The group published two smaller-circulation papers and had its own publishing house. It also established a health care fund, a legal defense team, and an arts center. The Freethinkers fought for civil mar-riage and school reform and continued their traditional struggle against the church. They attracted intellectuals to their cause, especially ones involved with adult education, such as Ludo Hartmann, Josef Friedjung and Wilhelm

---

50. Drehsen and Zander, "Rationale Weltveränderung," 225; Stadler, *Vienna Circle*, 183–88.

51. The journal was *Der Freidenker. Blätter für Humanität, Aufklärung, und Bildung.*

Börner. The Austrian Freethinkers' Association was one of the largest social organizations of the First Republic.[52]

The views expressed in *Der Freidenker* reveal the radicalization of progressive thought in the postwar period. The opening number of *Der Freidenker* presented its mission statement, though it is typically misread. Like Schlick a decade later, editor-in-chief Friedrich Haller declared the group to be an "apolitical association." However, this apolitical statement was a mere holdover from the late imperial period, when such disclaimers from social and cultural organizations were required. Haller quickly qualified this claim in the same paragraph: "Today's world order is built on a falsely conceived, antisocial world picture that violates the laws of experience.... [T]he most influential, self-centered and power-hungry individuals, parties and interests arrange and execute everything. The only way therefore to an ultimate improvement of our position is if a revolution in the mind [*Gehirn*] *follows the political and economic revolution* [*Umsturz*]."[53] Although their goal was a revolution of the mind, the Freethinkers saw that spiritual revolution could be achieved only after political and economic transformation. Though it is possible that Haller was referring to the November revolution, it is unlikely. By 1922, it was clear that the expectations of liberals and socialists had not been realized with the 1918 Central European revolutions. The SDAP had lost its position in the ruling coalition in 1920 and had entered into permanent opposition to the bourgeois parties. The conservative bloc had consolidated and grown more militant. Moreover, Austria's economic woes had reached a fever pitch with inflation so bad that the government was on the verge of laying off hundreds of thousands of employees and turning its finances over to the League of Nations in return for foreign loans. Evidently Haller envisioned a forthcoming revolution to rectify the problems of the First Republic. The Freethinkers would take active part in the struggle. Haller enumerated their enemies: the clergy, nobility, and large-scale capital. The inclusion of anticapitalist sentiments signaled the Freethinkers' shift from their nineteenth-century liberal origins. They had made a break from their bourgeois past and joined in the fight for social and economic equality.

From the outset, *Der Freidenker* exhibited militant tendencies. The rhetoric in the journal is redolent with military metaphors and battlefield imagery. In February 1922, the editor announced a "battle for the spirit." In June, every major article discussed the struggle ahead and recommended that its

---

52. Franz Roznal, "Bericht für Österreich," in *Protokoll 1931, IV. Kongreß der "Internationale Proletarischer Freidenker" (I.P.F),* (Vienna: 1931), 86–92; Stadler, *Vienna Circle,* 188–90.

53. Friedrich Haller, "Drei Jahre der Republik," *FD* 27 (January 1922): 2 (emphasis added).

readers be battle-ready (*kampfbereit*) and militant (*kämpferisch*). If any doubts remained about the radical convictions of the organization, the June article by Felix Panzer titled "Kapitalismus, Kirche, und Sozialismus" dispelled them. Panzer argued that the predominant form of violence in the contemporary world was capitalism. It had brought the church and aristocracy under its power and now employed their modes of repression for its own purposes. The church had long since ceased to be an organization devoted to love of one's fellow man and instead sought to instill ignorance in the people. Panzer concluded with an endorsement of Marxist socialism:

> Where do we find that striving, that love of one's neighbor or, in other words, the continual concern for the general good? The answer can only be: in Socialism! Socialism embodies the struggle against exploitation and oppression, these two factors that represent the core of capitalism. We must unite with socialism and from this standpoint decide which things will serve the good of the collective and those that oppose the general interest. We then must fight against these latter forces with all available means with the exception of personal violence. Out of the church! To Socialism![54]

Panzer stopped shorted of advocating terroristic violence, yet all other means were permissible in the class struggle against capitalism. The last two sentences in particular sum up the shift in the freethinker movement. Previously, the penultimate statement alone would have sufficed: the goal of the movement had been to leave the church and achieve a separation of church and state. By 1922, this was insufficient; Marxist socialism was the answer.

As the association grew in popularity, its position radicalized. In 1923, *Der Freidenker* launched a campaign to ensure that nonpracticing Catholics did not list themselves as Catholics in the upcoming census. This was partially because of the Freethinkers' atheistic tendencies; it also hinged on their distaste for Christian Social education and social policy. Beginning in 1922, the Christian Socials intensified their efforts to roll back the Glöckel educational reforms. Over the next five years, under the leadership of the "intransigent" Richard Schmitz, the conservatives attempted to turn the clocks back to 1855, when Catholic teaching was made mandatory for all students. The assault on free, secular education inspired greater resistance from within Red Vienna and the Freethinker Association.[55] Their *Austritt* campaign was designed to decrease the amount of state money committed to

---

54. Felix Panzer, "Kapitalismus, Kirche und Sozialismus," *FD* 27 (May 1922): 2.
55. Gulick, *Austria,* chap. 16, especially 565–78.

religious schools and conservative social programs. In bold block letters on the front page in February, *Der Freidenker* implored, "SOCIALISTS, OUT OF THE CHURCH!" and "WE ARE SOCIALISTS!"[56]

The Freethinkers turned increasingly to Marxist explanations for current problems. A series of long articles presented a materialist conception of history in an effort to understand the interaction between natural and historical laws. In a May 1923 article, the new editor claimed that 99 percent of all Freethinkers were proletarian, and he enjoined the Austro-Marxists to wage war against the church and the Austrian establishment. He also announced that the German Monist Association had joined them in the International Free-Minded (*freigeistige*) Workers' Community, thereby bringing monists, freethinkers, and working-class intellectuals into an official union. The Austrian Freethinkers were becoming a focal point of radical agitation in Central Europe.

In May 1924, the historian and future Ernst Mach Society executive Robert Endres took over editorship of *Der Freidenker* and used the opportunity to present the current freethinker movement as an organization steeped in socialist radicalism. The association remained dedicated to its traditional cultural ideals, yet it had also evolved in a proletarian direction:

> The freethinker movement of the nineteenth century was a purely bourgeois movement; it sprang up at the tail end of the struggle between the bourgeoisie and the nobility. Since the reactionary church essentially stood alongside the nobility and abetted the reaction, liberalism had to be anticlerical, too. Today the bourgeoisie has already long been in possession of power and has made its peace with the church. Even more: the bourgeoisie, threatened by the proletariat, seeks refuge behind the frock as the king once did behind the bourgeoisie. For these reasons, the proletariat now leads the battle against the church, as the bourgeoisie once did. The bourgeois freethinker movement is dead but the proletariat Freethinker movement lives on.[57]

This became the standard narrative of the freethinker movement. It was a proletarian movement engaged in class struggle against the church, nobility, and the bourgeoisie. To educate readers in socialist thinking, Endres published the works of leading socialists, past and present: Victor Adler, Otto Glöckel, Julius Tandler, and Max Adler were but a few contributors. Otto Neurath wrote for the journal, too. Moreover, the Austrian Freethinkers

---

56. *FD* 28 (February 1923): 1.
57. Robert Endres, *FD* 29 (June 1924): 3.

spearheaded the internationalization of their movement by creating the International Congress of Proletarian Freethinkers. This group asserted that an unbridgeable gap existed between the goals of the remaining bourgeois freethinkers and the ascendant proletarians. The Austrian Freethinkers saw this international program as a way of linking up with the Labor and Socialist International, the heir to the Vienna, or "Two-and-a-Half," International of the early 1920s. Within two years, the Vienna-based International Proletarian Freethinkers had a journal, *Der Atheist,* with a circulation in the tens of thousands. Edgar Zilsel published in its pages.[58] Interestingly, the views of the Freethinkers were so radical that the socialist leaders distanced themselves from the movement in their 1926 party platform for fear that voters might conflate the atheism of the Freethinkers with their own views on religion and education. The Austro-Marxists kept the organization at a distance through the 1927 elections, causing widespread disappointment in the ranks of the Freethinkers.

Of course, the consequences of such militant activity in a time of political polarization were predictable. Shortly after the Christian Social chancellor Engelbert Dollfuss suspended parliament in March 1933, he disbanded the Freethinkers, one of the first groups outlawed by the Austrofascist regime. After the 1934 civil war, Robert Endres backed away from his earlier militant socialism and anticlericalism.[59] Nevertheless, the history of the post-war Freethinker Association demonstrates that there was no confusion for interwar Austrians—conservative or radical, religious or atheist, political or apolitical—about the group. The Freethinkers constituted a revolutionary association, not a mere bourgeois or liberal reformist movement. A commitment to class struggle against the church, aristocracy, and capitalism was part of their program. The members of Vienna Circle were undoubtedly aware of this mission and shared many of their attitudes, meaning the affiliation with the Freethinkers in the Ernst Mach Society carried clear ideological valences.

The Ernst Mach Society

Contrary to popular belief, the Freethinkers, not the Vienna Circle philosophers, founded the Ernst Mach Society. Typically the 1928 announcement of the society is used to indicate its beginning, thereby granting the Vienna Circle primacy. However, the Austrian Freethinker Association took the first

---

58. Ronzal, "Bericht für Österreich," 86–92.
59. Glaser, *Austromarxismus,* 109–10.

steps, revealing that the society was as much a Freethinker institution as it was a logical empiricist one. In April 1927, the Freethinkers established the Ernst Mach Society for the Promotion of Scientific Education; no circle members were yet involved. The society was modeled on the adult education movement and intended to present lectures and papers, organize guided tours, and provide scientific literature.[60] Conceived in the wake of the 1927 elections, where the Social Democrats achieved their greatest electoral success, the society represented an optimistic engagement with social reform. Neurath, given his ties to the Freethinkers, was the first circle member who affiliated with the society, and he brought other philosophers aboard. Initially it was the Freethinkers' journal *Der Pionier* that published announcements and propagandized for the society. The society did not carry on public activities before 1928 and was officially established only in November of that year. The Freethinkers dominated the membership of the society even when circle members conducted most of the lectures. Moreover, it was the Freethinkers who solidified ties with the Viennese municipal government, since Julius Tandler and Josef Friedjung were on the society's board.[61]

By the time the Verein Ernst Mach went public, political conditions had shifted dramatically. The July 1927 Justizpalast fire and the subsequent conservative backlash dealt a massive blow to the confidence of the socialist movement. The bourgeois parties, especially the Christian Socials, turned increasingly to paramilitary, fascist organizations like the Heimwehr to ensure order. Chancellor Ignaz Seipel openly embraced the authoritarian rhetoric of Black Vienna, calling for a "true democracy" based on strong executive leadership; ethnic, religious, and political exclusion; and centralized power. He introduced authoritarian constitutional amendments, designed to enhance the power of the executive and curtail the freedom of the federal states, particularly Vienna. Austria seemed on the verge of either a civil war or a conservative revolution.[62] Black Viennese ideologues looked to the regimes of Italy, Hungary, Spain, and Portugal for aspirational models for their true state.

This background partially explains the radical content of the lectures in the society and the militant tone of the famous Vienna Circle manifesto, "The Scientific World-Conception," published in conjunction with the society. Lectures by socialists like Neurath, Bauer, Zilsel, Friedjung, and Josef Frank about economic and social issues corresponded with the aims of

---

60. Statutes of the Verein Ernst Mach, Wiener Stadt- und Landesarchiv.

61. Stadler, *Vienna Circle*, 328–34.

62. Gulick, *Austria,* chap. 20.

the freethinker and adult education movements. They promoted a socialist vision associated with the Austro-Marxism of Red Vienna. "The Scientific World-Conception," the manifesto of the Vienna Circle, presented the history of the group, emphasizing its radicalism and its contribution to contemporary intellectual, cultural, and political struggles. When Schlick was offered a chair in philosophy at Bonn, the authors implored him to stay in Vienna and lead the struggle against the rising tide of "metaphysical and theologizing" thought.[63] Neurath was particularly vexed with these forces, since the conservative newspaper the *Reichspost* had "misappropriated" his innovative graphical modeling system of "picture statistics" (*Bildstatistik*). In the final paragraph, Neurath issued a call to arms:

> Thus, the scientific world-conception is close to the life of the present. Certainly it is threatened with hard struggles and hostility. Nevertheless there are many who do not despair but, in view of the present sociological situation, look forward with hope to the course of events to come. Of course not every single adherent of the scientific world-conception will be a fighter. Some, glad of solitude, will lead a withdrawn existence on the icy slopes of logic; some may even disdain mingling with the masses and regret the "trivialized" form that these matters inevitably take on spreading. However, their achievements too will take a place among the historic developments. We witness the spirit of the scientific world-conception penetrating in growing measure the forms of personal and public life, in education, upbringing, architecture, and the shaping of economic and social life according to rational principles. *The scientific world-conception serves life, and life receives it.*[64]

Neurath acknowledged that not everyone would be a fighter; nevertheless, those "glad of solitude" were still part of the revolution. Even with its political and polemic tone, the manifesto met with overwhelming approval in the society. The scientific world-conception represented a worldview compatible with adult education, the Freethinkers, and the Social Democrats: weakening the influence of the church, improving the social condition of the masses, rationalizing the economy, and furthering science. The forces of metaphysical and theologizing thought were on the march; the only way to persevere was through political, social, scientific, and ideological struggle.

---

63. Otto Neurath, "Scientific World-Conception," in Neurath, Neurath, and Cohen, *Empiricism and Sociology,* 299–301, 317–18.
    64. Ibid., 317–18.

Although he objected to the style and content of the piece, Schlick accepted the circle's plea and remained in Vienna. The unanimous agreement of the other circle members with the manifesto cannot be denied. Although it was written by the left-wing members Neurath, Carnap and Hahn, the right-wing members Waismann and Feigl provided comments and contributions. The members of the Vienna Circle agreed upon the implications of their thought and their choice of allies, conceding that the Ernst Mach Society and even the Vienna Circle were in no way unpolitical. Given the intimate ties to adult education, the monists, and the freethinkers and the increasingly polarized historical circumstances of the late 1920s, this consensus comes as little surprise.[65]

In his 1934 letters Schlick realized that the assertions he had made about the political reliability of the society would not suffice. His initial argument showed only that the society was scientific, not that it was unpolitical. He had to assure the government on religious and political grounds that the society was not subversive. His argument employed several tacks. First, he argued that the association was not antireligion or atheistic: "The society has nothing to do with religion. Everyone familiar with empiricism knows that among its members (like any other philosophical orientation) are to be found both religious and skeptical spirits. The greatest American philosopher William James was a radical empiricist and he wrote the book *The Varieties of Religious Experience.*"[66] Schlick recognized that religion—more specifically, Catholicism—was a wedge issue for the Austrofascist regime and tried to meet its leaders halfway. He employed a technique similar to the one the socialists had used before the 1927 elections, when they argued that religion was a private matter (*Privatsache*) and that they did not support atheism. Of course, this strategy deliberately sidestepped the real political issue—the relationship of the society to the tenets of the Catholic Church and the new state. Even if the Ernst Mach Society was not radically antimetaphysical and militantly atheistic—a dubious claim at best—the new government would hardly have approved of the society's pluralist religious views. The endorsement of James's pragmatic philosophy of religion did little to help the cause.

Nor could Schlick adequately distance his association from the socialists. To do so, he had to address two concerns: why many prominent members of the society were avowed socialists and why Otto Bauer had been allowed to deliver a lecture in 1930. Schlick argued,

---

65. Feigl, "Wiener Kreis," 630–31.
66. Schlick to the Bundes-Polizei-Direktion, 3 March 1934.

It is purely coincidental [*zufällig*] that a few scholars... that have great interest in empiricist philosophy are members of that party and have attracted others to the group. I can attest that within the society they are in no way politically active, having neither the occasion nor the opportunity to act in such a manner. It should be clear that it is against the nature of the society to ask about a member's political convictions or to make membership dependent on such an avowal.[67]

Schlick was honest that the society required nothing more than a commitment to empirical science and an antimetaphysical worldview. However, those strictures effectively excluded most conservatives. As we have seen, it was precisely this omission of overt commitment to Catholicism and pan-Germanism that rankled conservatives throughout the educational debates of the 1910s and 1920s. Schlick's argument fell on deaf ears.

The claim that socialist members had no opportunity to discuss political matters also relied on a restrictive definition of politics, one out of keeping with the times. The lines between party political and political had increasingly blurred in the interwar years. It was therefore disingenuous to argue that theoretical discussions of political issues carried no practical political implications. For the Austrofascist authorities, the fact that many society lectures took up issues that fell squarely within the Austro-Marxist bailiwick rendered it politically suspect. Schlick's treatment of the Bauer lecture revealed this problem most clearly. First, he argued that Bauer had given only one lecture. The connection between the socialists and the Ernst Mach Society was only coincidental. Second, he asserted that Bauer "obviously was not permitted to speak there as a politician but exclusively as a sociologist."[68] Schlick did not elaborate on how he distinguished between sociological and political work. These determinations would have been even harder for him to make in this case since he had not attended the lecture. In this instance, the authorities did not need complicated formulas to demarcate politics and science; for them, the scientific world-conception was profoundly political. All these considerations made it impossible to accept Schlick's claim that the Ernst Mach Society was absolutely unpolitical. The Verein Ernst Mach had to be shut down.

---

67. Ibid.
68. Ibid.

CHAPTER 5

Österreichische Aktion and the New Conservatism

In the introduction to its 1927 manifesto, the Österreichische Aktion, the most important group of Austrian monarchists from the interwar era, demanded the creation of a new conservatism, steeped in traditional values yet sensitive to the present and future demands of modern Europe. "The future belongs to historically and sociologically consequential Conservatism, which knows what it wants and takes the present as it is, a Conservatism which...has the courage 'to stand with the Right and think with the Left,' that is, to be rooted in Tradition and yet to accommodate the demands and needs of the times, as leftist as they may seem, in the name of Tradition. [This conciliation of] Left and Right is found above all in the European Idea."[1] The writers envisioned a unified, peaceful Europe, achieved by forward-looking conservative governments and a federated organization of European states, led by a restored Habsburg Austria. These monarchists had reason for optimism, for the past year had produced important gains for European conservatism. The League of Nations ended its control of Austrian and Hungarian finances after four years, thanks to economic improvements under their respective conservative governments. Germany had joined the league at the urging of Gustav Stresemann, the German People's Party (DVP) politician and monarchist. A conservative French government began

---

1. Ernst Karl Winter, "Vorwort," in Knoll et al., *Österreichische Aktion*, 9–10.

withdrawal from the Rhineland. Finally, Fascist Italy and authoritarian Hungary signed a treaty of friendship, taking the first steps to the consolidation of a European bloc of radical conservative states against the Little Entente and France. Conservative politics appeared to be on the upswing; the Aktion hoped to capitalize on these developments.

Envisioned as a complement to the church's Catholic Action programs for social reform and as an Austrian analogue to the Action Française, the group advocated for the restoration of the Habsburg monarchy under Emperor Otto and the establishment of a cultural and political union of the traditional crown lands of Austria, Hungary, Bohemia, Croatia, and Poland. The appeal of the movement derived from the political and cultural landscape of interwar Europe, which encouraged new thinking about traditional concepts like legitimacy, monarchy, and authority. The "new" conservatism of the Aktion also responded to the tumult of the Great War and the collapse of the Habsburg Empire, since it was a restatement of traditional values in a changed world. The Aktion sought stability in a time when a wholesale return to the status quo was not a possibility. Interpreting this Austrian new Right, dedicated to a "European idea" of international peace and a "social idea" of rights and justice, therefore requires a close examination of the historical and ideological conditions of the Aktion's emergence. The ideas of Black Vienna and ascendant conservative ideologies like fascism were fundamental to this development.

Monarchism—even in its moderate variations—contributed significantly to the radicalization of First Republic politics and the rise of Austrian authoritarianism in the 1930s. For conservative intellectuals, the First Republic—with its secular constitution, high middle-class unemployment, divided parliamentary politics, and diminished geopolitical importance—became a target of their dissatisfaction. This led to various restorationist and revanchist proposals. Although the members of the Aktion presented themselves as political outsiders and intellectual innovators, the group did not occupy a fringe position in the ideological field of interwar Austria. In academic societies like the Leo-Gesellschaft, in fraternities like the Deutsche Studentenschaft, in organizations like the Spannkreis, and in journals like Das neue Reich and Die schönere Zukunft, they built bridges with other radical conservatives within Catholic and German nationalist circles. Common ground existed, based on their authoritarian, anti-Republic, antisocialist, and anti-Semitic worldview. This placed the Aktion at the forefront of Black Viennese intellectual developments.

Most interestingly, the commitment to a nonnationalist European idea, centered on the German traditions of the Habsburg Reich, allowed them

to compromise with many German nationalists on the "German question." Ideas of the Reich circulated widely in Europe during the interwar
era and took various forms. Although they rejected an *Anschluss* to Prussia-
dominated Germany, the Aktion still presented a vision of a federated *Mitteleuropa* that differed little from those of conservatives across Central Europe.[2]
The emphasis on a particular interpretation of Habsburg and German history showed the monarchists' attempt at a palingenetic nationalist tradition
of their own, one in line with efforts by other fascist movements of the
era.[3] The Österreichische Aktion's objection to political parties and liberal
democracy and its calls for a restoration of Austrian greatness drew directly
from the Action Française. The members' frequent favorable references
to Mussolini's revolution in Italy likewise signaled their political affinities.
Within the Catholic context, their interpretation of recent papal encyclicals
on political and social reform placed them on the radical end of the religious
community. The stridency of their demands therefore reflected the general
radicalization of Catholic politics in the first decades of the twentieth century across Europe.[4]

Prevailing interpretations of the monarchists' movement have centered on its "Catholic internationalism,"[5] its idiosyncratic and inconsistent
Romanticism,[6] and its "modernism,"[7] as demonstrated by its staunch anti-
Nazism.[8] Most studies focus on the action of monarchists in the mid-1930s,
when the fault lines between Nazism and Austrian conservatism—including
Austrofascism—were clearly drawn.[9] Despite post-*Anschluss* assertions about
their ideological moderation, the writings and actions of these monarchists
during the First Republic attest to a more ambiguous reality: they may have
opposed the Nazis but they still harbored an anti-republican, anti-Semitic,
and authoritarian worldview. The subsequent analysis of the Aktion shows
that Black Viennese formed a relatively coherent ideological field, bent
on crushing the socialists and subverting the political and cultural order
rather than preserving Austrian independence. Black Viennese intellectuals

---

2. See Breuning, *Vision des Reiches,* on *Reichsgedanken.* Seefried, *Reich und Stände,* demonstrates
the diversity of views on concepts like *Reich* and *Stand.*

3. See Griffin, *Nature of Fascism.*

4. Wolff and Hoensch, *European Radical Right,* 5–30, 67–91, 119–57. See also Feldman, Turda,
and Georgescu, *Clerical Fascism,* chaps. 9–15.

5. Hacohen, "Kosmopoliten."

6. Diamant, *Austrian Catholics,* 120–25, 203–7, 220–29.

7. Angerer, "De l'"Autriche germanique,'" 407–64.

8. Leser, *Grenzgänger,* 1:55–73, 107–66.

9. As a good example, see Blair R. Holmes, "The Austrian Monarchists, 1918–1938: Legitimism
versus Nazism," in Parkinson, *Conquering the Past,* 91–109.

belonged to the same societies, published in the same weeklies, and attended the same events. While hardly monolithic, this field was more integrated than has been assumed, especially before 1933.

The Aktion serves as a pivot for understanding Black Vienna. While not wholly comfortable in any *Lager,* members of the Aktion moved fluidly across a broader ideological space. Claiming political neutrality as long as the Republic existed, the monarchists stood aside and rejoiced as the First Republic collapsed before accepting patronage from the Austrofascist state. Their famous "split" from the national *Lager* occurred only *after* the Austrians had developed a fascist movement of their own.[10] A closer look at the ideology and activities of Austrian monarchists demonstrates the need for a careful reconsideration of the significance of politics and religion for conservative intellectuals. Black Vienna derived much of its strength from its successful appropriation of Catholic ideology and values. Moreover, Austria's new Right[11] figured prominently in the Europe-wide authoritarian turn, by disseminating European ideas to an Austrian audience and by reaching out internationally to radical conservative groups. It deserves the critical attention that similar phenomena in Germany, Spain, Hungary, France, and Italy have received.[12]

Postwar Crisis and the Early Development of Aktion Ideology

Defeated on the battlefield in October 1918, the leaders of the Austro-Hungarian state struggled to hold together the nationalities of the Empire. As the Empire's fortunes diminished, politicians explored a variety of state forms to stave off revolution.[13] Emperor Karl issued a manifesto on October 16, reshaping the Empire into a federation of autonomous nation-states. By the end of the month, Czechoslovakia, Galicia, and several southern Slavic territories withdrew from the union. On November 11 Karl renounced his political claims, and the following day the Republik Deutschösterreich was declared. A year later, the Treaty of Saint-Germain rendered Austria a rump

---

10. Thorpe, *Pan-Germanism,* chaps. 1–2, demonstrates the German nationalist affinities of Catholic conservatives well.

11. Hanebrink, *Christian Hungary,* 56.

12. Similar "Action" movements developed in Portugal, Spain, and Italy. See Payne, *Fascism in Spain,* 18–22. Hanebrink, *Christian Hungary,* and Robert Soucy's books on French fascism highlight the conservative, religious, and nationalist elements in the Hungarian and French cases, respectively. On the Italian example, see Blinkhorn, *Fascists and Conservatives,* 1–49.

13. See Renner, *Staat und Nation,* Bauer, *Die Nationalitätenfrage,* and Seipel, *Nation und Staat.*

state, severed from its former industrial holdings in Bohemia and Moravia, its agricultural wealth in Hungary, and its natural resources in Galicia. A political union with Germany was also foreclosed. From its inception, many doubted the viability (*Lebensfähigkeit*) of the new state.[14]

More than merely questioning the *Lebensfähigkeit* of the fledging republic, Austrian conservatives rallied to the Habsburg dynasty while simultaneously decrying the new state. Joseph Eberle's *Die Monarchie,* later renamed *Das neue Reich,* stated the journal's mission as Catholic and monarchist: "This periodical sees its main mission as: intensive discussion of general cultural questions from the Christian [i.e. Catholic] standpoint; discussion of current questions of religion and church, science, literature and art . . . which serve to strengthen the Christian position. . . . *Die Monarchie* advocates an internally secure and outwardly strong Austria-Hungary."[15] The editors crafted a diffuse program, accounting for the shifting political landscape. This mission included a clear restorationist impulse. Eberle argued "for a Christian monarchy, against a Jewish republic" in the first edition after the November revolution. Anti-Semitism would play a central role in future monarchists' arguments against the republican state form. The journal also advanced the idea of a "United States of Austria" under Habsburg leadership. The editors remained committed to the "ideal state administration and state leadership"—that is, the monarchy.[16] As we have seen, *Das neue Reich* served as the fulcrum for conservative discussions in early postwar Austria, attracting an eclectic mix of monarchists, conservatives, anti-Semites, and German nationalists. The founders of the Aktion—Ernst Karl Winter, Hans Karl Zessner-Spitzenberg, Alfred Missong, August Maria Knoll, and Wilhelm Schmid—emerged from this cultural milieu.

Winter and Zessner-Spitzenberg contributed to the earliest editions of *Das neue Reich,* advocating the restoration of Emperor Karl and denouncing the influence of Jews on the new, "illegitimate" Austrian state. Winter, born in 1895 in Vienna, was raised in the German nationalist and Catholic social reform movement associated with the Christian Social politician and founder of the Antisemitenbund, Anton Orel. While at the University of Vienna, he joined the Catholic fraternity Nibelungia, founded by the archaeologist and race theorist Oswald Menghin. Winter studied law under Othmar Spann. In these contexts, he developed a radical social critique that centered on anti-Semitism, German ethnic superiority, and Central European

---

14. On Austrian viability, see Pauley, "Austria's *Lebensunfähigkeit.*"
15. "Geschichte und Programm der Wochenschrift 'Die Monarchie'," *NR* 1 (1918–19): 2.
16. *NR* 1 (1918–19): 89, 91, 105.

unity. Winter's essays reflected his love of the Romantic era and his fear of the decline of modern civilization. He wrote about the significance of a unified *Mitteleuropa*—one including Germany and France—that could stave off the Asiatic Russian "barbarian" and materialistic British shopkeeper.[17] He rejected modern capitalism as a product of Renaissance humanism and Enlightenment individualism, both the work of the Jewish forces.[18] Opposed to the crass nationalism and "Prussianism" of the nineteenth century, he maintained that only a *Mitteleuropa* based on a pre-Enlightenment Habsburg model could unify Europe. Invoking a series of Catholic, nationalist, and anti-Semitic scholars, from the Austrian dramatist Richard Kralik and the German sociologist Werner Sombart to the French historian Ernst Renan and British author Houston Stewart Chamberlain, Winter presented a worldview that fit the ethnonationalist mood of the time. Despite his professions of toleration and international understanding based on Catholic ideas of brotherly love, he espoused traditional anti-Semitic ideals, lamenting the deleterious effect of *Rassenjude, Jüdlinge,* and *Mischlinge* on the Aryan population.[19] Though these views hardly distinguished Winter from many other intellectuals of the period, their stridency attests to his early immoderation.[20]

In his first essays, Zessner-Spitzenberg presented a more reasoned assessment of contemporary developments, arguing for a "people's state [*Volksstaat*] with a monarch at its head." Ten years Winter's senior, the Bohemian-born Zessner-Spitzenberg had studied jurisprudence at Charles University in Prague and was a member of the Catholic umbrella organization, the Cartellverband (CV). He served in three governmental positions in the late imperial period and became a constitutional adviser during the Republic. Nevertheless, he expressed strong reservations about the new state. He lamented that the Austrian people had not had the opportunity to vote via referendum on their desired state form. Like Winter, he asserted the Habsburgs' unifying and civilizing mission in *Mitteleuropa*. Contrary to his later anti-*Anschluss* views, he viewed a federated union with Germany as a potential positive development. After nearly a century of Prussian domination of German affairs, "the time has come, when the more adaptable southern Germans...must bring their true German ideas of peaceful cultural exchange and combination to the people of the east."[21] Austria, as the Ostmark, was a vital part of

---

17. Ernst Karl Winter, "Mitteleuropa als Kulturfrage," *NR* 1 (1918–19): 30.

18. Ernst Karl Winter, "Moderner Kapitalismus," *NR* 1 (1918–19): 220.

19. Ernst Karl Winter, "Die Juden," *NR* 1 (1918–19): 273.

20. Holzbauer, "Ernst Karl Winter," 13–46. On Austrian anti-Semitism, see Pauley, *Prejudice to Persecution.*

21. Hans Zessner-Spitzenberg, "Dem ganzen Volk gebührt das Wort," *NR* 1 (1918–19): 132.

the greater German nation, prepared to assume Central European leadership through a process of cultural imperialism.

Despite invocations of Christian democratic values, Zessner-Spitzenberg fundamentally rejected the liberal democratic state. The product of the "victory of Freemasonry" and "materialistic-plutocratic republicans," the new republic affronted Christian values. "Social monarchy" was the best alternative to the atheistic "rule of the streets" and the "rule of the greedy." This entailed the reinstallation of the Kaiser as a people's tribune, who would stand above classes and interests and rule autocratically. Only social monarchy and its authoritarian power structure could subdue the unruly, terroristic masses of modern democracy and represent the "true Christian majority." While Zessner-Spitzenberg's ideas tended toward the traditional, he recognized that a simple return to the past was impossible. A direct confrontation with the new political order was necessary.[22]

Winter and Zessner-Spitzenberg sharpened their respective critiques of the Austrian state and intensified their call for a restored monarchy in the coming years. They responded directly to the disappointment, shared by most Austrian conservatives, with the republic, the Treaty of St. Germain in 1919, and the prohibition of *Anschluss* with Germany. The disavowal of monarchy and the commitment to a secular form of popular sovereignty in the Austrian constitution exacerbated the anger of Austrian conservatives.[23] Winter and Zessner-Spitzenberg both questioned the legitimacy of the new state while examining the permissible grounds for resistance against its authority. Winter posited two forms of opposition: passive, which constituted nonconformism and civil disobedience (*Nichtbefolgen*), and active, consisting of willful actions directed against the state (*Widerstreben*). Citing Thomas Aquinas, Winter argued for the permissibility of *völkisch* antistate action: "A defensive or active resistance of this sort is no revolt, no revolution, but the emergency defense of the collective. . . . A tyrannical regime is not right because it is not oriented to the common good but to the private well-being of those with power."[24] Winter believed that mass democracy possessed a tyrannical potential and that only authoritarian rulers went beyond the egotistic self-interest of individuals and tended to the *Volk*.[25]

Zessner-Spitzenberg's distaste for liberal democracy was even more evident. He claimed his objection to the republic derived more from historical

---

22. Ibid., 131.
23. Hanisch, *Die Ideologie des politischen Katholizismus*, 9.
24. Ernst Karl Winter, "Die Frage des Widerstandes gegen eine tyrannische Staatsgewalt," *NR* 1 (1918–19): 431.
25. Ibid., 432.

grounds than from religious and philosophical ones. On the first anniversary of the November revolution, he attacked the Republic as an "empty void" (*ein leeres Nichts*). Referencing the Treaty of St. Germain and the League of Nations, Zessner-Spitzenberg castigated the Entente and the world conspiracies of Jews and Masons for the ills that had befallen Austria: "With hate-filled consequences the Jewish-Masonic world league has slandered, undermined, and deformed the hated Christian Austria with its mission of unifying and reconciling peoples."[26] This revanchist commentary bears strong resemblances to the work of the Viennese philosopher and German nationalist Hans Eibl, with whom Zessner-Spitzenberg interacted in the social science branch of the Leo-Gesellschaft. Both men believed that once the peoples of the former Empire realized what they had lost, "a new Austria would be created by the people, out of a consciously turbulent will, through strenuous effort and experience."[27] Alternately vengeful and nostalgic, Zessner-Spitzenberg only grudgingly accepted the new state. Ironically, he invoked the liberal right to free speech to defend his illiberal position: he was not necessarily advocating for a "putsch, rebellion, or counterrevolution"; he merely wanted to "persuade" Austrians of an authoritarian course.[28] These views not only corresponded to Black Viennese ideas but also placed him in the mainstream of Central European conservatives, who yearned for the repudiation of the Paris Peace Accords.

Appeals to public opinion and procedural democracy did not satisfy Zessner-Spitzenberg: to maintain conservative support for the republic, he demanded authoritarian constitutional reforms. Contrary to later contentions, these proposals were calls not for decentralization or local autonomy but for centralized authority. Shortly after the grand coalition of the Social Democrats and the Christian Socials collapsed in August 1920 and Vienna asserted its independent state status, thereby assuring socialist control of the city, Zessner-Spitzenberg argued that a new government would never succeed without a strong president, elected directly by the people. This new executive would preside over legislative affairs and break parliamentary impasses. He likely had in mind a provision similar to article 48 of the Weimar Constitution. Although his rhetoric harked back to the Middle Ages and the decentralized rule of the Holy Roman Emperors, in practice a strong Caesarist executive was required, one who could flout democracy in

---

25. Hans Zessner-Spitzenberg, "Der Glaube an Österreich," *NR* 2 (1919–20): 102.

27. Ibid., 103.

28. Hans Zessner-Spitzenberg, "Zum Jahrestag der Kaiserverbannung," *NR* 2 (1919–20): 426.

the name of the people.[29] This new ruler could undertake a comprehensive corporatist transformation of state and society:

> Is the true people's will expressed through today's bleak voting machinery, where each voter is nothing other than an atom in a great, formless, disorganized and inorganic mass . . . ? Is it not time to allow the decision making of the people to take place in the zestful, viable communities comprised by trades [*Beruf*] and estates [*Stand*]? In other words, should we not once again return to the creation and recognition of corporately organized associations [*berufsständisch gegliederten Verbänden*]?[30]

These views situated Zessner-Spitzenberg within the corporatist discourse of the period, which enjoyed particular appeal in Central and Eastern Europe.[31] As political and economic conditions deteriorated in the early 1920s, Zessner-Spitzenberg grew more impatient: "The Austrian republic is no legitimate state! If we Catholics nevertheless respect and observe its organization, in no way do we accept its legitimacy."[32] Catholics should openly declare themselves "legitimists" and act in ways that facilitated the restoration of the Kaiser.[33] Zessner-Spitzenberg and the legitimists consequently rejected the involvement of Catholics in the political parties of the First Republic, since political involvement only perpetuated the system. This rejection of parliamentarianism distanced the Aktion members from the Christian Social party, which had grudgingly accepted the Austrian constitution and democratic procedures.[34] Winter spoke bitterly about the failures of modern European Catholic parties: "The so-called Catholic parties of the last century have fulfilled their purpose of representing the religious and cultural interests of Catholicism so badly that they deserve to disappear—they would not be missed."[35]

These early political statements repeatedly invoked the criticisms offered by Othmar Spann, situating these monarchists at the border between Catholic

---

29. On the tension between corporatist ideals and centralization, see Wohnout, "Chancellorial Dictatorship," 143–61.

30. Hans Zessner-Spitzenberg, "Grundsätzliches vor den Neuwahlen in Österreich," *NR* 2 (1919–20): 813.

31. Maier, *Recasting Bourgeois Europe*, ix–xvi, 3–18.

32. Zessner-Spitzenberg, "Grundsätzliches," 808. The terms "monarchist" and "legitimist" were used almost interchangeably. If anything, "legitimist" carried a more intransigent tone, since it demanded the end of the "illegitimate" Republic.

33. Hans Zessner-Spitzenberg, "Legitimität und Gemeinwohl," *NR* 3 (1920–21), 833–36.

34. Hanisch, *Die Ideologie des politischen Katholizismus*, 1–24.

35. Ernst Karl Winter, "Die katholische und die österreichische Aktion," in Knoll et al., *Österreichische Aktion*, 259.

conservatives and German nationalists. Spann's philosophy of totality stressed the need for hierarchical social and political organization. He condemned the ideas of liberalism, socialism, democracy, and individualism as the fruits of the French Revolution and demanded an immediate return to corporate society under the leadership of a führer. Identified as a quintessential figure in the German national *Lager*, Spann attracted widespread support from Catholic conservatives and nationalists alike. The future members of the Aktion operated within this constellation. Winter, August Maria Knoll, and Alfred Missong studied under Spann and participated in his weekly seminar. They interacted closely with one another until the end of the 1920s. Although Spann and the members of the Österreichische Aktion eventually opposed one another on National Socialism, they traveled a similar path of political and ideological engagement for a decade.[36]

Three major historical events confronted the inchoate legitimist movement in 1922, resulting in a more radical turn: the death of Kaiser Karl, Chancellor Ignaz Seipel's successful negotiation of a loan from the Entente, and the Fascist March on Rome. The loans stabilized the Austrian economy after a period of hyperinflation and lent credibility to the Christian Social-led government. This divided pro- and antidemocratic conservatives more sharply. The death of Karl cut deeply, for the legitimists viewed him as the key to maintaining continuity with the former Empire. At the time of Karl's death, the rightful heir, Otto, was nine years old. While the idea of a child emperor would not have been problematic if the monarchists had espoused a divine-right model of legitimacy, their concept of "social monarchy" did not easily permit such an eventuality. The legitimate kaiser was supposed to be the "people's tribune," a leader who could conscientiously address the needs of a modern citizenry in a rationalized social order. Advocating for the installation of a nine-year-old smacked of absurdity. Finally, the rise to power of the Italian Fascists demonstrated that the possibility of radical conservative transformation was real if a powerful movement could be started. Monarchists therefore redoubled their efforts to build an Austrian paramilitary force in the Heimwehr.[37] In response to these developments, the legitimist movement and its ideas about the Reich fundamentally changed. Before 1922, conservatives had invoked the Reich as much as a practical program as a Romantic one. The restoration of the Habsburgs did not necessarily entail a utopian return to the Holy Roman Empire. A restored Reich could replace the Republic, restoring the status quo ante bellum. After Karl's death, the

---

36. Holzbauer, "Ernst Karl Winter," 34–36, 83–84, 136, 159–77.
37. On early Heimwehr activities, see Edmondson, *Heimwehr,* chap. 1.

Reich was reimagined as an ideal space free from the evils of the modern world. The retreat into the abstract allowed the monarchists to ignore current conditions and advocate radical social and political programs. Henceforth monarchists found more common ground with radicalizing Black Viennese intellectuals, whether nationalist or Catholic.

As chapter 1 demonstrated, the radicals of Black Vienna enjoyed a new-found popularity in the mid-1920s in their scholarly societies, fraternities, and journals. A tectonic shift shook the conservative field in September 1925 when Eberle left *Das neue Reich* to begin a new journal, *Die schönere Zukunft.* This schism confronted intellectuals with a fateful choice about the direction of Austrian conservatism: should it be tied to political parties, working primarily within the system for incremental change, or should it espouse radical transformation? As chapter 7 shows, *Die schönere Zukunft* embraced a full break with democracy, abandoning the politics of the Christian Socials and distancing itself from the social activism of the Catholic Action for authoritarian and nationalist positions. *Das neue Reich,* with editors Aemilian Schoepfer and Johannes Messner serving as its ideological leaders, tentatively committed to the democratic process and Catholic Action. This divide—and the internecine struggle it precipitated—dictated conservative debates for the remainder of the First Republic, with radicals gaining the upper hand as early as 1927. Friedrich Funder, Eberle's former mentor, endorsed *Die schönere Zukunft* in the *Reichpost,* the influential conservative daily.[38] Most Black Viennese cultural organizations radicalized at this time. The Deutsche Studentenschaft advertised first with *Das neue Reich* but quickly switched allegiances to *Die schönere Zukunft.* Both the Leo-Gesellschaft and the Cartellverband turned from discussions of Catholic doctrinal matters to political ones. After barely surviving the war, the Leo-Gesellschaft regrouped by turning to Catholic scholars with German nationalist convictions, such as Spann, Hans Eibl, and the *Germanist* Josef Nadler.

Interestingly, the exodus to *Die schönere Zukunft* included the monarchists around Zessner-Spitzenberg and Winter, none of whom wrote for *Das neue Reich* again. Their ideas formed an integral part of Eberle's program for a "more beautiful future," and they participated in discussions with Spann and Eibl on the re-creation of a true German and Catholic Reich. Given their reputation for moderation or even "leftism," what surprises is that the Aktion chose to ally with Spann and Eberle. After all, both *Das neue Reich* and the Aktion claimed to support the teachings of the church. Winter even asserted

---

38. Friedrich Funder, "Ein Wort zum katholischen Pressewesen in Mitteleuropa," *SZ* 2 (1926–27): 453–55. See also Pfarrhofer, *Friedrich Funder.*

the Aktion's "parallelism to the Catholic Action," invoking Pope Pius XI's call to lay Catholics to advance Catholic teachings in social matters. He also harked back to Leo XIII's encyclical "Rerum Novarum" and referenced the Catholic imperative to transform society and help the working classes.[39] However, as the theologian Oswald Nell-Breuning noted, many Austrians misinterpreted these encyclicals, viewing them as calls for radical transformation and not gradual reform. The Aktion was guilty of this, too.[40]

These two competing interpretations of Catholic social theory derived from distinct traditions: *Sozialpolitik* and *Sozialreform,* with the Aktion and *Die schönere Zukunft* representing the latter trend. Representatives of *Sozialpolitik* advocated for incremental change within the existing order. They viewed the state and economy as matters of indifference; their mission entailed spiritual reform in the direction of the church. They permitted the formation of sectarian political parties and collaboration with non-Catholic organizations. An early exemplar was Bishop Wilhelm Ketteler, who participated in the revolution of 1848 and pressed for reconciliation between Catholics and Protestants. His teachings shaped Leo XIII's pronouncements in "Rerum Novarum."[41] *Sozialreform,* on the other hand, demanded a restoration of the organic order of the Middle Ages. The cornerstone of this approach was a return to corporate guilds and the end of modern capitalism. *Sozialreform* required a hierarchical social and political structure—in other words, the repudiation of liberal democracy. The leading representative of *Sozialreform* (and one of the heroes of the Aktion) was Karl Vogelsang, the Catholic publicist and politician.[42] A neo-Romantic theorist and staunch anti-Semite, the Prussian-born Vogelsang provided Viennese anti-Semitism with cultural legitimacy. He played a pivotal role in the foundation of the Christian Social movement. By the end of his life, Vogelsang was an ideological mainstay in the Austrian capital, bringing together an eclectic assortment of reactionary Catholics and anti-Semitic nationalists.[43]

The Aktion's antidemocratic turn makes more sense in light of its *Sozialreform* views. *Sozialreform* also helps explain the group's idiosyncratic interpretation of the Catholic Action movement. For them, the Christian Social

---

39. Winter, "Vorwort," 8–9.

40. Hanisch, *Die Ideologie des politischen Katholizismus,* 24.

41. Diamant, *Austrian Catholics,* 16–22. For an alternate view, see Boyer, *Political Radicalism,* 174–75.

42. Diamant, *Austrian Catholics,* 42–7; Winter, "Vorwort," 9.

43. Boyer, *Political Radicalism,* 166–80. Boyer points out a delightful irony about Vogelsang that also applies to the Österreichische Aktion: though he professed allegiance to a brand of Romanticism, Vogelsang's ideology hewed closer to the statist and Enlightenment politics of Joseph II.

party had taken a wrong turn when it departed from Vogelsang's ideology, instead adopting Karl Lueger's pragmatic program. Winter demanded that conservatives move away from the political opportunism of Lueger and toward Vogelsang: "Above all Vogelsang was the creator of a social program, which most fully realized the Catholic-sociological tradition of the nineteenth century.... In this sense one must work against the Lueger myth."[44] Lueger had merely produced a reformist party that had lost sight of Catholicism's social goals. As an homage to Vogelsang, Wilhelm Schmid named his monarchist journal *Das Vaterland,* after Vogelsang's conservative journal. Because of their *Sozialreform* tendencies, Winter and Zessner-Spitzenberg preferred to ally with "apolitical," antidemocratic thinkers like Spann and Eberle than with Catholics of more moderate convictions.

The Manifesto and the Creation of the Aktion Movement

The radicalization of the Black Viennese field partially accounts for the monarchists' controversial name choice of the group in 1926. The Österreichische Aktion referenced the Catholic Action and, more significantly, Charles Maurras's recently condemned Action Française. Declaring itself a parallel movement to the Catholic Action allowed the Österreichische Aktion to assert its Catholic bona fides. Nevertheless, the Aktion's overt antidemocratic stance and political advocacy went against Leo XIII's agnostic stance on the proper state form in "Rerum Novarum"[45] and Pius XI's introduction of the Catholic Action as a movement solely for social and educational reform.[46] By appealing to the integral nationalism and antidemocratic values of the Action Française, the Austrian monarchists found an ideological antecedent for their social and political aims in one of the founding movements of the European new Right. Arguably Europe's first fascist organization,[47] the Action Française wedded traditional monarchist ideas and exclusionary nationalism into a novel political program. Under the leadership of Charles Maurras, Action Française generated broad support in France and other Catholic countries.[48] The Österreichische Aktion saw itself as heir to this ideology.

---

44. Winter, "Das conservative und liberale Österreich," in Knoll et al., *Österreichische Aktion,* 122.
45. "Rerum Novarum," May 15, 1891, paras. 32–33.
46. "Ubi Arcano Dei Consilio," December 23, 1922, 52–53.
47. See Nolte, *Three Faces of Fascism.* Sternhell, *Fascist Ideology,* makes a similar argument.
48. On the impact of the Action Française, see Weber, *Action Française.* See also Payne, *Fascism in Spain,* 18–22.

The Aktion chose an inopportune time to show its commitment to the Action Française program, for the pope condemned Maurras and his movement in 1926 for its opportunistic and instrumental use of Catholicism for political purposes. It was also chastised for its dangerous effect on Catholic youth. The Austrians' decision to stick with their name indicated that their political commitment to authoritarian rule and nationalism at least equaled their allegiance to Catholic social theory. Moreover, in the wake of the tumultuous events of 1927—the contentious April elections, the Justizpalast fire in July, the rise of the authoritarian Heimwehr—the monarchists believed the time propitious for a radical statement of aims. Winter attempted to sidestep criticism from Catholics over the name choice by differentiating between the means and ends of the Action Française: the church "judged the theories of the Action Française in the here and now, not, however, the concept of French authoritarianism or legitimism."[49] According to Winter, the pope condemned Maurras for a lack of Catholic conviction, not for his political or social goals. Reconciling Catholicism and the Action Française allowed the Aktion to have its cake and eat it too: it could appeal to Black Viennese intellectuals on either Catholic or nationalist grounds.

The affiliation with Action Française also suggests how the monarchists' antinationalism and Europeanism should be read. While they rejected nationalism, that only meant particular variants—either Prussian militarist or French liberal. The German nationalism of Habsburg restorationists did not fit those molds. It resembled Maurras's historical and cultural understanding of the nation, which permitted some variation among individuals as long as they remained true to the traditional leader. As Zessner-Spitzenberg proclaimed, the "Austrian idea" was a supranational (*übernational*) one, grounded in a shared historical (i.e., Habsburg) experience, which did not recognize ethnicities or minorities.[50] Whether Hungarians, Czechs, Poles, or any other national groups within the former monarchy desired such an "Austrian" state was beside the point: the Austrian idea of unity was crucial for European civilization.[51]

---

49. Winter, "Vorwort," 8.

50. Hans Zessner-Spitzenberg, "Das Völkerreich des Hauses Österreich," in Knoll et al., *Österreichische Aktion,* 61.

51. Steinberg, *Austria as Theater,* 84–90, introduces the concept of "nationalist cosmopolitanism" to capture the conservative ideology of Hugo Hoffmannsthal. Members of Die Aktion did not embrace the values of the German *Aufklärung* in asserting their cosmopolitanism, but their notion of "tolerance," predicated on German superiority in a multiethnic Habsburg Reich, resembled Hoffmannsthal's.

The 1927 programmatic statement of the group demonstrates that its ideology aligned its members with radical conservatives elsewhere in Europe and those in the so-called Catholic and nationalist *Lager* in Austria. Their manifesto consisted of fourteen essays and distilled their views on Austrian and European history and social and political theory. They called for the restoration of Austria's prominence in the European community as a cultural and political bridge between east and west and between German and Catholic heritages. In this manner, Austria would help Europe overcome the "barbarism of the Northeast"—that is, Bolshevism—and the chauvinistic militarism and industrialism of Prussia.[52]

The Aktion's program rested on a particular understanding of German and Austrian history that chronicled the Holy Roman Empire and the decline of post-Reformation Western civilization through a religious and racial lens. Its narrative skirted the line between traditional anti-Jewish, xenophobic rhetoric and modern racial theory. The ethnographic work of Wilhelm Schmid and the anthropological studies of Friedrich Wilhelm Foerster and Hermann Muckermann served as the foundations for their anthropology. Schmid and Muckermann, two noted Catholic race theorists, stressed that the northern race of Germans had inherited Greek culture and drove world history.[53] Foerster emphasized the prehistoric unity of Austria, Bohemia, and Hungary. Winter, Missong, and Schmid elaborated these basic positions, employing racial categories in defending the superiority of Germans over other Europeans and in recognizing the importance of racial difference in creating a new European order. For the Aktion, the invasion of "Asiatic and African elements" set off an era of militarism and industrialism that destroyed the peaceful world of Central Europe. These "oriental" forces had a particular impact on northern Germanic culture, characterized by Armin of Westphalen's defeat of Marbod of Bohemia in 17 AD. Since then, northern German history had been dominated by militarism, nationalism, and Aryanism. On the other hand, the Habsburgs remained true to pacifist, federalist, and Roman traditions. They were the rulers who could unite the Romance West (France, Italy, and Spain) with the Habsburg center (Austria, Hungary, and Bohemia) and the Slavic East (Poland and Croatia).[54] These thinkers emphasized

---

52. Winter, "Vorwort," 5–6.

53. Edouard Conte, "Völkerkunde und Faschismus?" in Stadler, *Kontinuität und Bruch,* 239–40. On Muckermann and Schmid, see Connelly, "Catholic Racism," 821–22.

54. Ernst Karl Winter, "Der europäische und der österreichische Raum," in Knoll et al., *Österreichische Aktion,* 12–25.

the impossibility of reconciling Prussianism and Austrianism. Austria alone carried the responsibility of joining Europe under its authority.[55]

The restoration of Habsburg greatness meant more than a return of the Habsburgs—it was also a spiritual reorientation. To achieve this, ethnic Germans needed to reimagine their past in terms of a counterreformation. Winter had been engaged in this "revision of the German historical concept" (*Revision der deutschen Geschichtsauffassung*) since the beginning of the Republic, arguing—along with Richard Kralik—that Austrian history deserved priority in German history. It was the distinctively Catholic and conservative events of Austrian history that accounted for German national distinction. The Leo-Gesellschaft, Gralbund, and *Die schönere Zukunft* spearheaded these discussions involving Winter, Kralik, Eibl, Srbik, and the Graz professor Raimund Kaindl. Though these scholars differed in their chosen points of emphasis, they all deemphasized Prussian history and played up the importance of religion in German history. Even Srbik, the most nationalist of these historians, recognized that only an autonomous and fully integrated Austria could produce a rebirth of German culture.[56] For the Aktion, the previous centuries represented a fall from grace, when Prussian ideas corrupted the purity of the German idea. The Habsburg Empire had collapsed because the taint of Prussian nationalism destroyed the unity of the Habsburg peoples by encouraging separatism. The compromise of 1867, for example, had been a failure of liberal diplomacy, granting rights solely to Magyars and not to the other ethnic groups within the realm.[57] Only a return to the Counter-Reformation and the Baroque could reunite Central Europe. Through its historical program, Die Aktion crafted a palingenetic myth of Austrian Catholic greatness from Clovis through Charlemagne to the Habsburgs.

These historical and philosophical positions suggest a tolerant and internationalist approach to Central European politics; however, tensions lurked close to the surface of this ideology. In discussing the unity of the Habsburg crown lands, the monarchists turned a blind eye to the experiences of non-German subjects, neglecting the painful defeats at Mohács in 1526 and White

---

55. Ernst Karl Winter, "Die österreichische Idee in der Geschichte," in Knoll et al., *Österreichische Aktion*, 26–33.

56. Richard Kralik, "Die Entdeckungsgeschichte des österreichischen Staatsgedankens," *Kultur*, 1917, 68–75; Hans Eibl, "Die Stellung der Nation im christlichen Weltbild," *Kultur*, 1924, 28–35, and "Vom Sinne der deutschen Geschichte," *SZ* 2 (1926–7): 755–57, 773–74; Heinrich von Srbik, "Unmethodische Geschichtsbetrachtung," *SZ* 3 (1927–28): 104–6; Raimund Kaindl, "Professor Srbik und mein Buch *Österreich, Preußen, Deutschland*," *SZ* 3 (1927–28): 126–30. For Srbik's views on Austria's role in German history, see *Österreich*, 71–78.

57. Alfred Missong, "Österreichs Politik," in Knoll et al., *Österreichische Aktion*, 92–112.

Mountain in 1620 that resulted in the subjugation of the Magyars and the Bohemians to Habsburg hegemony. They disregarded the Hussite rebellion and Thirty Years' War, instead portraying the Habsburg lands as peacefully unified under Catholicism. Theirs was a distinctively German interpretation of Central European unity, which left no room for pluralist views on national belonging or religious diversity. Rejecting the liberal rights tradition, they refused minority groups or individuals any protection under the law: "The transnational [übernationale] state knows no minorities and therefore no mere minority protections since it bestows or at least strives for equality for all participating minorities."[58] They did not recognize equality before the law, so guaranteed protections made little sense. Local autonomy, guaranteed by a strong emperor, sufficed to protect minority rights. While they paid lip service to the rights of all nationalities, it was a German emperor who remained at the top of the hierarchy.

Moreover, the Aktion's condemnation of all other forms of international cooperation, from the League of Nations to Richard Coudenhove-Kalergi's Paneuropa movement, belied their pacifist and cosmopolitan claims.[59] This position reflected the resentment that Central European conservatives felt about the Paris Peace Accords and the heavy-handed economic policies of the League of Nations and the Western European financial sector in the early 1920s. It was only in late 1926 that the League of Nations freed Austria and Hungary from direct financial supervision, a demeaning and humbling experience for the former Habsburg crown lands. The Aktion could not make peace with liberal movements like the league, which privileged economic and political exigencies over cultural, historical, and religious factors. Alfred Missong, Othmar Spann's student and an editor of *Die schönere Zukunft*, argued that the goal should not be equality among nations but an organic grouping of unequal nationalities under the leadership of a kaiser and the Catholic Church. There was no room for the "Jewish and Masonic" League of Nations: "The league should be rejected on fundamental sociological grounds as one rejects the modern parliamentary-democratic state. The same considerations however recognize it as *a necessary evil to tolerate as one tolerates the democratic Republic of Austria.*"[60] The Aktion abided liberal solutions only until a time came when its true state could emerge.

---

58. Zessner-Spitzenberg, "Völkerreich," in Knoll et al., *Österreichische Aktion*, 68.

59. It was only after the *Anschluss* that the pan-European and monarchist movements found common cause. Otto Habsburg headed the Pan-European Union from 1973 to 2004.

60. Alfred Missong, "Europa," in Knoll et al., *Österreichische Aktion*, 53–55. Emphasis added.

To achieve those long-term ends, the Aktion advanced a new form of conservatism "that has the courage to stand with the Right and think with the Left."[61] This clever formulation, which implied a commitment to Austrian tradition and a concern for modern social and ethnic issues, revealed the movement's radical character. In contradistinction to Catholic social reformers who addressed the problems of industrial society practically,[62] these thinkers approached social problems with neo-Romantic conceptions of the economy, drawn mostly from Spann's universalism and Vogelsang's *Sozialreform* program. Their attempt to transcend the Right-Left divide of politics loosely resembled the "neither Right nor Left" quality of French and Italian fascisms, though it lacked the Marxist undercurrents of those developments.[63] The followers of the Aktion wrote enthusiastically about Mussolini and the Fascists, especially in *Das Vaterland*. The support for new Right movements extended beyond the Fascists to the radical branch of the Heimwehr, where the monarchists had their firmest support.[64]

The Aktion's idiosyncratic and fanciful concept of "de-proletarianization" (*Entproletarisierung*) most clearly demonstrates its radical, quasi-fascist conservatism and unwillingness to think with the Left. The group's proposals reveal a deficient understanding of modern industrial society and a naive faith in corporatist reform. Zessner-Spitzenberg argued that the restoration of the kaiser as the head of a "social monarchy" would correct the economic problems of modern Central Europe. He maintained that only autocrats could serve social justice since they stood above parties and interests. His reforms centered on traditional family policies: every family should have a house; fathers should receive a family wage; women should not work outside the home; and small firms and artisans should receive favorable treatment from the state. All these aims, he asserted, were incompatible with democracy, requiring instead a strong authority figure. Overall he displayed a disdain for proletarian workers, accusing them of libertinism and contempt for tradition.[65] Missong ventured similar proposals, demonstrating a greater concern for restoring authority than aiding workers. Protecting people from falling into the proletariat was the priority, not helping those already "lost" to

---

61. Winter, "Vorwort," 9.

62. Diamant, *Austrian Catholics,* 210–14.

63. Sternhell, *Neither Right nor Left.*

64. Wilhelm Schmid, "Wege und Irrwege der Heimatwehr," *VL,* 1931, 5–8. See Holmes, "Monarchists," 92–96.

65. Hans Zessner-Spitzenberg, "Kaisertum und Proletariat," in Knoll et al., *Österreichische Aktion,* 188–89, 192–94, 198–210.

that class.[66] Missong's program combined reactionary and fascistic elements into an expressly Austrian solution: saving and promoting small shopkeepers and artisans; building a "new middle class" (*Mittelstand*); and requiring large industries to serve the public interest. Though he described this as a "kind of socialism," his program resembled European national socialist and fascist plans instead. Missong's friendly comments about fascism belied his socialist claims.[67] The "leftist" proposals of the Aktion emphasized its authoritarianism more than a commitment to social justice.

Despite the stress on a "spiritual, social, cultural and historical mission," the members of the Aktion did not deny that their work also had a political aspect, which encouraged the replacement of liberal nation-states with authoritarian ones. This was not just an appeal to monarchism. Zessner-Spitzenberg endorsed a non-Habsburg dictator if it meant the restoration of the Austrian idea: "In case no royal house is available, then a dictator, provided he honestly strives for de-proletarianization...could be set up in the future."[68] These thinkers wanted to do away with the independence of the successor states and establish a true state under a führer figure. Although this position entailed a theoretical rejection of *Anschluss* with Germany, it was not categorical. While denying the legitimacy of a unified German Reich under Prussian leadership, the Aktion offered an alternative: "an absolute rejection of any *Anschluss* to Germany, as long as Austria is deprived of its transnational ties."[69] If Austria were reconnected with its Habsburg holdings, then a unification of all German peoples could be considered. All these statements reveal that the Aktion desired not the end of nationalism or the promulgation of a cosmopolitan league of European nations but an Austrian- and German-dominated conservative *Mitteleuropa*. These writings evince a will to power that went beyond mere cultural hegemony toward a distinctive brand of imperialist internationalism.

Though the Aktion presented itself as an isolated group of true conservatives, many Austrian and central European conservatives expressed similar chauvinist and nationalist viewpoints. In fact, their ideology enjoyed ready support from the Eberle and Spann circles. The Aktion gained a wide hearing at the Leo-Gesellschaft, where its movement originated, and the increasingly nationalist student fraternities of First Republic Austria. The Aktion's position on *Anschluss,* often presented as its signature position, found

---

66. Alfred Missong, "Entproletarisierung," in Knoll et al., *Österreichische Aktion,* 216–22.

67. Ibid., 233–34. Only Winter condemned Italian Fascism as a distortion of conservatism. See Winter, "Souveränität," in Knoll et al., *Österreichische Aktion,* 155.

68. Zessner-Spitzenberg, "Kaisertum und Proletariat," 213.

69. Hans Zessner-Spitzenberg, "Die Zukunft des Hauses Österreich," in Knoll et al., *Österreichische Aktion,* 290.

resonance in the work of the nationalists Eibl, Srbik, Kaindl, and other Catholic German supporters of *Reichsgedanken,* both in Austria and in Weimar Germany. The Aktion therefore represented a movement at the intersection of Catholic conservatism and German nationalism. The group's ideas, combining nationalism, conservatism, and Catholicism, served as a focal point of Black Vienna and Central European radical conservatism.

Fascism, Nazism, and the Evolution of Die Aktion

Despite increasing tensions, German nationalist and Catholic conservatives remained largely unified in their antidemocratic and authoritarian ways through 1930–31. The success of the Nazis in the 1930 election precipitated a schism within the conservative camp, yet it did not produce a renewed commitment to democratic Austria. Black Viennese intellectuals, including the Aktion, supported the increasingly fascist tenor of Austrian politics as the government cracked down on socialists, liberals, and minorities, increased the authority of the chancellor, and eventually suspended parliament. The Aktion engaged directly in politics only after the suppression of democracy in March 1933. Subsequent calls by the monarchists for democracy and the reconciliation of classes under Austrofascism rang hollow given the ideological and political support the monarchists lent to the new government, which they declared legitimate, not because it restored the previous imperial state—as their definition of legitimacy would have prescribed—but because it negated the "illegitimate" Republic.

Between 1927 and 1930, the Aktion expanded into a full-fledged movement, recruiting followers in periodicals, organizing youth groups, and establishing connections with German and Central European political groups. Alfred Missong, an editor of *Die schönere Zukunft,* ensured that his comrades appeared regularly in that journal. This was the height of the popularity of the Eberle journal with a circulation of twenty-five thousand weekly copies. Despite retrospective claims that he and Eberle differed in their orientations to Germany, Missong's output during this period does not confirm this.[70] Missong published a fiery defense of Catholic anti-Semitism in 1928 that disavowed racial anti-Semitism yet demanded a re-Christianization of European society to stave off the threats of Judaism, liberalism, and capitalism.[71]

---

70. Missong and Missong, *Christentum,* 27–29.

71. Alfred Missong, "Wie Karl von Vogelsang über die Judenfrage dachte," *SZ* 3 (1927–28): 816–19. On the blurred lines between Catholic and modern race theories, see Connelly, *Enemy to Brother,* chaps. 1–2.

Zessner-Spitzenberg engaged in a renewed historical discussion with Eibl and Kaindl, affirming the role of Austria within the German cultural realm.[72] Wilhelm Schmid not only edited *Das Vaterland* but also reached out to youth organizations throughout Central Europe. He forged ties with Anton Orel's nationalist and anti-Semitic Bundesvereinigung der freien christlichen Jugend Österreichs, the Bund der deutschen katholischen Jugend Österreichs, and the Vaterländische Studentenbund Ostmark. These youth groups stressed the importance of German Catholic tradition in European culture. *Das Vaterland* also established connections to the Heimwehr and propagated a new myth of the Austrian *Heimat*.[73] Given all these popular activities, the Aktion enjoyed considerable renown. Its founders consequently established the Aktion as an official public association in 1930.[74]

The timing of this move proved inauspicious, for Austrian conservatism had reached a crossroads with the emergence of National Socialism. In the early years of the Great Depression, the Nazis made significant gains in Germany and Austria. The German president Paul von Hindenburg suspended parliament and established the first of a series of authoritarian presidential regimes. The end of democracy in Central Europe seemed near at hand. In Austria, similar developments forced conservatives to decide whether to make peace with National Socialism. The ensuing debates centered on Spann and Eberle. At first, Aktion members turned to radical conservatives and fascists for allies. Knoll and Winter wanted to form a common anti-capitalist and antidemocratic league with Spann, Orel, and others;[75] however, Aktion members ran afoul of Spann over Nazism. Despite attempts at reconciliation, Spann openly criticized Winter in 1929 and blocked his attempts to habilitate at the University of Vienna. A look at the habilitation records reveals that the rector of the university and key members of the law faculty agreed with Spann's doubts about Winter's political reliability.[76] Spurning Spann's suggestion that he contribute to an Austrian Nazi newspaper, Winter sealed his academic fate and began his anti-Nazi agitation.[77] Relations between Missong and Eberle soured for similar reasons. In 1931 Eberle published a gently critical treatise on Hitler and National Socialism. Although he

---

72. Hans Zessner-Spitzenberg, "Der österreichische Gedanke und die deutsche Frage," *SZ* 3 (1927–28): 922–24.

73. *VL* 1 (1927): 1–21, 37–44, 63–64.

74. Holzbauer, "Ernst Karl Winter," 94–98.

75. Knoll wrote enthusiastically about this "conservative front." See Holzbauer, "Ernst Karl Winter," 84.

76. Universitätsarchiv, Universität Wien, J PA 434, box 23.

77. Holzbauer, "Ernst Karl Winter," 136–69.

rejected the pagan and anticlerical elements in Nazi ideology, Eberle did not blame the Nazis for their radicalism. He saw them as a product of a degenerate time. Though he hoped that the Brüning government would radicalize its efforts to combat liberalism, socialism, and Judaism, he applauded the Nazis for forcing these issues to the fore.[78] Missong could not abide these views. His *Nazispiegel,* one of the period's most incisive criticisms of the National Socialist movement, appeared pseudonymously, for Missong remained editor of *Die schönere Zukunft* until 1938. He began a shadow career, writing under various noms de plume in anti-Nazi publications.[79] It was in this period between 1929 and 1931 that the cultural field of the First Republic truly split into three distinct *Lager.* This was also the moment when monarchism became synonymous with anti-Nazism and Austrian patriotism.

With the exception of Winter, however, the conservative rupture did not lead to a reconciliation with prodemocratic forces. The members of the Aktion kept their distance from the Christian Social party until 1933, preferring to continue their two-front campaign against Marxism and Nazism—with Marxism still drawing the bulk of their attention. They did not side with moderate Catholics on social and economic matters either. During the debate over the 1931 papal encyclical "Quadragesimo Anno," the monarchists endorsed the radical interpreters in *Die schönere Zukunft.* In the "moment of truth for German Catholics," the Aktion preferred authoritarianism to Catholic unity if the latter meant accommodation with democracy.[80] When Chancellor Dollfuss dissolved parliament and barred its assembly in March 1933, the monarchists rejoiced. Missong portrayed the collapse of parliamentary democracy with delight, identifying the current situation as "salvation" for Austria. While he recognized that rule by emergency decree could not last indefinitely, he welcomed the moment when the state would overcome the "constraints on the construction of a regime, established by the parliamentary constitution." Moreover, he pressed for a *Ständestaat* that resembled Fascist Italy and the Estado Novo in Portugal.[81]

Of the monarchist ideologues, only Winter recognized the danger of maintaining authoritarian views. He shifted from a position straddling the German nationalist and Catholic conservative camps to one between democratic

78. Eberle, *Kampf um Hitler,* 3–5, 45–53.

79. Alfred Missong, "Mein Leben," in Missong and Missong, *Christentum und Politik,* 30–33; Leser, *Grenzgänger,* 111–29.

80. Johannes Messner, "Die Schicksalsstunde der deutschen Katholiken in der 'schönere Zukunft,'" *NR* 14 (1931–32): 540. See chapter 7.

81. Hugo Diwald, "Staatsgestaltung im Geiste der Quadragesimo Anno," *CS,* December 3, 1933, 15.

Christian Socials and the socialists. Several interrelated political and personal developments contributed to this transformation. As Winter struggled to complete his *Habilitation,* he turned to the Marxist philosopher Max Adler and the jurist Hans Kelsen for support. These men inculcated in Winter a respect for Enlightenment concepts of human dignity and rights.[82] Kelsen in particular instilled a respect for liberal legal norms and structures, challenging Winter's earlier Romantic ideas. Subsequently Winter defended the Austrian constitution for its rationality and fairness against attacks from the Right. He believed that only if everyone—from Communists to fascists—banded together in a popular front would Austria survive as an independent nation.[83] The newly published writings of the young Karl Marx also shaped Winter's development, convincing him of some of the merits of modern socialism. Instead of viewing Marx as a deterministic, scientist theorist, Winter now appreciated the socialist for his moral and ethical concerns. This fueled a reconsideration of Austro-Marxism, which, through its housing, education, and welfare initiatives, embodied much of that humanistic spirit. On the fiftieth anniversary of Marx's death in 1933, Winter delivered a lecture on the "new Marx," extolling the early Marx's virtues.[84] Winter made overtures to the Austro-Marxists, befriending Otto Bauer and Otto Neurath. These developments precipitated a fracture in the Aktion, for Winter publicly opposed the "coup d'état" (*Staatsstrich*) of Dollfuss and demanded an immediate return to democracy while the others embraced the new state.[85]

Winter and the other members of the Aktion benefited directly from the events of 1933–34. After the violent suppression of the socialists during the civil war of February 1934 and the official establishment of the Austrofascist state in May, each individual experienced professional and political success. Dollfuss appointed Winter the third vice mayor of Vienna, responsible for the reconciliation of the working class to the new state. His outreach efforts, dubbed the Aktion Winter, provoked angry responses within the Austrofascist community.[86] Zessner-Spitzenberg became a member of the Federal Council on Culture (*Bundeskulturrat*). Missong, still an editor at *Die schönere Zukunft,* also wrote for the state-sponsored *Christlicher Ständestaat.* August Maria Knoll habilitated in 1934 under Spann and served as

---

82. Ernst Karl Winter, "Die Staatskrise in Österreich," *WPB,* April 16, 1933, and "Die Krise des Marxismus," WPB, June 16, 1933.

83. Ernst Karl Winter, "Brief an den Bundespräsidenten," *WPB,* April 16, 1933, 18–31.

84. Holzbauer, "Ernst Karl Winter," 78–92.

85. Winter, "Brief."

86. Winter, *Arbeiterschaft und Staat.* On the Aktion Winter, see Holzbauer, "Ernst Karl Winter," 192.

the editor-in-chief of the "coordinated" populist paper, *Das kleine Blatt*. Schmid's Vaterländische Aktion, an umbrella group for youth and monarchist organizations, served as an inspiration for Dollfuss's new Fatherland Front. Each man received state patronage in the form of a governmental or cultural appointment. This revealed the latent politicism that undergirded their "neutral" ideology. Previously the Aktion had declared the movement apolitical; it was merely the politics of the First Republic that did not suit its ambitions, however.

During the early years of the *Ständestaat,* the members of the Aktion made little mention of legitimism or monarchism, reinforcing the belief that their previous political and philosophical logic had been largely instrumental. In setting aside their agitation for legitimism, the monarchists revealed their priorities: a strong Austrian state with an authoritarian führer that paid lip service to a Catholic, corporatist order. The monarchists focused their attention on combating Nazism and providing the new state with a solid ideological foundation. As chapter 7 will show, this involved a rearguard action against their former friends and colleagues, Joseph Eberle and Othmar Spann, which met with little success.

Monarchism, on the wane for several years, enjoyed a resurgence after the Schuschnigg–Hitler accommodation of July 1936, since it was one of the few movements that stood for Austrian independence. In agreeing to terms with Hitler, Schuschnigg embarked on a German nationalist course that eased the road to *Anschluss.* The monarchists sensed that the *Ständestaat* had failed to unify Austrians against the Nazis. Recognizing the failure of their previous ideological strategy, which had sought reconciliation with nationalists, Aktion members retreated from the political sphere and returned to their Romantic preoccupations. Schuschnigg accepted Winter's resignation in late 1936. Schmid's *Vaterland* limped along, appearing less frequently and with lower circulation after 1936. Missong withdrew from daily activities with *Die schönere Zukunft* and entered into a correspondence with Otto Habsburg.[87] Zessner-Spitzenberg attempted to reconstitute the Aktion by reaching out to the Austrian Academy, which led to a new publication and a few new supporters. Nevertheless, the project made no mention of democratic reforms or reconciliation with the Left, dwelling instead in a realm of Romantic fantasy.[88]

Winter alone reimagined the monarchist project, incorporating the lessons learned during the previous decade. In founding the Volksmonarchische Aktion, he acknowledged his earlier mistaken beliefs: the complicity of

---

87. Missong, "Mein Leben," 31–35.
88. Fellner, *Geschichtsschreibung,* 175–77; Wolf, Heilig, and Görgen, *Österreich.*

Catholic conservatives with German nationalists, the fundamental significance of a democratic Austria, and the need for the inclusion of all Austrians in shaping the future. In his program he made his new goals explicit:

1. For a free, independent Austria. The Austrian state, the Austrian people, Austrian culture can be assured only through the legitimate monarchy.... Neither politically nor morally annexed to Germany....
2. For cultural success, social freedom and political equality for workers.... The reestablishment of constitutional rights...
3. For a new democracy....
10. For the cooperation [*Zusammenarbeit*] of European peoples.[89]

Winter understood that the earlier efforts of the Aktion had undermined the group's goal of "legitimate monarchy" by privileging authority over all other programmatic points (democracy, rights, international cooperation, etc.) and by confusing authoritarianism with legitimacy. He hoped with his new program to attract all non-Nazi Austrian patriots, from Communists to fascists. Although this belated attempt attracted virtually no supporters, Winter's evolution represented a first step toward a potential postwar Austrian reconciliation between socialists and conservatives.

Fueled by staunch anti–Nazism and Austrian nationalism, the conservatives of the Österreichische Aktion waged a courageous ideological battle against Nazism in the mid-1930s. With the arrival of the Nazis in March 1938, they suffered a victim's fate: persecution, exile, imprisonment, and even death. Zessner-Spitzenberg was one of the first Austrians to die in a concentration camp. Winter fled Austria for Switzerland in 1938, continuing his Austrian and monarchist agitation in exile. The gestapo arrested Schmid and Missong. After their releases, they emigrated to Vatican City and Switzerland, respectively. Only Knoll remained behind, enduring inner emigration. The memory of their resistance and sacrifice is an important one in Austrian history. In recognizing the righteousness of the Aktion members' anti-Nazi stance, however, one must not forget the more problematic elements of their program: the rejection of democracy and the First Republic, the advocacy of dictatorial means, and anti-Semitic and German chauvinist social theories. Prior to 1938, and especially before 1934, the conservatives of the Aktion belonged to a larger group of perpetrators who waged war on socialists, Jews, and democrats, advocating ideas aligned with and inspired by radical European conservatism and fascism.

---

89. Holzbauer, *Winter*, 342–43.

The Austrian conservative intellectual field in the 1920s differed from that of the 1930s. Instead of three *Lager* vying for hegemony within a fragile republic, there were two blocs: a minority socioliberal one and a hegemonic Catholic-nationalist one. Austrian conservatives formed a coherent, if not unified, ideological bloc, with the monarchists at one of its crucial pivots. Though they were rhetorically unique, little distinguished the Catholic monarchists of the Aktion from their German nationalist compatriots during the 1920s and early 1930s. They belonged to the same scholarly organizations, wrote in the same journals, and attended the same social events, forming a unified Black Viennese field. While Catholic conservatives seemed to do most of the "border crossing" between *Lager,* the cases of Heinrich von Srbik and Hans Eibl, explored more later, demonstrate that German nationalists were also willing to embrace the conservatism of a new Right. Ideological disparities regularly arose within the latter camp, but their shared hostility to the modern democratic state and Jewish influences and their espousal of pan-German nationalism assured general harmony. The commitment to authoritarian solutions trumped all others until 1930, when the Nazi threat forced a reevaluation of earlier alignments. By the time they recognized the need for democratic unity and patriotism—Winter in 1933, the others years after—it was too late. The case of the Austrian monarchists reflects the difficulties conservatives had in coming to terms with the post–World War I order and the new Austrian state.

Prior to 1933, conservatives *en bloc* undermined their own state before succumbing to the Nazi threat. The Nazi era has obscured the configuration of the First Republic conservative cultural field. Prior to the rupture caused by emergent Nazism, however, the divisions within Black Vienna were minimal and easy to overcome. When forced to choose between liberal democracy and internationalism on one hand and authoritarianism and exclusionary Austrian nationalism on the other, most opted for the radicalism of the latter.[90] The Aktion and the members of the Black Viennese cultural field drew on influences from abroad in their attempts to refashion the Austrian social landscape. Their palingenetic myths of true Austrian and German culture and their counterrevolutionary demands made compromise with moderates and leftists impossible. Despite claims of apoliticism and patriotism, Austrian conservatives, including the Aktion, actively contributed to the destruction of the First Republic and indirectly facilitated the *Anschluss.*

---

90. On the exclusionary nature of Austrofascist conceptions of citizenship, see Thorpe, *Pan-Germanism,* chaps. 5–6.

CHAPTER 6

The Rise and Fall of Politically Engaged Scholarship in Red Vienna, 1927–1934

As the writers of the Österreichische Aktion celebrated Chancellor Dollfuss's suspension of parliament and Black Viennese intellectuals trumpeted the successes of Hitler, Mussolini, and radical conservatism across Europe, a group of Viennese social scientists released a landmark study to little fanfare. The team of Marie Jahoda, Paul Lazarsfeld, and Hans Zeisel published their "sociographical" work on the working-class textile town of Marienthal in March 1933. Commissioned by the Social Democratic Party and largely funded by the American Rockefeller Foundation, *Arbeitslosen von Marienthal* examined the impact of long-term unemployment on people's daily lives. The conclusions directly criticized Black Viennese economic concepts, like the Aktion's *Entproletarisierung,* which claimed that corporatism would rectify Austria's "social question." They also rejected austerity programs that reduced welfare services, which the bourgeois political parties promulgated and the Social Democrats grudgingly accepted. Finally, they confronted the Social Democratic leadership, arguing that the party was too conciliatory and not activist enough. The Austro-Marxists should not expect a sudden uprising of workers against bourgeois capitalism or radical conservatism, since persistent unemployment and economic hardship suppressed revolutionary urges. *Marienthal* was thus more than a scientific study: it was an appeal for a radical reorientation by socialists and progressives in the face of mounting economic and social problems.

In many ways, *Marienthal* was the first study of its kind, combining elements of psychology, sociology, history, anthropology, demography, and economics to produce a comprehensive picture of a community suffering from the lingering effects of the Great Depression. It drew upon the investigators' interdisciplinary exposure in the intellectual environment of Red Vienna, combining socialist activism with Freudian psychoanalysis, Adlerian and Bühlerian psychology, Austro-Marxist sociology and economics, and the philosophy of the Vienna Circle of logical empiricism. It paved the way for subsequent social scientific studies conducted by the Frankfurt School, among others. Not only did the researchers conduct quantitative analysis of economic and political data—per capita income, voter and union participation—but they also assembled time sheets from townspeople that listed their daily activities and the way they budgeted their time. They immersed themselves in the town for nearly a year, distributing questionnaires and performing interviews with thirty families to gain firsthand knowledge of personal experiences and the town's inner workings. This added a qualitative element to their work.[1] *Marienthal* derived its richness from the waxing Marxist-progressive intellectual synthesis of Red Vienna, which had developed since the turn of the century and reached a peak in the late 1920s.

Given the robustness of the intellectual context within which the study originated and the extensiveness of the gathered data, the research bore fascinating fruit, producing a typology of responses to enduring immiseration and a startling revelation about the deleterious effects of poverty on political radicalism. The findings undermined traditional Marxist assumptions about the relationship between increasing poverty and the socialist revolution. Instead of finding a causal connection, the investigators argued for an inverse relationship between economic suffering and radicalism. Jahoda, Lazarsfeld, and Zeisel identified four categories of unemployed families (in order of increasing misery): unbroken (*ungebrochen*), resigned (*resigniert*), despairing (*verzweifelt*), and apathetic (*apathisch*). Of the 478 families in Marienthal, 23 percent were unbroken, 69 percent resigned, and only 8 percent broken—with 5 percent apathetic. The researchers noted that the number of broken families was on the rise, yet Marienthal endured hardship with remarkable resilience.[2] Despite the generally positive morale of the Marienthaler, the authors came to a startling and disappointing conclusion about the people's waning power of resistance (*Widerstandskraft*) to economic problems

---

1. For an overview of the study, see Christian Fleck, introduction to Jahoda, Lazarsfeld, and Zeisel, *Marienthal* (2002), vii–xxx.

2. Jahoda, Lazarsfeld, and Zeisel, *Marienthal,* 47–51.

and conservative policies. They found a direct correlation between monthly income and family disposition: the "wealthier" the family, the more likely it was unbroken; the poorer, the more apathetic it became. The final paragraph was part scientific conclusion and part moral exhortation:

> [W]e had the opportunity to present to the reader a few of the people with whom we have had such intimate contact these last months. With that we have come to the limits of our investigation and our methodology, which was directed to the general and characteristic. We stepped foot in Marienthal as scientists: we left with the wish that the tragic chance that provided grounds for such an experiment will soon be removed from our time.[3]

This was an urgent call for an end to economic hardship. It was also a wake-up call to the Social Democrats. The Marienthal scholars warned the Austro-Marxists that socialist revolution would not follow from economic immiseration. The socialists would lose their base, both in the working class and among progressive intellectuals, if conditions persisted and politicians stood idly by.

The publication and reception of the Marienthal study in Vienna revealed the frayed relations between the Austro-Marxists and their erstwhile supporters. Although the study was initially commissioned by the Social Democratic Party, its affiliated presses did not publish the book. The book was published in psychologist Karl Bühler's series, thereby limiting its circulation. The Austro-Marxist leader Otto Bauer, who inspired the study, did not endorse the project publicly. In fact, he never mentioned it. In total, only two reviews appeared in Austria, which was one fewer than in the United States, one fewer than in the city of Leipzig, and five fewer than in Germany overall.[4] It seems that the findings of the study—that political radicalism declined with increasing unemployment and poverty and that the socialists had not done enough to address the plight of Marienthalers—led the Austro-Marxist leadership to keep a critical distance from it.

The Marienthal example—its origins, findings, and reception—illuminates the waxing and waning of Marxist-progressive collaboration in Red Vienna in the late 1920s and early 1930s. Initially, progressive intellectuals saw the Austro-Marxist movement as the defender of the First Republic, of Enlightenment values, and of academic freedom, and they flocked to its ranks. As

---

3. Ibid., 88.
4. For a complete list of reviews, see http://agso.uni-graz.at/marienthal/bibliothek/rezensionen/07_03_00_00_Rezensionen.htm.

earlier chapters showed, this culture reached a climax in the late 1920s, when the "Announcement of Intellectual Vienna" appeared and the Verein Ernst Mach began its public phase. The mature Red Viennese cultural field was the product of a long evolution that benefited from the radicalization of Viennese intellectuals. Scholarship and socialism interpenetrated, transforming Vienna into a hothouse of interdisciplinary research. While traditional intellectuals eluded the Social Democrats, by the election of 1927 the socialists had assembled an impressive constellation of progressive thinkers in analytic philosophy, psychoanalysis, psychology, and the natural and social sciences. Through 1931, these intellectuals produced works that not only advanced their respective fields but also contributed to the socialist cause. Intellectuals were at the core of the great Red Viennese socialist experiment. The chapter suggests that it was not only Black Viennese scholarship that politicized and radicalized during the interwar era. We must therefore take seriously the political valences of the scientific output of Red Viennese intellectuals.[5]

While scholarship on Red Vienna has often emphasized the monolithic and unchanging aspects of the milieu, this chapter argues—alongside other recent scholarship—for the fluidity and historical contingency of this cultural field.[6] The Marxist-intellectual synthesis began to unravel around 1930 for a number of reasons. Red Viennese intellectuals intensified their calls for social and political transformation, even as the Social Democrats hesitated in the face of mounting pressure from fascists and conservatives. Unfortunately, the Austro-Marxists had become increasingly immobile after the 1927 Justizpalast fire. The Great Depression, mounting nationalism and anti-Semitism, and emergent fascism all contributed to the urgency of the situation. Without a coherent plan of action, the Austro-Marxists devoted much of their time to maintaining party discipline and defusing opposition movements. This led to growing alienation within the trade unions, youth organizations, and other groups with which Red Viennese intellectuals consorted.[7]

This process of politicization and radicalization was a dynamic one, subject to outside social, economic, and political developments. The Marienthal study demonstrated that intellectuals increasingly despaired about Austro-Marxist policy and theory and demanded a more muscular response to conservative counterforces. About half a decade later than Black Viennese

---

5. See Kraft, *Vienna Circle* and Gay, *Freud.* On this depoliticization, see Stadler, *Vienna Circle,* 12, and Reisch, *Cold War,* 191.

6. See Leser, *Zwischen Reformismus;* Leser, *Geistiges Leben;* Glaser, *Austromarxismus;* Stadler, "Spätaufklärung." Timms, "Cultural Parameters," and Stadler, *Studien zum Wiener Kreis,* argue for a more dynamic, historicized approach to Viennese intellectual history.

7. On left-wing affiliations and the subsequent alienation, see Rabinbach, *Crisis,* 32–79.

intellectuals, Red Viennese thinkers acknowledged that political parties might not provide an adequate defense for their values or ideas. They did not all respond to this crisis in the same fashion. One can identify several different reactions: some retreated into scholarly pursuits yet remained tacitly loyal to their earlier social and political visions (Lazarsfeld, Zeisel, Hans Kelsen, Alfred Adler); others, undaunted, plotted new courses, radical yet critical of the Bauer-led movement (Neurath, Jahoda, Wilhelm Reich, Manes Sperber and Ilona Duczynska); a final class resignedly accepted events as they came, including going along with the Austrofascists as the lesser of two authoritarian evils (Sigmund Freud, Moritz Schlick, and Karl and Charlotte Bühler). Before the destruction of the First Republic, before the *Anschluss* and World War II, and before the depoliticization that accompanied emigration, the concept of intellectual activism for these Viennese intellectuals underwent a critical shift, one that demonstrated the remarkable diversity *and* the tenuousness of the Red Vienna project in the late Republic.

The Marxist-Intellectual Synthesis of the Early Republic

The hothouse intellectual environment of Red Vienna, which produced the politicization of progressive science, resulted from a combination of personal, historical, and intellectual factors. As discussed earlier, the Austro-Marxists effectively reached out to the progressive intellectual circles of Vienna in the first years of the Republic, a process that culminated in the "Kundgebung des geistigen Wiens," an open letter signed by forty leading Viennese intellectuals that endorsed the Social Democratic party and its policies prior to the 1927 election. The significance of the signers (including Freud, Adler, Bühler, and Kelsen) increases when one considers that these men and women represented larger intellectual movements. Scholars of Austro-Marxism have highlighted the nondogmatic socialism of the movement's theoreticians and its pluralist epistemological views as attractive elements for progressive intellectuals, yet this only partially explains the phenomenon.[8] There was also a shared commitment to social reform that stemmed from their Enlightenment humanist values and a similar reaction to the hardships of the Great War. In particular, the socialists were the lone (albeit reluctant) patrons of Jewish intellectuals, whose involvement was resisted by other scholarly and political

---

8. Glaser, *Austromarxismus,* 33–76, 111–38; Bottomore and Goode, *Austro-Marxism,* 1–44.

associations.[9] A lack of opportunities in the conservative academy led intellectuals to band together in socialist-supported institutes and in salons and other organizations that welcomed "outsiders."[10] Most important, however, were the close personal connections between these members of the educated classes with each other and with Austro-Marxist leaders like Otto Bauer and Max Adler. Marie Jahoda—a personal friend of Bauer's, student of the Bühlers, coworker of Otto Neurath, and follower of the socialist Freudian Siegfried Bernfeld—represents this phenomenon aptly. As she noted in her biography, "In my Austrian time there was no one in my inner circle who was not at least a Socialist sympathizer."[11]

After 1918, the psychoanalytic movement hewed more closely to Austro-Marxism, in large part because of the activities of Paul Federn, Helene Deutsch, Siegfried Bernfeld, and Wilhelm Reich. Psychoanalysts viewed their discipline as an empirical science and *Geisteswissenschaft* that explored the nature of the human spirit and offered assistance to those who suffered. The shift to social activism began at the top with Freud himself. The Freudians committed themselves to social reform projects in 1918 when Freud announced that psychoanalysis had a duty to help the unfortunate.[12] Freud required that therapists devote one-fifth of their time to treating poor patients pro bono, and he encouraged the establishment of free clinics for working-class citizens across Europe. Freud's postwar output also underwent a sociological shift. While he continued to refine his psychological theories, the Great War prompted him to look at the underlying social forces that produced (and destroyed) civilization. In the works *Future of an Illusion, Group Psychology and the Analysis of the Ego,* and *Civilization and Its Discontents,* Freud focused more on group dynamics and criticized negative features of modern civilization. Most important, he attacked religion as a reaction to infantile helplessness and explained civilizational development as a process of sublimation of libidinal drives. His critical stance on religion, calls for rational restraint of the impulses, and Enlightenment humanism dovetailed with similar positions in the Austro-Marxist movement. His close relations with Victor Adler, Julius Tandler, and Josef Friedjung contributed to this burgeoning allegiance.

9. On the relationship between Jews and socialists, see Wistrich, *Socialism and the Jews.* See also Hacohen, *Karl Popper,* chap. 7.

10. "Outsider" is defined by Peter Gay in *Weimar Culture* as "Jews, democrats, socialists."

11. Jahoda, *"Ich habe die Welt,"* 36.

12. Danto, *Freud's Free Clinics,* 1–33.

Particularly important were the new social and sexual hygiene programs, which employed sexual knowledge in novel ways.[13]

Freud spearheaded a group of engaged intellectuals, yet he was also perhaps the least radical. It was his colleagues and disciples who regularly collaborated with the Austro-Marxists in social reform and educational projects, thereby politicizing the psychoanalytic movement. They also approached other social and cultural organizations and began to build a network of activist intellectuals. Paul Federn, one of the earliest members of Freud's circle, provided an early example. In 1919 he presented a lecture for a joint session of the Monist League and the Psychoanalytical Union, entitled "Vaterlose Gesellschaft," that he later published as *Zur Psychologie der Revolution.* The venue is important for, as we have seen, the Monist League was itself in the process of radicalization. Federn's lecture touched on a subject of major significance to the Viennese in the immediate wake of the war. With tens of thousands of Viennese fathers killed during the Great War, there were real concerns about a crisis of patriarchal authority and masculine virtue. The loss of the symbolic father figure, the Emperor, also loomed large. Federn addressed the problem of paternal authority from the vantage point of Freudian psychoanalytic categories, arguing for an embrace of a new revolutionary society.[14]

Federn welcomed the recent Central European revolutions as confirmation of Freud's sociological theories and expressed a hope for further transformative advances. Applying the phylogenetic theories Freud had advanced in *Totem and Taboo,* Federn argued that Austrian and German society had reached a crucial world-historical juncture, when paternal authority had to be replaced by fraternal cooperation. The "sons" (the masses) had killed the tyrannical father (the monarch) and had established a new social order based on equality. Federn embraced the new Austrian republic as a step forward in civilizational development. He maintained that a deeper understanding of Freud's principles would allow politicians to harness the will of the people and steer a course out of the respective crises of the Great War, masculinity and paternal authority.[15] Although Freud's lessons possessed a universal applicability, Federn believed that it was the Austro-Marxists and the proletariat who could best deploy his theories. "The same people who had long adapted to the powers that be, suddenly became insatiable, craving a renewal and demanding a rapid tempo of revolution. . . . This revolutionary radicalism

---

13. See McEwen, *Sexual Knowledge;* Logan, *Hormones, Heredity, and Race;* and Weindling, "A City Regenerated" on these evolving discourses.

14. Healy, *Vienna,* 258–62.

15. Ibid., 292–99.

was realized in the worker and soldier councils. . . . The political and social struggle must be taken up on their terms, if it is going to be won in favor of democracy against the dictatorship of the proletariat."[16] This statement showed Federn's approval of the Social Democratic party line that the best way to avoid the mistakes of the German Left was to wrest control of the soviets from the Bolsheviks through democratic means. Federn believed that the Austro-Marxist commitment to democracy and social reform provided the best answer to the authority vacuum produced by the dissolution of the Habsburg monarchy. At the core of this socialist transformation lay Austro-Marxism and Freudian theory.[17]

As Federn drew parallels between the emergence of proletarian class consciousness and Freudian patricide and embraced socialist leadership, his psychoanalytic colleagues focused on compatibilities between psychoanalysis, women's rights, and educational reform. Helene Deutsch, one of Freud's favorite students, contributed to Austro-Marxist publications like *Der Kampf,* lending her expertise on the psychology of working women to discussions of capitalist exploitation.[18] In the postwar years, she recommitted to the cause when she witnessed the suffering of the working class in Vienna and Berlin. She characterized her interwar involvement as "revolutionism," an attitude that embraced all that was new and recently won.[19] This attitude drove many of her colleagues too, providing the impulse behind the two Freudian free clinics, the polyclinic in Berlin and the Ambulatorium in Vienna.

The socialist vision of antiauthoritarian secular education attracted Freudian educators. As discussed earlier, Otto Glöckel, the driving force behind the school reform movement, advocated a strict separation of church and state in the classroom. He called for a turn away from the "drill school" pedagogical model to a more democratic one based on the collaboration of teachers, parents, and students.[20] Max Adler reinforced this position in his popular work *Neue Menschen,* in which he argued that nonrepressive education would produce a new type of individual. "*Neue Menschen!* That is the real goal of a revolutionary education, of an education that realizes the new society in the soul of each individual, which otherwise remains a mere objective possibility for realization because of the economic process."[21] This stance, combining socioeconomic analysis with pedagogical innovation, enjoyed a

---

16. Federn, *Psychologie der Revolution,* 2–3.
17. Ibid.
18. See Roazen, *Helene Deutsch.*
19. Deutsch, *Confrontations with Myself,* 82, quoted in Danto, *Freud's Free Clinics,* 3, 31.
20. Glöckel, *Drillschule, Lernschule, Arbeitsschule.*
21. Adler, *Neue Menschen,* 48. See also Glaser, *Austromarxismus,* 317–22.

broad resonance in progressive circles, as most thinkers recognized the need for public reform and assistance for Austrian youth.

August Eichhorn and Siegfried Bernfeld in particular took up the Austro-Marxist call for change. Aichhorn's engagement with the Freudian and Austro-Marxist movements emerged in the immediate postwar period. Previously he had conducted child welfare work in independent organizations. The Freudian focus on the power of unconscious drives for the treatment of neuroses became an effective tool for his work. So did socialist patronage.[22] Aichhorn's work with delinquent youth in Ober-Hollabrun and St. Andrä between 1918 and 1922 convinced him of the need for a new educational system, one that deemphasized discipline and stressed positive reinforcement. This social work culminated in the 1925 book *Wayward Youth,* which served as a manual for Austro-Marxist delinquent centers in Vienna. Freud wrote the book's introduction.

Siegfried Bernfeld, a leader in both the socialist and Zionist youth movements, also reconciled his revolutionary educational ideas with Marxism and psychoanalysis. Bernfeld ran summer camp colonies for Viennese youth; after the war he established a home for displaced proletarian youth. He became an inspirational figure for socialist youth such as Lazarsfeld, Zeisel, Jahoda, Reich, and the psychoanalyst Otto Fenichel. Like Aichhorn, he became more interested in psychoanalysis during the First Republic as he sought to make his education theory more scientific. The original intellectual foundations stemmed from a Marxian critique of capitalist society. He made this commitment explicit in his 1925 pedagogical work *Sisyphus:* "The school has its origin in the economic, financial, political forces of society and in the ideological requirements and cultural valuations that reflect those forces. It has its roots also in the nonrational views and valuations that are the unconscious product of the relations between the generations and of the prevailing class structure. Whatever direction these forces may take, they are more likely to deflect from than to aid the attainment of instructional objectives."[23] He argued that class society prevented children from all walks of life from enjoying the fruits of *Bildung.* Bernfeld explored these concerns in Marxist publications (*Der Kampf* and *Der sozialistische Arzt*) and psychoanalytic journals (*Die Zeitschrift für internationale Psychoanalyse* and *Imago*). He also played an active role training other analysts at the Viennese Psychoanalytical Union. Bernfeld's bona fides as both an activist and analyst led Freud to suggest him for a position in Berlin, though he remained involved in Vienna. Bernfeld's

---

22. Aichhorn, *Verwahrloste Jugend,* 10–23.
23. Bernfeld, *Sisyphus,* 16–17. On Bernfeld, see the preface by Peter Paret, ix–xxvii.

disciples—in psychoanalytic and youth organizations—played decisive roles in the leftist opposition to the Austro-Marxists in the 1930s.[24]

Otto Fenichel, Wilhelm Reich, and Eduard Hitschmann, the driving force behind the Ambulatorium,[25] were all products of Bernfeld's instruction. Reich, who had little initial concern for politics, became more engaged as a result of his training with Bernfeld. In 1920, he joined the Vienna Psychoanalytic Society, disseminating Freud's teachings among his university colleagues. Although his focus remained on "the politics of everyday life," Reich sought to alleviate the economic and social pressures placed on people and their sexuality. The founding of his Sex-Hygiene Clinics in 1922 and his later Sex-Pol work stemmed from these revolutionary social concerns. He often found support from the Viennese municipal government.[26]

There was much that recommended the Austro-Marxists to the Freudians in the early years of the Republic: their commitment to social welfare and education reform and their willingness to embrace new approaches to social questions. It also helped that leading members of the Red Viennese reform efforts either were well acquainted with Freud from the University of Vienna (Julius Tandler) or were practicing Freudians themselves (Josef Friedjung). This was not a marriage of convenience either; each side believed in the mission of the other. A look at interwar psychoanalytic journals demonstrates a growing concern with economic and social inequality. The main contributors to the *Internationale Zeitschrift für Psychoanalyse* and *Imago* were part of this Marxist-Freudian synthesis: Bernfeld, Deutsch, Hitschmann, Federn, Fenichel, Friedjung, and Reich. Although many of their articles were clinical or theoretical, the book and article reviews—such as Henrik de Man's "On the Psychology of Marxism," Fenichel's "Psychoanalysis and Socialism," and Reich's "Dialectical Materialism"—focused on topics of social and political interest. Articles discussed the role of psychology and psychoanalysis in socialist and democratic politics and suggested ways to enrich socialist discussions with Freudian insights. The Freud-Marx fusion in Austria and Germany was no accidental alliance; it represented a shared social, political, and intellectual commitment.

Similar affiliations developed between the Austro-Marxists and the individual psychologists around Alfred Adler and the empirical psychologists in Karl and Charlotte Bühler's circle, respectively. Like the Freudians, these groups had an interest in developmental and child psychology and hence

24. Rabinbach, *Crisis,* 59–79.
25. Danto, *Freud's Free Clinics,* 3, 9.
26. Ibid., 78, 115–20.

educational reform. They also believed that their ideas could help reshape a sick postwar world. Adler and the Austro-Marxists early found common cause, since both groups emphasized the role of environmental factors in developing individual character traits.[27] Influenced by his radical socialist wife, Raissa, who was in contact with exiled Russian revolutionaries after 1905, Adler developed distinctly socialist views in the prewar years. Even as his political attitudes shifted rightward during the First Republic, his students Manes Sperber, Alice and Otto Ruehle, and others picked up the Marxist banner.[28] Additionally, Sophie Lazarsfeld, Paul's mother, was an Adlerian who frequently contributed to socialist publications. She played a leading role in the evolving discourse of sexual knowledge in interwar Vienna.[29] She also hosted an influential salon, one that regularly included Otto Bauer, Friedrich Adler, Otto Neurath, and Karl Polanyi. Adlerian psychology gained a wide hearing in Red Vienna, for Adler lectured at the city-run Pedagogical Institute and helped establish a network of over twenty educational guidance clinics with the support of the municipal government. These centers provided a forum for parents, teachers, and students to deal with classroom problems or delinquent behavior.[30]

The Pedagogical Institute served as an important meeting point for Austro-Marxists, Adlerians, and Bühlerians. Founded in 1922 under the auspices of the Viennese city government and the University of Vienna, the institute quickly became a center of interdisciplinary interaction and radical reform, showcasing the politicization of progressive science. A subdivision of the Pedagogical Institute was the Bühlers' Psychological Institute, a center for empirical psychological and sociological research. In these forums, scholars lectured, engaged in discussion, and conducted research on child psychology, language acquisition, and pedagogical techniques. The Pedagogical Institute, along with the affiliated *Volkshochschulen,* provided a haven for embattled scholars from the increasingly conservative university. Lectures were not restricted to psychology; the jurist Hans Kelsen and the sociologist Wilhelm Jerusalem also worked with the institute.[31] Kelsen moved closer to the Austro-Marxists during the first years of the Republic because of their shared commitment to the new democratic state. Jerusalem, founder of the

27. See Logan, *Hormones, Heredity, and Race,* chap. 7. Logan downplays the commonalties between Adler's and Tandler's developmental theories, yet they were both interested in understanding the intersection of individual and social progress.

28. Stepansky, *In Freud's Shadow,* 210.

29. McEwen, *Sexual Knowledge,* 96–8, 110–13.

30. Ibid., 208–17.

31. Benetka, *Psychologie in Wien,* 19–21.

Austrian Society of Sociology and a member of the Monist League, discussed the sociology of education, empirical science, and American pragmatism.[32]

Institutional affiliations established through the collaboration of the Red Viennese intellectuals and socialists tell only part of the story of the Marxist-intellectual synthesis, for interpersonal relationships contributed significantly to the politicization of Red Viennese culture. Individuals involved in one field were often aware of developments in others through collaboration in political and cultural organizations. A willingness to engage critically with other methodological viewpoints characterized this hothouse culture, enriching all fields and providing the foundation for Red Vienna's reform agenda in the early Republic.

Interdisciplinary Interactions and the Radicalization of Thought

During the 1920s, Red Viennese intellectuals embraced interdisciplinarity in their scholarly endeavors. The expansion of opportunities to explore and apply scientific knowledge within socialist-sponsored vehicles produced a radicalization of science. Psychology in particular benefited from this vibrant environment. Karl Bühler's work provides an example of this new broadmindedness, while his students' output points to the radicalization that occurred in the application of new approaches. Bühler moved with his wife, Charlotte, from Germany in 1922 to take a professorship. Their school of psychology was the third in the capital. This made him acutely aware of the tensions within his own discipline. He likened the discipline of psychology to the Tower of Babel. Despite these difficulties, he viewed the crisis not as one of decline (*Zerfallskrise*) but as one of construction (*Aufbaukrise*), believing that the various subdisciplines could assemble their knowledge and reap the benefits. Bühler endeavored to show the common intellectual origins of the various traditions of thought embodied in contemporary psychology, offering a holistic vision of the field. A tour de force survey of the psychological landscape, his 1927 *Crisis of Psychology* had two main aims. First, he wanted to find a set of rules that would allow one group of scientists to examine the work of others through a system of verification. Invoking the verificationist techniques of the Vienna Circle of logical empiricism, his model enabled him to find scientific merit in other branches. Despite his criticisms of psychoanalysis, for example, he maintained that Freud was

---

32. Ludwig Nagl, "Jerusalems Rezeption des Pragmatismus," in Benedikt et al., *Totalitarismen*, 352.

one of the great system-builders in modern psychology and an absolutely first-rate "materialist thinker" (*Stoffdenker*). He believed Freud's theorizing belonged to the field of psychology as long as it was confirmed, as some of his research on drives had already been.[33] Second, Bühler argued for the unification of diverse scientific branches such as biology, sociology, and psychiatry, suggesting that the combined efforts of scholars would greatly advance human society.[34] He hoped to discover a monistic "logical-epistemological" philosophy of observation. This quest for holism paralleled similar efforts by the Vienna Circle, especially Bühler's University of Vienna colleague Moritz Schlick, along with Rudolf Carnap and Otto Neurath. In offering a liberal vision of scientific unification, Bühler's model counteracted the epistemological claims of Othmar Spann's philosophical school, whose emphasis on holism led to exclusion, chauvinism, and repression. It placed him centrally in the ongoing debates in Europe over the possibility of holistic science.[35]

Like their mentor, Bühler's students embraced an ecumenical approach that permitted social and political applications of interdisciplinary theories. In Paul Lazarsfeld's first monograph, *Jugend und Beruf,* he balanced the influences of Bernfeld, Freud, Alfred Adler, and the Bühlers in a study of proletarian youth. Charlotte Bühler had conducted extensive research on middle-class adolescents, but Lazarsfeld felt that working-class children underwent a qualitatively different formational experience. Influenced by Bernfeld's belief that these individuals had a lower level of aspiration and by Adler's focus on inferiority feelings, Lazarsfeld constructed a new type of social psychological investigation.[36] He also drew inspiration from thinkers outside psychology. In his memoir, he noted that Friedrich Adler, Ernst Mach, Henri Poincaré, and Albert Einstein had profoundly shaped his idiosyncratic approach. Although he denied any direct contact with members of the Vienna Circle in the early 1920s, their shared methodological interests permitted future collaborations in the Pedagogical Institute and Verein Ernst Mach.[37] Marie Jahoda became acquainted with the logical empiricists in the late 1920s when she worked at Otto Neurath's Social and Economic Museum. Neurath's work on pictorial statistics impressed her because of its ability to convey complex information in a simple, graphical fashion. She became involved in a student group for scientific cooperation, established by Carnap. In addition to the Bühler students Lazarsfeld, Jahoda, Zeisel, and

33. Bühler, *Krise der Psychologie,* 162–200.
34. Ibid., 1.
35. On holism in Central Europe, see Harrington, *Reenchanted Science.*
36. Paul Lazarsfeld, "A Memoir," in Fleming and Bailyn, *Intellectual Migration,* 277–80.
37. Ibid., 273.

Egon Brunswik, the radical Freudians Reich and Heinz Hartmann participated, as did the Vienna Circle members Herbert Feigl and Edgar Zilsel. Karl Polanyi, who became a fixture in these radical circles in the mid-1920s, also took part.[38] Despite their divergent scholarly interests, they recognized a common commitment to scientific research and social transformation.

Central to this interactive environment was Otto Neurath, a tireless organizer and loquacious interlocutor. Neurath's involvement in Red Vienna extended well beyond the social and philosophical radicalism of the Vienna Circle. For Jahoda, he was a larger-than-life figure: "He became a leading member of the Vienna Circle, a top mind in adult education for the party, founder and director of the city's Social and Economic Museum and God knows what else."[39] Neurath played a decisive role in a number of discussion groups: Otto Bauer's circle, the Vienna Circle, the Heinrich-Gomperz-Kreis, and the Richard-von-Mises-Zirkel. He knew members from many other intellectual groups personally and engaged them in spirited debates.[40] As we have seen, he engaged the Austro-Marxists on their plans for economic socialization in the early years of the Republic. His theories on socialization offered fodder for Karl Popper's earliest ruminations on economics.[41] As one of the last advocates of a moneyless economy, he drew the attention of the economists Ludwig Mises (with whom he had attended the prewar Böhm-Bawerk seminar) and Friedrich Hayek.[42] He inspired the economic ideas of another freethinking socialist, Karl Polanyi.[43] When Polanyi began a seminar at his house on socialist price calculation, Neurath's theories served as the starting point.[44] The Polanyi landmark study *The Great Transformation* had its origins in these economic discussions, which included Jahoda, Zeisel, Lazarsfeld, and the Hungarian émigré Aurel Kolnai. Despite their many differences, Polanyi and Neurath agreed on the social embeddedness of economic systems and the need for institutions that privileged social and moral well-being above individual acquisition and wealth. They remained intellectual allies into their respective exiles in the 1930s.[45]

---

38. Stadler, *Studien zum Wiener Kreis,* 627–39.

39. Jahoda, *"Ich habe die Welt,"* 38–39.

40. Stadler, *Studien zum Wiener Kreis,* 627–39. See also Nemeth, Heinrich, and Soulez, *Otto Neurath,* and Neurath, Neurath, and Nemeth, *Otto Neurath.*

41. Hacohen, *Karl Popper,* 88–90.

42. Steele, *From Marx to Mises,* 64, 124–25; Caldwell, *Hayek's Challenge,* 113–19.

43. See Eva Gabor, "The Early Formation of Karl Polanyi's Ideas," and Ilona Duczynska Polanyi, ' I First Met Karl Polanyi in 1920...." in Levitt and McRobbie, *Karl Polanyi,* 298–301, 310–11.

44. Felix Schaffer, "Vorgartenstrasse 203," in Levitt and McRobbie, *Karl Polanyi,* 329.

45. Michele Cangiani, "The Continuing Crisis of Democracy," in Levitt and McRobbie, *Karl Polanyi,* 38.

Polanyi brought these concerns to the economic magazine *Der öster-reichische Volkswirt,* edited by Paul Federn's brother, Walther, where Polanyi wrote on international affairs as the "red" member of the staff. Although Walther Federn considered himself a nineteenth-century liberal, he hewed to Polanyi's politics, arguing that no self-respecting liberal could make peace with the Christian Socials or German nationalists. After 1934, Federn identified himself as a socialist. Meanwhile *Der österreichische Volkswirt*'s high integrity and political and intellectual open-mindedness made it one of the sole journals that Karl Kraus read and esteemed.[46]

Neurath's views often encouraged his colleagues to take more combative intellectual and political positions. Not only did his ideas have an effect on Jahoda and Polanyi, but his interactions with Carnap moved the latter's work in a radical direction. Carnap admitted Neurath's influence on his thinking and on the work of the Vienna Circle: Neurath drew attention to the social and economic determinants that shaped the development of scientific and philosophical thought.[47] Thomas Uebel has demonstrated the role of the Neurath-Carnap exchanges in the development of Carnap's thought in the early 1930s,[48] yet Neurath was perhaps even more important for Carnap in the 1920s. The preface to Carnap's *The Logical Structure of the World* resounded with militant language reminiscent of the "The Scientific World-Conception." When Carnap discussed his antimetaphysical project, he identified himself as part of a larger movement:

> We do not deceive ourselves about the fact that movements in meta-physical philosophy and religion which are critical of such an orientation have again become very influential of late. Whence then our confidence that our call for clarity, for a science that is free from metaphysics, will be heard? It stems...from the belief that these opposing powers belong to the past. We feel that there is an inner kinship between the attitude on which our philosophical work is founded and the intellectual attitude which presently manifests itself in entirely different walks of life; we feel this orientation in artistic movements, especially in architecture, and in movements which strive for meaningful forms of personal and collective life, of education, and of external organization in general.[49]

---

46. Schaffer, "Vorgartenstrasse 203," 335–6; Timms, *Karl Kraus,* 2:95.
47. Rudolf Carnap, "Intellectual Biography," in Schilpp, *Rudolf Carnap,* 22–24.
48. See Uebel, *Empiricism at the Crossroads,* chaps. 4, 5, 7, and 8.
49. Carnap, *Logical Structure,* xvii–xviii.

Carnap drew attention to conservative metaphysical thinking while expressing optimism about its eclipse. He alluded to movements in architecture
such as the Bauhaus and Viennese public housing movement, with which
he was personally involved.[50] He also referenced the social commitment of
the Social Democrats and their focus on social and educational reform. He
recognized his work as a contribution to an ongoing struggle in science and
society. The language of the 1929 Vienna Circle manifesto, written by Carnap, Neurath, and Hahn, made the same points. The liberal Karl Menger recognized (and rejected) the dogmatic nature of Carnap's work, which pleased
Neurath no end: "As the academic year went on and Carnap got more radical, Neurath got more excited and aggressive."[51] Carnap's role as leader of an
interdisciplinary study group therefore reinforced the importance of social
and political concerns for this intellectual milieu.

The theoretical work of Neurath and Wilhelm Reich most clearly
reflected the willingness of logical empiricists and Freudians to engage with
Marxist teachings. A general agreement about Marx's importance for scientific inquiry helped to produce a convergence of thought in Red Vienna.
The contentious relations of these two thinkers with Austro-Marxism drove
them to similar critical assessments of radical scholarship and politics. They
both believed that social science required a full understanding of economic
and social conditions. Only scholars aware of exogenous influences could
produce true knowledge. Neurath tasked the proletariat with the development of scientific and antimetaphysical thought. He contended that although
the bourgeoisie downplayed the significance of Marxist thought for modern
science, the proletariat would vindicate Marxism.[52] He also developed the
methodological similarities between Marxism and social science, arguing that
socialism provided the foundation for a unified science.[53]

Likewise, Reich linked the revolutionary impulse of Marx with a comple-
mentary spirit in Freud. He maintained that Freudianism was not a comprehensive worldview, since it lacked a sociological, economic, or political
theory. To make full use of its findings required situating psychoanalysis
within a Marxist worldview and practice. It was only by understanding
psychoanalysis as a product of the socioeconomic conditions of capitalism
that it could be deployed. Its therapeutic techniques could have the desired
effect only in a classless society liberated from bourgeois social and sexual

50. Galison, "Aufbau/Bauhaus," 709–52.
51. Menger, "Vienna Meetings 1927–1930," 81.
52. Otto Neurath, "Lebensgestaltung und Klassenkampf," in Neurath, *Philosophische und Methodologische Schriften,* 1:287–93.
53. Otto Neurath, "Empirische Soziologie," in ibid., 449–55, 465–78.

repressions. He also directed criticisms at orthodox socialists who failed to see the applicability of Freudianism:

> Thus the Marxist critics are right when they reproach certain representatives of the psychoanalytic school with attempting to explain what cannot be explained by that method. But they are wrong when they identify the method with those who apply it, and when they blame the method for their mistakes. These two points lead on to a necessary distinction... between Marxism as a sociological doctrine—that is to say as scientific method—and Marxism as the philosophical practice of the proletariat. Marxist social theory is the result of the application of the Marxist method to problems of social existence. As a science, psychoanalysis is equal to Marxian sociological doctrine.[54]

As long as psychoanalysis is not extended beyond its proper function—"the psychological life of man in society"—it remains a valid science. The parallels with Neurath's calls for an empirical sociology are evident.

When Reich asserted the radical implications of Freud, he was not alone in the psychoanalytic community. Through the end of the 1920s, he was a leader in the movement and his Sex-Pol clinic (with the assistance of Bernfeld, Fenichel, Grete Bibring, and Anna Freud) was overrun with patients.[55] The Austro-Marxists agreed with Reich's assessment of psychoanalysis. *Die Stunde,* one of their papers, applauded Bernfeld and Freud in 1928 for their aid in the fight for social progress.[56] Reich and his colleagues successfully argued that Freudian psychoanalysis could account for the subjective factor in historical materialism and provide Marxists with guidance for their actions.

A consensus in Red Viennese circles about the compatibility of socialism and scientific work developed in the 1920s. Scientists in disparate fields found their work converging on a mission of radical social change and engaged science. Reich and Fenichel's work approached Carnap and Neurath's; Alfred Adler's educational theory approached those of the Freudians August Aichhorn and Franz Alexander.[57] Although "socialism" carried different connotations for each figure, a form of socialist empiricism predominated. The Austro-Marxists, through their epistemological pluralism and their support of various institutes and initiatives, provided a basis for intellectual innovation and social activism. Faced with conservative opposition on the meaning of

54. Wilhelm Reich, "Dialectical Materialism and Psychoanalysis," in Reich, *Sex-Pol,* 7–8.
55. Danto, *Freud's Free Clinics,* 115–20, 208–10.
56. *Die Stunde,* September 16, 1928, quoted in Danto, *Freud's Free Clinics,* 200–201.
57. Stepansky, *In Freud's Shadow,* 222–30.

science, philosophy, and politics, Red Viennese intellectuals aligned with and fought for the socialists throughout the 1920s, contributing to the remarkable efflorescence of ideas for which interwar Vienna in known.

The Decline of the Synthesis and the Disillusionment of the Intelligentsia

The sense of common purpose among Austro-Marxists and progressive Viennese intellectuals reached its climax in 1927 with the April national election. On 15 July, after the announcement of the acquittal of members of a conservative paramilitary group charged with the murder of a socialist Schutzbund member and a child, the masses took to the streets of Vienna. In the confusion, the crowd set fire to the Justizpalast. In the ensuing confusion, the police opened fire on the unarmed crowd, killing ninety people. The Austro-Marxist leadership, which had been caught by surprise by the protest and then reacted hesitantly, left many supporters disappointed.[58] Many leftists, including Wilhelm Reich, the future Communist leader Ernst Fischer, and the Nobel Prize–winning author Elias Canetti, described these events as the turning point in the Republic's history, when the socialists proved unwilling or unable to stand up to the rising fascist tide and the conservatives realized that radical tactics would work against the working class and its leadership. Intellectuals lost faith in the ability of the Social Democrats to defend the republic and advance the cause of social change.[59]

Although there was a decline in intellectual engagement after 1927, the process was uneven and gradual. The view of July 1927 as the turning point in the First Republic is a common one.[60] Undoubtedly it set a precedent for later developments, yet neither progressive nor conservative movements experienced a major change in fortunes in the immediate wake of these events. There was a wide array of responses on the right and the left. On the right, the Spannkreis intensified its appeals to fascist movements across Europe. The Österreichische Aktion doubled down on its authoritarian claims in *Die schönere Zukunft* and began organizing as a social movement. On the left, the events of July 1927 led a small segment of defiant intellectuals to seek more proactive alternatives to the Social Democrats. Ilona Duczynska, Karl Polanyi's wife, formed the Politische Arbeitsgemeinschaft,

---

58. See Hanisch, *Der große Illusionist,* 240–51, for a detailed account of the socialist response.

59. Canetti, *Memoirs,* 484–90; Reich, *People in Trouble,* 40–48; Fischer, *Erinnerungen und Reflexionen.*

60. As examples, see Leser and Sailer-Wlasits, *1927;* Botz, *Krisenzonen;* Gulick, *Austria,* vol. 1, chap 20.

the first organization to criticize the Austro-Marxists from within the party. She began to distance herself from the party, producing her own journal, *Der linke Sozialdemokrat.*[61] Duczynska criticized the fatalism of the Austro-Marxists and their unwillingness to rise in defense of their moral and political values. In a leaflet, she gave vent to her disappointment: "In the name of the masses of the Social Democratic party, justly filled with mistrust, the opposition raises its voice against the position of the party leadership. Because its indecisive and equivocal tactic has led to disaster, we call upon the leadership to assume responsibility and we raise the sharpest protest against its beginning movement to the right, for whose consequences we hold it ultimately responsible."[62] Duczynska permitted no "rightist" compromise with conservative forces and demanded that the leadership actually lead the workers' movement against fascism. Many of her fellow writers in the journal, including Joseph Buttinger and Otto and Käthe Leichter, later participated in underground resistance movements against the Austrofascist state.[63] When Polanyi left Austria in 1933, Duczynska stayed behind and became involved in the fight against fascism as part of the German underground organization Neu-Beginnen and the Revolutionary Socialists.

Unlike his defiant wife, Polanyi chose to retreat from party activism after 1927. A lifelong admirer of Red Vienna, he nevertheless criticized the dogmatism of contemporary socialism in an unpublished manuscript "Über die Freiheit."[64] His affiliation with the party had always been limited, yet his contacts after 1927 nearly disappeared. Previously, he had shared many positions with Otto Bauer and expressed himself positively on the Austro-Marxist economic policies. This ceased in the late 1920s.[65] He focused on his work with *Der österreichische Volkswirt,* writing primarily on the global economic crisis and the rise of fascism and Nazism. In his landmark book, *The Great Transformation,* Polanyi asserted that the inability of the Austro-Marxists to respond to the rise of the Heimwehr marked the moment of collapse for Viennese socialism: "The Heimwehr victory in Austria formed part of a total catastrophe of the national and social system."[66] Polanyi lauded the Viennese working-class experiment as a major achievement, yet he acknowledged that Viennese socialist leaders struggled to meet the authoritarian challenge head-on.

---

61. Rabinbach, *Crisis,* 50–52.

62. Kenneth McRobbie, "Ilona Duczynska: Sovereign Revolutionary," in Levitt and McRobbie, *Karl Polanyi,* 256–57; Congdon, *Exile and Social Thought,* 217–20.

63. Ilona Duczynska, "Genossen!," quoted in Rabinbach, *Crisis,* 51–52.

64. Duczynska Polanyi, "I First Met Karl Polanyi," 310–11.

65. Polanyi, *Chronik,* 2:31–33.

66. Polanyi, *Great Transformation,* 298.

Interestingly, with a few exceptions, intellectual engagement with socialism seemed to increase in the first years after the fire. The moment for decision had seemingly arrived, and Red Viennese intellectuals rose to the call. Wilhelm Reich did not officially join the Social Democratic party until July. The events of 1927 provided motivation for his "Dialectical Materialism and Psychoanalysis."[67] Karl Popper, the philosopher and political theorist, remained a party member until 1937 despite mounting concerns about the party.[68] The case of Aurel Kolnai demonstrates this intensification of commitment to Marxist socialism after 1927, even by intellectuals outside the socioliberal bloc. Kolnai moved from an unorthodox non-Marxist socialism in the early 1920s to a Catholic socialist position when he converted in the mid-1920s. Starting in early 1927, however, he advocated for the Religious Socialists, a small clan of practicing Catholics who believed in the compatibility of Marxism and Catholicism. Kolnai supported the Austro-Marxists in *Der österreichische Volkswirt* and the Religious Socialists' paper, *Der Menschheitskämpfer*. Kolnai joined the Social Democratic party itself in 1930, partly in reaction to the fascist turn of the Christian Socials in 1929.[69]

The events of 1927 alone did not break the alliance of Marxists and intellectuals; in some cases it strengthened the ties. Many intellectuals maintained connections with the Austro-Marxists into the 1930s. Nevertheless, the political developments of 1928–29, which culminated in the passage of an authoritarian constitutional amendment and the political alliance of the Christian Socials with the Heimwehr, alerted many intellectuals to the inability of the Social Democratic party to protect democracy and challenge conservative hegemony. In November 1928, Chancellor Ignaz Seipel announced his plan for the realization of a "true democracy" that would do away with the "pseudo-democracy" of party rule and extend the power of the executive. He argued for removing the two-thirds majority requirement for constitutional amendments, implying that he intended to cast off the constitution entirely. He also wanted to strengthen the executive branch and decrease the autonomy of Austrian *Länder*. These measures were aimed at weakening socialist influence, especially in Vienna.[70] A version of the constitutional amendments passed as civil unrest mounted. The Heimwehr staged rallies across the country with the backing of the Christian Socials.

67. Rabinbach, "Wilhelm Reich," 92.

68. Hacohen, *Karl Popper*, 290–1.

69. Congdon, *Exile and Social Thought*, 233–252. By 1932, Kolnai became dissatisfied with the Religious Socialists and shifted rightward. Although he criticized the Christian Socials, he endorsed the Austrofascist regime as a bulwark against communism and Nazism.

70. Ignaz Seipel, "Wahre Demokratie," *RP,* November 28, 1928; quoted in Gulick, *Austria,* 806.

Socialist leaders feared a conservative coup d'état, yet they did not mobilize their own forces, the Schutzbund. This unwillingness to confront force with force led some intellectuals to criticize the disjuncture between the party's revolutionary rhetoric and its quiescence.

The constitutional compromise provoked substantial criticism from progressive allies. The jurist Hans Kelsen viewed the proposed amendments as a violation of the democratic spirit of the original constitution and a blatant attack on the working class: "The purpose of the bill—as openly admitted, not by the government but by the Heimwehr leaders—is to break the power of the Socialist party."[71] Kelsen feared the meddling of the fascist paramilitary group and its potential to destroy socialism and the Republic. Despite controlling two-fifths of the legislative assembly—making it possible to block any such amendments—the Social Democrats entered into negotiations. Eventually a version passed that allowed for an expansion of executive power and a weakening of Vienna's position in the state. The socialists hoped this compromise would prevent further rightward movement of the Christian Socials and decrease the influence of the Heimwehr. This was a classic example of what Ernst Hanisch has called Otto Bauer's politics of *Einerseits/Anderseits*—hesitating in the face of a momentous decision, caught between his radical rhetoric and pragmatic political decisions.[72] Kelsen and his colleague Adolf Merkl responded with dismay at the perceived abrogation of the original constitution. They asserted that this amendment would not have the desired conciliatory effect.[73] Kelsen, long one of the most hated professors at the University of Vienna and a target of anti-Semitic attacks,[74] grew tired of the combative nature of academic politics and pessimistic about the prospects for democracy in Austria. He left for Cologne in 1930, becoming one of the first intellectual émigrés from Red Vienna.[75]

In an article from the socialist *Arbeiter-Zeitung* from July 1930, the editors acknowledged the alarming precedent that Kelsen's departure signified, for both the Marxist-intellectual synthesis and the Austrian academy. The essay examined the difficulties scholars from non-Catholic backgrounds or progressive worldviews had in acquiring tenured positions at the University of Vienna. The discussion focused on what Kelsen meant for Vienna

---

71. Hans Kelsen, "Die österreichische Verfassungsreform," *ÖV* 22 (October 26, 1929), 99. See Gulick, *Austria From Habsburg to Hitler*, 862–79.

72. Hanisch, *Der große Illusionist*, 273–7.

73. Gulick, *Austria*, 875.

74. Thomas Olechowski, "Hans Kelsen und die Universität Wien," in *Kelsen und die Bundesverfassung*, 32–39.

75. Robert Walter, "Hans Kelsens Emigration," in Stadler, *Vertriebene Vernunft*, 2:463–5.

and the Republic: "He is no social democrat. He is an opponent of Marxism, but he is undoubtedly the most important jurist at the University of
Vienna and...the creator of the mechanisms of our constitution. How did
it come to pass...that the regime let him go to Cologne? Everyone knows
that today's Austria is in an era of 'Antimarxism'!"[76] The socialists' ambivalence about Kelsen reveals some of the enduring biases the Austro-Marxists
had about bourgeois and Jewish intellectuals. Kelsen had long endorsed the
Social Democratic party, even as he argued with his university colleague
Max Adler about the shortcomings of Marxist theory.[77] The Austro-Marxists
relished Kelsen's endorsement of the party in 1927, yet his more recent criticisms had produced a rift. The article identified major problems in how the
regime appointed professors, but it also disingenuously blamed the bourgeois
intellectuals in Kelsen's circle for opposing Austro-Marxist measures and tacitly allying with conservatives instead.[78] The Kelsen case reveals how mistrust
began to emerge on both sides of the Marxist-intellectual synthesis.

Wilhelm Reich also saw his close alliance with the Austro-Marxists end
abruptly in 1929. Reich's disengagement coincided with similar actions by
other activist analysts. For several years, the most radical psychoanalysts had
made their way to Germany, where the employment and political situation
seemed more favorable: Otto Fenichel left in 1922, Helene Deutsch in 1923,
and Siegfried Bernfeld in 1925. The focal point for Marxist social scientific
research, including psychoanalysis, had shifted, especially with the emergence
of the Institute for Social Research in Frankfurt, first under the Viennese
expatriate Carl Grünberg and then under Max Horkheimer. While hardly
isolated, Reich became the leftist Freudian par excellence in Vienna. In 1929,
he made a trip to Moscow and came back with a newfound appreciation for
Bolshevism and its advances in sexual reform. On his return, Reich formed
an oppositional political organization, the Kommitee Revolutionärer Sozi-
aldemokraten, which brought him in contact with Ernst Fischer and future
underground leaders. He spoke out angrily against the appeasement tactics
of the Social Democrats. "This is always the strange tactic practiced by
the leaders. That is, on the one hand, to act sharply, be radical and egg the
workers on, and on the other hand to brake the struggle, and when a worker
attacks this policy, to gag him and make it impossible for him to exist in the
party."[79] He also wrote "The Sexual Misery of the Masses," which linked

---

76. *AZ,* 11 Juli 1930, 2.

77. See Kelsen, *Sozialismus und Staat.*

78. *AZ,* 11 Juli 1930, 2–3.

79. Allgemeines Verwaltungsarchiv, Vienna, SD Archiv, Karton 88, Protokolle in Angelegenheit
Reich, December 13, 1929. Quoted in Rabinbach, *Crisis,* 69.

socioeconomic factors with the current repressive state of sexual politics. This text, which looked at the negative effects of everyday politics on the oppressed classes, laid the groundwork for his famous works "What Is Class Consciousness?" and *The Mass Psychology of Fascism*. His criticisms were not confined to repressive conservatives. Reich's criticism of the bourgeois sexual politics of the Social Democrats, especially Julius Tandler, led to his expulsion from the party in January 1930.[80] With his emigration to Germany in 1929, Reich severed all ties with the Austro-Marxists and joined the Communist Party. He remained a radical adherent of Marxism, even after the Communists banished him in 1933, and became part of the circle, led by Fenichel, that circulated letters discussing the revolutionary psychological, political, and social implications of Freudian theory.[81]

While Freudian analysts maintained their radical psychological and social agendas in the late 1920s and early 1930s,[82] actual exchange with the Social Democrats largely ended. Analysts chose to focus more on their clinical work as the socialists descended into arcane debates. As Helene Deutsch noted, the increasingly doctrinal concerns of the socialists had little to do with the revolutionary impulses that she possessed: "There were of course other elements in socialism that were devoid of the revolutionary spirit and limited to party politics and short-term improvement of the workers' lot. This was not the form of socialism to which I...subscribed."[83] Likewise, Siegfried Bernfeld, who returned to Vienna in 1932, scarcely interacted with Bauer, Tandler, or other Austro-Marxists anymore.[84]

As the Reich, Kelsen, and Kolnai cases show, after 1929 intellectuals increasingly questioned their allegiances to the Austro-Marxists—even then, the process of disengagement was uneven and contingent upon a variety of factors. At the same time, a similar dissatisfaction emerged within the Social Democratic party itself, where leftist opposition groups challenged the stasis of the Otto Bauer-led executive.[85] This opposition came predominantly from activists involved with socialist youth groups, whose members had close interactions with Red Viennese intellectuals. Duczynska represented an early example; many more were to follow. By 1932, the radical Viennese intelligentsia had mostly distanced itself from the Austro-Marxists: some emigrated

80. Rabinbach, "Politicization of Wilhelm Reich," 94–97.

81. On the *Rundbriefe,* see Jacoby, *Repression of Psychoanalysis.*

82. Danto, *Freud's Free Clinics,* 183–249.

83. Deutsch, *Confrontations with Myself,* 84.

84. Rudolf Ekstein, Kurt Fallend, and Johannes Reichmayr, "Too Late to Start Afresh: Siegfried Bernfeld auf dem Weg ins Exil," in Stadler, *Vertriebene Vernunft,* 2:230–41.

85. Rabinbach, *Crisis,* chaps. 2, 3, and 5.

to better professional and political situations; others shifted political allegiances; some withdrew into their work.

The Marienthal study, with its concepts of defiance, resignation, desperation, and apathy, provides a useful spectrum of the different responses that radical intellectuals evinced during the crisis of Austrian socialism and the First Republic. The Marienthal scholars themselves illuminate this well. Marie Jahoda sought out other radicals. In 1932 she befriended a member of the radical socialist organization Neu-Beginnen and joined the resistance movement Der Funke in 1933. The latter group began preparations for taking the Austrian socialist movement underground, where it could better fight against the fascists.[86] She was involved in resistance activities until 1936, when she was arrested and then freed under the condition that she emigrate.[87] Hans Zeisel and Paul Lazarsfeld, on the other hand, dedicated their time to a new research center that pursued market research.[88] Lazarsfeld's memoir highlights the tension between his early Marxist commitment to class struggle and the Austro-Marxist stress on nonviolent, gradualist electoral struggle. This produced a "curious and important functional displacement."[89] Lazarsfeld resolved his own displacement problem by turning away from the class struggle in pursuit of financial and academic stability. He abandoned work on socialist youth for research on occupational patterns. After he completed *Jugend und Beruf*—a work with "a visible Marxist tinge"—in 1931, he downplayed issues of exploitation in the name of science, at the behest of his adviser and friend Charlotte Bühler. His subsequent work possessed a depoliticized, "descriptive and naturalistic, instead of critical" tone.[90]

Disenchantment among the logical empiricists came slightly later. The years 1929–31 represented the high point of the Vienna Circle's involvement in the cultural and intellectual affairs of the city.[91] The lectures offered by the Verein Ernst Mach attested to the interdisciplinary nature of the organization, its scientific world-conception, and its social and political radicalism. Josef Frank, the leader of the Viennese public housing project, lectured on modern worldviews and architecture, linking modernist architecture to Marxism. Carnap offered a speech drawing from "Pseudo-Problems in

---

86. Ibid., 115–16.

87. Jahoda, *"Ich habe die Welt,"* 50–62.

88. Fleck, "Vor dem Urlaub. Die intellektuelle Biographie der Wiener Jahre Paul F. Lazarsfelds," in Wolfgang Langenbucher, ed., *Paul F. Lazarsfeld. Die Wiener Tradition der empirischen Sozial- und Kommunikationswissenschaften* (Munich: Ölschläger, 1990), 65–66.

89. Lazarsfeld, "Memoir," 278–79.

90. Ibid.

91. Stadler, *Studien zum Wiener Kreis,* 252–66, 364–75.

Philosophy," arguing for a radical reorientation in social and political values. Neurath delivered a talk entitled "Unity of Science and Marxism," introducing his utopian vision for a unitary scientific community committed to socioeconomic transformation. Josef Friedjung, Wilhelm Reich, Heinz Hartmann, Karl Polanyi, and Egon Brunswik all presented work. The clearest signal of the connection between the circle and Austro-Marxism was Otto Bauer's lecture on industrial rationalization and science.

By 1931, as the country lurched toward fascism and the economic depression deepened, a noticeable change in content and participation took place. First, there was a decline in the involvement of non-Vienna Circle members. Austro-Marxist thinkers no longer presented their work; members of the Freudian, Bühler, and Adlerian camps rarely did, either. This was accompanied by a shift toward rarefied scientific lectures. Carnap and Neurath presented their highly abstract work on protocol sentences and physicalism. Edgar Zilsel, who had previously offered Marxist *Ideologiekritik,* spoke on theories of scientific induction, and Moritz Schlick discussed logical empiricist ethics. There were no more explicit references to Marxism, social politics, or economic policies.[92]

The actions of members of the left wing of the circle clearly demonstrate the break. Carnap took a job at Charles University in Prague in 1931 and disengaged from Austrian political affairs. Zilsel, who had long been one of the Vienna Circle's most active participants in adult education and *Der Kampf,* forcefully declared his disagreement with Austro-Marxist dogmatism. The occasion for the contretemps was Max Adler's book on historical materialism. Zilsel rejected Adler's neo-Kantian reliance on a priori categories as metaphysical and unscientific. This was a significant challenge, since Adler himself was on the left wing of the Austro-Marxist establishment and had long encouraged oppositional thinking within the party.[93] Nevertheless, Adler continued to advocate for a utopian, idealist Marxism. Zilsel believed that what was revolutionary in Marxism was its willingness to seek sociological and historical knowledge on the basis of empirical investigation, which was then applied to socioeconomic issues. "Real science and real philosophy, bound with the proletariat, move toward the culmination of a four hundred-year journey. Much as the proletariat has not destroyed the Machine Age but has completed it, so will empirical-rational research into

92. Ibid.
93. Rabinbach, *Crisis,* 103–5.

all events lead to an end."[94] Zilsel could not abide by Adler's complacent, professorial constructions. This debate between Adler and Zilsel raged for a year and a half, at the end of which Zilsel categorically rejected the Adlerites, retorting, "What new results in the exact sciences have emerged thanks to neo-Kantian inspiration?"[95] Zilsel did not believe that the Austro-Marxists were sufficiently committed to change and were thus playing into the hands of "school philosophers" and politicians that were set on a "revolution of the Right."[96] After the debate, Zilsel retreated into research.

Otto Neurath's disaffection carried perhaps the most weight of all. His political activism had long made his Vienna Circle colleagues slightly uncomfortable.[97] He, too, curtailed his political output starting in 1931, restricting his political commentary to letters to friends.[98] In the wake of the Zilsel debate, Neurath published only one more article in *Der Kampf*. In that article, he picked up where Zilsel had left off, attacking the educational system in Austria, which allowed philosophers to present "magical, theological and antiquated scientific outlooks." Neurath made one final call for Marxists to band together with the Vienna Circle to fight the metaphysical attitudes of "bourgeois ideology" and to facilitate the "revolutionary reform of today's social and economic order."[99] His outrage had a few targets—not all on the right, however. First, there were the school philosophers—he named Othmar Spann and Martin Heidegger—who preached the most nefarious philosophies. These thinkers offered obsolete theories to contemporary youth and blocked scientifically oriented thinkers from the academy. The second target was other thinkers who foisted bourgeois ideology on their students. This group included Max Adler. The claim that the most radical Austro-Marxist theoretician was in fact abetting the bourgeois status quo amounted to a repudiation of the party's mission. Neurath's writings after 1931 displayed a pronounced shift to methodological and philosophical concerns. In addition to conducting protocol-sentence and physicalism debates with Schlick and Carnap, he wrote increasingly of a depoliticized unity of science. Whereas previously Neurath linked the unity of science with Marxism and social revolution, he now offered a cosmopolitan and apolitical vision. He had not

94. Edgar Zilsel, "Soziologische Bemerkungen zur Philosophie der Gegenwart," *K* 23 (1930): 424.

95. Edgar Zilsel, "Partei, Marxismus, Materialismus, Neukantianismus," *K* 24 (1931): 216.

96. Edgar Zilsel, review of *Die geistige Situation der Zeit* and *Die Revolution von Rechts, K* 24 (1931): 172–76.

97. Carnap, "Intellectual Biography," 22.

98. Galison, "Aufbau/Bauhaus," 740–44.

99. Otto Neurath, "Die 'Philosophie' im Kampf gegen den Fortschritt der Wissenschaft," *K* 25 (1932): 385–89.

given up his beliefs; however, he no longer viewed (Austro-)Marxism as a cornerstone of the solution.[100]

Neurath's and Zilsel's retreat from political involvement was part of a larger trend among the intelligentsia away from Austro-Marxism in the early 1930s. Whereas Red Viennese intellectuals had previously contributed to the ideology and sociopolitical activities of the socialists, these contacts dried up by 1931. Although no single justification can account for this withdrawal, growing disappointment with the inaction and fatalism of the party played a decisive role. Progressive intellectuals had allied with the Austro-Marxists because of the conviction that the socialists shared their commitment to Enlightenment values, empirical scientific research, and social change. As the years advanced, the Austro-Marxists seemed to reject both the urgings and the findings of the progressive Viennese intelligentsia, settling on an ineffectual course of empty theorizing and internal debate.

In late 1931, intellectuals watched as the Social Democrats twice rejected overtures from the Christian Socials to enter into a coalition to solve the country's economic woes. The socialists then negotiated half-hearted austerity measures, which only worsened matters. They witnessed a putsch attempt by the Heimwehr, the subsequent acquittal of its leaders, and its rapprochement with the Christian Social party. During this time, unemployment increased by tens of thousands, the salaries of civil servants were cut, and unemployment benefits were curtailed.[101] This combination led to skepticism among the radical yet heterodox supporters of Austro-Marxism. They saw their own work marginalized and felt the party was untrue to its professed intellectual, social, and political goals. Red Viennese intellectuals therefore backed away from their earlier involvement. Well before the dissolution of parliament in 1933, the civil war in February 1934, or the official end of the First Republic, the Austro-Marxists had lost the support of one of their core constituencies: Red Viennese intellectuals. As one of Red Vienna's landmark studies would show, the socialists also had reason to worry about their working-class base.

Marienthal Redux

The reviews of the Marienthal study in Austria were striking in their scarcity, location, and tone, evidence that the Austro-Marxist leadership was distancing itself from the project. The only reviews came from members of leftist

---

100. Jahoda reveals that he had already made connections with underground movements.
101. Gulick, *Austria,* 922–71.

opposition groups in journals that had been critical of the party leadership. No reviews appeared in the largest organs of the party, the *Arbeiter-Zeitung, Das Kleine Blatt,* or *Der Kampf.* Käthe Leichter, a Social Democratic central committee member, member of the Workers' Chamber (*Arbeiterkammer*), and leader in the women's rights movement, wrote the first review in *Arbeit und Wirtschaft,* the trade unions' official paper. The unions had been disappointed by the Austro-Marxist leadership's decision to stay out of a coalition and worried whether the party's efforts were sufficient to combat the growing economic crisis. Leichter became one of Otto Bauer's sharpest critics in 1932 and 1933. She argued that Bauer's commitment to socialism was in danger of becoming a "worthless phrase," since he overestimated the role of objective factors in producing socialist reform.[102] *Marienthal* therefore was a perfect text with which to confront Bauer. Overall, Leichter was complimentary. She commended the writers for attempting to fill the gaps that existed in studies of unemployment—between a dry statistical analysis and sensationalistic reportage. After outlining the main points of the study and endorsing many of the findings, she offered only a few challenges. While pleased that the study had revealed the plight of industrial workers, Leichter hesitated to endorse the pessimistic conclusions about worker apathy. She recommended that the researchers return in a year to investigate whether their assumptions were correct. Ambivalence pervaded Leichter's review. On the one hand, she commended the Marienthal study on its scientific findings; on the other, she did not want to make a complete break with the party's social, economic, and ideological beliefs. She saw the value of the piece in critiquing Bauer's policies on the Great Depression, yet she refused to accept that workers' activism and revolutionary faith were on the wane. She wished to support the Marienthal researchers, all of whom she had interacted with at the Psychological Institute, yet she could not abandon hope for a proletarian revolt.[103]

The other review, written by Lazarsfeld and Jahoda's friend Ludwig Wagner, appeared in the small-circulation illustrated, *Der Kuckuck,* and served as a weapon with which to attack the Austro-Marxist leadership. Wagner and Ernst Fischer were the leaders of the radical student opposition movement. They had broken with the party leadership in the early 1930s because of their commitment to armed antifascist resistance.[104] They were friends with Lazarsfeld from his socialist youth. Wagner's review ran through all the hardships enumerated in the work, presenting the study as a condemnation of

---

102. Hanisch, *Der große Illusionist,* 287; Rabinbach, *Crisis,* 152–54.
103. Käthe Leichter, *"Die Arbeitslosen von Marienthal,"* *Arbeit und Wissenschaft,* July 1, 1933, 204–6.
104. Rabinbach, *Crisis,* 77, 85, 96, 100–103.

poverty and "the technical development of capitalist civilization." He used the review as an opportunity to attack the capitalist system and at the same time to raise criticisms of the slow responses of the party leadership.[105] The Marienthal study became a weapon for the opposition against the dogmatic and dilatory policies of the Austro-Marxist leadership.

Marienthal and its reception history reveal that the dissatisfaction of progressive intellectuals dovetailed with that of the left-wing socialist opposition to the Austro-Marxist leadership. A study that owed its origins to the richness of Red Viennese culture and the interaction between intellectuals and the Social Democrats—the Pedagogical and Psychological Institutes, *Volkshochschulen,* counseling centers, and interdisciplinary discussion groups—ultimately revealed the tensions within that collaboration and the decline of politicized thought at the end of the First Republic.

Whether because of a lack of reception from the party or a growing unease with the direction of Austro-Marxism, the three individuals involved with *Marienthal* all moved away from the Social Democratic party. Marie Jahoda, ever defiant, became more radical politically, while Paul Lazarsfeld and Hans Zeisel retreated into their scholarship. In these choices, they were representative of the Red Viennese intellectual community. Initially attracted to the Austro-Marxist movement for its commitment to democratic political reform and wholesale social and economic change, these intellectuals endorsed the socialist agenda in their scientific output and sociopolitical activities. They helped make the Austrian Social Democrats one of the strongest and most dynamic socialist parties in Europe. Their engagement also spawned remarkable interdisciplinary interactions that contributed to an efflorescence of social scientific and philosophical work. From the highpoint of the 1927 national election, however, this synthesis eroded as intellectuals began to doubt the Marxists' willingness and ability to bring about change. They also questioned the Austro-Marxist commitment to actual science as the party's "illusory" predilections became more evident.[106]

After years of economic depression and political turmoil were met with half-hearted actions and craven compromise by the Social Democrats, most Red Viennese intellectuals left Austro-Marxism behind. They did this in a variety of ways: some defiantly sought more radical political options; others retreated into their intellectual communities (while maintaining their democratic and socialist beliefs); a few resignedly rode the waves of instability and

---

105. Ludwig Wagner, "Das Leben in Marienthal. Forschungsreise in ein Arbeitslosendorf," *Der Kuckuck,* July 2, 1933, 14, 16.

106. On the "illusions" of the party leadership, see Hanisch, *Der große Illusionist,* introduction.

eventually endorsed the Austrofascist state as the lesser of two authoritarian evils. By the end of the Republic intellectuals had largely abandoned the Austro-Marxist project because of the latter's waning "power to resist" (*Widerstandskraft*). When the socialists faced their moment of truth during the civil war of February 1934, the direst predictions of the Red Viennese intelligentsia were borne out. The workers' will to resist had been sapped by all the years of hardship. Ineffectual leadership hamstrung the resistance even before it began.

Despite the shortcomings of the Austro-Marxist leadership and its approach to intellectual matters, it is not accurate to blame the socialists for the collapse of the Republic. They helped to build a remarkable progressive and democratic movement in Red Vienna and remained committed to the defense of the nation until the end. To explain the end of the Republic and the rise of fascism in Austria, we need to give closer scrutiny to Black Viennese ideologues of the 1920s and 1930s. After all, it was radical conservatives who denied progressive intellectuals jobs, who incited students with their anti-Semitic and nationalist rhetoric, and who forged alliances with anti-democratic forces across Europe. We now turn to the final victory of radical Black Viennese circles in the late Republic and *Ständestaat*.

CHAPTER 7

The Triumph of Radical Conservatism in the Austrofascist State, 1933–1938

On 22 June 1936 at 9:20 a.m., philosophy professor Moritz Schlick made his way across the courtyard of the University of Vienna. As he ascended the stairs to a lecture hall, Hans Nelböck, a thirty-two-year-old former student of Schlick's, confronted him, drew a pistol, and fatally shot Schlick four times in the chest. Police arrived on the scene and apprehended Nelböck, a man who had long suffered from psychotic episodes and had recently been released from a Viennese psychiatric center, Am Steinhof. Nelböck confessed to the crime and was sent to police headquarters for psychological evaluation. For several days, Vienna was abuzz about the case.[1] Nelböck, who suffered from paranoia and bouts of schizophrenia, harbored feelings of resentment toward Schlick, maintaining that Schlick had failed to secure him an academic job. He had sent Schlick death threats before, yet nothing had come of them before that June morning.

In *Erkenntnis,* the philosophical journal Schlick had cofounded in 1930, the outpouring of grief was massive. Philipp Frank mourned the death of the Vienna Circle founder.[2] The Berlin philosopher Hans Reichenbach wrote,

---

1. *Das Kleine Blatt*'s lead story was about the murder. The *Reichspost* carried articles for three consecutive days. The *Neue Freie Presse* started its article above the fold on page one. Only *Das Kleine Blatt* offered any information on Schlick; the focus remained primarily on Nelböck. The papers focused on an alleged love triangle between him, Schlick, and a female student.

2. Philipp Frank, "Nachruf auf Moritz Schlick," *Erkenntnis* 6 (1936): 141–42.

"How is it possible that Moritz Schlick was killed by a human being? Moritz Schlick—this genuine, irreproachable character, friend of his students, warm and helpful man, whose lessons affirmed life and youth. . . . We cannot comprehend it; we can only register it as a senseless accident."[3] Even intellectual adversaries paid tribute to Schlick. In *Der christliche Ständestaat*, the unofficial journal of the Austrofascist government, the Catholic theologian and professor Dietrich Hildebrand expressed the feelings of many conservative scholars: "Anyone who knew this noble, good, amiable man, who fell victim to this frightful act, must feel shaken to their depths. . . . All members of the Philosophical Faculty will miss him as an especially loyal, friendly, objective colleague. His philosophical orientation was not ours. . . . But these objective differences of opinion cannot lessen our deep pain over the loss."[4] The eulogies from friends and colleagues characterized Schlick as sincere and compassionate and condemned the senselessness of his murder.

Only one major Viennese journal did not join in these sentiments: Joseph Eberle's *Die schönere Zukunft*. Johann Sauter, a professor of political science at the University of Vienna and a student and ally of Othmar Spann's, wrote an article under the pseudonym "Dr. Austriacus" in which he blamed Schlick for Nelböck's madness and cast the victim as perpetrator:

> The world famous thinker Schlick, so it is said, has become the regrettable victim of a psychopath. However, everything written thus far about the case deals only with the surface; it does not address the *true* circumstances. . . . For this reason, one must delve one level deeper, namely in the stratum in which the great struggle between Nelböck and Schlick was actualized. This level is the struggle over worldviews [*Weltanschauungskampf*], which played out in the spiritual depths of the young, lonely Dr. Nelböck under the influence of Professor Schlick over the course of many years.[5]

Sauter questioned whether Schlick was Nelböck's victim or whether the roles were reversed. The most salient fact of the case, according to Sauter, was that Nelböck had not always been a psychopath; his madness arose only after exposure to Schlick's corrosive philosophy. Thus the bullet that killed Schlick was guided not by the logic of a lunatic but by that of a betrayed soul. Many students had lost their faith in "God, the world and humanity"

---

3. Hans Reichenbach, "Moritz Schlick," *Erkenntnis* 6 (1936): 11.

4. Dietrich Hildebrand, "Ein Furchtbares, in der Geschichte der Universitäten Unerhörtes hat sich ereignet," *CS*, June 28, 1936, 624.

5. Austriacus, "Der Fall Moritz Schlick—eine Mahnung zur Gewissenserforschung," *SZ* 11 (1935–36): 1079.

as a result of Schlick's lessons. Nelböck had avenged them and revealed the toxic effects of Schlick's lessons.

Sauter showed Schlick no quarter, assailing his philosophy, his students, and his legacy in the name of conservative, *völkisch* values and idealist philosophy. He castigated the features of Schlick's worldview: materialism, Bolshevism, Freemasonry, and especially "Jewishness." He asserted that Schlick was not a philosopher but rather a physicist who reduced all metaphysical and moral questions to physical ones. Schlick's arrogant, atheistic, and antimetaphysical work had made him popular within "materialist" (i.e., Bolshevik) and Masonic (i.e., Jewish) circles. Bolsheviks, seeking to destabilize the German *Volk,* populated Schlick's Ernst Mach Society. Moreover, the murder demonstrated the pernicious influence of Jewish thinking on the German soul. Schlick surrounded himself with Jewish assistants, male and—even worse—female, serving as an idol to the Jews. According to Sauter, it made sense for Jews, who were naturally antimetaphysical, materialist, and positivist, to celebrate Schlick's accomplishments, yet Austria was a German Catholic state and had the responsibility to eradicate such worldviews from the *Volk.* Therefore, Jews must be restricted to Jewish cultural institutions, and university positions should be left to real Germans and Catholics. If this peaceful segregation proposal were rejected, then only violent resolutions would remain. Sauter used the Schlick murder as an opportunity to endorse racist and violent actions in the name of the Austrian state and German identity.[6]

The Sauter article provoked heated debate in Vienna. Schlick's son enlisted Professor Richard Meister to write the rector of the university to clear his father's name. He demanded that the Federal Ministry for Education reject Sauter's claims and issue a formal defense of Schlick. The ministry never took action.[7] Dietrich Hildebrand's journal, *Der christliche Ständestaat,* condemned Sauter's morbid schadenfreude.[8] In response, *Die schönere Zukunft* offered a rebuttal to Hildebrand, making no apology and accusing the attackers of misreading the patriotic Sauter.[9] As for Nelböck, he was put on trial in early 1937 and sentenced to ten years in prison. He received a conditional release by the Nazi government in 1938; his sentence was commuted in 1943.

---

6. Austriacus, "Moritz Schlick," 1079–80. Lisa Silverman makes the compelling argument that the murder of Schlick, a Lutheran, was coded "Jewish" by the press as a product of the interwar Viennese focus on the category of "Jewish difference." See Silverman, *Becoming Austrians,* chap. 1.

7. Stadler, *Wiener Kreis,* 920–61.

8. Dietrich Hildebrand, "Verleumdung eines Toten," *CS,* June 28, 1936, 696.

9. Hans Sievering, "Noch einmal—die Philosophie Moritz Schlicks," *SZ* 11 (1935–36): 1196.

The Schlick murder has received frequent attention over the years,[10] yet several significant historical problems remain unresolved. First, it is surprising that Sauter's article attracted so much attention in 1936 Austria. By that time, the socialist threat had been neutralized by the Austrofascists, and Jewish influences had been suppressed.[11] The Social Democrats had been outlawed in 1934, their leaders forced to flee and the workers' unions destroyed. Attacking Bolshevism, Freemasonry, and materialism seems to have been tilting at windmills. Furthermore, Schlick was hardly the "menace" he had been earlier. The new government had disbanded the Freethinkers in 1933 and the Ernst Mach Society in March 1934. The Vienna Circle curtailed all public activities. Many of its scholars emigrated; the government monitored those who remained. Moreover, Schlick openly supported the *Ständestaat* as a bulwark against National Socialism. This attitude placed him squarely within the ideological spectrum of the *Ständestaat,* which propagated an "Österreich-Ideologie" that supported an autonomous, German Christian, non-Nazi Austria.[12] Sauter's selection of the Protestant Schlick as a target, especially in the wake of his murder, seemed to have questionable merit.

Nevertheless, Sauter's article appeared prominently in *Die schönere Zukunft,* the largest intellectual weekly in Central Europe, and the editors went out of their way to reiterate their defense of Sauter's position, thereby revealing the tenacity of radical conservative Black Viennese values. The timing of the debate—which coincided almost perfectly with the July agreement between Kurt Schuschnigg and Adolf Hitler at Berchtesgaden that set Austria and Germany on the road to *Anschluss*—allowed it to serve as a synecdoche for larger discussions about *völkisch* values and the Austrian state. The debate revealed that a substantial gulf existed between official Austrian state ideology, as represented by *Der christliche Ständestaat,* and the prevailing views in the Black Viennese cultural field, a gap that has heretofore received little attention. As earlier chapters have shown, tensions within Austrian, particularly Viennese, conservatism had existed since the founding of the Republic, sometimes taking a backseat to conflicts with socialists and other times rearing up in debates over politics, religion, society, and economics. Conservative groups grew together during the Republic, united in their pan-German, antidemocratic, antisocialist, and anti-Semitic views. Tensions reemerged only in the early thirties, becoming most pronounced in 1933 and 1934 with the rise

---

10. A partial list: Stadler, *Wiener Kreis,* 920–62; Botz, *Gewalt in der Politik,* 289; Segar and Warren, *Austria in the Thirties,* 298; Silverman, *Becoming Austrians,* chap. 1.

11. On repression measures, see Neugebauer, "Repressionsapparat," 298–320.

12. Staudinger, "'Österreich-Ideologie,'" 28–52.

of Nazism in Germany and Austrofascism in Austria. The discourse around the Schlick murder fits into this broader story. The Schlick case demonstrates that Austria's rightward shift hardly stopped with the inception of the *Ständestaat*. There was a sizable group of disaffected intellectuals that yearned for radical, *völkisch* social and political solutions. Even if Nazi supremacy was not necessarily the ideal, Black Viennese intellectuals pushed for a more radical and more totalistic answer even after 1934. Therefore, they were hardly blameless in the lead-up to the *Anschluss*.

This chapter explores the evolution of the Black Viennese cultural field in the late 1920s and 1930s from a period of relative consensus through its tensions in the early Austrofascist state to the eventual triumph of the radicals before the *Anschluss*. An examination of the conservative intellectual landscape through its leading publications—*Das neue Reich, Die schönere Zukunft,* and *Der christliche Ständestaat*—and the scholarly works published by central thinkers such as Hans Eibl, Johannes Messner, and Eric Voegelin, reveals the ideological rift in Black Vienna. While a contingent of intellectuals supported the *Ständestaat* and accepted the opportunities it provided, most tolerated the new government only grudgingly. As we saw with the Österreichische Aktion, its unwillingness to make common cause with republicans and socialists against the ostensible enemy, the Nazis, revealed the shortcomings of "moderate" conservatism. As the Austrian state struggled to consolidate its power and Hitler's Germany continued its ascendancy, the calls for a *völksich* revolution only increased. Austrofascist ideology never achieved the status of a cultural dominant—the more radical Black Viennese ideas of German nationalism, fascism, and anti-Semitism predominated. By the time of Schlick's murder, the *Ständestaat* and its exponents had already lost the struggle over worldviews *(Weltanschauungskampf)*. Despite a general uneasiness about the Nazis, the vast majority of Black Viennese intellectuals, because of the ongoing radicalization of their conservative ideology, bear some responsibility for the Nazi triumph.

Conflict and Consensus in Black Vienna at the End of the Republic

Divisions within the conservative camp gradually emerged in the early 1930s after a period of general consensus and collective radicalization. As seen in chapter 1, conservative Viennese formed a relatively unified bloc of intellectuals in the early postwar years, opposed to socialism, Judaism, capitalism, and democracy. These shared aims brought together members of the Catholic conservative and German nationalist *Lager* in a common front to do away with the new Republic and restore Austrian, German, and Catholic greatness. In forums like the Leo-Gesellschaft, Cartellverband, and the Deutsche Studentenschaft, intellectuals championed new Right ideas for the postwar era. The attendant ideology of the Black Viennese bloc presented itself most vocally in Joseph Eberle's publication *Das neue Reich,* the most-read intellectual weekly in German-speaking Central Europe. A new era began in late 1925, however, when Eberle left *Das neue Reich* to form a new journal, *Die schönere Zukunft,* which espoused a more radical ideology. The next five years revealed a general coherence within the Black Viennese bloc even as *Das neue Reich* and *Die schönere Zukunft* vied with each other for readers and revenue.

After Eberle's departure from *Das neue Reich,* the journal rebranded itself as a more moderate offering, appealing to democratic Christian Socials and members of the Catholic Action social movement. The editors also reached out to political Catholics from other European nations. Fundamentally, the periodical changed only slightly. It remained focused on the "re-Christianization of our thought and life." This entailed several responsibilities. First, the journal must examine the "major cultural problems of the day" with the tools of the "true philosophy" of the Catholic religion. Second, *Das neue Reich* supported a distinct "Austrian cultural idea" that emphasized Austrian centrality for German-Christian culture. It supported an independent Austria and rejected a Prussia-dominated *Anschluss.* Third, it remained the implacable enemy of "individualistic" capitalism, socialism, Judaism, and Bolshevism. From a political perspective, the editors called for the return of "authoritarian thinking" and the institution of a *völkisch* "true democracy." They rejected "corrupt" democracy, "weak" pacifism and "chauvinistic" rationalism in favor of Christian harmony and peace between nations. This meant the end to the liberal constitution of the Republic and the restoration of the monarchy. Catholic social theory, as expressed by Leo XIII in his encyclical "Rerum Novarum," served as the social and economic model. The editors declared their full sympathy with both the working classes and the middle classes and stated that a corporatist state would help those constituencies.[13] Under Aemilian Schoepfer and Johannes Messner, *Das neue Reich* changed its tone but not its content.

Die schönere Zukunft, which slowly became the more popular journal over the next few years, sought to distinguish itself by espousing a more vital and radical form of conservatism, which was better connected to international trends. The editors, including Eberle, the Spannian Eugen Kogon, and Österreichische Aktion founder Alfred Missong, declared war on "bad press,"

---

13. *NR* 7 (1924–25): 1210–11.

characterized by "Jewish hacks," in the name of the *Volk*. Eberle lambasted the bankruptcy of modern, non-Christian culture and demanded a return to the world of the old church. He celebrated the Counter-Reformation, the Baroque, the Romantic, and Richard Kralik's Grail movements as authentic expressions of the German Christian ideal. He extolled the Holy Roman Empire as the true exemplar of the German nation. He explained, "The way into the more beautiful future [*schönere Zukunft*] is the way of the crusader." This future is "expressly Central European, expressly international; international not in the sense of a fuzzy internationalism that condemns national values, but one that observes such values as those strongly rooted in Vienna and Austria." Like the Österreichische Aktion, Eberle excoriated liberal cosmopolitanism and lauded the "Habsburg myth" of a transnational Austria and a powerful *Großdeutschland*. He elaborated his journal's main subjects thus: "State, Tradition, Authority, Monarchy, Nobility, Democracy, Parliamentarianism, Republic, Marxism, Plutocracy, Jewishness, Freemasonry; questions on the organic formation of Central Europe, on the possibility of solving the social question, clarification and overcoming the oppositions in the Catholic camp."[14] He and his colleagues believed the new journal would organize a new, militant Catholic conservative movement in Central Europe.

To distinguish the journal from *Das neue Reich*, Eberle enlisted international support for his vision of the new authoritarian European order. He established ties to fifteen European Catholic journals; their respective articles were serialized. He named forty international contributors that would grace the pages of *Die schönere Zukunft*, including the French Catholic philosopher Jacques Maritain, the British intellectuals Hilaire Belloc and G. K. Chesterton, and the American industrialist and anti-Semite Henry Ford. He argued that intellectuals must transform postwar Central European politics and society behind strong centralized leadership.[15]

While the two journals vied for the same followers and competed for market share, their substance varied more in degree than in kind in the late 1920s. Many of the central figures of the Black Viennese bloc—Richard Kralik, Hans Eibl, Oswald Menghin, Friedrich Funder, Sigmund Waitz—published in both venues, as did international contributors such as Béla Bangha, Maritain, Belloc, and Gonzague de Reynold. Representatives from the Christian Social party—including Ignaz Seipel—the German Center Party, DVP, and German National People's Party (DNVP) wrote in both. Though *Das neue Reich* offered a modicum of support for the Republic and

---

14. Joseph Eberle, "Die schönere Zukunft," *SZ* 1 (1925–26): 1–2.
15. Ibid.

democratic ideals, this endorsement was ambivalent. It encouraged participation in the democratic process around election time to ensure that socialists would not take over the state. The rest of the time it attacked parliamentary democracy. Finally, while *Das neue Reich* brought Catholicism more to the fore, these Catholic theologians and writers—including members of the German and Italian Solidarist camp that later opposed the Spannkreis and *Die schönere Zukunft*—used Eberle's publication nearly as often. Although members of Spann's circle and the Österreichische Aktion moved fully into the radical camp, most Viennese and European conservatives initially viewed the two periodicals as ideologically alike.

The journals engaged in minor skirmishes in the late 1920s, particularly during the heady events of 1927, yet this remained a case of narcissism of minor differences. In 1926, Eberle, Eibl, and Kralik entered into a debate with the German journal *Hochland* and the German Catholic academic society, the Görres-Gesellschaft, over objective versus politically engaged science. Leading figures in the Görres-Gesellschaft supported "value-free" scientific activity and wanted to raise Catholic science to the level of its secular peers. Eberle, Kralik, and Eibl favored research that served Catholic political and social aims.[16] *Das neue Reich* supported the former position, publishing excerpts from Görres-Gesellschaft meetings. These debates came to nothing. The events of 1927—the April elections and the Justizpalast fire—seemed to have little impact on the orientation of the Black Viennese field. The relative publication numbers of *Die schönere Zukunft* and *Das neue Reich* bear this out, as neither publication saw major changes to its support. At the beginning of 1927, Eberle announced that the weekly was publishing between eleven thousand and twelve thousand copies. By this point, *Die schönere Zukunft* and *Das neue Reich* stood on equal terms. By the end of the year, the number had climbed to fourteen thousand, with incremental bumps coming in May, October, and November. Undoubtedly the journal's hardline stance on the July "Bolshevik Revolts" contributed to the upturn, especially since *Das neue Reich* was relatively laconic on the subject. Overall, the growth of *Die schönere Zukunft* was organic and gradual; subsequent years saw similar annual growth.[17]

With the deteriorating political and economic situation in Austria and Europe in the late 1920s and early 1930s, the strident tone of *Die schönere Zukunft* gained the upper hand in Black Viennese circles. The journal had

---

16. Weiß, *Rechtskatholizismus*, 57–71.

17. Publication numbers of *Das neue Reich* are lacking after Eberle's departure, yet they stood at fifteen thousand in late 1925.

long advocated ethnonationalist and authoritarian views, yet these extreme positions did not fully manifest themselves until the Austrian fascist turn after 1929. This was best exemplified by the closer alliance with the fascist Spannkreis. As seen in chapter 3, Spann and his acolytes engaged with fascist movements across the continent, a practice that culminated in the creation of the Korneuburg oath for the Austrian Heimwehr, repeated meetings with Mussolini, and involvement in several Nazi cultural organizations, all around 1930. They also brought their activist ideas to the Leo-Gesellschaft and *Die schönere Zukunft*. Tension within the conservative camp reached a climax in 1931–32 with the rise of Nazism in German Central Europe and the publication of the papal encyclical "Quadragesimo Anno," which the two major Viennese factions embraced for different reasons. Writing in *Das neue Reich*, Oswald Nell-Breuning, author of the encyclical, and his colleague Gustav Gundlach published several articles to clarify the church's position, which called for gradual social reform by working within constraints set by the state. In its efforts at disseminating the message of "Quadragesimo Anno," *Das neue Reich* solicited work from theologians such as Dietrich Hildebrand, who shared this moderate interpretation.

Invited by Eberle to offer a universalist reading of the encyclical, Spann rejected this moderate assessment and its "crypto-individualism," arguing that Solidarism was a social order that was worse than either socialism or liberal individualism. Spann advocated for a true state with fascistic, corporatist elements. Messner responded angrily with a list of reasons why Spann's article and Eberle's decision to include it were "criminal," given the threats posed to German Catholics by "Jewish" Bolsheviks and Nazis:

> 1. If we Catholics stand today at a fateful hour [*Schicksalsstunde*] ... then it is absolutely a crime to instigate a new conflict in social Catholicism, as *Die schönere Zukunft* has done. 2. Even more so when *Die schönere Zukunft* professes to commit itself to a corporatist order like Solidarism, which is the central idea of "Quadragesimo Anno"... 3. It is absolutely grotesque when Spann writes in *Die schönere Zukunft* that Dr. Messner and *Das neue Reich* "dare" to speak of a corporatist order ... when one would search in vain in *Die schönere Zukunft* for contributions to corporatist thought.[18]

Messner decried the divisiveness of Eberle's and Spann's work. Faced with the joint threats of Bolshevism and fascism, he believed that Catholics must band together in this "fateful hour." If Eberle and Spann succeeded in fragmenting

---

18. Messner, "Schicksalsstunde," 540.

the German Christian bloc, then Central European society would founder. To prevent dissolution, *Das neue Reich* rallied Waitz, Hildebrand, Gundlach, and Nell-Breuning to defend Solidarism and criticize universalism.[19] This was a shining moment of resistance as Eberle retreated from his pro-Spann position. Messner showed himself to be Eberle's intellectual superior.

Despite winning the intellectual battle, Messner and *Das neue Reich* lost the ideological war for Black Vienna. Ironically, it was *Die schönere Zukunft* that unified Austrian conservatives in this fateful hour. Only two months after the "Quadragesimo Anno" debate, Messner announced that the two publications were merging under Eberle's leadership. Messner tried to downplay the defeat. He admitted that readers might be surprised that the two could join, given their differences, but the merger actually made sense. If one examined the cultural landscape, he reasoned, it was necessary for all Catholics to join together to achieve their goals. It was incumbent on intellectuals to cooperate in times of economic hardship and political turmoil, since recovery stemmed from spiritual health. He stressed that merging the journals ensured intellectual fertility and debate. The new *Schönere Zukunft* would now be the sole focal point for Central European Catholic intellectual life, a united front against heretical worldviews.[20] These words rang hollow. As Eberle commented triumphantly, his journal was now "the mouthpiece of the leading personalities in German Catholicism." By the end of 1932, it had a weekly circulation of between 20,000 and 25,000 copies, reaching a readership of 120,000, spread across German-speaking lands. The journal was now the most widely read weekly in Central Europe.[21] Eberle's publication had shown that it better represented radical conservatism in Vienna and Central Europe.

After the merger, the journal continued its rightward shift in conjunction with the radicalization of European politics. Whereas earlier polemics in *Die schönere Zukunft* had voiced outrage over the post-Versailles European order and invoked millennial visions of a *Großdeutsch* empire, by the 1930s Eberle and his colleagues had directed their attention to contemporary social and

---

19. Sigmund Waitz, "Solidarismus und Katholizismus," *NR* 14 (1931–32): 650; Dietrich Hildebrand, "Weder Individualismus noch Universalismus," *NR* 14 (1931–32): 693; Gustav Gundlach, "Staat, Gesellschaft und Wirtschaft," *NR* 14 (1931–32): 870; Oswald Nell-Breuning, "Zwei Ganzheitslehren," *NR* 14 (1931–32): 708–10, "Ein Jahr *Quadragesimo Anno,*" *NR* 14 (1931–32): 732, "Die falsche Ganzheitslehre: Universalismus," *NR* 14 (1931–32): 749–51, and "Die wahre Ganzheitslehre: Solidarismus," *NR* 14 (1931–32): 769–71.

20. Johannes Messner, "*Das Neue Reich* und *Die Schönere Zukunft* vereinigen sich," *NR* 14 (1931–32), 1003–4.

21. Hofer, "Joseph Eberle," 106–9, and Ziegerhofer-Prettenthaler, "*Schönere Zukunft,*" in Grunewald and Puschner, *Das Katholische Intellektuellenmilieu,* 395–96.

political movements for the attainment of a new Reich and beautiful future: Fascism and Nazism. Initially, Eberle hewed closer to the Italians. After some initial hesitation about Mussolini—particularly about attitudes to the church and ambitions in the Tirol—Eberle invited positive articles on the movement after the Italian concordat with the Vatican.[22]

Eberle's support of Nazism followed a similar trajectory. Shortly after the Nazis made parliamentary gains in 1930, Eberle authored a series of admonitory essays. In his 1931 brochure "Zum Kampf um Hitler," he expressed pro-Brüning, anti-Hitler thoughts: "It is regrettable that the crises of the period allow movements like the Nazis to become so large. These movements can only wreak havoc because they stem from and are interlarded with false ideas."[23] He argued that German Catholics had better solutions for the problems of Weimar Germany and that the anticlericalism and primitiveness of the Nazi program were troublesome. He explicitly rejected the "socialist" elements in the Nazi platform. Although he criticized the Nazis, he recognized that they were an important force combating the evils of the period: Bolshevism, plutocracy, Jewry, and democracy.[24] Eberle's solution to the turmoil in Germany was to provide the chancellor with dictatorial power, which would undercut the Weimar Republic and strip Hitler of his appeal.

Black Viennese attitudes on the Nazis softened as Hitler consolidated power. The *Reichspost* and its editor, Friedrich Funder, applauded the rejuvenated German nationalism associated with the movement, beginning a process of "bridge building" with the Nazis.[25] By the Nazi seizure of power in March 1933, Eberle had also adopted a position of tacit endorsement. Instead of focusing on the "un-Christian" and "barbaric" qualities of the movement, Eberle now stressed the reasons that Nazism was a necessary development:

> Nazism is therefore a reaction against the inadequacies of the parliamentary system, against the program of Western democracy. This does not seem to be a system for Germans. History also shows that peoples are not raised up [*emporgebracht*] from emergencies and failures through discussion but by authority.... Nazism owes its upswing ultimately to a

---

22. Some examples: "Einen Vergleich zwischen dem napoleonischen und dem italienischen Konkordat," *SZ* 5 (1929–30): 151–52; "Vergötzter Faschismus," *SZ* 5 (1929–30): 331; "Bilanz des ersten faschistischen Jahrzehnts," *SZ* 8 (1932–33): 269.

23. Eberle, *Kampf um Hitler*, 3.

24. Ibid., 19–29.

25. Busshoff, *Das Dollfuss-Regime*, 14–19. See also Thorpe, *Pan-Germanism*, 113–14.

reaction of natural feelings of the people [*natürliche Volksgefühle*] against the overwhelming Jewification of Germany.[26]

The echoes of Carl Schmitt's critique of deliberative democracy and the anti-Semitic discourse of integral German nationalism are unmistakable. Eberle may still have viewed the Nazis as an unsavory symptom of the post-Versailles order, yet he accepted them as superior to the alternatives. While Eberle cautioned the Nazis against excluding German Catholics from the *Volksgemeinschaft,* he characterized Hitler's achievement as "extraordinary" and a first step toward a federated *Großdeutschland.*

Emboldened by the Nazis, Black Viennese intellectuals advocated a new, more muscular "German mission" that included territorial expansion into southern and Central Europe. Hans Eibl and Heinrich Srbik provided credibility for these projects, since they were both full professors in Vienna, members of the Leo-Gesellschaft, and authors of best-selling books on the subject: Eibl's 1933 *Vom Sinn der Gegenwart* and Srbik's 1936 *Österreich in der deutschen Geschichte.* While Srbik remained on the fringes of the *Schönere Zukunft* circle, he pressed Catholic intellectuals and nationalist historians to recognize Austria's position in a broader Germanic historical context. He endorsed a revised *gesamtdeutsch* idea, unifying Germany and Austria on equal, federative terms. His views led him to become a staunch Nazi sympathizer by the mid-1930s.[27]

Eibl's *Vom Sinn der Gegenwart* merits closer scrutiny, for it demonstrates the growing affinities between German nationalism and Nazism within Black Viennese discourse. It foreshadows the possibility of collaboration between Austrian conservatives and the Germans, given their shared commitment to radical ideas of the Reich and the *Volk.* In his introduction, he expressed his desire for a Third Reich: "I have characterized the cultural synthesis, which also belongs as part of the present political struggles of Germans, with the Romantic philosophical term 'The Third Reich.'... That the idea of the Third Reich is for me strongly suffused with politics is only natural."[28] Eibl knew the historical origins of the term "Third Reich" in medieval German lands. As a nationalist and polemicist, he also appreciated that the concept carried Nazi connotations by 1933. He viewed the present moment in

26. Joseph Eberle, "Nur weniger als je politische Ausschaltung der deutschen Katholiken," *SZ* 8 (1932–33): 575.

27. Fritz Fellner, "Heinrich von Srbik," in Lehmann and Melton, *Paths of Continuity,* 171–86; Martina Pesditschek, "Heinrich (Ritter von) Srbik (1878–1951)," in Hruza, *Österreichische Historiker,* 2:263–65, 284–314.

28. Eibl, *Von Sinn der Gegenwart,* viii.

apocalyptic terms: "As far back as our historical memory extends, there is no period that, with respect to the depths of the upheavals and the breadth of their reach, compares to the present. . . . The present world-historical moment is a chosen time, in which a glimpse onto a new, comprehensive order of values is afforded."[29] The new German order of values, exemplified by the coming Third Reich, was the manifestation of a higher human consciousness and superior political and social universe.

The first section of the book elaborated his cosmological vision and argued for the integral role of intellectuals in reshaping society. This was an attitude shared by members of the Black and Red Viennese fields during the First Republic. In quasi-Hegelian fashion, Eibl maintained that history advances from states of dissolution (*Auflockerung*) to elevation (*Erhöhung*). During periods of dissolution, the desire for unification (*Streben nach Vereinheitlichung*) promotes human progress. The main actors are always scientists (*Wissenschaftler*) and other professionals, such as politicians, artists, engineers and businesspeople—those with the greatest stake in society. Change occurs more quickly with more intellectuals involved. As these individuals strive for unity in their own disciplines, they create coherent cultural formations for the *Volksgemeinschaft*. Eibl asserted that contemporary society, with its abundance of intellectuals, was ripe for revolutionary change.[30] These holistic and universalistic ideas of social improvement squared well with Black Viennese writers like Spann, Kralik, and Eberle and matched similar claims about intellectuals made by the Austro-Marxists.

In the concluding section, "the German Reich," Eibl called on his compatriots to carry out the German mission—violently, if necessary. "The three main tasks for Germans are (1) combating the peace treaty as murderous and morally bankrupt; (2) a struggle for a new legal order; (3) a struggle for a new Kingdom of God."[31] Militant language and imagery characterized all his demands—everything was a "battle" or "struggle." He called for crusading zeal in the fight for God and country. Only through the combined efforts of all Germans under the leadership of a strong führer could a respiritualized German nation and Western civilization emerge. "The strongly connected Third Reich will be a powerful focal point not only for Germans but for all peoples, German and non-German."[32] For Eibl, Germans possessed a messianic mission among the peoples of the world; this justified German imperialism. Even if he

---

29. Ibid., 5.
30. Ibid., 5–10.
31. Ibid., 286.
32. Ibid., 380.

did not mention the Nazis by name at this point, his aims and theirs largely coincided. Before long, Eibl began writing defenses of Nazi ideology in the Austrian press. He represented an early example of a *Brückenbauer*, a German nationalist intellectual who facilitated the rise of National Socialism in Austria.

Though the first stirrings of Nazi support were now present in Austrian scholarly books and journals, this was not a position taken by many conservative Austrians. Even as Eibl wrote pro-expansionist and pro-Nazi pieces with titles like "Mehr Lebensraum," most Black Viennese intellectuals still looked to domestic alternatives, adopting fascist views free of Nazi influence.[33] At first, this resulted in diverse discussions and little acrimony within the conservative field, since differences over Nazism were largely masked by a shared disdain for liberalism, socialism, and republicanism. Black Viennese conservatives revealed their dictatorial predilections in these exchanges. By 1932, writers in *Die schönere Zukunft*, the *Reichspost*, and the Leo-Gesellschaft's journal *Die Kultur* had abandoned any support for Austrian democracy.[34] As the next section shows, through late 1936 even the supporters of a more moderate authoritarianism in *Der christliche Ständestaat* unswervingly supported Austrofascism and Italian Fascism rather than a broad anti-Nazi coalition. In addition, anti-Semitic articles appeared with greater frequency, with Catholic theorists adopting problematic attitudes on concepts like *Rasse* and *Volk*.[35]

With the demise of the First Republic, Black Viennese thinkers got an opportunity to see some of their ideas come to fruition. On March 4, 1933, the three presidents of the national assembly resigned their positions during the course of a procedural vote. This left no one to end the session or call for a new one. Chancellor Dollfuss used this opportunity to end parliamentary democracy in Austria by refusing to call for new elections. On March 7 he announced he would rule by decree, and on March 15 he summoned the police to prevent the presidents of the assembly from reconvening the body. Dollfuss moved to consolidate power through the formation of the Vaterländische Front and the restriction of activities by the Social Democrats and National Socialists. His regime censored rival papers, disbanded the socialist paramilitary organization, the Schutzbund, and prevented opponents from organizing.[36]

Black Viennese intellectuals looked expectantly to Dollfuss as an Austrian Mussolini or Hitler, someone who would restore the country to greatness.

---

33. Busshoff, *Dollfuß-Regime*, 130–31.
34. Ibid., 278–79.
35. Connelly, *From Enemy to Brother*, 13–25, 65–85.
36. Jelavich, *Modern Austria*, 194–200.

Gregor Uhlhorn wrote an ecstatic eulogy for the parliament and a paean to Dollfuss: "The Austrian Parliament dissolved itself during the course of one of its trivial arguments over the order of business.... This result is also of symbolic significance: it is the most obvious proof of the incapacity for survival [*Lebensunfähigkeit*] and fruitlessness of radical parliamentarianism in Austria. The parliament committed suicide, thereby admitting its inability to master the prevailing emergency conditions."[37] After asserting that Dollfuss had no dictatorial intentions and that only some authoritarian constitutional amendments were necessary, Uhlhorn declared the present moment propitious for the creation of a state along the lines of the 1931 papal encyclical, "Quadragesimo Anno." Like most conservatives, Uhlhorn believed that the problem for Austria's future was the socialists, not the Nazis. He quoted Dollfuss, who had argued that it was just a matter of time before the Nazis made common cause with other conservatives. Since the Nazis shared many values with the Fatherland Front, they should work in league against the reds. Once the socialists had been defeated, then the Nazi movement would lose its modus vivendi.[38]

For the next year, little disagreement over Austria's political course appeared in Black Viennese discussions. While Eberle, Eibl, and Uhlhorn wrote laudatory pieces about both the Nazis and Fatherland Front, such "moderates" from the now-defunct *Neues Reich* as Johannes Messner and Andreas Posch contributed articles that advocated for authoritarian government predicated on the leadership principle (*Führer- und Autoritätsprinzip*).[39] They agreed with the government's attacks on socialism, Red Vienna, and Jewish influences. As for the Nazis, moderates tolerated them as long as their activities did not challenge Catholicism or Austrian autonomy. Messner openly endorsed the July 1933 *Reichskonkordat* between Hitler and the Catholic Church, offering the following justification: "[The concordat] is a recognition of the secular mission of the German people for the Christian West, a recognition that appears petty if one... views it as the recognition of a new state form or the worldview standing behind it. As if the Church had not always asserted that it is not its place to recognize or reject state forms if they harmonize with the moral order of the world!"[40] While the first sentence conveys Messner's lack of enthusiasm for the Nazi movement, the second offers a tacit acceptance of the Nazi regime and its legitimate contribution to the "moral order of the world." Messner's comments

---

37. Gregor Uhlhorn, "Regierungskurs des Reformwillens," *SZ* 8 (1932–23): 603.
38. Ibid., 604.
39. See *SZ* 8 (1932–33) and 9 (1933–34) for articles from Eibl, Eberle, Messner, Spann, and others.
40. Johannes Messner, "Nach dem Reichskonkordat," *SZ* 8 (1932–33): 1099.

highlight the ambiguous relationship that developed between the church, conservative intellectuals, and the Nazis in the interwar era.[41]

Black Viennese intellectuals discussed more than political developments, yet their cultural agenda was always an extension of sociopolitical beliefs. As Friedrich Funder acknowledged, *Die schönere Zukunft* and the *Reichspost* complemented each other in their radical challenges to the political order: they "complete one another insofar as *Die schönere Zukunft* tries to clarify different questions of politics, business, culture and religion from a fundamentally Catholic standpoint, while *Die Reichspost* wants to achieve this standpoint through the analysis of the daily political struggle."[42] Funder and Eberle took seriously the task of criticizing the Austrian cultural landscape in the name of creating a better order. In *Die schönere Zukunft,* Hans Eibl contributed to this political and cultural mission, lauding the new German and Austrian states for their anti-Western and antiliberal militancy:

> The meaning of this struggle is the uprooting of two axioms of Western thought that have predominated for four centuries and have increasingly destroyed our moral consciousness: the belief that humans are solitary beings left to their own devices and that humans as a species are the measure of all things and the creators of the moral order [*Wertordnung*]. Today the old truth survives... that human souls are a priori bound up with metaphysical values and placed into a moral order that they do not create but can only discover and actualize.[43]

Like Messner, Eibl invoked the idea of order as a justification for the fascist turn of 1930s politics. They could brook no compromise with the "atheistic" Freudians, "antimetaphysical" positivists or "nihilistic" Marxists. Helmuth Burgert, a *Dozent* in philosophy, applauded the recent renaissance in metaphysics. "Kantianism of all forms has run its course [*abgewirtschaftet*].... The strict positivists have only built a sect and those phenomenologists following Husserl, who anxiously closed themselves off from metaphysics, are finished. Husserl's most important students and supporters—Scheler, Heidegger, Hildebrand, Moritz Geiger, Edith Stein, etc.—have given up the methodological narrowness of pure ontological research [*Wesensforschung*] and have become metaphysicians."[44] Burgert argued that a revolution in thought and spirit had accompanied the ongoing political changes

---

41. On Catholics and the Nazis, see Hastings, *Roots of Nazism;* Krieg, *Catholic Theologians;* Lewy, *Catholic Church;* Phayer, *Catholic Church;* Spicer, *Hitler's Priests;* Steigmann-Gall, *Holy Reich.*
42. Quoted in Busshoff, *Das Dollfuss-Regime,* 15.
43. Hans Eibl, "Die Scheidung der Geister," *SZ* 9 (1933–34): 142.
44. Hans Burgert, "Der katholische Beitrag zur Metaphysik," *SZ* 9 (1933–34): 210–11.

of 1933–34. The Christian worldview would show the way out from this *Weltanschauungskampf*. Positivists such as Schlick and phenomenologists such as Husserl were representatives of a moribund order, which the current revolutions seemed destined to overcome.

As Burgert's comments suggest, conservative intellectuals held a paranoid conviction that liberals and socialists dominated the Viennese and Central European cultural landscape. This produced a sense of solidarity in Black Vienna in the early 1930s. Intellectuals saw the conservative and nationalist University of Vienna as a hotbed of subversive activity, which the new government had to eradicate. Burgert elaborated on the corrosive nature of Austrian philosophy:

> While today's Austrian government has worked with all available means to allow good conservative and Catholic forces to come to prominence in all cultural areas, university philosophy still has an outdated, highly liberal face. Particularly in Vienna since Mach, positivism has found a home. Schlick, also Carnap and Frank…are its modern…advocates. It is clear that these philosophers in their antimetaphysics and atheism do not fit with the cultural program of the Austrian government…. They do not see that empiricism refutes itself [*sich selbst aufhebt*], since its claims [about metaphysics] are themselves not empirically verifiable…. Of the philosophers who have formed the opposition to this coarse, metaphysics-less scientism, we mention above all Richard von Kralik, Hans Eibl, Lorenz Fuetscher, Othmar Spann.[45]

Burgert invoked Eric Voegelin's concept of "scientism" to attack the ideological assumptions of the logical empiricists.[46] Of the dangerous philosophers identified by Burgert, only Schlick lived in Austria—Carnap and Frank both had posts in Prague. Moreover, Schlick was no radical, openly expressing his support for the new regime. Groups like the logical empiricists had curtailed their public activities by 1933 and many Red Viennese intellectuals left the country.[47] The conservatives were attacking straw men, yet this provided a unifying impetus. Burgert argued the state must abet the efforts of Catholic philosophers in combating positivists, since science and politics were inextricably connected. Much as the new state did not tolerate resistance from socialists, its intellectual supporters could not permit philosophical challengers.

---

45. Hans Burgert, "Philosophie in Österreich," *SZ* 9 (1933–34): 309.
46. Voegelin, *Race and State,* 8–12.
47. On Austrian intellectual migration, see Stadler, *Vertriebene Vernunft.*

The united front of Black Viennese thinkers largely endured through the end of the Republic. During this time, the political landscape shifted tremendously in Central Europe. With the removal of their main ideological and political enemies, tensions reemerged in Vienna over alternate visions of German fascism.[48] *Lager* thinking—implying a divide between Catholic conservatism and German nationalism—reappeared as politicians and intellectuals wrestled with new concerns. In particular, the formation of the Austrofascist state presented an opportunity for pro-Austrian Catholics to gain political influence and develop a distinctive Austrian ideology. Ironically, it was a German political émigré who figured most prominently in the Black Viennese schism, offering the stiffest challenge to hegemonic Black Viennese radicalism. Dietrich Hildebrand and *Der christliche Ständestaat* offered a principled and consistent anti-Nazi position that forced the Viennese to confront problematic aspects within their respective ideologies. They also raised important questions about the role of Catholicism in Viennese conservatism. The struggle between these factions sheds light on the radicalization of Austrian thought in the mid-1930s and the difficulties in drawing clear ideological distinctions in interwar Central Europe.

Der Christliche Ständestaat and the Conservative Schism in Authoritarian Vienna, 1934–1936

In early 1933 the anti-Nazi Catholic theologian Dietrich Hildebrand fled Germany to avoid arrest. He resettled in Vienna, where he made connections in the university and the Dollfuss government. He chose Austria, for he believed the country to be the best hope for a Catholic German state and the last bastion against "economic materialism" (i.e., Marxism) and "materialism of the blood" (Nazism). Hildebrand decided to found a publication that would advance an "Austrian mission" and warn against the twin evils on the left and right. In December 1933 *Der christliche Ständestaat* first appeared. According to Rudolf Ebneth, Hildebrand and his fellow contributors had several goals in mind, including the reduction of the influence of *Die schönere Zukunft,* the attraction of Catholic intellectuals to moderate Catholic cultural goals, and the strengthening of political Catholicism.[49] Since these ambitions coincided with Chancellor Dollfuss's vision, the journal became an unofficial organ for the Austrofascist state. From the outset, *Der christliche Ständestaat* received most of its money from the Austrian government, and the regime purchased a large

---

48. On Austria's two fascisms, see Mann, *Fascists,* 208.
49. Ebneth, *Die österreichische Wochenschrift "Der Christliche Ständestaat,"* 22–35.

number of the journal's editions.[50] The support helped the fledgling periodical survive despite a lack of advertising revenue, a small contingent of writers, and intense competition in the Viennese press.

Hildebrand established the journal's anti-Nazi, pro-Austrian position from the start, presenting Austria as Europe's hope for a Christian future and a third way between political extremisms. "Europe, the Christian West and true Germandom turn their eyes with expectation on Austria, which has chosen a Christian, German *Ständestaat* as a program. This program goes well beyond the boundaries of politics; it demands a profound, spiritual clarification of worldview. False and erroneous conceptions, economic materialism and materialism of the blood, liberal individualism and heathen totalitarianism [*Staatsomnipotenz*], must be opposed by the great classical formulations of Western thought."[51] Hildebrand proffered the "Austrian idea" as a political and spiritual answer to the crises of modern Central Europe. He advocated a "Christian, German" state—preferably, an authoritarian one. Hildebrand may have been a moderate Catholic, but he was neither a liberal nor a democrat.[52] Austria must be Catholic and German; exclusion of others was acceptable: "This paper will serve the ideological conquest of Austria. Outside all party politics it will help work for . . . the development of a fully flourishing life, which is captured in the words of the man entrusted with the leadership of the great, truly German, Christian future [Dollfuss]: 'Austriam instaurare in Christo' (Austria will be restored in Christ)."[53] Hildebrand did not see that one could not stand outside party politics while endorsing an Austrofascist program that embraced anti-Semitism, denied the rights of socialists and liberals, and promulgated xenophobic legislation.[54]

Given that *Der christliche Ständestaat* represented more moderate conservative views, it was clear before the end of the Republic that Black Viennese thinkers had abandoned any efforts to work within the republican political system. For them, the Fatherland Front had a responsibility to the country to protect it from the antidemocratic Social Democrats and National Socialists. In their respect for true democracy, moderates argued they had to do away

---

50. Kromar, *Der "Österreich-Mythos,'"* 114. Kromar estimates that weekly circulation was about five thousand, with one thousand copies going to Italy, five hundred to Alsace and Lorraine, and "hundreds" to the Austrian government. Other estimates suggest that the weekly numbers were about four thousand, with almost half going to the regime. See Seefried, "Reich und Ständestaat," in Grunewald and Puschner, *Das Katholische Intellektuellenmilieu,* 421.

51. Dietrich Hildebrand, "Was wir Wollen," *CS,* December 3, 1933, 3.

52. Seefried notes no support for the Weimar Republic in Hildebrand's earlier writings. See "Reich und Ständestaat," 418–19.

53. Hildebrand, "Was wir Wollen," 3.

54. On the fascistic qualities of Austrofascist legislation, see Thorpe, *Pan-Germanism,* chaps. 4–6.

with democracy to save it. Eric Voegelin, then an emerging political theorist and moral philosopher, captured this irony when he argued that the Christian Socials acted in self-defense by destroying the Republic:

> The democrats [Christian Socials] were under an obligation to cling to the letter of the constitution until the antidemocratic forces [socialists and Nazis] were strong enough to do away with it. The rules of the constitution had to be observed, according to this opinion, although the social reality to which they should be applied was lacking. The "democratic" contents of the constitution should be the guiding rule for the government, in spite of the fact that there existed no Austrian "demos."[55]

Why preserve a democracy against Nazism or socialism when there was no Austrian *demos,* Voegelin argued. The unrest of 1933 and 1934 impelled "loyal" conservatives to move against "national-socialist propaganda" and "class-war ideology." This necessitated the circumvention of the constitution and the rise of Austrofascism. Of course, the socialists had never expressed an intention to circumvent the law of the land, a subject on which Voegelin remained mum. He also had little use for questions of legitimacy or legality, for he believed that the First Republic and its constitution lacked legitimacy. Members of the Dollfuss movement were wasting their time trying to demonstrate the *Ständestaat* to be the rightful successor of either the Republic or the earlier monarchy. Using Max Weber's language, Voegelin argued that the Austrofascists possessed legitimacy because they monopolized the legal use of violence after February 1934. Simply put, might determined right.[56]

Despite the inconsistencies in the views of Black Viennese moderates, many intellectuals rallied to the Austrofascist cause in 1934 in the wake of the May constitution and the assassination of Chancellor Dollfuss by Nazi terrorists in July. This was a moment of decision for Black Vienna: either it could support the *Ständestaat* in its time of crisis or it could endorse fascism theoretically, while leaving the door open for solutions other than Austrofascism. *Die schönere Zukunft* chose the latter approach by taking an ambivalent stance on the Dollfuss assassination. While the journal condemned the act and included articles honoring the dead, it did not reject the Nazis outright.[57] A closer look at *Die schönere Zukunft's* financial base and audience

---

55. Eric Voegelin, "Government and Constitution," in Voegelin, *Published Essays 1934–1939,* 104. On the young Voegelin, see Cooper, *Beginning the Quest.*

56. Voegelin, *Authoritarian State,* 223–46.

57. Ebneth, *Die österreichische Wochenschrift "Der Christliche Ständestaat,"* 103–11.

partially explains this equivocation. Nearly 40 percent of its readership resided in Germany, and a substantial portion of its advertising also came from across the border. To maintain the journal's preeminent position in Central Europe, Eberle could not afford to antagonize the German government, which had just promulgated the Thousand-Mark Law—which charged Germans one thousand marks if they wished to visit Austria—and hoped to weaken the Austrian economy at every turn.

Many Black Viennese intellectuals could not abide this pragmatism, nor could they brook compromise with the Nazis. As we have seen, members of the Österreichische Aktion stopped writing for *Die schönere Zukunft*. Johannes Messner, like his fellow editor Alfred Missong, remained on the editorial board of the journal until 1938, though he rarely wrote articles after 1934. He turned his intellectual attentions to the university, where he was appointed professor, and the government, where he served as an adviser to Kurt Schuschnigg. His dismay over Eberle's coverage of the assassination prompted him to write a hagiographic Dollfuss biography in 1934.[58]

Der christliche Ständestaat was the primary beneficiary of the schism within Black Viennese circles. In the first few months of its existence, the weekly scraped along, consisting primarily of articles by Hildebrand, fellow German exiles, and Austrian government officials. By March, Hildebrand had enlisted a wide variety of intellectuals, including the author Richard Schaukal, former Aktion member Hans Zessner-Spitzenberg, the *Sozialreform* theorist Wiard Klopp, the composer Ernst Krenek, and the psychiatrist Victor Frankl. *Der christliche Ständestaat* became a dynamic forum for the discussion of international affairs, the Austrian state, and the German religious and cultural mission. It was also one of the earliest forums for antitotalitarian discussions[59] and new thinking on Catholic anti-Semitism.[60] In May 1934 the increasingly confident Hildebrand began to attack *Die schönere Zukunft*.[61] When Eibl wrote a piece for Eberle's journal that argued for the compatibility of racial politics and Christianity and applauded the Nazi concern for maintaining a healthy race,[62] Hildebrand pounced. He castigated this support for Nazi racism and argued that there was no way for a true conservative to square Nazi racial ideas with Catholic dogma. He identified Eibl as part of a dangerous group of Catholics that tacked toward Nazism despite its heretical

58. Messner, *Engelbert Dollfuss*.

59. Chappel, "Catholic Origins," 561–90.

60. Connelly, *From Enemy to Brother*, 108–33.

61. From May until July, there were two or three articles a month directed at Eberle's journal and its problematic relationship to the Nazis.

62. Hans Eibl, "Um Fragen und Zielsetzung in Deutschland," *SZ* 9 (1933–34): 787–88.

tendencies.[63] Hildebrand and his fellow contributors missed no opportunity to criticize Eibl, Eberle, Spann, and others when they showed sympathy for Nazism.

In the first couple of years of the Austrofascist state, the moderate wing seemed to gain traction, both in the academy and in government. Hildebrand, Messner, Voegelin, and Zessner-Spitzenberg received professorships at the University of Vienna, and Josef Dobretsberger became a full professor. This signaled a shift in ideology in the academy, for appointments had previously gone to scholars with strong German nationalist convictions.[64] By comparison, Othmar Spann's students, who had enjoyed great academic success through 1933, saw their opportunities dry up. Likewise, Austrofascist intellectuals wrested control of the Leo-Gesellschaft away from the radicals.[65] Dobretsberger, Messner and Ernst Karl Winter also took positions within the Austrofascist government—Dobretsberger as minister of social affairs, Messner as a constitutional adviser, and Winter as the third vice mayor of Vienna.

The Christlicher Ständestaat conservatives crafted their own political and philosophical ideology in new forums. Though it was distinctively Austrian and clearly anti-Nazi, it was fascist, authoritarian, and antidemocratic. They saw themselves as part of a broader European trend away from Enlightenment values. Hildebrand stressed his rejection of parliamentary democracy in favor of strong leadership (*Führertum*):

> Today's desire for an authoritarian state is more the consequence of disappointment with the political feasibility of exaggerated parliamentarianism. Not only is it the awareness that democratic parliamentarianism is an unfeasible state form, which must be replaced for a healthy political life to thrive, but it is also a true desire for authority *as such* in the state, because of the virtue and majesty that only true authority can establish.[66]

According to Hildebrand, authority qua authority was the sole basis for politics. This signaled a clear break with recent instructions from the church on political matters. A mere two years earlier, Pope Pius XI had promulgated the encyclical "Quadragesimo Anno," which expressed a willingness to work

---

63. *CS*, May 20, 1934, 22–23.

64. On the politics of the academy, see Weinzierl, *Universität und Politik,* and Wimmer and Fischer, *Der geistige Anschluss.*

65. A survey of lectures in the society suggest that the German nationalists no longer participated to the same degree after 1933. See Theodor Innitzer, *Leo-Gesellschaft 1933–1934* (Vienna: Verlag der Leo-Gesellschaft, 1934) and *Leo-Gesellschaft 1935–1938* (Vienna: Verlag der Leo-Gesellschaft, 1934).

66. Dietrich Hildebrand, "Autorität und Führertum," *CS,* December 3, 1933, 6.

within democratic states for a Catholic social program. As discussed earlier, Hildebrand and others had defended this course, which lay in the tradition of Catholic *Sozialpolitik,* against the radical interpretation offered by Spann and Eberle. By 1933, even the Hildebrand circle categorically rejected compromise with liberal democratic forms.[67]

The major monographs of this circle stressed the incompatibility of Christian social theory and democracy. Johannes Messner, a so-called realistic theorist who rejected the more utopian elements of Catholic *Sozialreform,*[68] argued for major social changes in his two books from the Austrofascist period. The first book criticized the capitalist economic order and its individualist, rationalist ethos for the impoverishment of contemporary society. Messner attacked the "sham equality" of democratic states and lamented the loss of "true democracy" characteristic of "organic," hierarchical societies. He contrasted "formal" democracy with "real" democracy: "If the common good remains the unconditional norm for state leadership [in authoritarian democracy], in formal democracy the regime is wholly bound to the majority will, which is all too easily corrupted by chance and party egotism. It is in real democracy that the weight of each individual's voice is categorized according to their social responsibility."[69] For Messner, formal democracy was pseudodemocracy, prone to demagogic manipulations and distortions. Only if individualism, socialism, and capitalism were overcome would a Christian world once again thrive. Messner invoked both Spann and Carl Schmitt in making his argument for authoritarian democracy and cited Eibl on the nature of the German *Volk.* A new state had to be established, which prioritized the social and economic well-being of all its subjects by attending to the needs of the nation's various estates and professions. The only way for such a state to appear would be under a unitary leader who wielded power over the social, political, and economic order.[70] In drawing these conclusions, Messner saw the merit of Nazi economic programs: "Even if the economic picture of National Socialism is only now recognizable in outline, it is nevertheless clear that a thoroughgoing agreement with the fundamental principles of Christian *Sozialreform* exists."[71]

Messner's views on race, anti-Semitism, and eugenics also placed him in the mainstream of Central European Catholic racial thinking.[72] Though he

---

67. Diamant, *Austrian Catholics,* 169–207.
68. Ibid., 195–202.
69. Messner, *Soziale Frage,* 172.
70. Ibid., 488–90.
71. Ibid., 422. See also 167–84, 556.
72. Connelly, *From Enemy to Brother,* chap. 1.

denied the Nazis' claims about the purity of the Aryan race and the possibility of pure races at all, he nevertheless supported Hermann Muckermann's assertions that premature (*unfertig*) races existed, which must be prevented from breeding with the German *Volk*. Messner called for a "national eugenics" to protect Germandom from corruption. Eugenics was an absolute necessity, tied to principles of natural rights and the common good. Messner advocated positive pronatalist measures and restrictions on marriage and procreation for "tubercular, alcoholic, feeble-minded or criminal families."[73] Clear overlaps existed between Messner's social and racial views and those of the German nationalists and Nazis he decried.

Messner's second book defended the Austrofascist state as a valid attempt to institute an organic order. He saw the state as the sole defense against the perils of socialism and capitalism. While he did not equate the "corporate order" *(berufsständische Ordnung)* with the Austrian *Ständestaat*, he saw the latter as an important first step to a restored, authoritarian German nation. Messner distinguished between authoritarian and führer rule, preferring the former, because it lacked the personal, charismatic character of the latter and was less susceptible to corruption. Nevertheless, he recognized the need "in the present cultural crisis" for a führer who could open the eyes of the *Volk* and reintroduce national values.[74] Messner was referring to more than just Hitler; he saw the importance of a Mussolini, Dollfuss, Salazar, or Franco for European communities. For example, he spoke favorably of the constitutions in Portugal and Italy and of Fascist corporatist reforms.[75] Though he distinguished the authoritarian state from a total state, he demanded that the state oversee all aspects of economic and social life in the name of the common good.[76] Messner—a leading moderate in Black Vienna, Dollfuss's adviser, and Eberle's stalwart opponent—expressed ideas that situated him squarely in the middle of European fascist discourse. He was not a Nazi, to be sure, but neither was he a moderate or a realist.

Like Messner, Eric Voegelin glorified authoritarianism, the Austrofascist state, and power politics in his writings from the mid-1930s. The 1936 *Authoritarian State* had three purposes: to present a history of Austrian constitutionalism, a critique of the First Republic, and a defense of the new state. Despite its academic pretensions and claims of critical objectivity, the

---

73. Messner, *Soziale Frage,* 557–60.
74. Messner, *Berufsständische Ordnung,* 4–15, 259–60.
75. Ibid., 284–85, 299–300.
76. Ibid., 69–78.

book carried an illiberal bias and propagandistic intent. Voegelin expressed his intention to investigate the essence of the authoritarian state and to advocate for the increase of its power: "The significance of the organization of the authoritarian state and the possibility of strengthening it in the direction of totalitarianism or weakening it must be evaluated with a view to historical factors."[77] Although he claimed that strengthening and weakening the state were both possibilities, he argued against weakening the state through democratic measures and for totalitarian measures. His contention that the 1934 constitution stemmed from a liberal tradition was deceptive, for the Austrofascists had done away with parliament, political parties, and elections while eliminating basic civil liberties. Despite the political biases embedded in his recommendations, he argued that this book would leave political ideologues disappointed, since it offered no endorsement of any given system. Everywhere he cloaked his Austrofascist political convictions in academic jargon, a fact that even he later came to admit.[78]

Voegelin dealt with questions of legality and legitimacy, offering a *völkisch* interpretation of Austrofascism. He posited that the new Austrian state was the first legitimate state that Austrians had had. He rejected the strict division of legality and legitimacy advocated by Hans Kelsen and Max Weber, whereby the rule of law established by a constitution (legality) assured the legitimacy of the political system. Employing ideas based on Carl Schmitt's theories of dictatorship and the state of exception, as well as Spann's notions of a true state, Voegelin claimed that only strong leadership insured legitimacy. "Rulership is legitimate when its relationship to an institution is one of representation; the ruler himself as representative of the institution gives it its ruling order; his position cannot be legitimated through a rule of law. The demand for 'legality' is a misunderstanding...of the processes of legitimation."[79] Strong rulership assured legitimacy; the rule of law (legality) had no legitimacy without strong leadership. Practically speaking, Voegelin attacked the First Republic as a legal order without legitimacy or leadership, while claiming that the post-1933 government possessed all essential components.

Voegelin stated his reservations about Nazi ideology in 1933 and noted that Austrian national sentiment had emerged only in the face of its potential

---

77. Voegelin, *Authoritarian State,* 47.

78. In his *Autobiographical Reflections,* he wrote that *The Authoritarian State* had been written in response to receiving his academic appointment at the University of Vienna.

79. Voegelin, *Authoritarian State,* 223. See also 235, 245–46.

elimination from the European map.[80] Nevertheless, his conception of Austrian unity—shared by fellow moderate Black Viennese thinkers—excluded liberals, democrats, non-Germans, and Jews. These were not moderate positions; rather, they represented a fascist middle way between Nazism and democracy. Undoubtedly distinct from Nazism, their views fit well within European fascist discourse. More problematic still was that they offered little on a political, philosophical, or theoretical level that substantively differentiated their ideological position from that of the radicals like Spann and Eberle. This lack of clear differentiation spelled trouble for moderates in their *Weltanschauungskampf* for Black Vienna.

The Reassertion of Radical Hegemony and the Decline of the *Christliche Ständestaat*

Political Catholicism enjoyed a resurgence during the *Ständestaat,* a fact that many scholars have emphasized.[81] As Julie Thorpe has shown, however, German nationalist ideology and radical authoritarianism continued to exert considerable influence.[82] While moderate Catholics gained a hearing, their views were ultimately drowned out. Much like the state they endorsed, *Ständestaat* intellectuals like Messner and Hildebrand failed to effect a change in the Black Viennese *Weltanschauung.*

When Dietrich Hildebrand delivered his introductory lecture in the philosophy department of the University of Vienna in 1934, around six hundred students showed up to protest, signaling their displeasure at the appointment of an anti-Nazi and antinationalist intellectual.[83] These students dismissed the German émigré Hildebrand's call for an independent, Catholic Austria and hoped for a unified German Reich. Like these nationalist students, the radical *Schönere Zukunft* contributors intensified their critique of the Austrian state and its affiliated intellectuals while simultaneously softening their stance on the Nazis. Hildebrand and his colleagues at *Der christliche Ständestaat* faced difficulties in positing a viable alternative to the hegemonic vision for Austria represented by Spannians, Nazis, and other German nationalists.

After reaching a high-water mark of twenty-five thousand weekly editions in October 1932, *Die schönere Zukunft* saw its numbers decrease

---

80. His two 1933 books, *Race and State* and *The History of the Race Idea,* questioned the scientific validity of Nazi racial theory while leaving open the possibility of a credible race science.

81. See Diamant, *Austrian Catholics;* Hanisch, *Die Ideologie des politischen Katholizismus;* Weiß, *Rechtskatholizismus;* and Prinz, *Politischer Katholizismus.*

82. Thorpe, *Pan-Germanism,* introduction.

83. Kromar, *Der "Österreich-Mythos,"* 116.

to twenty thousand by 1936.[84] While myriad reasons contributed to this trend, the largest factor was *Der christliche Ständestaat*. Eberle, ever the shrewd publicist, knew this. Consequently, he and his collaborators set about differentiating their position from Hildebrand's, engaging in skirmishes over conservative ideology. Hans Eibl instigated conflict with an essay arguing that Catholicism and racial theory were reconcilable. Hildebrand responded, asserting that such a statement tacitly endorsed Nazi ideology.[85] Eberle and his minions tarred *Der christliche Ständestaat* as an uncritical, sycophantic government rag. They frequently mentioned that this "Austrian" publication was written by non-Austrians. Hildebrand replied with admonitory essays about the dangers of Hitlerism. The conflict expanded to include the *Reichspost* by late 1934, reaching a high point when the paper endorsed Bishop Alois Hudal's tract, *The Foundations of National Socialism,* which reconciled "healthy" National Socialism with the Catholic worldview.[86] Hudal, a frequent contributor to Eberle's publications and the Leo-Gesellschaft, found vocal support at the university, where he was a professor (and later rector). *Der christliche Ständestaat* found itself fighting on multiple fronts against an implacable Black Viennese foe.

In late 1934 Othmar Spann again became a focal point for his derisive comments about the *Ständestaat*. In his book *Kämpfende Wissenschaft* he mocked the new state as an "uncanny carnivalesque joke" (*unheimliche Fastnachtsscherz*). Spann felt his theories had been misappropriated and the new government was heir to the individualist ideas of 1789. As with the debates about "Quadragesimo Anno," *Der christliche Ständestaat* attacked Spann and universalism. Otto Maria Karpfen called Spann a dangerous crypto-Nazi elitist who favored a total state like the one "to the north."[87] Aurel Kolnai dismantled Spann's philosophy, calling it a heathen system.[88] These writers distanced themselves from Spannian (and Nazi) totalitarianism and argued for an independent Austria guided by corporatist policies. The Spannkreis responded to these criticisms with disdain, noting the ineffectiveness and unpopularity of the new government.

Making matters more difficult was the delicate ideological tightrope that Austrofascist intellectuals had to negotiate, attacking the German nationalists for totalitarian tendencies and anti-Catholicism while also supporting the

---

84. Ebneth, *Die österreichische Wochenschrift "Der Christliche Ständestaat,"* 130.

85. Dietrich Hildebrand, *CS,* May 20, 1934, 22–23.

86. Ebneth, *Die österreichische Wochenschrift "Der Christliche Ständestaat,"* 103–23. See also Connelly, *From Enemy to Brother,* 25–27.

87. Otto Fidelis, "Ist Österreich ein totaler Staat?" *CS,* September 16, 1933, 8–9.

88. See the November 1934 editions of *CS.*

regimes in Italy, Hungary, Portugal, and Spain.[89] That left little room for them to carve out a distinctive *Weltanschauung* or "third way" conservatism. Like the government they supported, these intellectuals found themselves caught between Italy and Germany. Hildebrand and his colleagues advanced many positive ideas in their weekly, which served as a forum for antitotalitarian and antiracist thought, but they also supported the imperialist adventures of Italy in Abyssinia and the Nationalists in Spain during its civil war. They made frequent attempts to distinguish Nazism from Fascism and argued in favor of the latter system over other alternatives, including democracy.[90] In a piece discussing Carl Schmitt's *Concept of the Political* that compared conservative ideologies, the author argued that Fascism was exemplary for all ethnic group and states: "Fascism is an adequate political form for modern Italianness [*Italientum*], which indicates very well a model character in a conservative direction for other states."[91] Thus, even as they distanced themselves from Nazi thought, they remained bound to other forms of fascism, imperialism, and racism.

A perceptible shift took place in the polemical style of *Der christliche Ständestaat* as the editors realized that their offensive against radical Black Viennese intellectuals had not had the desired effect. Whereas articles from 1934 and 1935 offered a critical refutation of Black Viennese universalism and nationalism, subsequent submissions descended into personal attacks. The changing geopolitical situation played a role at this stage, since Italy had retreated from its unequivocal support of an independent Austria in 1936 and the gentleman's agreement between Hitler and Schuschnigg left anti-Nazis feeling isolated and betrayed. Spann was the primary target of these verbal assaults. Articles portrayed him as "caught between two chairs"— Catholic authoritarianism and Nazism. They reveled in Spann's political failures, invoking his phrase *Fastnachtsscherz* to characterize his own work.[92] Hildebrand argued that only a tolerant state would allow an enemy like Spann to remain in its employ. This claim was riddled with irony, for Spann's continued employment demonstrated the weakness of the Austrofascist state's

89. P. Albert Müller, "Ständestaat Portugal," *CS,* September 2, 1934; "Latinität," January 6–13, 1935.

90. "Nationalsozialismus und Faschismus sind nicht Gleich!" *CS,* September 9, 1934; "Mussolini über Österreichs historische Mission," *CS,* February 24, 1935; Otto Karpfen, "Italien und der österreichische Gedanke," *CS,* March 24, 1935.

91. Richard Behrendt, "Die Totalität des Politischen," *CS,* June 16, 1935, 572. On Italian imperialism and racism, see Ben-Ghiat, *Fascist Modernities,* 123–30.

92. "Klarheit gegen Othmar Spann," *CS,* January 5, 1936, 25, and Junius Austriacus, "Henlein und Spann," *CS,* July 5, 1936, 639–41.

ideological position. Had the Austrofascists been in a position to remove Spann, they would have. The Nazis did not hesitate to do so in 1938.

By late 1936, it was apparent that the *Ständestaat* ideologues, much like the state itself, had to bow to pressure from the radical right. As the new chancellor Schuschnigg hewed closer to the Nazis, *Der christliche Ständestaat* lost its mandate. The government withdrew financial support in 1936 at the time of the gentleman's agreement. Sensing the changing political winds, Hildebrand resigned from his position as editor in 1937. Attacks on Spann, the *Reichspost,* and *Die schönere Zukunft* disappeared. *Der christliche Ständestaat* was reduced to an exile publication, mostly of literary and cultural essays.[93] Meanwhile, *Die schönere Zukunft* continued to operate through the *Anschluss,* closing only in 1941. The Nazis, who cracked down on all offending intellectuals and cultural organizations, saw *Die schönere Zukunft* as a permissible periodical. Its intellectuals, who made up the core of the Black Viennese cultural field, managed to bridge the gap between Catholic conservatism, German nationalism, and National Socialism.

"God protect us from such Catholics!"[94] Dietrich Hildebrand issued this pronouncement in response to Johann Sauter's essay on Moritz Schlick. As noted earlier, it seemed odd that in 1936 there would be such heated debate centering on a progressive yet pro-*Ständestaat* intellectual whose influence had long been in eclipse. Given the ideological tensions prevalent in Black Vienna, however, the debate becomes more comprehensible. For the conservatives of interwar Austria, Schlick's case came at the culmination of a protracted debate about Catholicism, conservatism, and the state. On one side, moderates such as Dietrich Hildebrand, Johannes Messner, and Eric Voegelin condemned the heinous act *tout court* and eulogized Schlick as a good scholar, a good Austrian citizen, and a good Christian man. On the other side, Sauter, Joseph Eberle, Hans Eibl, and the Spannkreis saw Schlick's destructive Enlightenment ideas as the cause of his own downfall. Nobody in this debate actually *defended* Schlick's views or his right to hold them, for this was not a debate about tolerance or liberalism. Rather, it was a microcosmic struggle between intellectual elites who were vying for hegemony in the Austrofascist state and Central European fascism. It was a conflict over the use of violence and the necessity of authoritarianism camouflaged as one about Enlightenment thought. Both sides longed for strong leadership and loathed democracy. They both rejected Enlightenment values, disagreeing

---

93. Seefried, "Reich und Ständestaat," 421–43.
94. Hildebrand, "Verleumdung eines Todes," 696.

but slightly on the extremity of their solutions. While in the 1920s and early 1930s, conflict within the right was relatively muted, by the mid-1930s it had broken out again between radicalized conservative factions. While moderate *Ständestaat* intellectuals seemed to make inroads, this was largely illusory, for they never gained much influence beyond their own ranks. Their enduring inability to distinguish their views—grounded in notions of power politics, national unity, and race—from those of Eberle and Spann ultimately undermined their cause.

The failure of the Christlicher Ständestaat movement can be traced back to its fundamental tenets. The only major distinguishing characteristic of the upstart ideological group was its endorsement of the *Ständestaat* and rejection of Nazism. Otherwise, the two Viennese blocs differed in tone more than substance. When the new state failed to develop a popular following, its associated intellectual basis lost its purchase too. The Schlick case, which Sauter identified as a *Weltanschauungskampf* between Left and Right, good and evil, was actually a struggle between conservatives over power politics, or, as Michael Mann has put it, two Austrian fascisms. According to all participants, whichever state could guarantee unity and stability had a legitimate claim on total authority. The Schlick controversy, which reaffirmed the hegemony of radical Black Viennese ideology, revealed that the major discursive battles within Vienna had been resolved by early 1936. With the victory of *Die schönere Zukunft* over *Der christliche Ständestaat,* Black Viennese intellectuals announced a rejection of the Austrofascist *Weltanschauung* a full year and a half before the *Anschluss.*

Conclusion

The *Anschluss* had a profound effect on intellectual life in Vienna. There were a few possible outcomes for progressive thinkers. A few, including the Vienna Circle member Viktor Kraft, remained in inner exile; others, such as Sigmund Freud, emigrated; the psychoanalyst Bruno Bettelheim and the philosopher Jean Amery ended up in concentration camps, where the least fortunate, among them Käthe Leichter, perished. There were no truly desirable alternatives. Emigration was often a struggle, and many Viennese, including Egon Brunswick, Edgar Zilsel, and Karl Bühler, struggled to adapt to their new home countries.[1] The developments of the 1930s capped a process of persecution, alienation, and expulsion that amounted to the destruction of the greatest socialist laboratory in interwar Europe.

After the *Anschluss,* Black Viennese intellectuals likewise suffered degradations, though typically less severe in degree. Many professors were released from their positions, some were arrested, and a few ended up in concentration camps.[2] Intellectuals retreated from the public sphere and focused on their scholarly interests. As we discussed in chapter 3, on the day of the

---

1. On Austrian intellectual exile, see Stadler, *Vertriebene Vernunft.*
2. The impact of the *Anschluss* at the University of Vienna has been researched extensively. For a recent summary, see Ash, Nieβ, and Pils, *Geisteswissenschaften im Nationalsozialismus,* 22–8.

Anschluss, Othmar Spann was arrested by the gestapo.[3] He spent five months in prison before he was allowed to return to his estate. His closest associate, Walter Heinrich, who had given enthusiastic speeches to Nazi audiences in 1933, was also arrested that day. He spent a year and a half in Dachau. Wilhelm Andreae, Jakob Baxa, and Hans Riehl all lost their academic positions and either were imprisoned briefly or were forced to work in relative obscurity.[4] The monarchists of the Österreichische Aktion also suffered victims' fates. Hans Zessner-Spitzenberg was one of the first Austrians to die in a concentration camp, suffering kidney failure in August 1938 at Dachau. Ernst Karl Winter fled Austria for Switzerland in 1938. The gestapo arrested Wilhelm Schmid and Alfred Missong. After their respective releases, they emigrated to Vatican City and Switzerland. Only August Maria Knoll remained behind, enduring inner emigration.

Conservatives in the Joseph Eberle and Johannes Messner circles experienced mixed outcomes. Although the Nazis allowed *Die schönere Zukunft* to continue publishing until 1941, they restricted its content to cultural and religious matters. The gestapo subjected Eberle to frequent questionings, and he eventually had to give up his editorship in 1940. He was arrested in 1941 and sent to a concentration camp. He was released three months later.[5] Nevertheless, *Die schönere Zukunft* was relatively fortunate: it continued to exist under Nazi rule, long after most cultural organs had ceased to appear. According to Eberle, this was due to the intercessions by several members of his circle—Hans Eibl, Heinrich von Srbik, and Hans Sperl. Although these men did not enjoy the same degree of support from the Nazis as the famous academic collaborators Josef Nadler and Oswald Menghin, they retained their academic positions. Though Nazi authorities rejected Eibl's application for party membership, he never faced further harassment.[6] Srbik, after advocating *Anschluss* as the sole viable *gesamtdeutsch* possibility after 1933, was a fixture at the University of Vienna during the Nazi era. He even supported Nazi racial policy and their imperialist adventures publicly.[7] Johannes Messner, Josef Dobretsberger, and Dietrich Hildebrand, on the other hand, lost their academic appointments and fled to England, Turkey, and France, respectively. Viennese intellectuals, black and red, endured hardships at the

---

3. Salomon, *Fragebogen,* 218.

4. Schneller, *Zwischen Romantik und Faschismus,* 18–20.

5. Eberle, *Los der christlichen Press,* 2–9.

6. Korotin, "Deutsche Philosophen," 45–65.

7. Pesditschek, "Heinrich (Ritter von) Srbik (1878–1951)," in Hruza, *Österreichische Historiker,* 2:292–314.

hands of the Nazis. After the war, members of both groups asserted their victimhood.

The Austrian victim narrative has a long history. It has occupied a central position in Austrian collective memory since 1945, serving as a pillar for the founding myth of the Second Republic. The myth states that Austria was the first victim of Nazi aggression. As a consequence of a shared concentration camp experience, Austrians of all political convictions learned to set aside their ideological differences. The first official declaration of this understanding was the 1943 Allied conference in Moscow, and it was reaffirmed in the post–World War II constitution.[8] This story encouraged Austrians to overlook past conflicts and to blame the Germans alone for their nation's earlier problems. This required a healthy dose of historical amnesia, especially for conservatives. Despite the willing participation in the destruction of First Republic, the brutal suppression of Austrian workers in February 1934, and the establishment of the Austrofascist state, Viennese conservatives downplayed their role in the Austria's fascist turn.[9] Memories of post-*Anschluss* persecution encouraged conservatives to reinterpret and justify their earlier actions as patriotic and defensive. Historical events belie this view. In 1938 neither the Austrian Nazis nor their German brethren expected such an easy *Anschluss;* even the Austrian Nazis favored an autonomous and Catholic Austria. Black Vienna, it turns out, was not so much an impediment to the Nazi takeover of Austria as a facilitator. Their debates in favor of authoritarianism, fascism, and anti-Semitism paved the way for Hitler—an inconvenient truth that was lost when conservatives themselves became victims.[10]

With the defeat of the Nazis, most Black Viennese intellectuals returned to their prewar activities. The restoration of intellectual life in postwar Vienna strengthened Black Viennese culture. It also led to the elision of problematic aspects of conservative intellectual life from the First Republic, *Ständestaat,* and Nazi eras. While politicians remained mum about their past actions,[11] intellectuals actively recast their past, reinterpreting their work and actions in apolitical terms. They presented themselves as bystanders rather than participants in the political and social turmoil of the previous era. They chalked up the failures of the First Republic to a broken party structure, a

---

8. On coming to terms with the past and the victim myth, see Parkinson, *Conquering the Past,* and Utgaard, *Remembering and Forgetting Nazism.*

9. Utgaard, *Remembering and Forgetting Nazism,* 11–15.

10. See Bruce F. Pauley, "The Austrian Nazi Party before 1938: Some Recent Revelations," and Maurice Williams, "Captain Josef Leopold: Austro-Nazi or Austro-Nationalist?," in Parkinson, *Conquering the Past,* 34–71, and Pauley, *Hitler and the Forgotten Nazis,* 179.

11. Parkinson, *Conquering the Past,* 327–8.

rancorous parliamentary system, and unbridgeable political and ideological antagonisms. Alfred Missong, now an editor of the conservative Austrian People's Party's (ÖVP) newspaper, blamed the socialists for those problems and for failing to develop patriotic sentiments: "A not unimportant symptom of the sickness of the democratic state was also readily visible: despite the ever-clearer appearance of the danger to the sovereignty of Austria posed by the expansive all-German tendencies of Hitler-Germany, the necessity of a gathering together of all patriots, regardless of party, was not really recognized by the Social Democrats. At that time, we in no way heard from the Social Democratic side any unambiguous commitment to Austria."[12] Lest we forget, Missong never advocated for the First Republic or recommended reconciliation with the Social Democrats. Of the members of the Aktion, only Ernst Karl Winter suggested such a course. Missong was still the editor of the increasingly radical *Schönere Zukunft,* only offering pro-state sentiments after the triumph of Austrofascism. He rejoiced at the destruction of the Social Democrats in the civil war of 1934. His disingenuous statements blatantly ignored that the socialists had defended the parliamentary system and the Republic against the attacks of the Christian Socials, Heimwehr, and the Nazis. It also overlooked the fact that the Social Democrats had committed to the Austrian state by renouncing any *Anschluss* to a Hitler-led Germany.

In addition to recasting First Republic events, many Black Viennese intellectuals made decisive turns away from overt political involvement, which seemed to strengthen their claims of objectivity and detachment. This depoliticization mirrored a similar phenomenon among exiled Red Viennese intellectuals, though the reasons differed.[13] Eibl, after nearly two decades of political writing, returned to classical philosophy. He managed to avoid a de-Nazification review. Joseph Eberle moved to Salzburg and wrote an exculpatory memoir.[14] Othmar Spann's last works covered logic, Mozart, and the philosophy of religion. When his *Complete Works* was published, the editors presented Spann not only as the most influential intellectual figure of interwar Vienna but also as an Austrian freedom fighter.[15] Even Srbik, one of the most implicated "bridge builders," was rehabilitated, albeit posthumously, in 1958.[16]

---

12. Alfred Missong, "Wie kam es 1933/38 zur Krise der österr. Demokratie?," *Österreichische Monatshefte,* November 1945, 19–20, quoted in Missong and Missong, *Christentum und Politik,* 345.

13. See Kraft, *Vienna Circle,* Stadler, *Vienna Circle,* 12; and Reisch, *How the Cold War Transformed Philosophy of Science,* 191.

14. Eberle, *Los der christlichen Presse,* and *Erlebnisse und Bekenntnisse.*

15. Walter Heinrich, "Leben und Lebenswerk," in Spann and Heinrich, *Othmar Spann,* 17.

16. Peditschek, "Srbik," 315–24.

Eberle passed away in 1947. Spann, Srbik, and Eibl died in 1950, 1951, and 1958, respectively. While none of them regained their academic or intellectual positions, their Black Viennese colleagues and students had little problem resuming their activities. After a brief and incomplete period of de-Nazification between 1945 and 1949, almost all restrictions on academics were abandoned.[17] Of course, these postwar strictures hardly affected Black Viennese intellectuals since they were not Nazis, just radical conservatives. Members of the Spannkreis, including Walter Heinrich, Wilhelm Andreae, and August Maria Knoll, resumed their work. Johannes Messner returned from exile to the University of Vienna and worked on social theory. The conservative education ministry, dominated by ÖVP politicians, facilitated this restoration.[18] Conservative student bodies, which still possessed some German nationalist predilections, predominated for the next two decades.[19] These factors all contributed to the ease with which the Black Viennese past was forgotten and a "new" ideological order was founded on similar foundations.[20]

Conspicuously absent from the preceding discussion of postwar restoration is *any* mention of Red Viennese intellectuals. This is no accident, since few progressive intellectuals wished to return, and, more important, neither the state nor the universities invited them back.[21] Not only were the former ideological positions of those émigrés viewed as undesirable, but the return of progressives also would have challenged the narrative of the interwar past constructed by conservatives. The blacklisting of red intellectuals had a deleterious effect on the Second Republic as postwar Austria suffered through an intellectual brain drain that endured for decades. Even as Red Vienna became a subject of pride in Austrian and Viennese history, its leading figures were excluded by Black Viennese intellectuals and their followers. It was not until the 1980s that official overtures were made to the lost generations of Viennese intellectuals.[22]

---

17. On Austrian de-Nazification, see Stiefel, *Entnazifizierung in Österreich,* and Meissll Mulley, and Rathkolb, *Verdrängte Schuld, verfehlte Sühne.*

18. See Koenig, "Entstehung eines Gesetzes," and Grandner, Heiss, and Rathkolb, *Zukunft mit Altlasten.*

19. On postwar students, see Reinhard Gärtner, "Right-Wing Student Politics in Austria after 1945," in Parkinson, *Conquering the Past,* 279–93.

20. See Grandner, Heiss, and Rathkolb, *Zukunft mit Altlasten.*

21. See Christian Fleck, "Rückkehr unerwünscht," in Stadler, *Vertriebene Vernunft,* 182–213, and "Wie Neues nicht entsteht."

22. Friedrich Stadler, "Die Emigration der Wissenschaft," in Stadler, *Vertriebene Vernunft,* 9–41.

This brief overview of the postwar Austrian intellectual climate—in particular, the restoration of a Black Viennese ideological apparatus and the exclusion of countervailing trends—reinforces several key arguments of this book, since the ideological conflicts of the Second Republic continued the battles from the First Republic. The first point is that interwar Vienna was hardly a red fortress, especially intellectually. For the hundreds of intellectuals who participated in the classes, institutes, and meetings around Schlick, Freud, and Bühler, there were also thousands listening to Spann, Eibl, Srbik, and Kralik. Conservative scholarly societies dwarfed progressive ones in size, with participation a prerequisite for advancement. Black Viennese professors and ministers crafted Austrian culture in their image and strove to drive reds out—either into alternative institutions or into exile. In striving for intellectual and cultural hegemony, Red Viennese intellectuals fought a rearguard action against those in control of the institutions of knowledge and power. This struggle politicized and radicalized intellectual life in Vienna. Despite occasional glimmers of hope for the reds—the 1919 and 1927 elections, the rare appointments of progressive professors, the establishment of new research centers by the Viennese government—intellectual life in Red Vienna rarely provided relief from the antidemocratic, anti-Semitic, Catholic, authoritarian, and fascist onslaught.

Second, this book demands a reevaluation of the relationship between Catholicism, conservatism, and fascism in interwar Austria. Scholars in fascist studies generally present the ideology of the *Ständestaat* and First Republic conservatives as authoritarian,[23] "parafascist,"[24] or clerical authoritarian, a distinctive amalgam of Catholic social theory and modern authoritarian thought. These interpretations tend to distance Austrian developments from those across Europe.[25] They also tend to overlook the radicalism of Black Viennese ideology. The intellectuals within this field saw themselves as part of a European-wide trend toward radical conservatism, corporatism, and fascism. As Julie Thorpe has pointed out, fascism itself is a process of state and civic construction. This necessarily entailed a struggle for hegemony. Black Viennese intellectuals were instrumental in the construction of a fascistic ideology during the First Republic and the implementation of these ideas in the *Ständestaat*. In other words, Austria was a fascist state well before 1938.[26] The intellectuals behind Black Vienna were

---

23. Payne, *History of Fascism,* 14–19.
24. Griffin, *Nature of Fascism,* 124–25, 240.
25. See Paxton, *Anatomy of Fascism.*
26. Thorpe, *Pan-Germanism,* 232.

nationalistic, anti-Semitic, militant, and authoritarian, exhibiting most of the key elements of the "fascist minimum."[27]

Though some scholars maintain that Austrofascists were indeed fascist,[28] this view has become less prevalent with the passage of time. One of the complicating factors has been the issue of religion. In contrast to the secularism of Italian Fascism and Nazism, Catholicism was at the core of most Black Viennese intellectuals' ideational universe. Standard definitions of fascism cannot reconcile the secular (and sometimes pagan) elements of a "palingenetic ultranationalism" with the Catholic-inspired or universalist ideas of Viennese intellectuals. However, scholars of southern and eastern European radical movements have begun to reconsider the potential overlap between religious conservatism and fascism.[29] Broadening the historical discussion beyond political and economic affairs to include intellectual and cultural life leads to a more radical reading of the Austrian landscape. Although Black Viennese intellectuals by no means belonged to a single monolithic bloc and cannot be uniformly cast as fascists, they advocated for radical solutions that pushed the bounds of interwar conservative discourse. These solutions impelled Christian Socials to radicalize by issuing stronger nationalist and imperialist claims and explicitly antidemocratic and authoritarian proposals. Black Viennese intellectuals also searched across Europe for movements that shared their views, finding allies in Germany, Italy, Hungary, France, and Spain. The struggle for intellectual Vienna reveals the compatibility of religious and fascist thought as conservatives fought against democracy, socialism, liberalism, and Jewishness.

Third, the connection between politics, science, and philosophy in interwar Vienna was not an accidental one—it was unavoidable. A commitment to new scientific and philosophical methods almost invariably entailed affiliations with Austro-Marxist ideological circles. There was little space for free-floating intellectuals in an era of "fighting science." These fights were carried out on the academic and intellectual level and in political arenas, as the struggles for intellectual and political hegemony overlapped. Freudians, Adlerians, logical empiricists, and other reds recognized they could not thrive without a transformation of the state and educational system. They therefore

---

27. Black Viennese intellectuals fit Michael Mann's definition of fascists as those in "pursuit of a transcendent and cleansing nation-statism through paramilitarism." Mann, *Fascists,* 13.

28. Tálos, "Zum Herrschaftssystem des Austrofaschismus: Österreich 1934–1938," in *Autoritäre Regime in Ostmittel- und Südeuropa 1919–1944,* ed. Erwin Oberländer (Paderborn: Schöningh Verlag, 2001), 143–62.

29. See Feldman, Turda, and Georgescu, *Clerical Fascism;* Wolff and Hoensch, *Catholics;* and Blinkhorn, *Fascists and Conservatives* and *Fascism and the Right in Europe.*

made common cause with radicals in the socialist camp, and they strove together to achieve their intellectual and social goals. While the municipal government of Vienna offered some aid, it was not enough to overcome the imbalance in the universities, the bureaucracy, and the national government. The many successes of Red Viennese thought in the face of long odds attest to the robustness and resourcefulness of that field.

The radicalism of Red Viennese intellectuals becomes evident in the analysis of hegemonic conflict in interwar cultural and intellectual forums, showing the profound changes wrought by the Great War. Undoubtedly, most interwar intellectual movements had their origins in the reform-based "socio-liberal cultural movements" of the fin-de-siècle late Enlightenment and the liberal cosmopolitanism of assimilated Viennese Jewish life.[30] The First World War was a moment of rupture that revolutionized this project, however. As in Weimar Germany, "outsider" intellectuals—Jews, democrats, and socialists—faced the prospect of continued exclusion or radical oppositional engagement.[31] The defense of a secular, social democratic state and a liberal educational system represented an extreme position in an archconservative country dominated by thoughts of Habsburg restoration and authoritarianism, Catholic religious and educational views, and illiberal political and social ideas. Philosophical and scientific ambitions informed social and political engagement, as they had elsewhere in the Atlantic world.[32] The desire not merely to gain an academic hearing but also to defend the Republic against radical conservative views signaled a new activism on the left. As Helene Deutsch and Paul Federn noted, a spirit of "revolutionism" inspired Red Viennese intellectuals. They saw themselves on the front line of a contest for Europe's soul. For them, Vienna was not a fortress under siege; it was a battlefield. This gave the city its hothouse quality and its edge. Ideas developed through interdisciplinary exchanges with sympathizers and through hegemonic confrontations with opponents.

On the right, Black Viennese intellectuals were also instrumental in the radicalization of First Republic discourse and culture. From the outset, the Spannkreis, the Kralik circle, and writers for *Das neue Reich* and *Die schönere Zukunft* demanded radical transformation. Intellectuals generally supported the overthrow of the postwar state and the establishment of an authoritarian, Catholic, and German Reich. Most were prepared to employ violent means to eradicate the blights of socialism, liberalism, and Jewish

30. Stadler, "Spätaufklärung," and Hacohen, "Kosmopoliten."
31. Gay, *Weimar Culture,* 3.
32. See Kloppenberg, *Uncertain Victory.*

influence. We have seen how radical conservative ideas incubated in the Austrian capital—not just in Nazi circles but across the Black Viennese field. Examining Black Viennese ideas in the contexts of the First Republic and interwar European conservatism illuminates how dictatorship emerged so easily in 1933–34 and why *Anschluss* faced so little resistance in 1938. Black Viennese intellectuals may not have supported Nazism, but they certainly paved the way for its successes.

BIBLIOGRAPHY

Archives

Allgemeines Verwaltungsarchiv des österreichischen Staatsarchiv, Vienna, Austria
    Sozialdemokratisches Parteiarchiv
Archiv der Geschichte der Soziologie in Österreich, Graz, Austria
    Othmar Spann Papers
    Walter Heinrich Papers
Archiv der Universität Wien, Vienna, Austria
    Juristisches Fakultätsarchiv
    Philosophisches Fakultätsarchiv
Institute Wiener Kreis, Vienna, Austria
    Moritz-Schlick-Nachlass
    Otto-Neurath-Nachlass
International Institute of Social History, Haarlem, the Netherlands
    Friedrich Adler Archive
    Otto Bauer Archive
Museum für angewandte Kunst, Vienna, Austria
    Plakat-Sammlung
Verein für Geschichte der Arbeiterbewegung, Vienna, Austria
    Adler-Archiv
Vienna Circle Foundation, Amsterdam, the Netherlands
Wienbibliothek im Rathaus, Vienna, Austria
    Richard-Kralik-Nachlass
    Wiener Stadt- und Landesarchiv

Books and Articles

Achleitner, Friedrich, ed. *Österreich—geistige Provinz?* Vienna: Forum-Verlag, 1965.
Achs, Oskar, and Albert Krassnigg. *Drillschule, Lernschule, Arbeitsschule: Otto Glöckel und die österreichische Schulreform in der Ersten Republik, Pädagogik der Gegenwart.* Vienna: Jugend und Volk, 1974.
Adler, Friedrich. *Ernst Machs Überwindung des mechanischen Materialismus.* Vienna: Ignaz Brand, 1918.
Adler, Max. *Der Sozialismus und die Intellektuellen.* Vienna: Wiener Volksbuchhandlung, 1910.
———. *Neue Menschen.* 2nd ed. Berlin: Laub, 1926.
Aichhorn, August. *Verwahrloste Jugend.* Leipzig: Internationaler Psychoanalytischer Verlag, 1925.

Albers, Detlev. *Otto Bauer und der "dritte" Weg: Die Wiederentdeckung des Austro-marxismus durch Linkssozialisten und Eurokommunisten.* Frankfurt am Main: Campus, 1979.

———. *Versuch über Otto Bauer und Antonio Gramsci: Zur politischen Theorie des Marxismus.* Berlin: Argument-Verlag, 1983.

Alda, Patricia. *Karl Kraus' Verhältnis zur Publizistik.* Bonn: Alda!, 2003.

Anderson, Harriet. *Utopian Feminism: Women's Movements in Fin-de-Siècle Vienna.* New Haven: Yale University Press, 1992.

Andics, Hellmut. *Der Staat, den keiner wollte: Österreich von der Gründung der Republik bis zur Moskauer Deklaration.* Vienna: Molden, 1968.

———. *Luegerzeit: Das schwarze Wien bis 1918.* Vienna: Jugend und Volk, 1984.

Angerer, Thomas. "De l'Autriche germanique' à l'Autriche européenne'," In *Le rôle et la place des petits pays en Europe au XXe siècle,* edited by Gilbert Trausch, 407–64. Brussels: Bruylant, 2005.

Apitzsch, Ursula, and Peter Alheit. *Neurath, Gramsci, Williams: Theorien der Arbeiterkultur und ihre Wirkung, Argument-Sonderband.* Hamburg: Argument-Verlag, 1993.

Ardelt, Rudolf G. *Friedrich Adler: Probleme einer Persönlichkeitsentwicklung um die Jahrhundertwende.* Vienna: Österreichischer Bundesverlag, 1984.

———. *Zwischen Demokratie und Faschismus. Deutschnationales Gedankengut in Österreich 1919–1930.* Vienna: Geyer, 1972.

Ash, Mitchell G. *German Universities, Past and Future: Crisis or Renewal.* Providence, RI: Berghahn Books, 1997.

Ash, Mitchell G., Wolfram Nieß, and Ramon Pils, eds. *Geisteswissenschaften im Nationalsozialismus. Das Beispiel der Universität Wien.* Vienna: Vienna University Press, 2010.

Ash, Mitchell G., and Alfons Söllner, eds. *Forced Migration and Scientific Change: Emigre German-Speaking Scientists and Scholars after 1933.* Cambridge, UK: Cambridge University Press, 1996.

Ash, Mitchell G., and William Woodward. *Psychology in Twentieth-Century Thought and Society.* Cambridge: Cambridge University Press, 1987.

Aussermair, Josef. *Kirche und Sozialdemokratie: Der Bund der religiösen Sozialisten, 1926–1934.* Vienna: Europaverlag, 1979.

Baader, Gerhard, Veronika Hofer, and Thomas Mayer, eds. *Eugenik in Österreich. Biopolitische Strukturen von 1900 bis 1945.* Vienna: Czernin, 2007.

Barnett, William P., and Michael Woywode. "From Red Vienna to the Anschluss: Ideological Competition among Viennese Newspapers during the Rise of National Socialism." *American Journal of Sociology* 109 (June 2004): 1452–99.

Bauer, Otto. *Der Weg zum Sozialismus.* Vienna: Ignaz Brand, 1919.

———. *Die Nationalitätenfrage und die Sozialdemokratie.* Vienna: Ignaz Brand, 1907.

———. *Die österreichische Revolution.* Vienna: Wiener Volksbuchhandlung, 1923.

———. *Zwischen zwei Weltkriegen.* Bratislava: E. Prager, 1936.

Beller, Steven. *A Concise History of Austria.* Cambridge: Cambridge University Press, 2007.

———, ed. *Rethinking Vienna 1900.* New York: Berghahn Books, 2001.

———. *Vienna and the Jews, 1867–1938: A Cultural History.* New York: Cambridge University Press, 1989.

Benedikt, Heinrich, ed. *Geschichte der Republik Österreich.* Munich: R. Oldenbourg, 1954.

Benedikt, Michael, Reinhold Knoll, and Cornelius Zehetner, eds. *Im Schatten der Totalitarismen: Vom philosophischen Empirismus zur kritischen Anthropologie; Philosophie in Österreich 1920—1951.* Vol. 5 of *Verdrängter Humanismus—verzögerte Aufklärung.* Vienna: Turia & Kant, 2005.

Beneka, Gerhard. *Psychologie in Wien: Sozial- und Theoriegeschichte des Wiener Psychologischen Instituts, 1922–1938.* Vienna: WUV-Universitätsverlag, 1995.

———. *Zur Geschichte der Institutionalisierung der Psychologie in Österreich: Die Errichtung des Wiener Psychologischen Instituts.* Vienna: Geyer, 1990.

Ben-Ghiat, Ruth. *Fascist Modernities: Italy, 1922–1945.* Berkeley: University of California Press, 2001.

Beniston, Judith. *Welttheater: Hofmannsthal, Richard von Kralik, and the Revival of Catholic Drama in Austria, 1890–1934.* Leeds, UK: W.S. Maney, 1998.

Beniston, Judith, and Ritchie Robertson, eds. *Catholicism and Austrian Culture.* Edinburgh: Edinburgh University Press, 1999.

Beniston, Judith, and Robert Vilain, eds. *Culture and Politics in Red Vienna.* Leeds, UK: Maney, 2006.

Bernfeld, Siegfried. *Psychoanalyse und Marxismus.* Frankfurt am Main: Suhrkamp, 1970.

———. *Sisyphus.* Translated by Frederic Lilge. Berkeley: University of California Press, 1973.

Binder, Dieter A., and Ernst Bruckmüller. *Essay über Österreich: Grundfragen von Identität und Geschichte 1918–2000.* Vienna: Verlag für Geschichte und Politik, 2005.

Bischof, Günter, and Anton Pelinka, eds. *Austrian Historical Memory and National Identity.* New Brunswick, NJ: Transaction, 1997.

Bischof, Günter, Anton Pelinka, and Alexander Lassner, eds. *The Dollfuss/Schuschnigg Era in Austria: A Reassessment.* New Brunswick, NJ: Transaction, 2003.

Bischof, Günter, Fritz Plasser, and Peter Berger, eds. *From Empire to Republic: Post-World War I Austria.* New Orleans: University of New Orleans Press, 2010.

Blackmore, John T., R. Itagaki, and S. Tanaka. *Ernst Mach's Vienna, 1895–1930.* Boston: Kluwer, 2001.

Blau, Eve. *The Architecture of Red Vienna, 1919–1934.* Cambridge, MA: MIT Press, 1999.

Blinkhorn, Martin. *Fascism and the Right in Europe, 1919–1945.* New York: Longman, 2000.

———. *Fascists and Conservatives: The Radical Right and the Establishment in Twentieth-Century Europe.* Boston: Routledge, 1990.

Böck, Susanne. "Volksbildung oder Volk-Bildung. Die Wiener Volkshochschulen von 1918 bis 1934." PhD diss., University of Vienna, 1992.

Börner, Wilhelm. *Friedrich Jodl.* Stuttgart: Cotta, 1911.

Bottomore, T. B., and Patrick Goode. *Austro-Marxism.* Oxford: Clarendon Press, 1978.

Botz, Gerhard. *Gewalt in der Politik: Attentate, Zusammenstösse, Putschversuche, Unruhen in Österreich 1918 bis 1934.* Munich: W. Fink, 1976.

———. *Krisenzonen einer Demokratie: Gewalt, Streik und Konfliktunterdrückung in Österreich seit 1918.* Frankfurt: Campus, 1987.

Botz, Gerhard, Ivar Oxaal, Michael Pollak, and Nina Scholz, eds. *Eine zerstörte Kultur: Jüdisches Leben und Antisemitismus in Wien seit dem 19. Jahrhundert.* Vienna: Czernin, 2002.

Botz, Gerhard, and Gerald Sprengnagel. *Kontroversen um Österreichs Zeitgeschichte: Verdrängte Vergangenheit, Österreich-Identität, Waldheim und die Historiker.* Frankfurt: Campus, 1994.

Bourdieu, Pierre. *The Field of Cultural Production: Essays on Art and Literature.* Edited by R. Johnson. New York: Columbia University Press, 1993.

Boyer, John W. *Culture and Political Crisis in Vienna: Christian Socialism in Power, 1897–1918.* Chicago: University of Chicago Press, 1995.

——. *Karl Lueger (1844–1910). Christlichsoziale Politik als Beruf.* Vienna: Böhlau, 2010.

——. *Political Radicalism in Late Imperial Vienna: Origins of the Christian Social Movement, 1848–1897.* Chicago: University of Chicago Press, 1981.

——. "Silent War and Bitter Peace: The Revolution of 1918 in Austria." *Austrian History Yearbook* 34 (2003): 1–56.

Braunthal, Julius. *History of the International.* 2 vols. New York: Praeger, 1967.

Breuning, Klaus. *Die Vision des Reiches: Deutscher Katholizismus zwischen Demokratie und Diktatur (1929–1934).* Munich: Hueber, 1969.

Bronner, Stephen Eric, and F. Peter Wagner, eds. *Vienna: The World of Yesterday, 1889–1914.* Atlantic Highlands, NJ: Humanities Press, 1997.

Bruckmüller, Ernst. *Österreichbewusstsein im Wandel. Identität und Selbstverständnis in den 90er Jahren.* Vienna: Signum, 1994.

Bryant, Chad. *Prague in Black: Nazi Rule and Czech Nationalism.* Cambridge, MA: Harvard University Press, 2007.

Bühler, Karl. *Die Krise der Psychologie.* Jena: Fischer, 1927.

Bukey, Evan Burr. *Hitler's Austria: Popular Sentiment in the Nazi Era, 1938–1945.* Chapel Hill: University of North Carolina Press, 2000.

——. *Jews and Intermarriage in Nazi Austria.* New York: Cambridge University Press, 2011.

Busshoff, Heinrich. "Das Dollfuss-Regime in Österreich als geistesgeschichtliches Problem unter besonderer Berücksichtigung der 'Schöneren Zukunft' und der 'Reichspost.'" PhD diss., University of Würzburg, 1964.

Caldwell, Bruce. *Hayek's Challenge: An Intellectual Biography of Friedrich Hayek.* Chicago: University of Chicago Press, 2005.

Canetti, Elias. *The Memoirs of Elias Canetti.* New York: Farrar, Straus and Giroux, 1999.

Carnap, Rudolf. *The Logical Structure of the World: Pseudoproblems in Philosophy.* Berkeley: University of California Press, 1967.

Carsten, F. L. *Fascist Movements in Austria: From Schönerer to Hitler.* London: Sage, 1977.

——. *Revolution in Central Europe, 1918–1919.* Berkeley: University of California Press, 1972.

Cartwright, Nancy, Jordi Cat, Lola Fleck, and Thomas Uebel. *Otto Neurath: Philosophy between Science and Politics.* Cambridge: Cambridge University Press, 1996.

Chappel, James. "The Catholic Origins of Totalitarianism Theory in Interwar Europe." *Modern Intellectual History* 8 (2011): 561–90.

Chase, Stephanie M. "The Three Phases of Austro-Marxism: Max Adler, Otto Neurath, and Karl Popper." Master's thesis, University of Portland, 2007.

Coen, Deborah R. *Vienna in the Age of Uncertainty: Science, Liberalism, and Private Life.* Chicago: University of Chicago Press, 2007.

Cohen, Gary. "Nationalist Politics and the Dynamics of State and Civil Society in the Habsburg Monarchy 1867–1914." *Central European History* 40 (2007): 241–78.

——. "Neither Absolutism nor Anarchy: New Narratives on Society and Government in Late Imperial Austria." *Austrian History Yearbook* 29 (1998): 37–61.

Collini, Stefan. *Absent Minds: Intellectuals in Britain.* Oxford: Oxford University Press, 2006.

Congdon, Lee. *Exile and Social Thought: Hungarian Intellectuals in Germany and Austria, 1919–1933.* Princeton, NJ: Princeton University Press, 1991.

Connelly, John. "Catholic Racism and Its Opponents." *Journal of Modern History* 79 (December 2007): 813–47.

——. *From Enemy to Brother.* Cambridge, MA: Harvard University Press, 2012.

Conway, John. *Nazi Persecution of the Churches, 1933–1945.* New York: Basic Books, 1968.

Cooper, Barry. *Beginning the Quest: Law and Politics in the Early Work of Eric Voegelin.* Columbia: University of Missouri Press, 2009.

——. *Eric Voegelin and the Foundations of Modern Political Science.* Columbia: University of Missouri Press, 1999.

Cornwall, Mark. *The Devil's Wall: The Nationalist Youth Mission of Heinz Rutha.* Cambridge, MA: Harvard University Press, 2012.

——. *The Undermining of Austria-Hungary: The Battle for Hearts and Minds.* New York: St. Martin's, 2000.

Cornwall, Mark, and R. J. W. Evans, eds. *Czechoslovakia in a Nationalist and Fascist Europe.* Oxford: Oxford University Press, 2007.

Dahms, Hans-Joachim. *Philosophie, Wissenschaft, Aufklärung: Beiträge zur Geschichte und Wirkung des Wiener Kreises.* Berlin: De Gruyter, 1985.

Danneberg, Robert. *Zehn Jahre neues Wien.* Vienna: Wiener Volksbuchhandlung, 1929.

Danto, Elizabeth Ann. *Freud's Free Clinics: Psychoanalysis and Social Justice, 1918–1938.* New York: Columbia University Press, 2005.

Deutsch, Helene. *Confrontations with Myself: An Epilogue.* New York: Norton, 1973.

Diamant, Alfred. *Austrian Catholics and the First Republic: Democracy, Capitalism, and the Social Order, 1918–1934.* Princeton: NJ: Princeton University Press, 1960.

Drehsen, Volker, and Walter Sparn. *Vom Weltbildwandel zur Weltanschauungsanalyse: Krisenwahrnehmung und Krisenbewältigung um 1900.* Berlin: Akademie Verlag, 1996.

Dunkmann, Karl. *Der Kampf um Othmar Spann.* Leipzig: Quelle & Meyer, 1928.

Dvorak, Johann. *Edgar Zilsel und die Einheit der Erkenntnis.* Vienna: Löcker, 1981.

Eberle, Joseph. *Das Los der christlichen Presse im Dritten Reich.* Bregenz: E. Rusz, 1945.

——. *De profundis.* Innsbruck: Verlagsanstalt Tyrolia, 1921.

——. *Die Überwindung der Plutokratie.* Vienna: Tyrolia, 1918.

——. *Erlebnisse und Bekenntnisse.* Stuttgart: Schwabenverlag, 1947.

——. *Grossmacht Presse.* Vienna: Verlagsanstalt Herold, 1920.

——. *Zertrümmert die Götzen!* Vienna: Tyrolia, 1918.

——. *Zum Kampf um Hitler. Ein Reformprogramm für Staats-, Wirtschafts-, und Kulturpolitik zur Überwindung des Radikalismus.* Vienna: Verlag Schönere Zukunft, 1931.

Ebneth, Rudolf. *Die österreichische Wochenschrift "Der Christliche Ständestaat": Deutsche Emigration in Österreich 1933–1938*. Mainz: Matthias-Grünewald-Verlag, 1976.

Edmondson, Clifton Earl. *The Heimwehr and Austrian Politics, 1918–1936*. Athens: University of Georgia Press, 1978.

Eibl, Hans. *Vom Sinn der Gegenwart*. Vienna: Braumüller, 1933.

El Refaie, Elisabeth. "Keeping the Truce: Austrian Press Politics between the 'July Agreement' (1936) and the *Anschluss* (1938)." *German History* 20, no. 1 (2002): 44–66.

Eppel, Peter. *Zwischen Kreuz und Hakenkreuz: Die Haltung der Zeitschrift "Schönere Zukunft" zum Nationalsozialismus in Deutschland 1934–1938*. Vienna: Böhlau, 1980.

Fallend, Karl. *Siegfried Bernfeld, oder, Die Grenzen der Psychoanalyse*. Basel: Stroemfeld/ Nexus, 1992.

Fassmann, Heinz, and Emmerich Talos. *Handbuch des politischen Systems Österreichs: Erste Republik 1918–1933*. Vienna: Manz, 1995.

Federn, Paul. *Zur Psychologie der Revolution: Die vaterlose Gesellschaft*. Vienna: Anzengruber-Verlag, 1919.

Feldman, Matthew, Marius Turda, and Tudor Georgescu, eds. *Clerical Fascism in Interwar Europe*. London: Routledge, 2008.

Fellner, Fritz. *Geschichtsschreibung und nationale Identität*. Vienna: Böhlau, 2003.

——. "The Problem of the Austrian Nation after 1945." *Journal of Modern History* 60, no. 2 (1988): 264–89.

Filla, Wilhelm, Elke Gruber, and Jurij Jug. *Erwachsenenbildung in der Zwischenkriegszeit*. Innsbruck: Studien Verlag, 1999.

Fischer, Ernst. *Erinnerungen und Reflexionen*. Reinbeck bei Hamburg: Rowohlt, 1969.

Fleck, Christian. "The Restoration of Austrian Universities after World War II." Working paper, Center of Austrian Studies, 1995.

——. *Rund um "Marienthal."* Vienna: Verlag für Gesellschaftskritik, 1990.

——. "Wie Neues nicht entsteht." *Österreichische Zeitschrift für Geschichtswissenschaften* 11 (January 2000): 129–78.

Fleming, Donald, and Bernard Bailyn, eds. *The Intellectual Migration: Europe and America, 1930–1960*. Cambridge: Belknap Press, 1969.

"Forum: Habsburg History." *German History* 31, no. 2 (June 2013): 225–38.

Frank, Philipp. *Modern Science and Its Philosophy*. Cambridge, MA: Harvard University Press, 1949.

Frank, Tibor. *Double Exile: Migrations of Jewish-Hungarian Professionals through Germany to the United States, 1919–1945*. Oxford: Peter Lang, 2009.

Frei, Alfred Georg. *Rotes Wien: Austromarxismus und Arbeiterkultur: Sozialdemokratische Wohnungs- und Kommunalpolitik, 1919–1934*. Berlin: DVK-Verlag, 1984.

Galison, Peter. "Aufbau/Bauhaus: Logical Positivism and Architectural Modernism." *Critical Inquiry* 16 (1990): 709–52.

Gardner, Sheldon, and Gwendolyn Stevens. *Red Vienna and the Golden Age of Psychology, 1918–1938*. New York: Praeger, 1992.

Gay, Peter. *Freud: A Life for Our Time*. New York: Norton, 1988.

——. *Weimar Culture: The Outsider as Insider*. New York: Norton, 1968.

Gee, Malcolm, and Tim Kirk, eds. *Printed Matters: Printing, Publishing and Urban Culture in Europe in the Modern Period*. Aldershot, UK: Ashgate, 2002.

Geehr, Richard S. *The Aesthetics of Horror: The Life and Thought of Richard von Kralik.* Boston: Brill, 2003.

Gehler, Michael. "Korporationsstudenten und Nationalsozialismus in Österreich: Eine quantifizierende Untersuchung." *Geschichte und Gesellschaft* 20 (1994): 1–28.

Gellott, Laura S. *The Catholic Church and the Authoritarian Regime in Austria, 1933–1938.* New York: Garland, 1987.

———. "Defending Catholic Interests in the Christian State: The Role of Catholic Action in Austria, 1933–1938." *Catholic Historical Review* 74 (1988): 571–89.

———. "Recent Writings on the Ständestaat, 1934–1938." *Austrian History Yearbook* 26 (1995): 207–38.

Glaser, Ernst. *Im Umfeld des Austromarxismus: Ein Beitrag zur Geistesgeschichte des österreichischen Sozialismus.* Vienna: Europaverlag, 1981.

Glöckel, Otto. *Drillschule, Lernschule, Arbeitsschule.* Vienna: Verlag der Wiener Volksbuchhandlung, 1928.

Goller, Peter. *Otto Bauer—Max Adler: Beiträge zur Geschichte des Austromarxismus (1904–1938).* Vienna: Klahr, 2008.

Gramsci, Antonio. *Selections from the Prison Notebooks of Antonio Gramsci.* Edited by Quintin Hoare and Geoffrey Nowell-Smith. New York: International Publishers, 1972.

Grandner, Margarete, Gernot Heiss, and Oliver Rathkolb, eds. *Zukunft mit Altlasten. Die Universität Wien 1945 bis 1955.* Vienna: Studien-Verlag, 2005.

Gregor, A. James. *Marxism, Fascism, and Totalitarianism: Chapters in the Intellectual History of Radicalism.* Palo Alto: Stanford University Press, 2009.

Gretic, Goran, and Marion Heinz, eds. *Philosophie und Zeitgeist im Nationalsozialismus.* Würzburg: Königshausen & Neumann, 2006.

Griffin, Roger. *The Nature of Fascism.* London: Palgrave Macmillan, 1991.

Gruber, Helmut. "Red Vienna and the 'Jewish Question.'" *Leo Baeck Institute Yearbook* 38 (1993): 99–118.

———. *Red Vienna: Experiment in Working-Class Culture, 1919–1934.* New York: Oxford University Press, 1991.

Grunewald, Michel, and Uwe Puschner, eds. *Das katholische Intellektuellenmilieu in Deutschland, seine Presse und seine Netzwerk (1871–1963).* Bern: Lang, 2006.

Gulick, Charles Adams. *Austria from Habsburg to Hitler.* 2 vols. Berkeley: University of California Press, 1948.

Haag, John. "Heinrich von Srbik." In *Encyclopedia of Historians and Historical Writing,* edited by Kelly Boyd. London: Fitzroy Dearborn, 1999.

———. "'Knights of the Spirit': The Kameradschaftsbund." *Journal of Contemporary History* 8, no. 3 (1973): 133–53.

———. "Othmar Spann and the Politics of 'Totality': Corporatism in Theory and Practice." PhD diss., Rice University, 1969.

Hacohen, Malachi Haim. "The Culture of Viennese Science and the Riddle of Austrian Liberalism." *Modern Intellectual History* 6, no. 2 (2009): 369–96.

———. *Karl Popper, the Formative Years, 1902–1945: Politics and Philosophy in Interwar Vienna.* Cambridge: Cambridge University Press, 2000.

Haeckel, Ernst. *Der Monismus als Band zwischen Religion und Wissenschaft.* Bonn: Kroner, 1893.

Haider, Markus Erwin. *Im Streit um die österreichische Nation: Nationale Leitwörter in Österreich 1866–1938.* Vienna: Böhlau, 1998.

Haller, Rudolf. "Der erste Wiener Kreis." *Erkenntnis* 22 (1985): 341–58.

———. "Gibt es eine österreichische Philosophie?" *Wissenschaft und Weltbild* 3 (1979): 173–81.

Haller, Rudolf, and Friedrich Stadler, eds. *Ernst Mach—Werk und Wirkung.* Vienna: Hölder-Pichler-Tempsky, 1988.

Hanebrink, Paul. *In Defense of Christian Hungary: Religion, Nationalism and Antisemitism, 1890–1944.* Ithaca, NY: Cornell University Press, 2006.

Hanisch, Ernst. *Der große Illusionist. Otto Bauer (1881–1938).* Vienna: Böhlau, 2011.

———. "Der katholische Literaturstreit." In *Der Modernismus: Beiträge zu seiner Erforschung,* edited by E. Weinzierl, 125–60. Vienna: Verlag Styria, 1974.

———. *Der lange Schatten des Staates: Österreichische Gesellschaftsgeschichte im 20. Jahrhundert.* Vienna: Ueberreuter, 1994.

———. *Die Ideologie des politischen Katholizismus in Österreich 1918–1938.* Vienna: Geyer, 1977.

Hans Kelsen und die Bundesverfassung. Katalog zur Ausstellung im BM Josefstadt. Vienna: Manz, 2010.

Hanzer, Stefan. "Die Zeitschrift 'Das Neue Reich' (1918–1925) zum restaurativen Katholizismus in Österreich nach dem ersten Weltkrieg." PhD diss., University of Vienna, 1973.

Harrington, Anne. *Reenchanted Science: Holism in German Culture from Wilhelm II to Hitler.* Princeton: Princeton University Press, 1996.

Hartmann, Gerhard. *Der CV in Österreich: Seine Entstehung, seine Geschichte, seine Bedeutung.* 4th ed. Vienna: Lahn-Verlag, 2011.

Hastings, Derek. *Catholicism and the Roots of Nazism: Religious Identity and National Socialism.* New York: Oxford University Press, 2009.

Hausmann, Otto. "Othmar Spann und seine Schule." PhD diss., University of Vienna, 1962.

Healy, Maureen. *Vienna and the Fall of the Habsburg Empire: Total War and Everyday Life in World War I.* Cambridge: Cambridge University Press, 2007.

Heimann, Siegfried, and Franz Walter. *Religiöse Sozialisten und Freidenker in der Weimarer Republik, Solidargemeinschaft und Milieu.* Bonn: J.H.W. Dietz, 1993.

Heinrich, Walter. *Der Faschismus.* Munich: F. Bruckmann, 1932.

Heinz, Karl Hans, and Ernst Karl Winter. *E.K. Winter, ein Katholik zwischen Österreichs Fronten, 1933–1938.* Vienna: Böhlau, 1984.

Heiss, Gernot, Siegfried Mattl, Sebastian Meissl, Edith Saurer, and Karl Stuhlpfarrer, eds. *Willfährige Wissenschaft. Die Universität Wien 1938–1945.* Vienna: Österreichische Texte zur Gesellschaftskritik, 1989.

Herf, Jeffrey. *Reactionary Modernism: Technology, Culture, and Politics in Weimar and the Third Reich.* Cambridge: Cambridge University Press, 1986.

Heer, Friedrich. *Der Kampf um Österreichs Identität.* Vienna: Böhlau, 1996.

Hochman, Erin. "Staging the Nation, Staging Democracy: The Politics of Commemoration in Germany and Austrian 1918–1934." PhD diss., University of Toronto, 2010.

Hofer, Barbara Maria. "Joseph Eberle: Katholischer Publizist zwischen 'Monarchie' und 'Schönere Zukunft.'" PhD diss., University of Vienna, 1995.

Holmes, Deborah, and Lisa Silverman, eds. *Interwar Vienna: Culture between Tradition and Modernity*. Rochester, NY: Camden House, 2009.

Holzbauer, Robert. "Ernst Karl Winter (1895–1959)." PhD diss., University of Vienna, 1995.

Hruza, Karel, ed. *Österreichische Historiker. Lebensläufe und Karrieren 1900–1945.* 2 vols. Vienna: Böhlau, 2008–12.

Hudal, Alois. *Die Grundlagen des Nationalsozialismus.* Leipzig: Günther, 1937.

Hughes, H. Stuart. *Consciousness and Society: The Reorientation of European Social Thought.* Cambridge, MA: Harvard University Press, 1958.

Ingrisch, Doris, Ilse Korotin, and Charlotte Zwiauer. *Die Revolutionierung des Alltags: Zur intellektuellen Kultur von Frauen im Wien der Zwischenkriegszeit.* Frankfurt am Main: Lang, 2004.

Jacoby, Russell. *The Repression of Psychoanalysis: Otto Fenichel and the Political Freudians.* New York: Basic Books, 1983.

Jahoda, Marie. *"Ich habe die Welt nicht verändert": Lebenserinnerungen einer Pionierin der Sozialforschung.* Edited by Steffani Engler. Frankfurt: Campus-Verlag, 1997.

Jahoda, Marie, and Christian Fleck. *Arbeitslose bei der Arbeit: Die Nachfolgestudie zu "Marienthal" aus dem Jahr 1938.* Frankfurt: Campus Verlag, 1989.

Jahoda, Marie, Paul Felix Lazarsfeld, and Hans Zeisel. *Die Arbeitslosen von Marienthal: Ein soziographischer Versuch über die Wirkungen langandauernder Arbeitslosigkeit.* Frankfurt am Main: Suhrkamp, 1933.

———. *Marienthal: The Sociography of an Unemployed Community.* New Brunswick, NJ: Transaction, 2002.

Janik, Allan. *Wittgenstein's Vienna Revisited.* New Brunswick, NJ: Transaction, 2001.

Janik, Allan, and Stephen Toulmin. *Wittgenstein's Vienna.* New York: Simon and Schuster, 1973.

Jedlicka, Ludwig, and Rudolf Neck, eds. *Das Juliabkommen von 1936: Vorgeschichte, Hintergründe und Folgen.* Vienna: Verlag für Geschichte und Politik, 1977.

Jeffery, Charlie. *Social Democracy in the Austrian Provinces, 1918–1934: Beyond Red Vienna.* London: Leicester University Press, 1995.

Jehly, Eduard. *Zehn Jahre rotes Wien.* Vienna: Genearlsekretariat der Christlichsozialen Partei Österreichs, 1930.

Jelavich, Barbara. *Modern Austria: Empire and Republic, 1815–1986.* New York: Cambridge University Press, 1987.

Johnston, William M. *The Austrian Mind: An Intellectual and Social History, 1848–1938.* Berkeley: University of California Press, 1972.

Judson, Pieter M., and Marsha L. Rozenblit, eds. *Constructing Nationalities in East Central Europe.* New York: Berghahn Books, 2005.

Judt, Tony, and Timothy Snyder. *Thinking the Twentieth Century.* New York: Penguin, 2012.

Kadrnoska, Franz, ed. *Aufbruch und Untergang: Österreichische Kultur zwischen 1918 und 1938.* Vienna: Europaverlag, 1981.

Keller, Robert. "Wiener Kreis und Volksbildung." Working paper, Institut Wiener Kreis, 1991.

Kaufmann, Fritz. *Sozialdemokratie in Österreich.* Vienna: Amalthea, 1978.

Kerekes, Lajos. *Abenddämmerung einer Demokratie: Mussolini, Gömbös und die Heimwehr.* Vienna: Europa, 1966.

Kindermann, Gottfried Karl. *Österreich gegen Hitler: Europas erste Abwehrfront 1933–1938.* Munich: L. Müller, 2003.

Kirk, Timothy. *Nazism and the Working Class in Austria: Industrial Unrest and Political Dissent in the National Community.* Cambridge: Cambridge University Press, 1996.

Kitchen, Martin. *The Coming of Austrian Fascism.* London: Croom Helm, 1980.

Klemperer, Klemens von. *Ignaz Seipel: Christian Statesman in a Time of Crisis.* Princeton, NJ: Princeton University Press, 1972.

Kloppenberg, James. *Social Democracy and Progressivism in European and American Thought, 1870–1920.* New York: Oxford University Press, 1988.

Kluge, Ulrich. *Der österreichische Ständestaat, 1934–1938: Entstehung und Scheitern.* Munich: Oldenbourg, 1984.

Knapp, Vincent J. *Austrian Social Democracy, 1889–1914.* Washington, DC: University Press of America, 1980.

Knoll, August M. et al. *Die Österreichische Aktion.* Vienna: Selbstverlag, 1927.

Koenig, Thomas. "Die Entstehung eines Gesetzes: Österreichische Hochschulpolitik in den 1950er Jahre." *Österreichische Zeitschrift für Geschichtswissenschaft* 23, no. 2 (November 2012): 57–81.

Konrad, Helmut, and Wolfgang Maderthaner, eds. *Das Werden der Republik:…der Rest ist Österreich.* 2 vols. Vienna: Gerold, 2008.

Köster, Roman. *Die Wissenschaft der Außenseiter. Die Krise der Nationalökonomie in der Weimarer Republik.* Göttingen: Vandenhoeck & Ruprecht, 2011.

Korotin, Ilse. "Deutsche Philosophen aus der Sicht des Sicherheitsdienstes des Reichsführers SS." In *Philosophie und Zeitgeist,* edited by M. a. G. G. Heinz, 45–65. Würzburg: Königshausen & Neumann, 2006.

Kos, Wolfgang, and Sándor Békési, eds. *Kampf um die Stadt: Politik, Kunst und Alltag um 1930.* Vienna: Czernin, 2010.

Kraft, Viktor. *The Vienna Circle.* New York: Philosophical Library, 1953.

Kreissler, Felix. *Der Österreicher und seine Nation: Ein Lernprozess mit Hindernissen.* Vienna: Böhlau, 1984.

Kriechbaumer, Robert. *Die grossen Erzählungen der Politik: Politische Kultur und Parteien in Österreich von der Jahrhundertwende bis 1945.* Vienna: Böhlau, 2001.

Kromar, Richard. "Der 'Österreich-Mythos.' Die Funktion der Presse im 'Ständestaat.'" PhD diss., University of Vienna, 2000.

Kutalek, Norbert, and Hans Fellinger. *Zur Wiener Volksbildung.* Vienna: Jugend und Volk, 1969.

Larsen, Stein Ugelvik, Bernt Hagtvet, and Jan Petter Myklebust. *Who Were the Fascists? Social Roots of European Fascism.* Bergen: Universitetsforlaget, 1980.

Lauridsen, John T. *Nazism and the Radical Right in Austria 1918–1934.* Copenhagen: Museum Tusculanum Press, 2007.

Lazarsfeld, Paul Felix. *Jugend und Beruf.* Jena: G. Fischer, 1931.

Lenin, Vladimir Ilíich. *Materialism and Empirio-criticism.* 2nd ed. New York: International Publishers, 1927.

Leonard, Robert J. "Ethics and the Excluded Middle: Karl Menger and Social Science in Interwar Vienna." *Isis* 89, no. 1 (1998): 1–26.

———. *Von Neumann, Morgenstern, and the Creation of Game Theory.* Cambridge, UK: Cambridge University Press, 2010.

Leser, Norbert, ed. *Das geistige Leben Wiens in der Zwischenkriegszeit.* Vienna: Öster-reichischer Bundesverlag, 1981.

——. *Grenzgänger: Österreichische Geistesgeschichte in Totenbeschwörungen.* 2 vols. Vienna: Böhlau, 1981.

——. *Zwischen Reformismus und Bolschewismus. Der Austromarxismus als Theorie und Praxis.* Vienna: Europa Verlag, 1975.

Leser, Norbert, and Paul Sailer-Wlasits, eds. *1927, als die Republik brannte: Von Schat-tendorf bis Wien.* Vienna: Va Bene, 2001.

Levitt, Kari, and Kenneth McRobbie, eds. *Karl Polanyi in Vienna: The Contemporary Significance of the Great Transformation.* 2nd ed. Montreal: Black Rose, 2006.

Lewis, Jill. *Fascism and the Working Class in Austria, 1918–1934: The Failure of Labour in the First Republic.* New York: St. Martin's, 1991.

——. *Workers and Politics in Occupied Austria, 1945–55.* Manchester: Manchester University Press, 2008.

Lewy, Guenter. *Catholic Church and Nazi Germany.* New York: McGraw-Hill, 1964.

Lindemann, Walter, and Anna Eichberg Henning. *Die proletarische Freidenker-Bewegung: Geschichte, Theorie, Praxis.* Münster: Lit, 1981.

Loew, Raimund. "The Politics of Austro-Marxism." *New Left Review*, no. 118 (1979): 15–51.

Logan, Cheryl. *Hormones, Heredity, and Race: Spectacular Failure in Interwar Vienna.* New Brunswick, NJ: Rutgers University Press, 2013.

Low, Alfred D. *Die Anschlussbewegung in Österreich und Deutschland, 1918–1919, und die Pariser Friedenskonferenz.* Vienna: W. Braumüller, 1975.

Luebbert, Gregory M. *Liberalism, Fascism, or Social Democracy: Social Classes and the Political Origins of Regimes in Interwar Europe.* New York: Oxford University Press, 1991.

Lüer, Andreas. "Nationalismus in Christlichsozialen Programmen 1918–1933." *Zeit-geschichte* 14, no. 4 (1987): 147–66.

Luft, David S. *Robert Musil and the Crisis of European Culture, 1880–1942.* Berkeley: University of California Press, 1980.

Lukács, Georg. *History and Class Consciousness: Studies in Marxist Dialectics.* Translated by Rodney Livingstone. Cambridge, MA: MIT Press, 1971.

Maderthaner, Wolfgang, and Lutz Musner. *Unruly Masses: The Other Side of Fin-de-Siècle Vienna.* New York: Berghahn Books, 2008.

Maier, Charles. *Recasting Bourgeois Europe: Stabilization in France, Germany, and Italy in the Decade after World War I.* Reprint ed. Princeton, NJ: Princeton University Press, 1988.

Manfred, Seper. "Ideengeschichte der Gemeinwirtschaft in der österreichischen Zwischenkriegszeit: Konzept und Analyse." PhD diss., Vienna University of Eco-nomics and Business, 2002.

Mann, Michael. *Fascists.* Cambridge: Cambridge University Press, 2004.

Mannheim, Karl. *Conservatism: A Contribution to the Sociology of Knowledge.* Edited by David Kettler, Volker Meja, and Nico Stehr. London: Routledge, 1986.

——. *Ideology and Utopia: An Introduction to the Sociology of Knowledge.* Translated by Louis Wirth and Edward Shils. New York: Routledge, 1936.

Matysik, Tracie. *Reforming the Moral Subject: Ethics and Sexuality in Central Europe, 1890–1930.* Ithaca, NY: Cornell University Press, 2008.

McEwen, Britta. *Sexual Knowledge: Feeling, Fact, and Social Reform in Vienna, 1900–1934*. New York: Berghahn Books, 2012.

——. "Welfare and Eugenics: Julius Tandler's Rassenhygienische Vision for Interwar Vienna." *Austrian History Yearbook* 41 (2010): 170–90.

McGrath, William J. *Dionysian Art and Populist Politics in Austria*. New Haven: Yale University Press, 1974.

Meissl, Sebastian, Klaus-Dieter Mulley, and Oliver Rathkolb, eds. *Verdrängte Schuld, verfehlte Sühne: Entnazifizierung in Österreich, 1945–1955*. Vienna: Verlag für Geschichte und Politik, 1986.

Menger, Karl. "Vienna Meetings 1927–1930." In *Unexplored Dimensions: Karl Menger on Economics and Philosophy (1923–1938)*, edited by Giandomenica Becchio, 69–86. Bingley, UK: Emerald, 2009.

Messner, Johannes. *Die berufständische Ordnung*. Innsbruck: Tyrolia, 1936.

——. *Die soziale Frage der Gegenwart*. 4th ed. Innsbruck: Tyrolia, 1934.

——. *Dollfuss*. Innsbruck: Tyrolia, 1935.

Mises, Ludwig. *Memoirs*. Translated by Arlene Oost-Zinner. Auburn, AL: Ludwig von Mises Institute, 2009.

Missong, Alfred, and Alfred Missong, Jr. *Christentum und Politik in Österreich: Ausgewählte Schriften 1924–1950*. Vienna: Böhlau, 2006.

Mohler, Armin. *Die konservative Revolution in Deutschland 1918–1932*. 2nd ed. Darmstadt: Wissenschaftliche Buchgesellschaft, 1972.

Mosse, George L. *The Crisis of German Ideology: Intellectual Origins of the Third Reich*. New York: Grosset & Dunlap, 1964.

Müller, Albert. "Dynamische Adaptierung und 'Selbstbehauptung': Die Universität Wien in der NS-Zeit." *Geschichte und Gesellschaft* 23 (1997): 592–617.

Müller, Reinhard. *Marienthal: Das Dorf—die Arbeitslosen—die Studie*. Innsbruck: StudienVerlag, 2008.

Nemeth, Elisabeth. *Otto Neurath und der Wiener Kreis: Revolutionäre Wissenschaftlichkeit als politischer Anspruch*. Frankfurt: Campus, 1981.

Nemeth, Elisabeth, Richard Heinrich, and Antonia Soulez. *Otto Neurath: Rationalität, Planung, Vielfalt*. Vienna: Oldenbourg, 1999.

Nemeth, Elisabeth, and Friedrich Stadler. *Encyclopedia and Utopia: The Life and Work of Otto Neurath (1882–1945)*. Boston: Kluwer, 1996.

Neurath, Otto. *Gesammelte philosophische und methodologische Schriften*. Edited by Rudolf Haller. 2 vols. Vienna: Verlag Hölder-Pichler-Tempsky, 1981.

Neurath, Otto, Paul Neurath, and Elisabeth Nemeth, eds. *Otto Neurath, oder, Die Einheit von Wissenschaft und Gesellschaft*. Vienna: Böhlau, 1994.

Neurath, Otto, Marie Neurath, and R. S. Cohen, eds. *Empiricism and Sociology*. Dordrecht, Neth.: Reidel, 1973.

Nolte, Ernst. *Three Faces of Fascism: Action Française, Italian Fascism, National Socialism*. New York: Holt, Rinehart and Winston, 1966.

Parkinson, F., ed. *Conquering the Past: Austrian Nazism Yesterday and Today*. Detroit: Wayne State University Press, 1989.

Pauley, Bruce F. *From Prejudice to Persecution: A History of Austrian Anti-Semitism*. Chapel Hill: University of North Carolina Press, 1992.

——. *Hitler and the Forgotten Nazis: A History of Austrian National Socialism*. Chapel Hill: University of North Carolina Press, 1981.

Paxton, Robert. *The Anatomy of Fascism*. New York: Alfred Knopf, 2004.

Payne, Stanley. *Fascism in Spain, 1923–1977*. Madison: University of Wisconsin Press, 1999.

——. *A History of Fascism, 1914–1945*. New York: Routledge, 1995.

Pelinka, Anton. "The Great Austrian Taboo: The Repression of the Civil War." *New German Critique* 43 (1988): 69–82.

——. *Zur österreichischen Identität. Zwischen deutscher Vereinigung und Mitteleuropa*. Vienna: Ueberreuter, 1990.

Pelinka, Anton, and Erika Weinzierl, eds. *Das große Tabu: Österreichs Umgang mit seiner Vergangenheit*. Vienna: Österreichische Staatsdruckerei, 1987.

Pfabigan, Alfred. *Karl Kraus und der Sozialismus: Eine politische Biographie*. Vienna: Europaverlag, 1976.

Pfarrhofer, Hedwig. *Friedrich Funder. Ein Mann zwischen Gestern und Morgen*. Graz: Styria, 1978.

Pfoser, Alfred. *Literatur und Austromarxismus*. Vienna: Löcker, 1980.

Phayer, Michael. *Catholic Church and the Holocaust, 1930–1965*. Bloomington: University of Indiana, 2000.

Pichler, Johann Hanns. *Othmar Spann, oder, Die Welt als Ganzes*. Vienna: Böhlau, 1968.

Polanyi, Karl. *Chronik der grossen Transformation*. Edited by Michele Cangiani, Claus Thomasberger, and Kari Levitt. 3 vols. Marburg: Metropolis, 2002.

——. *The Great Transformation: The Political and Economic Origins of Our Time*. 2nd ed. Boston: Beacon Press, 2001.

Popp, Gerhard. *CV in Österreich, 1864–1938: Organisation, Binnenstruktur und politische Funktion*. Vienna: Böhlau, 1984.

Posch, Herbert, Doris Ingrisch, and Gert Dressel, eds. *"Anschluss" und Ausschuss 1938. Vertriebene und verbliebene Studierende der Universität Wien*. Vienna: LIT-Verlag, 2008.

Prinz, Josef. "Politischer Katholizismus in Österreich. Zur politischen Rolle und sozialer Funktion der katholischen Kirche in der Ersten Republik bis zur Konstituierung des 'Autoritären Ständestaates' unter besonderer Berücksichtigung der katholischen Soziallehre." Diploma thesis, University of Vienna, 1986.

Puchner, Martin. "Doing Logic with a Hammer: Wittgenstein's 'Tractatus' and the Polemics of Logical Positivism." *Journal of the History of Ideas* 66, no. 2 (2005): 285–300.

Pyrah, Robert. *The Burgtheater and Austrian Identity: Theatre and Cultural Politics in Vienna, 1918–38*. London: Legenda, 2007.

Rabinbach, Anson, ed. *The Austrian Socialist Experiment: Social Democracy and Austromarxism, 1918–1934*. Boulder, CO: Westview, 1985.

——. *The Crisis of Austrian Socialism: From Red Vienna to Civil War, 1927–1934*. Chicago: University of Chicago Press, 1983.

——. "The Politicization of Wilhelm Reich: An Introduction to 'The Sexual Misery of the Working Masses and the Difficulties of Sexual Reform.'" *New German Critique* 1 (1973): 90–97.

Reich, Wilhelm. *Dialectical Materialism and Psychoanalysis*. London: Socialist Reproduction, 1972.

——. *The Mass Psychology of Fascism*. New York: Farrar, Straus & Giroux, 1970.

——. *People in Trouble*. New York: Orgone Institute Press, 1953.

——. *Sex-Pol; Essays, 1929–1934.* New York: Random House, 1972.

Reisch, George A. *How the Cold War Transformed Philosophy of Science: To the Icy Slopes of Logic.* New York: Cambridge University Press, 2005.

Renner, Karl. *Staat und Nation. Zur österreichischen Nationalitätenfrage.* Vienna: Dietl, 1899.

Rentetzi, Maria. *Trafficking Materials and Gendered Experimental Practices: Radium Research in Early 20th Century Vienna.* New York: Columbia University Press, 2008.

Resele, Gertraud. "Othmar Spanns Ständestaatskonzeption und politisches Wirken." Diploma thesis, University of Vienna, 2003.

Richardson, Alan W. *Carnap's Construction of the World: The Aufbau and the Emergence of Logical Empiricism.* New York: Cambridge University Press, 1998.

Rill, Robert. *CV und Nationalsozialismus in Österreich.* Vienna: Geyer, 1987.

Ringer, Fritz K. *The Decline of the German Mandarins: The German Academic Community, 1890–1933.* Cambridge, MA: Harvard University Press, 1969.

Roazen, Paul. *Encountering Freud: The Politics and Histories of Psychoanalysis.* New Brunswick, NJ: Transaction, 1990.

——. *Helene Deutsch: A Psychoanalyst's Life.* Garden City, NY: Anchor Press/Doubleday, 1985.

Rose, Alison. *Jewish Women in Fin de Siècle Vienna.* Austin: University of Texas Press, 2008.

Rozenblit, Marsha L. *The Jews of Vienna, 1867–1914: Assimilation and Identity.* Albany: State University of New York Press, 1983.

——. *Reconstructing a National Identity: The Jews of Habsburg Austria during World War I.* Oxford: Oxford University Press, 2001.

Saage, Richard. *Politische Ideengeschichte in demokratietheoretischer Absicht: Das Beispiel Hans Kelsens und Max Adlers in der Zwischenkriegszeit.* Leipzig: Verlag der Sächsischen Akademie der Wissenschaften, 2003.

Salomon, Ernst. *Der Fragebogen.* Hamburg: Rowohlt, 1951.

Sandner, Günther. *Engagierte Wissenschaft: Austromarxistische Kulturstudien und die Anfänge der britischen cultural studies.* Vienna: LIT, 2006.

Sarkar, Sahotra, ed. *The Emergence of Logical Empiricism: From 1900 to the Vienna Circle.* New York: Garland, 1996.

——, ed. *The Legacy of the Vienna Circle: Modern Reappraisals.* New York: Garland, 1996.

Schilpp, Paul, ed. *The Philosophy of Rudolf Carnap.* La Salle, IL: Open Court, 1963.

Schindler, Franz Martin. *Die Leo-Gesellschaft 1891–1901.* Vienna: Verlag der Leo-Gesellschaft, 1902.

Schlesinger, Therese. *Die geistige Arbeiterin und der Sozialismus.* Vienna: Heller, 1919.

Schlick, Moritz. *General Theory of Knowledge.* New York: Springer-Verlag, 1974.

Schmidt-Dengler, Wendelin. *Ohne Nostalgie. Zur österreichischen Literatur der Zwischenkriegszeit.* Vienna: Böhlau, 2002.

Schmitt, Carl. *The Concept of the Political.* New Brunswick, NJ: Rutgers University Press, 1976.

——. *Political Romanticism.* Cambridge, MA: MIT Press, 1986.

——. *Political Theology.* Cambridge, MA: MIT Press, 1985.

Schneller, Martin. *Zwischen Romantik und Faschismus: Der Beitrag Othmar Spanns zum Konservativismus in der Weimarer Republik.* Stuttgart: E. Klett, 1970.

Schorske, Carl E. *Fin-de-Siècle Vienna: Politics and Culture.* New York: Knopf, 1979.

———. *Thinking with History.* Princeton: Princeton University Press, 1998.

Seefried, Elke. *Reich und Stände. Ideen und Wirken des deutschen politischen Exils in Österreich 1933–1938.* Düsseldorf: Droste, 2006.

Segar, Kenneth, and John Warren, eds. *Austria in the Thirties: Culture and Politics.* Riverside, CA: Ariadne Press, 1991.

Seipel, Ignaz. *Nation und Staat.* Vienna: Braumuller, 1916.

Sieferle, Rolf Peter. *Die konservative Revolution.* Frankfurt am Main: Fischer Taschenbuch, 1995.

Seifert, Josef. *Dietrich von Hildebrands Kampf gegen den Nationalsozialismus.* Heidelberg: C. Winter, 1998.

Siegfried, Klaus-Jörg. *Klerikalfaschismus: Zur Entstehung und sozialen Funktion des Dollfussregimes in Österreich.* Frankfurt am Main: Lang, 1979.

———. *Universalismus und Faschismus.* Vienna: Europaverlag, 1974.

Silverman, Lisa. *Becoming Austrians.* Oxford: Oxford University Press, 2012.

Silverman, Paul. "Law and Economics in Interwar Vienna: Kelsen, Mises and the Regeneration of Austrian Liberalism." PhD diss., University of Chicago, 1984.

Smith, Barry. *Austrian Philosophy: The Legacy of Franz Brentano.* Chicago: Open Court, 1994.

Soucy, Robert. *French Fascism.* Vol. 1, *The First Wave, 1924–1933.* New Haven: Yale University Press, 1986.

———. *French Fascism.* Vol. 2, *The Second Wave, 1933–1939.* New Haven: Yale University Press, 1995.

Spann, Othmar. *Der wahre Staat.* Leipzig: Quelle & Meyer, 1921.

———. *Kämpfende Wissenschaft.* 2nd ed. Edited by Wolfgang Steffanides. Graz: Akademische Druck- und Verlagsanstalt, 1969.

———. *Kategorienlehre.* Jena: G. Fischer, 1924.

———. *Othmar Spann, Leben und Werk.* Edited by Walter Heinrich. Graz: Akademenische Druck- und Verlagsanstalt, 1979.

Der Spann-Kreis. Gefahren und Auswirkungen. Bericht des Reichssicherheitshauptamtes vom Mai 1936. Berlin, 1936.

Spector, Scott. "Beyond the Aesthetic Garden: Politics and Culture on the Margins of 'Fin-de-Siècle Vienna.'" *Journal of the History of Ideas* 59 (1998): 691–710.

Spicer, Kevin. *Hitler's Priests: Catholic Clergy and National Socialism.* Dekalb: Northern Illinois University, 2008.

Srbik, Heinrich. *Deutsche Einheit.* Munich: F. Bruckmann, 1935.

———. *Österreich in der deutschen Geschichte.* Munich: F. Bruckmann, 1936.

Stadler, Friedrich, ed. *Kontinuität und Bruch 1938–1945–1955. Beiträge zur österreichischen Kultur- und Wissenschaftsgeschichte.* Hamburg: Lit-Verlag, 2004.

———. *Österreichs Umgang mit dem Nationalsozialismus. Die Folgen für die naturwissenschaftliche und humanistische Lehre.* Vienna: Springer, 2003.

———. *Studien zum Wiener Kreis: Ursprung, Entwicklung, und Wirkung des logischen Empirismus im Kontext.* Frankfurt am Main: Suhrkamp, 1997.

———, ed. *Vertriebene Vernunft: Emigration und Exil österreichischer Wissenschaft, 1930–1940.* 2 vols. Vienna: Jugend und Volk, 1987/8.

———. *The Vienna Circle: Studies in the Origins, Development, and Influence of Logical Empiricism.* Translated by Camilla Nielsen. Vienna: Springer, 2001.

———. *Vom Positivismus zur "wissenschaftlichen Weltauffassung": Am Beispiel der Wirkungsgeschichte von Ernst Mach in Österreich von 1895 bis 1934.* Vienna: Löcker, 1982.

Staudinger, Anton. "Zu den Bemühungen katholischer Jungakademiker um eine ständisch-antiparlamentarische und deutsch-völkische Orientierung der Christlich-Sozialen Partei." In *Beiträge zum wissenschaftlichen Symposion des Dr. Karl Renner-Institutes,* edited by Heinz Fischer, 221–31. Vienna: Verlag der Wiener Volksbuchhandlung, 1984.

Steele, David Ramsay. *From Marx to Mises: Post-Capitalist Society and the Challenge of Economic Calculation.* La Salle, IL: Open Court, 1992.

Steigmann-Gall, Richard. *Holy Reich: Nazi Conceptions of Christianity, 1919–1945.* Cambridge: Cambridge University Press, 2003.

Steinberg, Michael P. *Austria as Theater and Ideology: The Meaning of the Salzburg Festival.* Ithaca, NY: Cornell University Press, 2000.

———. "Jewish Identity and Intellectuality in Fin-de-Siècle Austria: Suggestions for a Historical Discourse." *New German Critique* 43 (1988): 3–33.

Steininger, Rolf, Günter Bischof, and Michael Gehler, eds. *Austria in the Twentieth Century.* New Brunswick, NJ: Transaction, 2002.

Stepansky, Paul E. *In Freud's Shadow: Adler in Context.* Hillside, NJ: Analytic Press, 1983.

Stern, Frank, and Barbara Eichinger. *Wien und die Jüdische Erfahrung 1900–1938: Akkulturation, Antisemitismus, Zionismus.* Vienna: Böhlau, 2009.

Stern, Fritz. *The Politics of Cultural Despair: A Study in the Rise of the Germanic Ideology.* Berkeley: University of California Press, 1961.

Sternhell, Zeev. *The Birth of Fascist Ideology: From Cultural Rebellion to Political Revolution.* Translated by Mario Sznajder. Princeton: Princeton University Press, 1994.

———. *Neither Left nor Right: Fascist Ideology in France.* Translated by David Maisel. Berkeley: University of California Press, 1986.

Stiefel, Dieter. *Entnazifizierung in Österreich.* Vienna: Europaverlag, 1981.

Stöckler, Horst-Christian. "Otto Neuraths Gesellschafts- und Wirtschaftsmuseum und die Wiener Bildstatistik 1925–1934." Diploma thesis, Vienna University of Economics and Business, 1989.

Storm, Gerd, and Franz Walter. *Weimarer Linkssozialismus und Austromarxismus: Historische Vorbilder für einen "Dritten Weg" zum Sozialismus.* Berlin: Europäische Perspektiven, 1984.

Stourzh, Gerald. *Der Umfang der österreichischen Geschichte: Ausgewählte Studien 1990–2010.* Vienna: Böhlau, 2011.

———. *From Vienna to Chicago and Back: Essays on Intellectual History and Political Thought in Europe and America.* Chicago: University of Chicago, 2007.

———. *Vom Reich zur Republik: Studien zum Österreichbewusstsein im 20. Jahrhundert.* Vienna: Atelier, 1990.

Suppanz, Werner. "Die Gesellschaft als Körper. Organizistisches Denken in der Staats- und Gesellschaftstheorie Othmar Spanns." In *Einheit und Vielheit. Organologische Denkmodelle in der Moderne,* edited by B. a. S. R.-K. Boisits, 225–54. Vienna: Passagen, 2000.

———. "Othmar Spann: Soziologie—Zeitdiagnose—Politik." In *Soziologie in und aus Wien,* edited by A. a. G. M. Balog, 105–27. Frankfurt: Peter Lang, 2004.

——. "'Was ist deutsch?' Deutschnationale Volkstumideologie im Kontext von Othmar Spanns Lehre des Universalismus." In *Sprache—Denken—Nation. Kultur- und Geistesgeschichte von Locke bis zur Moderne,* edited by V. a. K. N. Munz, 223–41. Vienna: Passagen, 2005.

Suval, Stanley. *The Anschluss Question in the Weimar Era: A Study of Nationalism in German and Austrian 1918–1932.* Baltimore: Johns Hopkins University Press, 1974.

Tálos, Emmerich, Herbert Dachs, Ernst Hanisch, and Anton Staudinger, eds. *Handbuch des politischen Systems Österreichs 1918–1933.* Vienna: Manz, 1995.

Tálos, Emmerich, Ernst Hanisch, and Wolfgang Neugebauer, eds. *NS-Herrschaft in Österreich, 1938–1945.* Vienna: Verlag für Gesellschaftskritik, 1988.

Tálos, Emmerich, and Wolfgang Neugebauer, eds. *"Austrofaschismus": Beiträge über Politik, Ökonomie und Kultur, 1934–1938.* 6th ed. Vienna: Verlag für Gesellschaftskritik, 2012.

Thaler, Peter. *Ambivalence of Identity: The Austrian Experience of Nation-Building in a Modern Society.* West Lafayette, IN: Purdue University Press, 2001.

Ther, Philipp. "Beyond the Nation: The Relational Basis of a Comparative History of Germany and Europe." *Central European History* 36, no. 1 (2003): 45–73.

Thorpe, Julie. "Austrofascism: Revisiting the 'Authoritarian State' 40 Years On." *Journal of Contemporary History* 45 (2010): 315–43.

——. *Pan-Germanism and the Austrofascist State, 1933–38.* Manchester: Manchester University Press, 2011.

Timms, Edward. *Karl Kraus, Apocalyptic Satirist.* Vol. 1, *Culture and Catastrophe in Habsburg Vienna.* New Haven: Yale University Press, 1986.

——. *Karl Kraus, Apocalyptic Satirist.* Vol. 2, *The Post-War Crisis and the Rise of the Swastika.* New Haven: Yale University Press, 2005.

Timms, Edward, and Jon Hughes. *Intellectual Migration and Cultural Transformation: Refugees from National Socialism in the English-Speaking World.* Vienna: Veröffentlichungen des Institut Wiener Kreis, 2003.

Turda, Marius, and Paul J. Weindling, eds. *"Blood and Homeland": Eugenics and Racial Nationalism in Central and Southeast Europe, 1900–1940.* Budapest: CEU Press, 2007.

Uebel, Thomas E. *Empiricism at the Crossroads: The Vienna Circle's Protocol-Sentence Debate.* Chicago: Open Court, 2007.

——. *Rediscovering the Forgotten Vienna Circle.* Dordrecht, Neth.: Kluwer, 1991.

——. *Vernunftkritik und Wissenschaft: Otto Neurath und der ersten Wiener Kreis.* Vienna: Springer, 2000.

Uebel, Thomas E., and Alan W. Richardson, eds. *The Cambridge Companion to Logical Empiricism.* Cambridge: Cambridge University Press, 2007.

Utgaard, Peter. *Remembering and Forgetting Nazism: Education, National Identity, and the Victim Myth in Postwar Austria.* New York: Berghahn Books, 2003.

Voegelin, Eric. *The Authoritarian State.* Translated by Ruth Hein. Edited by Gilbert Weiss. Columbia: University of Missouri Press, 1999.

——. *Autobiographical Reflections.* Edited by Ellis Sandoz. Baton Rouge: Louisiana State University Press, 1989.

——. *Published Essays: 1922–1928.* Edited by Thomas W. Heilke and John von Heyking. Columbia: University of Missouri Press, 2003.

——. *Published Essays, 1929–1933.* Edited by John von Heyking and Thomas W. Heilke. Columbia: University of Missouri Press, 2004.

——. *Race and State.* Translated by Ruth Hein. Edited by Klaus Vondung. Columbia: University of Missouri Press, 1997.

Waismann, Friedrich. *Wittgenstein und der Wiener Kreis.* Oxford, UK: Blackwell, 1967.

Wandruszka, Adam. "Österreichs politische Struktur. Die Entwicklung der Parteien und politischen Bewegungen." In *Geschichte der Republik Österreich,* edited by Heinrich Benedikt, 289–485. Munich: Oldenbourg, 1954.

Weber, Eugen. *Action Française: Royalism and Reaction in Twentieth Century France.* Palo Alto: Stanford University Press, 1962.

Weidenholzer, Josef. *Auf dem Weg zum "neuen Menschen": Bildungs- und Kulturarbeit der österreichischen Sozialdemokratie in der Ersten Republik.* Vienna: Europaverlag, 1981.

Weihsmann, Helmut. *Das rote Wien: Sozialdemokratische Architektur und Kommunalpolitik, 1919–1934.* 2nd ed. Vienna: Promedia, 2002.

Weinzierl, Erika. *Der Februar 1934 und die Folgen für Österreich.* Vienna: Picus Verlag, 1995.

——. *Universität und Politik in Österreich.* Salzburg: Pustet, 1969.

Weinzierl, Erika, and Ursula Schulmeister. *Prüfstand: Österreichs Katholiken und der Nationalsozialismus.* Mödling: St. Gabriel, 1988.

Weinzierl, Erika, and Kurt Skalnik, eds. *Österreich, 1918–1938.* Graz: Styria, 1983.

Weiß, Otto. *Rechtskatholizismus in der Ersten Republik: Zur Ideenwelt der österreichischen Kulturkatholiken 1918–1934.* Frankfurt: Lang, 2006.

Werner, Ruth. *Die Wiener Wochenschrift 'Das Neue Reich' (1918–1925).* Breslau: Priebatsch, 1938.

Whiteside, Andrew. *The Socialism of Fools: Georg Ritter von Schönerer and Austrian Pan-Germanism.* Berkeley: University of California Press, 1975.

Williams, Raymond. *Politics of Modernism.* London: Verso, 1989.

Wimmer, Franz Martin, and Kurt Rudolf Fischer, eds. *Der geistige Anschluss: Philosophie und Politik an der Universität Wien, 1930–1950.* Vienna: WUV-Universitätsverlag, 1993.

Winter, Ernst Karl. *Monarchie und Arbeiterschaft.* Vienna: Gsur, 1936.

Wippermann, Wolfgang. *Europäischer Faschismus im Vergleich (1922–1982).* Frankfurt: Suhrkamp, 1983.

Wistrich, Robert S. *Socialism and the Jews: The Dilemmas of Assimilation in Germany and Austria-Hungary.* Rutherford, NJ: Fairleigh Dickinson University Press, 1982.

Wittgenstein, Ludwig. *Tractatus Logico-Philosophicus.* Edited by David Pears and Brian McGuinness. New York: Routledge, 2001.

Wolf, Julius, Konrad Josef Heilig, and Hermann Matthias Görgen. *Österreich und die Reichsidee.* Vienna: Österreichischer Verlag für Kunst und Wissenschaft, 1937.

Wolff, Richard J., and Jörg K. Hoensch. *Catholics, the State and the European Radical Right, 1919–1945.* Boulder, CO: Social Science Monographs, 1987.

Wolin, Richard. *The Seduction of Unreason: The Intellectual Romance with Fascism from Nietzsche to Postmodernism.* Princeton: Princeton University Press, 2004.

Woods, Roger. *The Conservative Revolution in the Weimar Republic.* New York: Macmillan, 1996.

Zeps, Michael J. *Education and the Crisis of the First Republic.* Boulder, CO: East European Monographs: New York, 1987.

Ziegler, Meinrad, Waltraud Kannonier, and Marlene Weiterschan. *Österreichisches Gedächtnis: Über Erinnern und Vergessen der NS-Vergangenheit.* Vienna: Böhlau, 1993.

Zilsel, Edgar. *Die Entstehung des Geniebegriffes.* Tübingen: Mohr, 1926.

——. *Die Geniereligion.* Frankfurt am Main: Suhrkamp, 1990.

——. *The Social Origins of Modern Science.* Edited by Diederick Raven, Wolfgang Krohn, and R. S. Cohen. Boston: Kluwer Academic, 2000.

Zöllner, Erich. *Der Österreichbegriff: Formen und Wandlungen in der Geschichte.* Vienna: Geschichte und Politik, 1988.

Zulehner, Paul Michael. *Kirche und Austromarxismus. Eine Studie zur Problematik Kirche-Staat-Gesellschaft.* Vienna: Herder, 1967.

INDEX

Action Française, 14, 31, 133–34, 144–45

Adler, Alfred, 47, 53, 68, 113n22, 159, 162, 167–68, 170, 174, 224

Adler, Friedrich, 54, 58–62, 72, 111, 168, 170

Adler, Max, 52, 56, 60, 63–65, 74, 80, 87, 89, 119, 126, 154, 163, 165, 179, 182–83

Adler, Victor, 23, 51, 54, 126, 163

adult education institutes. See *Volkshochschulen*

Aichhorn, August, 166, 174

Akademische Legion, 90

Amery, Jean, 218

Andreae, Wilhelm, 86, 91, 219, 222

"Announcement of Intellectual Vienna," 47, 51, 72–73, 161–62

Anschluss, 8, 14, 27, 44, 73, 105, 134, 137–38, 150, 155–57, 162, 191–93, 218–21, 226

anti-Nazism, 76, 134, 152–53, 155–56, 201, 205–6, 209, 212–13, 217

Antisemitenbund, 6, 8, 31, 136

anti-Semitism, 3, 5–8, 13, 18, 21–22, 29–38, 41, 59, 80, 84, 101–3, 133–39, 143, 146–48, 151–52, 156, 161, 178, 187, 190–202, 206, 208–211, 220, 224–26. *See also* Jews

apolitical science, 11, 13–14, 18, 30, 75–77, 81–82, 99, 104, 107–9, 119, 124, 130–31, 144, 155, 157, 183, 212, 220–21

Arbeiter-Zeitung, 19, 47, 116, 178, 185

Arbeitslosen von Marienthal, 158–61, 181, 184–86

Arendt, Hannah, 86

Arrow Cross (Hungary), 94

Der Atheist, 127

austerity, 43, 49, 66, 158, 184. *See also* Geneva Protocols

Austria, idea of, 16–18, 27, 30–31, 44–45, 139, 145–47, 152–56, 191–93, 205–6, 209, 212–14

Austrian civil war, 3, 103, 106, 154, 184, 187, 207, 220–21

Austrian Freethinkers' Association, 108–9, 120, 123–29. *See also* Freethinkers

Austrian Monist Association. *See* Monist League

Austrian People's Party (ÖVP), 221–22

Austrian School (economics), 67, 110, 115. *See also* marginal utility

Austrian victimhood, 9, 105, 220

Austrittsbewegung, 122–23, 125–26

Austrofascism, 8, 12–14, 18, 72–76, 98, 103–8, 130–31, 134–35, 151, 154, 187, 189–92, 201, 205–212, 216–17, 220–24; constitution of, 103–6, 207, 212

Austro-Marxism, 1–4, 12–14, 23, 47–54, 58–59, 72, 154, 162–68, 171, 174–75, 182–87, 224; attitudes toward intellectuals, 48–50, 55–63, 65–72, 108, 113, 116–19, 122, 126–31, 158–63, 177; opposition to, 167, 173, 176–86. *See also* Social Democrats

authoritarianism, 6, 18, 31–33, 37, 40–42, 45, 76, 80, 85, 93, 99–103, 128, 133–35, 138–39, 142, 145, 149–57, 176–77, 187, 193–96, 201–2, 206, 209–216, 220, 223–25

Bach, David Josef, 54, 111

Bahr, Hermann, 15, 24, 59

Bangha, Béla, 194

Bauer, Helene, 67

Bauer, Otto, 30, 52, 58–59, 68, 84, 117, 120, 128–31, 154, 160–63, 168, 171, 176–82, 185

Bauhaus (architecture), 115, 173

Baxa, Jacob, 86, 91, 95–96, 219
Belloc, Hilaire, 194
Berchtesgaden, 155, 191, 215
Bernfeld, Siegfried, 68, 163, 166–67, 170, 174, 179–80
Bernstein, Eduard, 52
Bettelheim, Bruno, 218
Bibring, Grete, 174
Black Vienna, idea of, 5–9, 12–14, 18–19, 28–31, 34–37, 40–46, 72–73, 77–78, 81, 95–98, 105, 133–35, 139–44, 187, 191–97, 204–217, 220–26
Bolshevism, 1–3, 18, 30–32, 40–41, 56–59, 84, 100, 146, 165, 179, 190–98
Boltzmann, Ludwig, 111
Börner, Wilhelm, 122n49, 123–24
Bourdieu, Pierre, 12n46, 109n11
Brand, Walter, 92, 94
"bridge building" (Nazis), 198, 201, 221
Brunswik, Egon, 171, 182, 218
Bühler, Charlotte, 68, 91, 113n22, 162, 167–70, 181
Bühler, Karl, 47, 68, 91, 113n22, 159–62, 167–70, 218, 223
Burgert, Helmuth, 203–4
Buttinger, Joseph, 176

Canetti, Elias, 175
capitalism: criticism of, 7, 13, 21–22, 29–30, 35, 60, 69, 77, 83, 95–97, 100, 104, 110, 117–18, 124–27, 137, 143, 148, 151–52, 165, 173, 186, 192–93, 198, 210–11; debates over, 5, 19, 52
Carnap, Rudolf, 110, 120, 130, 170–73, 181–83, 204
Cartellverband (CV), 21, 137, 142, 193
Catholic Action, 45, 133, 142–44, 193
Catholicism, Catholics, 4, 9, 13, 18, 20–23, 29–33, 38, 42–44, 83, 86, 96, 125–27, 130–36, 140–48, 151–58, 193–99, 201–8, 214–16, 223–24; social theory of, 7, 21, 31, 34, 38–39, 43–44, 95–98, 134, 137, 143–45, 153, 193, 196, 210, 223–25
Chamberlain, Houston Stewart, 137
Chesterton, G. K., 194
Christian Social party, 2–3, 6–8, 11, 16–26, 30, 35–37, 43–45, 48–49, 57, 66, 98–99, 125–28, 136, 139–44, 153–54, 172, 177–78, 184, 193–94, 207, 221, 224
Der christliche Ständestaat, 98, 154, 189–90, 192, 205–6, 208–9, 213–17

Communism, 35, 40, 154, 180. See also Bolshevism
conservatism, 4, 6, 8–9, 11–14, 16–19, 22–31, 33–46, 55–59, 69–72, 76–86, 90, 94–98, 103, 105, 108–119, 124–28, 131–42, 144–52, 156–57, 173–80, 187–99, 201–9, 214–17, 219–26. See also new conservatism; new Right
constitutionalism, 211
corporatism, 6–7, 20, 31, 44, 69, 84–85, 94–106, 140–43, 149, 155, 193, 196, 210–11, 214, 223. See also Sozialreform
Coudenhove-Kalergi, Richard von, 148
counterreformation, 38, 81, 147, 194

Danneberg, Robert, 3, 48, 57
democracy: Catholics and, 96, 98, 141; opposition to, 7n26, 8, 13, 17–18, 26, 30–32, 36, 40–43, 66, 69, 72, 75, 77, 81, 83, 85, 93–94, 97–104, 119, 134, 138–44, 148–57, 187, 191–95, 198–201, 209, 212, 215–16, 221, 224; support of, 155–56, 165–68, 178, 186–87, 194–95, 207–9, 225; "true democracy," 2, 32–33, 128, 177, 193, 206–7, 210
de-Nazification, 221–22
de-proletarianization, 64, 149–50, 158
Deutsch, Helene, 11, 68, 163, 165, 167, 179–80, 225
Deutsche Studentenschaft, 6, 8, 71, 90, 96, 133, 142, 193
dictatorship, 40, 150, 156, 165, 198, 201, 212, 226. See also authoritarianism
Dilthey, Wilhelm, 87
Dobretsberger, Josef, 209, 219
Dollfuss, Engelbert, 37, 103, 127, 153–55, 158, 201–2, 205–8, 211
Duczynska, Ilona, 162, 175–76, 180
Duhem, Pierre, 110
Dunkmann, Karl, 88

Eberle, Joseph, 11, 17–19, 27–30, 33, 36–40, 43–45, 64, 66, 78, 95–98, 108, 111, 136, 142, 144, 150–55, 189, 193–202, 208–217, 219–22
educational reform, 23, 39, 51, 55, 64, 110, 113–14, 122, 125, 144, 165–68, 173. See also Free School movement
Eibl, Hans, 19, 26, 36, 95, 111–12, 139, 142, 147, 151–52, 157, 192–95, 199–204, 208–210, 214, 216, 219–23

Einstein, Albert, 110, 170
emigration, 3, 114, 156, 162, 171, 178–81, 191, 218–22
empiricism, 52–54, 59–60, 77, 88, 107–115, 119, 122, 130–31, 163, 167–69, 174, 182–84, 204
Endres, Robert, 126–27
Engel, Alfred, 61–62
Erkenntnis, 107, 188
Estado Novo (Portugal), 153
Ethical Society, 54, 122n49, 123
eugenics, 210–11
Europe, idea of, 132–34, 206

Die Fackel, 16–17, 45
fascism, 5–6, 9, 13–14, 33, 40–46, 66, 76–77, 94, 97–101, 133–35, 144, 149–56, 175–78, 181–82, 187, 192, 196, 198, 201, 203, 205–217, 220, 223–24. *See also* Austrofascism
Fascism (Italy), 41–42, 76, 93–96, 99–101, 133–35, 141, 149, 153, 198, 201, 211, 215, 224
Fatherland Front (Vaterländische Front), 155, 201–2, 206
February 1934. *See* Austrian civil war
Federn, Paul, 163–67, 225
Federn, Walther, 172
Feigl, Herbert, 109n8, 110, 113–15, 119–20, 123, 130, 171
Fenichel, Otto, 166–67, 174, 179–80
Fifth German Sociological Conference, 70, 86–90
fin-de-siècle period, 4, 109–110, 121
First Republic (Austria), 2–3, 8, 18–19, 35–37, 40, 43, 46, 48, 80, 109, 134–42, 148, 153, 156–57, 162, 164, 168, 175, 178–81, 184–87, 201, 207, 220–21, 224–26; constitution of, 2, 47, 72, 80, 115, 128, 133, 138–40, 154, 177–78, 191, 193, 207, 211
First Vienna Circle, 110–11. *See also* Vienna Circle
Fischer, Ernst, 175, 179, 185
Foerster, Friedrich Wilhelm, 146
Ford, Henry, 194
Frank, Josef, 68, 111, 120, 128, 181
Frank, Philipp, 68, 109n8, 110–11, 120, 188, 204
Frankl, Victor, 208
Freemasonry, 31, 37–38, 75, 138–39, 148, 190–91, 194

Free School movement (*Freie Schule*), 23, 38, 51–52, 55, 112, 122–23. *See also* educational reform
Freethinkers, 54, 106, 120–21, 124, 126, 130, 191. *See also* Austrian Freethinkers' Association
Frege, Gottlob, 110
Der Freidenker, 121–26
French fascism, 135n12
Freud, Anna, 113n22, 174
Freud, Sigmund, 3, 47, 51, 53, 68, 120, 159, 162–70, 173, 203, 218, 223–24
Friedjung, Josef, 68, 113, 120, 123, 128, 163, 167, 182
führer, idea of, 7, 33, 40, 83, 94, 99–100, 141, 150, 155, 200, 202, 209, 211
Funder, Friedrich, 1, 29, 49, 142, 194, 198, 203

Ganzheitsphilosophie. *See* universalism
Geistkreis, 81
Geneva Protocols, 43, 95, 124, 141
German Monist Society, 121–22, 126. *See also* Monists
German nationalism, 6, 13–14, 16–19, 21–34, 43–46, 74–76, 81, 83, 90, 94–98, 105, 131–38, 140, 142, 145, 147, 151–57, 190, 192, 194, 197–201, 204–6, 209, 211–16, 219, 222
Gessmann, Alfred, 21
Gleichschaltung, 101, 103
Gleispach, Wenzel, 95, 104
Glöckel, Otto, 39, 113, 125–26, 165
Goldscheid, Rudolf, 67, 122
Gomperz, Heinrich, 91, 116
Görres-Gesellschaft, 20, 195
Gralbund, 17, 19, 43–44, 147, 194
Gramsci, Antonio, 10–12, 49, 56, 60–63. *See also* hegemony
Great Depression, 93, 98, 152, 158, 161, 176, 182, 185
Grünberg, Carl, 179
Gundlach, Gustav, 196–97

Haberler, Gottfried, 81
Habsburg, Karl von (emperor), 135–36, 141
Habsburg, Otto, 133, 141, 148n59, 155
Habsburg Empire, 16, 30, 35, 44, 57, 65, 80, 132–41, 146–48, 165, 194, 225. *See also* Holy Roman Empire
Haeckel, Ernst, 121–22

Hahn, Hans, 68, 71, 110–11, 120, 130, 173
Haller, Friedrich, 124
Hartmann, Heinz, 171, 182
Hartmann, Ludo, 71, 113, 123
Hayek, Friedrich, 81, 171
hegemony, 10–13, 49, 60–61, 77, 105, 109, 116, 119, 157, 216–17, 223–25
Heidegger, Martin, 183, 203
Heimwehr, 2, 13, 49, 72, 76, 91, 93–94, 99, 115, 128, 141, 145, 149, 152, 176–78, 184, 196, 221
Heinrich, Walter, 76, 91–102, 105, 219, 222
Henlein, Konrad, 75–76, 94
Herbst, Edgar, 123
Hildebrand, Dietrich, 14, 189–90, 196–97, 203–210, 213–16, 219
Hilferding, Rudolf, 52, 70
Hindenburg, Paul von, 152
Historical School (economics), 74, 78, 110
Hitler, Adolf, 6, 13, 43, 75, 98, 101–3, 152, 155, 158, 191–92, 198–99, 201–2, 215, 220–21
Hitschmann, Eduard, 167
Holy Roman Empire, 30–33, 44, 139, 141, 146–47, 194
Horkheimer, Max, 179
Horthy, Miklós, 40–41, 43
Hudal, Alois, 28, 36, 39, 214
Hungary, 40–41, 133, 215
Hussarek, Max, 21–22, 35
Husserl, Edmund, 203–4
hyperinflation, 43, 49, 66, 93, 95, 124, 141. *See also* Geneva Protocols

individualism, 77, 81–82, 84, 88–89, 96–97, 99, 137, 141, 196, 206, 210, 214
integralism, 22
intellectuals: Austrian, 66, 71, 197; Austro-Marxist, 50, 67, 224; Black Viennese, 7–14, 17, 19, 22, 25–30, 33–44, 69, 72, 78, 81, 91, 95–97, 105, 128, 133–37, 142, 145, 151, 161–62, 192–94, 198–209, 213–25; definitions of, 10–14, 33–39, 43, 48–50, 55–56, 59–65, 69–72, 85, 99, 103, 200; progressive, 5, 47, 50, 53–59, 67, 105, 108–9, 112–13, 119–24, 159–62, 175, 178, 184, 186–87, 216, 218, 222; Red Viennese, 5, 11–14, 72, 108–9, 113, 161–62, 169, 174–76, 180–81, 184, 186, 204, 219–25
International Congress of Proletarian Freethinkers, 127

International Proletarian Freethinkers, 127. *See also* Freethinkers
Inthal, Kaspar, 40–41
Isotype. *See* picture statistics

Jahoda, Marie, 4, 113n22, 158–63, 166, 170–72, 181, 185–86
James, William, 130
Jehly, Eduard, 3
Jerusalem, Wilhelm, 168–69
Jews, 27, 31–33, 37–38, 55, 67, 80, 112–13, 119n40, 120, 136, 139, 156, 162–63, 190, 225. *See also* anti-Semitism
Jodl, Friedrich, 122
Justizpalast fire, 2, 94, 128, 145, 161, 175, 177, 195

Kaindl, Raimund, 44, 147, 151–52
Kameradschaftsbund, 92, 94
Kammerer, Paul, 123
Der Kampf, 13, 45, 51–54, 58–59, 67–68, 70, 72, 165–66, 182–85
Kassel, Richard, 62–63, 65
Die Kategorienlehre, 77, 86–88
Kautsky, Karl, 51, 58
Kelsen, Hans, 3, 47, 51, 80, 91, 116, 154, 162, 168, 178–79, 212
Kerschagl, Richard, 95
Ketteler, Wilhelm von, 97, 143. *See also* *Sozialpolitik*
Keynes, John Maynard, 67
Kinderfreunde, 122. *See also* educational reform
Klopp, Wiard, 208
Knoll, August Maria, 136, 141, 152, 154–56, 219, 222
Kogon, Eugen, 95, 193
Kolnai, Aurel, 171, 176, 214
Korneuberg Oath, 93–94, 97, 196
Kraft, Viktor, 109n8, 110, 112–14, 119, 218
Kralik, Richard von, 11, 15–17, 22–27, 29–34, 39, 43–44, 59, 69–70, 111, 137, 147, 194–95, 200, 204, 223, 225
Kraus, Karl, 16–17, 32, 172
Krenek, Ernst, 208
Kulturkampf, 22, 55, 61

Labor and Socialist International. *See* Vienna International
Lager model, 8–9, 14, 24, 44, 46, 95, 135, 141, 146, 153, 157, 192, 205
late Enlightenment, 4–5, 109, 225

Lazarsfeld, Paul, 55, 113n22, 158–62, 166, 168–71, 181, 185–86
Lazarsfeld, Sophie, 55, 168
League of Nations, 24, 31, 124, 132, 139, 148
Lebensraum, 27, 201
legitimacy, 37, 86, 133, 136–41, 145, 151, 155–56, 207, 212, 217. *See also* monarchism
Leichter, Käthe. *See* Pick, Käthe
Leichter, Otto, 70–71, 176
Lenin, Vladimir, 52, 54, 56
Leo-Gesellschaft, 8, 12, 15, 17–28, 34, 44, 54, 71, 95, 133, 139, 142, 147, 150, 193, 196, 199, 201, 209, 214
Leopoldstadt, 113
Ley, Robert, 75, 102
liberalism, 4–5, 22–23, 51, 72–75, 108–120, 124, 154, 157, 170–73, 225; opposition to, 7, 18, 29–31, 34, 38–40, 75–84, 94–97, 101–4, 126–27, 134, 138–41, 147–52, 193–96, 201–6, 210–11, 216, 224
Liechtenstein, Alois von, 30, 32, 35–36
Little Entente, 133
logical empiricism, 117, 128, 173, 181–82, 204, 224. *See also* Vienna Circle
Logical Structure of the World, 172–73
Lueger, Karl, 7, 18, 21, 23–24, 144
Lukács, Georg, 60, 63, 117
Lux, Josef August, 39, 48, 96
Luxemburg, Rosa, 52, 70

Mach, Ernst, 52, 54, 59–60, 107, 110–11, 116, 170, 204
Machlup, Fritz, 81
Mahler, Alma, 47
Mannheim, Karl, 34, 60, 62
marginal utility (economics), 52, 67, 79, 110
Marienthal. *See* *Arbeitslosen von Marienthal*
Maritain, Jacques, 194
Marx, Karl, 31–32, 53, 89, 115, 117, 154
Marxism, 2, 37–8, 49–54, 56, 58–60, 75, 84–85, 97–99, 101–2, 115–19, 125–26, 153, 159, 166, 173–74, 177–83, 194, 203, 205. *See also* Austro-Marxism
Marxist-intellectual synthesis, 48, 159–61, 167, 169, 175–79, 183, 186
Maurras, Charles, 144–45
May Constitution. *See* Austrofascism: constitution of

Mein Kampf, 101–2
Meister, Richard, 190
Menger, Karl, 120, 173
Menghin, Oswald, 28, 36, 95, 136, 194, 219
Merkl, Adolf, 178
Messner, Johannes, 19, 37, 40, 72, 142, 192–93, 196–97, 202–3, 208–213, 216, 219, 222
Minor, Daisy, 47
Mises, Ludwig, 3, 79, 81, 84, 115n30, 171
Missong, Alfred, 136, 141, 146, 148–56, 193, 208, 219, 221
Mitteleuropa, 7, 27, 134, 137, 146–48, 150
Die Monarchie. See *Das neue Reich*
monarchism, 6, 14, 29, 32, 37, 44, 81, 132–42, 144–57, 193–94. *See also* Österreichische Aktion
monism, 117, 121, 170
Monist League, 54, 67, 120, 122–23, 164, 169
Monists, 120–23, 126, 130. *See also* Monist League
Morgenstern, Oskar, 81
Muckermann, Hermann, 146, 211
Müller, Adam, 7, 86
Musil, Robert, 47, 51
Mussolini, Benito, 40–43, 66, 100, 149, 158, 196–98, 201, 211

Nadler, Joseph, 28, 142, 219
nationalism, 41, 46, 49–52, 58, 78, 103, 108, 122, 134, 135n12, 137, 142–50, 156–57, 187, 194, 196, 215, 217, 224. *See also* German nationalism
Nazism, 9, 13, 49, 72–76, 83, 86, 92–93, 98–106, 134, 141, 151–53, 157, 176, 191–92, 196, 198, 201–8, 211, 213–16, 219–24, 226. *See also* anti-Nazism
Nelböck, Hans, 188–90
Nell-Breuning, Oswald, 143, 196–97
Das neue Reich, 8, 13, 15, 17, 19, 28–37, 40–46, 69, 95–98, 133, 136, 142, 192–97, 202, 225
Neurath, Otto, 11, 60, 67–68, 110–16, 119–20, 123, 126–30, 154, 162–63, 168–73, 182–84
new conservatism, 14, 35, 38, 41, 46, 132–33, 149. *See also* conservatism
new Right, 9–10, 19, 34–35, 38, 41, 46, 133, 135, 144, 149, 157, 193

Oppenheimer, Franz, 87
Orel, Anton, 21, 31, 36, 136, 152
Österreichische Aktion (manifesto), 132, 144, 146
Österreichische Aktion (movement), 8, 14, 31, 81, 92, 96, 132–36, 140–41, 143–57, 192–95, 208, 219, 221
Der österreichische Volkswirt, 172, 176–77
Ottakring, 113

Paneuropa movement, 148
Pan-Germanism, 6–8, 26, 43–44, 157, 191, 199, 221. *See also* German nationalism
Panzer, Felix, 125
Paris Peace Accords, 16, 27, 30, 80, 139, 148. *See also* treaties
Pawel, Karl, 97
Pedagogical Institute, 168, 170, 186
Pick, Käthe, 67, 176, 185, 218
picture statistics, 116, 129, 170
Poincaré, Henri, 110, 170
Polanyi, Karl, 67, 113n22, 168, 171–72, 176, 182
political Catholicism, 6, 18, 140, 193, 205, 213
Popp, Adelheid, 55
Popper, Karl, 3, 11, 59, 113n22, 171, 177
Posch, Andreas, 44, 202
positivism, 39, 121–22; opposition to, 81, 190, 203–4
progressives, 5, 47, 50, 53–59, 67, 105, 108–9, 112–13, 119–24, 159–62, 166, 168, 178, 187, 216, 223. *See also* intellectuals: progressive
Prohászka, Ottokár, 41
psychoanalysis, 68, 159, 161–70, 173–74, 179–80
Psychological Institute, 68, 168, 185–86
psychology, 47, 53–54, 68, 169–70, 182

"Quadragesimo Anno," 96–97, 103, 153, 196–97, 202, 209–210

race and racial theory, 9, 31, 36, 75–76, 100–105, 136–37, 146, 151, 190, 201, 208–211, 213n80, 214–17, 219
re-Christianization, 38–39, 41. *See also* counterreformation
Red Vienna, 1–5, 8, 12, 14, 17–18, 28, 46, 50–51, 61, 67, 72, 105, 109, 111, 119–20, 125, 129, 154, 158, 168, 171, 174–78,

184–87, 222, 224; public settlement movement of, 111–12, 115–16, 160–62, 173
Reich, ideas about, 7, 19, 26–27, 43–45, 133–34, 141–42, 150–51, 197–200, 213, 225
Reich, Wilhelm, 162–63, 166–67, 171, 173–77, 179–80, 182
Reichenbach, Hans, 188–89
Reichskonkordat, 202
Reichspost, 1, 15–17, 21, 29–30, 48, 116, 129, 142, 198, 201, 203, 214, 216
Religious Socialists, 177
Renner, Karl, 56, 58, 61
"Rerum Novarum," 20, 95, 143–44, 193
Reynold, Gonzague de, 194
Riazanov, David, 117
Riehl, Hans, 91, 93, 101, 219
Riehl, Walter, 76, 93
Rivera, Primo de, 43, 66
Roloff, Ilse, 101–2
Romanticism, 86, 95–96, 98, 119, 134, 137, 141, 143, 149, 154–55, 194, 199
Rosenberg, Alfred, 75, 94, 102, 104–5
Rutha, Heinz, 75–76

Salomon, Ernst von, 92–93
Sauter, Johann, 81, 189–91, 216–17
Schaukal, Richard, 38, 208
Scheler, Max, 203
Schindler, Franz, 20–21, 26
Schlesinger, Therese, 55, 71
Schlick, Moritz, 13, 91, 106–114, 116–23, 129–31, 162, 170, 182–83, 204, 223; murder of, 188–92, 216–17
Schmid, Wilhelm, 136, 144, 146, 152, 155–56, 219
Schmidt, Wilhelm, 39
Schmitt, Carl, 40, 86, 199, 210, 212, 215
Schmitz, Richard, 125
Schoepfer, Aemilian, 30–31, 35, 45, 142, 193
Schönerer, Georg von, 7
Die schönere Zukunft, 8, 17, 19, 45–46, 51, 69, 95–98, 133, 142–43, 147–48, 151–55, 175, 189–201, 203, 205–8, 213–17, 219, 221, 225
Schumpeter, Joseph, 67, 70
Schuschnigg, Kurt von, 155, 191, 208, 215–16
Schutzbund, 175, 178, 201

"The Scientific World-Conception," 114, 121, 128–31, 172–73. *See also* Verein Ernst Mach; Vienna Circle

Seipel, Ignaz, 1–2, 26, 33, 49, 66, 128, 141, 177, 194

Seitz, Karl, 55

Sex-Pol, 167, 174. *See also* Reich, Wilhelm

sexual politics and sexual reform, 164, 167–68, 179–80

Social and Economic Museum, 68, 112, 116, 170–71

Social Democrats, 1–3, 6, 11, 13, 25–26, 35–36, 47–48, 51–52, 55, 57, 66, 68, 72, 80, 84, 91, 94, 106, 111–12, 123–24, 127–29, 160–62, 173–80, 184–86, 191, 201, 206, 221. *See also* socialism

socialism, 3, 8, 22–23, 30–32, 38, 42, 49, 52, 56–57, 67, 74, 81–82, 97, 99, 109, 112–17, 123–30, 141, 150–56, 159–69, 172–82, 184–87, 190–96, 201–2, 206–7, 211, 218, 221, 224–25

socialization, 67, 84, 110, 115, 171

Société Henri Poincaré, 107

Society for Empirical Philosophy, 107

sociology, 87–89, 115, 163, 168–70, 174

sociology of knowledge, 34, 60

Solidarism, 96–98, 103, 195, 197

Sombart, Werner, 74, 84, 87–88, 90, 100, 137

Sozialpolitik, 96–97, 143, 210

Sozialreform, 20, 97, 143–44, 149, 210

Spann, Othmar, 11, 13, 21, 28, 34, 36, 70–74, 75–78, 84–93, 95, 97–105, 111, 136, 140–44, 149, 152–55, 189, 196–97, 200, 204, 209–216, 219, 221–23; biography of, 78–81. *See also* Spannkreis

Spann, Rafael, 94

Spannkreis, 13, 36, 69, 72–78, 85, 90–98, 102–5, 133, 150, 193–96, 209, 214–17, 219, 222, 225

Spengler, Oswald, 84

Sperber, Manes, 162, 168

Srbik, Heinrich von, 20–21, 27, 44, 95, 147, 151, 157, 199, 219–23

Ständestaat, 2, 8, 12, 18, 72–75, 97, 103, 107, 153–55, 191–92, 204–217, 220, 223. *See also* Austrofascism

Ständisches Leben, 78, 92, 98–103

Stresemann, Gustav, 132

Sudetenland, 13, 75–76, 86, 90, 92, 94, 104

Tandler, Julius, 68, 113, 126, 128, 163, 167, 180

Third Reich, 102; idea of, 27, 199–200

Tönnies, Ferdinand, 75, 87, 90

totalitarianism, 206, 212, 214–15

Tractatus Logico-Philosophicus, 107–8

treaties: of Saint-Germain, 135–36, 138–39; of Versailles, 27, 198–200. *See also* Paris Peace Accords

Trebitsch, Oskar, 61–62

Trotsky, Leon, 56

Uhlhorn, Gregor, 202

unions, 61–62, 65, 106, 161, 185, 191

universalism, 71, 74–82, 84–90, 93–105, 140, 149, 196–97, 214–15, 224. *See also* Spann, Othmar

University of Vienna, 28, 71, 80–81, 90, 110–13, 119, 136, 152, 167–68, 178–79, 189, 204, 208, 213–14, 218–19, 222

Das Vaterland, 144, 149, 152, 155

Verdross, Alfred, 28, 72

Verein Ernst Mach, 13, 68, 106–9, 114, 120–22, 126–31, 161, 170, 181, 190–91. *See also* Vienna Circle

Vienna: interwar, 10–14, 17; municipal government of, 2–3, 21, 54, 64, 68, 72, 109, 112–13, 119, 128, 167–68, 223, 225. *See also* Black Vienna; Red Vienna

Vienna Circle, 13, 68, 91, 107–115, 119–22, 127–30, 159, 169–72, 181–83. *See also* Verein Ernst Mach

Vienna International, 58, 127

Voegelin, Eric, 3, 28, 72, 81, 88, 192, 204, 207, 209–212, 216

Vogelsang, Karl von, 20, 31, 97, 143–44, 149

völkisch ideology, 6, 7n26, 23, 27, 32–33, 39–43, 74–75, 83–85, 91–94, 99–103, 138, 190–94, 199–201, 211–12

Volkshochschulen, 22, 28, 64, 68, 109–124, 128–29, 168, 171, 182, 186

Wagner, Ludwig, 185

Der wahre Staat, 69, 74, 77–78, 81–85, 95, 103. *See also* Spann, Othmar

Wahrmund affair, 23, 111

Waismann, Friedrich, 109n8, 110, 112–14, 119–20, 130

Waitz, Sigmund, 38, 59, 194
Wandruszka, Adam, 8
Weber, Max, 87, 207, 212
Webern, Anton, 47
Wellesz, Egon, 47
Werfel, Franz, 47
Westphalen, Friedrich, 91
Wiese, Leopold von, 87–90
Winter, Ernst Karl, 31, 44, 92, 136–37, 140–47, 152–56, 209, 219, 221

Wittgenstein, Ludwig, 3, 107
women, women's rights, 47, 55, 149, 165, 185

Zehentbauer, Franz, 95
Zeisel, Hans, 113n22, 158–62, 166, 170–71, 181, 186
Zessner-Spitzenberg, Hans, 36, 136–42, 145, 149–56, 208–9, 219
Zilsel, Edgar, 68, 91, 110–20, 127–28, 171, 182–84, 218

www.ingramcontent.com/pod-product-compliance
Lightning Source LLC
Chambersburg PA
CBHW020846270326
41928CB00006B/576